Virginia Rounding

THE BURNING TIME

THE STORY OF THE SMITHFIELD MARTYRS

PAN BOOKS

First published 2017 by Macmillan

This paperback edition first published 2018 by Pan Books
an imprint of Pan Macmillan
20 New Wharf Road, London N1 9RR
Associated companies throughout the world
www.panmacmillan.com

ISBN 978-1-4472-4108-9

1 3 5 7 9 8 6 4 2

A CIP catalogue record for this book is available from the British Library.

Typeset by Palimpsest Book Production Ltd, Falkirk, Stirlingshire
Printed and bound by CPI Group (UK) Ltd, Croydon, CR0 4YY

Visit **www.panmacmillan.com** to read more about all our books
and to buy them. You will also find features, author interviews and
news of any author events, and you can sign up for e-newsletters
so that you're always first to hear about our new releases.

FOR NICK AND SARAH,

AND FOR BEATRICE,

AND IN MEMORY OF ANTHONY

Now we see in a glass even in a dark speaking, but then shall we see face to face. Now I know unperfectly, but then shall I know even as I am known.

1 Corinthians 13:12 [The Matthew Bible]

The same cometh often to pass, when as men be of diverse opinions, concerning their faith and religion: for albeit that many other matters make one to hate another, yet nothing is there that breedeth so deadly hatred, as diversity of minds, touching religion.

John Christopherson,
An exhortation to . . . beware of rebellion, 1554

How long has Western culture been identified with democracy, toleration and respect for individual human rights? A clear-eyed examination of the record will show that, a few centuries ago, we were all – as it were – Islamic fundamentalists.

Thomas M. Franck,
'Is Personal Freedom a Western Value?', 1997

Contents

✠

A Note on Language

✠

When quoting from contemporary sources in this book, whether from Foxe's *Acts and Monuments*, *Letters and Papers* or various chroniclers, I have taken certain liberties in the interests of comprehensibility and immediacy. At times, particularly when recounting lively exchanges at trials or 'examinations' for heresy, I have chosen to paraphrase or use deliberately modern idioms when recounting, or re-imagining, conversations, in order to convey the spirit if not necessarily the letter of the discussion. At other times, I have retained the exact wording as recorded by contemporary (or near-contemporary) chroniclers, not wanting to detract from their characteristic vividness. At all times, I have used modern spelling. My choices throughout have been dictated by the desire to put no unnecessary obstacles between the twenty-first-century reader and the voices of their sixteenth-century forebears.

List of Illustrations

✠

Section Two

Acknowledgements

✠

Many people have supported me in the writing of this book, and it has given me particular pleasure to have had the support of those who may in a way be regarded as 'descendants' of the people caught up in the religious turmoils in sixteenth-century Smithfield – that is, both the current community of believers at the Priory Church of St Bartholomew the Great; and the representatives of the City authorities, members of the Court of Common Council of the City of London Corporation, both Aldermen and 'commoners'.

Among the latter group, my thanks go to: Ann Holmes, Michael Snyder, Stephen Haines, Philip Woodhouse, Jeremy Simons, Wendy Mead, Michael Welbank, George Abrahams, Jeremy Mayhew, Charles Bowman, Julian Malins, Peter Estlin, Catherine McGuinness, Joyce Nash, Henry Colthurst, William Russell, Marianne Fredericks, Billy Dove, Mark Wheatley, Emma Edhem, Nigel Challis, Richard Regan, Anthony Eskenzi, Nick Bensted-Smith, Graham Packham, Ian Seaton, Peter Dunphy, Chris Hayward, Vincent Keaveny, Tom Sleigh, Fiona and Nicholas Woolf, and Bill Fraser.

And at St Bartholomew's, I acknowledge the support of: Nick and Sarah Kelsey, Monica Darnbrough, Nigel and Lilian Reid, Nandini Sukumar, Beatrice and the late Anthony Perch, Richard and Sue Plaskett, Karen Falkner, Dominique Lazanski and Marc Sidwell, Geoff and Irina Cowley, Zoë McMillan, Nicholas Riddle and Patrick Stutz, and Maurice Hughes.

In addition, I have received valuable support from: Dr Maria Grasso and Dr James H. Pedersen, Dr Mary Hogan Camp, Emma Kirkby, Fionnuala Tennyson and Evelyn Pickup, Simon Woodroffe, Alexandre

Tissot Demidov, Tony and Anthea Peck, Tim Statham, John Morgan, Peter Rose, Vivien Gainsborough Foot, Una Riley, Nick and Joy Gravestock, Eddie and Pat Stevens, Michael Thompson, Jane Holt, Dr Maria Starkova-Vindman, Jane Miles Elliston, Leigh Richards, Michael Hopkins, Holly and Catriona McDavid, Alan and Hazel Birchenough, and Andrew Gillett.

Thanks are also due to Howard Doble, Senior Archivist (City Records), London Metropolitan Archives for finding the only mentions in the records of Town Clerk William Pavier; to Professor Bernard Knight and Dr Elayne Pope for providing details of the physiological and pathological effects of burning; and to the Revd Dr Martin Dudley, 25th Rector of St Bartholomew the Great, for much illuminating theological discussion and for being my first reader. I am also grateful to Charles Spicer of St Martin's Press for having conceived of the idea of a book about the Smithfield martyrs and to my agent, Clare Alexander, for suggesting I might be the person to write it. Georgina Morley has also been consistently encouraging, as has the whole team at Macmillan.

Introduction

SETTING THE SCENE

✠

> The past cannot be changed but we are responsible for how we
> remember it. What we extract and carry forward from what has
> gone before creates possibilities for the future or closes them off.
> In a sense we remember the future.
>
> The Rt Hon. and Rt Revd Dr Richard Chartres,
> the 132nd Bishop of London[*]

'UNDER ITEM 2, there are no resolutions. Under Item 3, the
Right Honourable the Lord Mayor to report on his overseas visits.
Under Item 4, there is no statement. Under Item 5, the book is on
the table.'

Such sentences, pronounced in the sonorous tones of the
gowned and bewigged Town Clerk of the City of London Corporation, are a standard part of the ritual of the monthly meetings of
the Court of Common Council, of which I am an elected member,
and which take place in the Great Hall of Guildhall, a ten-minute
walk from the site of the horrific events which are central to this
book. Being a member of the Court is in certain respects much
like being a local councillor anywhere else – we are elected by
people who live (and unusually, in the City, though nowhere else
in the United Kingdom, by people who work) in one of the
twenty-five 'Wards' or small districts which make up the 'Square

* From an address preached at 'Waterloo 200: A National Service of Celebration' at
St Paul's Cathedral on 18 June 2015.

Mile' of the City of London to represent their interests, and some of our time is indeed taken up with matters of parking, late-night noise from licensed premises, and litter collection. Our wider interests – the City has responsibility for managing some of London's most famous open spaces, for instance, including Hampstead Heath and Epping Forest – and our support for the UK's business interests, both at home and abroad, may also sound fairly familiar, and we all spend a lot of time in committee meetings. But other aspects of being a Common Councilman (as we one hundred 'Commoners' are resolutely called, irrespective of gender) bear no resemblance to anything you are likely to find elsewhere in the modern world. Our ceremonial resembles that of a royal court somewhere in eighteenth-century Europe, and is nowhere more striking than in the annual 'Silent Ceremony', when the new Lord Mayor (chosen from among the twenty-five Aldermen, one per Ward) takes office, the only sounds the measured pacing (backwards) by officials as they present the various symbols of office, the scratching of the pen as the Lord Mayor signs his (or, occasionally, her) name, and the swishing of the tricorne hat as that of the outgoing Lord Mayor is replaced by that of the incoming. Then there are the state banquets we get to attend, with the state trumpeters relaying their fanfares from one end of the Great Hall to the other, and the speeches from Prime Ministers, Lord Chancellors and visiting heads of state.

But most of all, perhaps, there is the sense of history itself, the awareness of being part of a tradition that may appear, at least on the surface, barely to have changed since the Middle Ages, members of the Court of Common Council having been elected by Wards in the City since 1384. There are many differences, of course, in my experience of being a member of the Court from those of my predecessors in the sixteenth century who witnessed – and, indeed, participated in – the events described in this book, the principal one being that I, despite being a Council*man*, am a woman, which would have been unthinkable for most of the City Corporation's history – but when we Commoners don our mazarine-blue gowns, and the Aldermen their scarlet, to march off in procession to some civic occasion, it's not so very hard to imagine we're setting off to watch some poor heretic being burnt at the stake.

Actually that is an imaginary scene – there are no records of Common Councilmen being ordered to attend burnings, though the Lord Mayor and Aldermen were frequently in attendance, and the two City Sheriffs were generally in charge of the proceedings. What is not imaginary, however, is the tablet on the wall of the Great Hall of Guildhall, more or less opposite where I sit every month (always on a Thursday, at one o'clock in the afternoon), headed: 'A list of some important trials held in this hall'. The very first entry on the list commemorates 'Anne Askew: a protestant martyr [who] was tried in 1546 for heresy. Afterwards she was tortured on the rack in the Tower of London, carried in a chair to Smithfield and burnt aged twenty-five.'

There are many questions arising from these two brief sentences. The first must be: who was Anne Askew, and what had she done to bring such a horrible end on herself at the age of only twenty-five? Who else was involved in Anne's story, and why were the beliefs of this young woman of such concern to her contemporaries that they were prepared to set her on fire for them, and she was prepared to embrace that fate? This book will attempt to answer these, and other, questions.

Anne Askew was burnt at the stake along with John Lascelles (a lawyer and Gentleman of the King's Privy Chamber), John Hadlam (a tailor from Essex) and John Hemsley (a former Franciscan friar), on 16 July 1546. A great stage was built at Smithfield for the convenience of Chancellor Wriothesley, other members of the Privy Council and City dignitaries, to watch the burning in comfort. Anne herself, having been broken on the rack, was unable to stand, and was chained to the stake in a sitting position. John Louth, the Archdeacon of Nottingham, who witnessed the execution, described Anne as smiling throughout her torment and looking like an angel, and insisted that, at the moment of her death, there was 'a pleasant cracking from heaven'. Whether that was the sound of the flames, or summer lightning, or merely a figment of the imagination, cannot now be determined; nor can we know how, or if, the witnesses could actually have identified the precise moment of death.

So what was the terrible crime that Anne was deemed to have committed and that led her to this appalling end? Why was being a 'Protestant' or 'reformer' considered so heinous, and what was this 'heresy' with which she was charged?

A word deriving from the Greek, 'heresy' originally meant merely 'choice', but by the Middle Ages it had come to mean 'wrong choice', especially in matters of religion. In Europe, and particularly Spain, the 'Inquisition' had been set up to identify heretics, with the aim of their contaminating heresy being cut out of society, like a cancer. Heretics were given one chance to 'abjure' or 'recant' – effectively, to make a public confession that they had been wrong, to accept some kind of 'shaming' penance (such as standing in front of a church congregation wearing a white sheet or being paraded through the streets on a cart), and to agree to follow 'orthodox' belief ('orthodoxy' meaning both 'right doctrine' and 'right worship') from now on. If a heretic, having recanted, fell back into his or her old ways, there was to be no second chance. They were to be handed over by the Church to the civic authorities for punishment – which meant death by burning.

But the nature of what constituted heresy kept changing, particularly in England during the tumultuous years of the mid-sixteenth century. There were several types of possible heretical belief under the respective reigns of the three monarchs which constitute the burning time (the period which saw the greatest number of burnings for heresy) in Tudor England – Henry VIII, Edward VI and Mary I. Some were based entirely upon interpretations of religious doctrine; some hinged on changes in society and questions of authority and were linked to the increased availability of the printed word; others were dictated by the whim of the individual monarch.

Purely religious heresies were associated with the new doctrines of Protestantism, originating from the teachings of Martin Luther and others. Luther's central doctrine was that of 'justification by faith alone', which implied that the whole paraphernalia of the traditional Church, with its pilgrimages, processions and prayers to saints, was at best unnecessary and at worst wicked and a form of idolatry. The nature of priesthood was also called into question, including whether or not priests should be celibate. But the most important issue in the religious disputes of the time – and the one on which the fate of Anne Askew hinged – concerned what was believed to take place during celebrations of the Eucharist, or the Mass (or what Protestants referred to as Holy Communion). In the mid-1540s, to declare in the wrong quarters that the Eucharist was a commemoration of the sacrifice of Christ, rather than a sacrifice in itself, was to risk one's life.

For the Protestant, or evangelical, reformers, the 'word' (that is, the Bible – rather than the Catholic emphasis on 'the Word of God' as Christ himself) took precedence over the Mass. One of the things which most disturbed the orthodox about the teaching of Luther and his followers was that it involved ordinary people being encouraged to read the Bible, in their own language, for themselves. Previously, the faithful would only have heard selected extracts from the Bible, in the context of church services, being said or chanted in Latin (though there was a move, in the late 1530s and under Henry VIII's authority, for English versions of the lessons – or readings – at Mass to be read out after the Latin). It was for the priest to understand the content of the Bible, as interpreted by the traditions of the Church, and for him to convey that interpretation to his flock. It was not up to his flock to decide for themselves what the word of God meant: so at least the hierarchy thought, and this became one of the main strands of opposition to the 'Gospellers', as the Protestants were sometimes known.

The centrality of the question of authority also helps to explain why heresy was often closely aligned with treason. If people were allowed to interpret the scriptures for themselves, without the mediation of legitimately authorized priests and theologians, anything could happen – or so it seemed to those desperate to preserve (for reasons either of power or of genuine belief, or of a combination of the two) the approved interpretation as the only possible truth. Sir Thomas More, for instance, was convinced that such a relaxation of ecclesiastical authority and of inherited systems of belief would unleash mayhem on the world and lead to the collapse of the entire social order.

In the time of the Tudor monarchs and before, most people maintained an unquestioning belief in the virtue of obedience to authority, whereas we, especially in the Western hemisphere, have now become very unused to the idea of authority being exercised over us – particularly over elements of what we consider to be our personal lives, of which our religious or spiritual beliefs (or lack of them) are seen as the most personal and private. But for many people living under Henry, Edward or Mary (and later under Elizabeth), having to negotiate the changes and chances of each reign, the most natural reaction to religious laws was to obey them with as little question – but maybe with as much covert grumbling – as the laws dictating which classes of people could wear which sorts of dress. This was what it meant to be a subject, and obedience, at least in outward things (including speech), was the surest way to survive. If you are used to being told what to wear (and sumptuary laws, or 'acts of apparel', were still being rigorously enforced in the reign of Elizabeth), perhaps you will also accept being told what to believe – at least until you begin to discover for yourself that what you are being told may not be right, or at best may not present the complete picture. This is the kind of realization that came to Anne Askew and people like her, a realization fostered by their own reading.

Of the three monarchs whose reigns span the burning time, it was at least possible to know where Edward and Mary stood and therefore, in theory at least, to avoid ending up on the wrong side. They were, however, diametrically opposed – Edward being a firm, some might say bigoted, Protestant, while his half-sister Mary was a correspondingly staunch Catholic. So to remain 'orthodox' when one reign succeeded the other, their subjects had to perform some extreme voltes-face. Henry was more of a problem. It could be argued that he was responsible for the initiation of the whole process of heresy-hunting in England, as it was he who split off the English Church from Rome. Though his motives were primarily bound up with his desire to have his marriage to Katherine of Aragon annulled so that he could marry Anne Boleyn and have an heir by her, he also had some sympathies with the 'new men' or Protestants, particularly during the years he was in love with Anne, as she was herself a Protestant sympathizer. But on the other hand, Henry remained largely faithful to most Catholic doctrine, and it was mainly for falling foul of traditional religious beliefs – as Anne Askew did – that 'heretics' were burnt during his reign.

Burnings typically took place on a wooden platform, some three feet from the ground, on which the victims were bound to the stake by chains. Bundles of brushwood, rods and sticks tied together to form 'faggots' – more usually used for kindling in the domestic hearth, or as the principal fuel of the city's bakeries and brew-houses – were stacked around the victims' legs, and the official in charge of the proceedings – sometimes the Lord Mayor of London – would cry out 'Fire the faggots!' and 'Let justice be done!' as the signal for the executioner to light the pile of wood with a flaming torch. There would always be a crowd gathered round (though not too close) – some sympathizers there to support the victims, others come to enjoy the spectacle – all waiting for the moment when the bodies, charred and melted by the flames, would topple over from their chains and into the fire. The faggots were intended to kindle quickly to produce a short hot blaze, before flesh and body-fat provided fuel for the fire. But every burning was different; if the fire 'caught', it could be over relatively quickly, but on damp days, or when the wind persisted in blowing the flames away from the body, it could take up to an hour for the condemned person to die, an hour of excruciating agony.

Of the burnings which took place in England between 1529 and 1558 by far the largest number occurred in one small area of London – the area known as (West) Smithfield. Just outside the City walls though still within its bounds, not far from Newgate prison, ten minutes' walk from both the Guildhall and St Paul's Cathedral on Ludgate Hill (the old pre-Fire of London cathedral, over 600 feet in length and with a spire rising to some 500 feet), this was a convenient place to take people to die, with space enough to erect viewing stands from which 'the great and the good' could watch the spectacle. Smithfield, originally known as 'Smoothfield', had been a place of public execution for over 400 years; many witches and heretics had been burnt, roasted or boiled alive there. It was here that the Scottish hero and patriot, Sir William Wallace, was hanged, drawn and quartered in 1315, and where Wat Tyler, the leader of the Peasants' Revolt, was fatally stabbed by the Lord Mayor in 1381. Many tournaments had also taken place there, royal jousts having begun in Smithfield in the reign of Edward III (1327–77). The other activity for which the area was (and is) famous was the craft of butchery, meat having been traded in Smithfield since the tenth century.

Adjacent to the open space of Smithfield was the great Augustinian Priory of St Bartholomew, one of the City's most important monasteries. The annual Bartholomew Fair was held on the priory's land, attracting all manner of people – cloth merchants from all around Europe mingling with jugglers, acrobats, inn-keepers and pickpockets. It was also an area which drew the poor and the sick, the monastery's sister-foundation, St Bartholomew's Hospital (still world-famous as 'Barts'), offering relief for the body while the prior and canons (as the members of an Augustinian community were known) offered prayers for the soul.

Of the 288 people estimated to have been burnt for heresy during the five-year reign of Mary Tudor, forty-eight were burnt in Smithfield. The next-highest numbers were eighteen in Lewes in Sussex, seventeen in Stratford-atte-Bow (now Bow in East London), fourteen in Canterbury and seven in Maidstone (both these latter in the county of Kent). Some seventeen people had suffered the same fate in Smithfield under Henry VIII, as had two 'Anabaptists' (extremists whom even Protestants regarded as heretics) during the brief reign of Edward VI.

However interesting, and harrowing, the lives and deaths of individual 'martyrs' (and the meanings of that emotive word will be considered in due course), my hope is that this book will be more than a compilation of biographies. During the time I have been working on it, the questions that the stories of the Smithfield martyrs provoke have become ever more pertinent, the need for answers (if any exist) ever more urgent. What is it that makes people kill other people in the name of religion? Why are some people prepared to die – or kill – for their beliefs, while the rest of us are content to muddle along with compromise and uncertainty? What led to this 'burning time' in the history of England? Could it have been avoided and how was it overcome? Could it happen again? And, most importantly, is there anything we can learn from this dark period in our history to help bring an end to today's deathly religious conflicts – or are we doomed to go on repeating the same mistakes, in different parts of the world, until we finally succeed in annihilating humankind altogether? The instances of heroism that emerge from the stories of the martyrs, the occasional glimpses of a different kind of light from that produced by flames, suggest it is worth struggling on.

There are several parallels between Tudor England and our own world today. One of the most obvious concerns technological developments, the revolution in information technology having an arguably even greater impact than the invention of printing had on the authoritative delivery of information. Now anyone really can find out anything for themselves, and intermediaries are no longer required. This in turn means that questions of interpretation and discrimination – how does one determine which information is reliable? – are ever more insistent. The proliferation and dissemination of 'authority' in Islam that has occurred with the growth of the Internet is addressed by Vit Šisler of Charles University in Prague in an article entitled 'The Internet and the Construction of Islamic Knowledge in Europe', in which he argues that 'a new paradigm has emerged in the construction of Islamic knowledge and interpretative authority. Within this new paradigm established "traditional" authorities operate in coexistence with Internet-based muftis, online fatwa databases and individual Islamic blogs.' Of particular resonance is Šisler's observation that: 'The Internet highlights the myriad concepts, movements and sects of Islam, but it also highlights the differences between them. In particular, the younger Muslims living in Europe pay close attention to these differences.

They search for an original or "true" Islam, which they can distinguish from the Islam of their parents.' This is very reminiscent of the sixteenth-century Protestants' adherence to what they perceived as the beliefs and practices of the early Church, reconstructed from their reading of the New Testament and which they characterized as original or 'true' Christianity. It is a form of 'primitivism', characteristic of reformatory movements.

To return to Smithfield, if we open our story in the year 1530 or thereabouts, we find little to suggest the turmoil to come – apart from the King's increasing impatience with Rome, and the rise of Lutheranism in parts of Europe. (Soon after Luther's teachings had been condemned by the Pope in 1521, his works had been publicly burnt in Oxford, Cambridge and at Paul's Cross – the site of the open-air pulpit outside St Paul's Cathedral – in London.) Henry was still married to Katherine of Aragon, though becoming increasingly desperate to cast her off and marry Anne Boleyn. He had been insinuating to Pope Clement VII that, if the Pope would not hurry up and make it possible for him to divorce Katherine, a way of dispensing with papal authority might be sought. In 1529 Henry had dismissed Cardinal Thomas Wolsey from the post of Lord Chancellor, under pressure from Anne, and replaced him with Thomas More. The disgraced Wolsey died in November 1530. Earlier that year, in July, John Stokesley, who was supportive of the King's campaign for a divorce and involved in the making of the case for an annulment under canon law, was appointed Bishop of London in succession to Cuthbert Tunstall, who had become Bishop of Durham.

At the helm of the small community of Augustinian canons living in St Bartholomew's Priory was William Bolton, who had been the prior since 1505. Now nearing the end of his life, Bolton had in his heyday been not only a cleric but also a builder of some eminence, having been employed as 'master [or clerk] of the works' by both Henry VII and Henry VIII. (The word 'builder' in this context implies something more akin to architect or project manager in modern terms, rather than someone involved in the physical work of construction.) Bolton's main work for Henry VIII had involved the rebuilding of New Hall in Essex, which the King had procured from Thomas Boleyn, the Earl of Wiltshire, and grandfather of Anne. The prior had also undertaken large building operations at St Bartholomew's itself and at Canonbury Tower in Islington, which formed part of the monastery's possessions (and from where its water supply was derived). Another notable commission entrusted to Bolton had been the ordering of the chimney pots for Cardinal Wolsey's palace at Hampton Court. But by 1530 Bolton's active life was over; in addition to his post at St Bartholomew's, he had for the last eight years been Rector of Harrow on the Hill, in Middlesex, but he was by now about eighty years old and virtually immobile. He died in April 1532.

Within the Priory Church, as was common in monastic churches, a chapel was set aside for the use of parishioners – the lay people who lived and worked in the monastic close. The parish also had its own priest, who would celebrate Mass in the chapel and look after the general spiritual welfare of the parishioners. It is not known who was fulfilling this role around the time of Prior Bolton's death, but by the end of the decade the post was held by a man who remained a constant presence at St Bartholomew's throughout all the turmoil of the burning time. This was Sir John Deane, the last parish priest of the chapel and subsequently the first rector of the parish church. In the early 1530s, Deane was already connected to the monastery, being Rector of Little Stanmore in Middlesex, one of the possessions of St Bartholomew's.

Meanwhile, steadily making his way up a different professional ladder, negotiating the twists and turns of Tudor politics, was a lawyer of the Middle Temple called Richard Rich, in 1530 aged thirty-four and recently returned as Member of Parliament for the borough of Colchester in Essex. His is a name that is already well-known, if in fictionalized form, to readers of Hilary Mantel's *Wolf Hall* and of C. J. Sansom's Shardlake series – where he appears as the principal villain – as well as to viewers of Robert Bolt's *A Man for All Seasons*. Rich's life would intersect with that of John Deane at many points over the following years, and both men would be witnesses at close quarters to all the horror of the burning time.

Nothing they had known before 1530, in their respective careers, could quite have prepared them for the sights, sounds and smells they would encounter over the next thirty years, as many of their closest acquaintances were consumed in the fires of Smithfield.

Chapter One

BOILING, BURNING AND AMBITION

✠

And whereas in the translation of the New Testament [Tyndale] covered and dissimulated himself as much as he could, yet, when he perceived his cloaked heresies espied and destroyed, then shewed he shortly himself in his own likeness, sending forth first his wicked Book of Mammon, and after his malicious Book of Obedience. In which books he sheweth himself so puffed up with the poison of pride, malice and envy, that it is more than marvel that the skin can hold together.

Thomas More,
from *A Dialogue Concerning Heresies*, 1529

ON 5 APRIL 1531 a cook, known both as Richard Roose and Richard Coke, and employed in the household of Bishop Fisher of Rochester, was boiled to death in Smithfield. He was convicted of having attempted to poison the bishop, and indeed several people of the household had become ill after eating the pottage or gruel which he had prepared. Two people – a member of the bishop's staff and a widow who had been among the poor people to whom leftovers from the kitchen were distributed – had actually died. The bishop himself had not eaten any of the pottage and so, in the unlikely event of this having been an assassination attempt, it failed.

For this case of food poisoning, the poor cook was boiled in a cauldron. According to Ambassador Eustace Chapuys, reporting the incident in a despatch to the Holy Roman Emperor Charles V, the cook had confessed to having thrown a powder into the pottage, which he had been told was some kind of a joke – probably involving a laxative – that wouldn't cause anyone real harm. There was no joke about the method of execution; he was immersed several times in boiling water – 'locked in a chain and pulled up and down with a gibbet at divers times till he was dead'.

Not only was it believed that the poisoning was deliberate (and so the alleged crime was given the name of 'high treason' and made the subject of a new statute entitled 'An Acte for Poysoning'), there was even a suspicion of involvement of people very close to the King, Chapuys specifically mentioning the possible involvement of 'the lady and her father' (that is, of Anne Boleyn and her father Thomas). Chapuys's speculation, while based on unreliable or non-existent evidence, nevertheless gives an indication of the atmosphere surrounding the King and those closest to him at this time, an aura of fear in which such conspiracy theories could arise and flourish. Bishop Fisher, an ascetic ecclesiastic of great personal integrity, thin-faced and clear-eyed, was known to be one of the chief supporters of Katherine of Aragon – and hence one of the greatest opponents of Anne Boleyn. His support for Katherine was based more on his belief in the indissolubility of marriage than on personal grounds, and no threat of poison would be likely to make him change his mind.

Around the same time as the alleged poisoning in the bishop's kitchens, in February 1531, an agreement had been made that a large fine be paid by the Church, all the clergy contributing, to the King in exchange for a pardon for offences committed under *praemunire*. (Chapuys had implied in his despatch to the Emperor that this decision – along with the clergy being forced to acknowledge Henry as the supreme head of the Church of England 'as far as the law of Christ allows', this latter phrase being added as a result of Fisher's efforts – is what had made the bishop ill, rather than any poison.) The so-called *praemunire* charge is what had been levelled at Cardinal Wolsey to bring about his downfall. Briefly, *praemunire* referred to the criminal offence of having introduced into England a foreign or papal authority that might limit the royal authority and, Wolsey having been convicted of it, all the clergy – especially the bishops – were deemed to have committed it as well by the mere fact of their having previously given obedience to the cardinal. It was therefore a word to inspire fear, particularly among the higher clergy, who did not wish to go the same way as the late disgraced Wolsey. And it was the higher clergy who had agreed to the fine, on behalf of their subordinates as well as of themselves. Some of those subordinates did not take this decision well, particularly in London. Meeting some resistance from the London clergy to contribute to the fine, the new Bishop of London, John Stokesley, summoned all the priests of his diocese to St Paul's Cathedral in late August, intending to see them in groups of six or eight and persuade them to have their benefices assessed (so that it could be determined how much they could each afford to pay). But the six hundred or so priests who assembled at St Paul's, encouraged by lay supporters, refused to submit to this effort to manipulate them and, rather than waiting to be invited in small groups, a larger group of them forced their way into the chapter house to confront the bishop. In response to his attempts to convince them that they had inadvertently offended the King through their 'frailty and lack of wisdom' and that the King was being 'merciful' in accepting a fine of only £100,000 to be paid over five years, the priests insisted they had never had anything to do with the cardinal so could not be implicated in *praemunire* and they neither could nor would pay up. The argument soon got out of hand, several of the bishop's servants were 'buffeted', and eighteen of the priests and a smaller number of the laymen present were arrested and imprisoned. They were eventually charged not only with riotous assembly, but with conspiring to murder Bishop Stokesley. The records of any ensuing trials have been lost – but, whatever else may have happened, the London clergy, like all the others, had to contribute to the fine.

Fears of being implicated in *praemunire* offences, or of difficulty in raising money to pay the fine, were minor in comparison to the ordeal facing another priest that same year of 1531. On 20 November, a Monday, Bishop Stokesley pronounced these words against one Richard Bayfield, a former Benedictine monk, before a number of high-ranking officials and clerics gathered in St Paul's:

> We John by the permission of God, Bishop of London, rightly
> and lawfully proceeding in this behalf, do dismiss thee Richard
> Bayfield, alias Somersam, being pronounced by us a relapsed
> heretic, and degraded by us from all ecclesiastical privilege, out
> of the Ecclesiastical Court, pronouncing that the secular
> power here present should receive thee under their jurisdic-
> tion, earnestly requiring and desiring in the bowels of Jesus
> Christ, that the execution of this worthy punishment, to be
> done upon thee, and against thee in this behalf, may be so
> moderated, that there be neither overmuch cruelty, neither
> too much favourable gentleness, but that it may be to the
> health and salvation of thy soul, and to the extirpation, fear,
> terror, and conversion of all other heretics unto the unity of
> the Catholic faith. This our final decree by this our sentence
> definitive, we have caused to be published in form aforesaid.

Prior to being handed over to the City authorities ('the secular
power here present'), Bayfield had to be 'degraded' – that is,
stripped of his orders as a priest – the ceremony of degradation not
only consisting of words but also including a powerful dramatic
element. In a symbolic reversal of the process of ordination, the
bishop struck Bayfield on the chest with his crosier as he knelt
before the altar, and then pushed him backwards down the altar
steps, so forcefully that he hit his head on the floor. He was then
handed over to the sheriffs and burnt in Smithfield on 4 December.
His was a particularly excruciating death, as the flames were reluctant to take hold, and he stood chained to the stake for half an hour,
slowly roasting. According to John Foxe in his *Acts and Monuments*,
'when the left arm was on fire and burned, he rubbed it with his
right hand, and it fell from his body, and he continued in prayer to
the end, without moving'.

Richard Bayfield had been born at Hadleigh in Suffolk, took
his monastic vows at the Abbey of Bury St Edmunds in 1514, and
was ordained priest four years later. In the early 1520s he had the
responsibility of looking after visitors to the Abbey (the provision
of hospitality being an important aspect of Benedictine life) and
this was how he came to be acquainted with the man who would

change his life – Robert Barnes, who had come to the Abbey to
meet with a former fellow student at Louvain (or Leuven) University in the Duchy of Brabant (now in Belgium). At the time of his
meeting with Bayfield, Barnes was based at the University of Cambridge and was one of a group of scholars and preachers who used
to gather informally at the town's White Horse tavern to exchange
ideas about biblical texts and the new doctrines coming out of
Germany. Barnes gave Bayfield a copy of the Latin translation of
the New Testament by the humanist scholar Desiderius Erasmus
(whom Barnes would have encountered at Louvain). Erasmus's text
had been published in 1516, and comprised a new edition of the
New Testament in Greek with his Latin translation printed on the
facing pages. Conservative elements in the Church had been perturbed at the idea of this new translation presenting a challenge to
the old and accepted Latin version by St Jerome, known as the
Vulgate, and Erasmus's annotations to his Greek text also at times
differed from the tradition. But Bayfield seems to have been
hungry for knowledge and soon found himself drawn to the new
ideas espoused by Barnes and his friends. In addition to Erasmus's
Greek and Latin New Testament, Bayfield was given (by two
'godly men of London', who were travelling with Barnes) William Tyndale's translation of the same text into English, along
with two other books by Tyndale. These were *The Parable of the
Wicked Mammon* (which comprised an argument in defence of the
Lutheran doctrine of justification by faith) and *The Obedience of a
Christian Man*.

Such straying from the paths of orthodoxy did not go down
well with Bayfield's superiors, and two years later – two years
during which he had spent much of his time reading and thinking
– his abbot confined him to the abbey prison, in the hope that he
would come to his senses. Instead, after about nine months (during
which time Bayfield was allegedly whipped, gagged and placed in
the stocks), Robert Barnes managed to negotiate his release from
the prison (Barnes was clearly skilled in the art of persuasion) and
took him back with him to Cambridge. In the atmosphere of
learning, discussion and enthusiasm which he encountered there,

Bayfield became ever more convinced of the rightness of the new teachings.

One year after Bayfield had been ordained to the priesthood in 1518, another young man – John Deane, the future Rector of St Bartholomew's in Smithfield – went through the same process (though he had chosen the secular, rather than the monastic, route). Both men were probably aged around twenty-four at the time of their ordination, this being the earliest age at which men could be ordained priest in the early sixteenth century. John Deane came from a family of yeomen farmers who owned a small amount of land in Shurlach, near the village of Davenham. The town of Northwich, where Deane states in his will that he was born, was just under two miles away and was itself about eighteen miles east of Chester, close to the border between England and Wales.

Nothing is known for sure about John Deane's education, but any man presenting himself for ordination was likely to have received elementary education as a boy. He would have learnt how to read and particularly how to say his prayers, in both Latin and English. Prior to putting himself forward for ordination to the lowest of the main, or holy, orders – that of subdeacon – he may have been admitted to the minor orders, and served as an acolyte in his local parish church (St Wilfrid's, Davenham, in the young Deane's case). The next step would be to prepare for his 'examinations', at which he would have to demonstrate that he fulfilled a number of criteria. He had to be of legitimate birth, at least eighteen years old, and unmarried. He must never have murdered anyone, be able to demonstrate that he was not seeking a clerical position through simony (that is, through having bought the position) or fraud, and he must also not be suffering from any physical disability. (Readers of C. J. Sansom's Shardlake novels will recall the hunchbacked lawyer's bitterness at having had his early vocation to the priesthood rejected on these grounds.) It was possible to apply for a papal dispensation in the case of disability, but this could be a costly business, with no guarantee of success. These 'examinations' into the candidate's personal circumstances and suitability generally took place a few days before the ordination to the subdiaconate.

A further examination would be required before a subdeacon could proceed to ordination as a deacon (for which the minimum age requirement was nineteen). This time a sound knowledge of scripture, music (at least such musical skill and knowledge as were necessary to sing the services) and liturgy was expected of the candidate. By the time the deacon was ready to become a priest (at the age of twenty-four), he would need to be able to demonstrate his competence in Latin. (In a report on the archdeaconry of London in 1561–2, towards the end of his ministry, Deane was described in the following terms: '*latine aliquid intelligit*' – 'he has some understanding of Latin'.) In practice, men were often not ordained as subdeacon until they had reached, or nearly reached, the age at which they could also become a priest, so that the whole process – that is, the three ordinations – might take place over the course of eighteen months or so.

In addition to passing the various tests of eligibility, it was at the first of these stages – at the point of ordination as a subdeacon – that a man had to provide evidence of his ability to support himself financially; this meant he had to prove either that he had the 'title' to a benefice – that he had, in modern parlance, a church job already lined up – or that he had a private income, deriving from his family. Once all these hurdles had been overcome, the young men seeking ordination would appear before the bishop of their diocese, at a ceremony advertised in advance by archdeacons and rural deans. Ordinations generally took place four times a year on the so-called Ember Days – that is, on the Saturdays in the third week of Advent (December), the first week of Lent (February or March), immediately before Trinity Sunday (May or June) and closest to the feast of the Nativity of the Virgin (September). The ceremony of ordination involved the laying on of hands by the bishop; a new priest would also be invested with a chasuble, paten and chalice, symbolic of the fact that he was now able to celebrate the Mass.

At no point did most candidates for the priesthood have to demonstrate an ability to preach, and only those who attended university (not the majority) or who were members of a preaching order such as the Dominicans received any training in how to do so. Preaching sermons was of less importance to the ordinary parish priest than celebrating the Mass and, when such a priest was called upon to preach, there were collections of homilies he could use – either as a basis for his own words or as a straightforward text to be read out verbatim. There were plenty of such texts available for use, one of the principal aids to preaching being the *Festial* compiled by John Mirk, an Augustinian canon, in 1508 which gathered together improving stories about the saints, many of them drawn from the medieval *Golden Legend*. Collections of sermons were also produced by various learned men of the Church, including Bishop Fisher of Rochester and Bishop Longland of Lincoln, with the intention of helping priests combat the spread of Lutheran ideas in their parishes.

At the time John Deane and his contemporaries were seeking ordination, there was an insufficient supply of benefices to meet the demand, and consequently it often fell to a religious house – a priory, convent or monastery – to act as a patron to a young man by providing him with a 'title'. Deane, who was ordained priest by the Bishop of Lichfield on 18 June 1519, was sponsored by Vale Royal Abbey, a Cistercian foundation situated between Northwich and Winsford.

Given the sponsorship of Vale Royal, which was local to his home, it is likely that John Deane began his priestly ministry in Cheshire, though there are no records of his having done so. By 1535 he had moved south, to Middlesex, where he was Rector of Little Stanmore, the largest single estate of St Bartholomew's Priory; his parishioners would not have numbered more than a couple of hundred (in 1547 the number of communicants in Little Stanmore totalled 127, of whom 91 were adult males). His stipend was £6 13s 4d.

The connection between John Deane and St Bartholomew's, offering an explanation as to how he came by this fairly lucrative rectory, so far from his origins in Northwich, is to be found in Sir Robert Blagge, near whose chapel in the quire of the Priory Church John Deane requested to be (and is) buried. Blagge was also born in Northwich, and Deane's request to be buried near him, along with the age gap between the two men (Blagge was considerably older than Deane), suggests that Blagge may have acted as Deane's patron and mentor.

At the time of Deane's ordination to the priesthood, Sir Robert Blagge was a long-standing inhabitant of the parish of St Bartholomew and one of its most influential parishioners. He had served as Remembrancer to King Henry VII, was listed as a baron of the exchequer in 1511 and held various other Crown appointments. From 1515 he had been joint Surveyor of Crown Lands and in 1519 was Surveyor General in the counties of Chester and Flint. He died in 1522, and his funeral was held at St Bartholomew's, with Prior William Bolton officiating (Sir Robert having made this particular request in his will). It is tempting to imagine the young priest John Deane in attendance, making his first acquaintance with the Priory Church which was to play such a large part in his life, then still in its glorious days as part of a great monastic complex. Sir Robert may also have been instrumental in furthering Prior Bolton's career, Bolton having taken over the responsibilities of Master of the King's Works in 1504, when Sir Robert was the King's Remembrancer. The connection between the Blagges and St Bartholomew's extends to Stanmore, for it was here that Sir Robert's son George died a somewhat untimely death in 1551. There is therefore strong circumstantial evidence to support the suggestion that Sir Robert, between Deane's ordination in 1519 and his own death in 1522, persuaded his friend Prior Bolton to award the living at Little Stanmore to his young protégé from Northwich.

The acquisition of an influential patron was of prime importance in sixteenth-century England, in all walks of life, particularly for young men whose own families were not wealthy or well placed. The fortunes of Richard Rich, whose life we are tracing in parallel with that of John Deane, improved considerably once he had identified and secured a useful patron. It is entirely in keeping with Rich's character that a degree of uncertainty exists as to his origins. There were a number of branches of the Rich family, and Richard appears to have laid claim to various relatives throughout his life as and when it suited him. Though the evidence is not definitive, it is generally agreed that he was born in Basingstoke in 1496 or 1497 to John Rich of Penton Mewsey, Hampshire, and his wife Agnes. The family may have been prominent in the Mercers' Company (the foremost livery company of the City of London), a succession of men called Richard, Thomas or John Riche having been Master Mercer in the fifteenth and early sixteenth centuries. Our Richard's father John owned a house in Islington, Middlesex, which he left to his son in 1509, and the young Richard may have grown up in, or at least near, the City (Thomas More, definitely a Londoner, claimed at his trial to have known him in his youth) and he may have been educated at Cambridge University. (He is listed in Venn's *Alumni Cantabrigiensis* as 'probably sometime a member of the university'.) What is certain is that he was admitted to the Middle Temple as a lawyer in February 1516.

The Middle Temple and the other three Inns of Court (the Inner Temple, Gray's Inn and Lincoln's Inn) were established by the middle of the fourteenth century, with the exclusive right of calling their members to the English Bar as barristers. The name 'Temple' derives from the Knights Templar who had been in possession of the Temple site for over 150 years, until they were dissolved in 1312. Middle Temple (along with its neighbouring Inner Temple – there is, confusingly, no 'Outer Temple') was – and still is – a so-called liberty, an area independent of any parish and consequently outside the ecclesiastical jurisdiction of the Bishop of London; neither was it, historically, governed by the City of London Corporation. So, though it falls geographically within the boundaries of the City, it can be thought of as an independent enclave.

The young Rich does not appear to have done anything in particular to distinguish himself from the other young lawyers at Middle Temple, beyond being very ambitious. In his *Records of St Bartholomew's Priory*, E. A. Webb expressed the opinion that Rich 'does not seem to have been a deeply read lawyer, but such knowledge as he had, added to great astuteness, carried him a long way'. John Lord Campbell, in his *Lives of the Lord Chancellors* of 1846, had little good to say about Rich, describing him as 'through life a very consistent character in all that was base and profligate'. He also considered that Rich 'early displayed an aspiring genius, and a determination to have all the pleasures of life without patient industry, or being very scrupulous about the means employed by him to gain his objects'.

Rich demonstrated his ambition in 1526 by standing for election for the common serjeantship of the City of London, a senior legal position, but unsurprisingly he lost to the Crown's nominee, William Walsingham. Two years later he was appointed a Commissioner of the Peace (or magistrate) for Essex and Hertfordshire, and it was through contacts in Essex that he found the breakthrough he had been looking for. Two significant men now appear among Rich's close acquaintance. One was John de Vere, an Essex magnate and the 15th Earl of Oxford, a member of whose council Rich had become by 1529. The earls of Oxford, in common with other members of the nobility, used their councils to conduct administrative matters, particularly when they themselves had to be absent from their estates, and to provide legal advice over such business as the sale or purchase of land, the management of trusts and the arrangement of marriages. The second man of importance to Rich was born in the village where the earls of Oxford had their manor, Earls Colne: the barrister and judge Thomas Audley. Rich would already have known Audley by sight, as he too was a Middle Temple lawyer, but it was with his appointment as a magistrate for Essex that he came into closer contact with him, as Audley had been appointed to the same role in 1521. It is likely that it was Audley who introduced him to John de Vere – but Audley himself was the real prize for Rich. Once the connection had been made, where Audley went, Rich was never far behind.

In 1523 Audley had become the Member of Parliament for Essex and he continued to represent this constituency in subsequent parliaments. In 1527 he held a position at Henry VIII's court as Groom of the Chamber and also became a member of the household of Cardinal Wolsey. On Wolsey's fall in 1529, Audley was made Chancellor of the Duchy of Lancaster and the same year became Speaker of the House of Commons, presiding over the

famous assembly which came to be known as the Reformation
Parliament (lasting from 1529 to 1536) and which included among
its achievements the abolition of papal jurisdiction over the Church
of England. Audley was joined in that parliament by Richard Rich,
who was returned as the member for the borough of Colchester,
a seat in the virtual control of Rich's other patron, the Earl of
Oxford.

A central figure during the early years of the Reformation
Parliament was the Lord Chancellor, Sir Thomas More, whose
intensity, concentration and unwavering focus are conveyed clearly
in the portrait painted of him in 1527 (two years before he became
Lord Chancellor) by Hans Holbein the Younger. One of More's
principal preoccupations – alongside his ultimately unwinnable
struggle to maintain his loyalty to both King and Pope – was the
battle against heresy, and against Lutheranism in particular. A man
on whom he had his eye in this regard was Thomas Bilney, a
graduate fellow of the University of Cambridge, a priest, and one
of the 'new men' encountered in that town by the Benedictine
monk Richard Bayfield, after he had been rescued by Robert
Barnes from incarceration in his abbey.

Bilney, often referred to as 'Little Bilney' on account of his
diminutive stature (though it has been pointed out that a more
fitting description might have been 'aggressive' or 'tough-minded'
Bilney), was an adherent of the central Lutheran doctrine of justification by faith alone. Though he condemned superstition and
corruption in the Church, he did not view himself as a 'Protestant'
and did not depart from many traditional teachings, including the
headship of the Pope. Bilney had himself been converted to the
cause of evangelical reform by reading Erasmus's Latin New Testament. In 1527 he had embarked on a preaching tour around the
country, though he was licensed to preach only in the diocese of
Ely, and he also distributed copies of Tyndale's English translation
of the New Testament which, having gone on sale in London early
in 1526, had been banned by Thomas More's friend Cuthbert Tunstall, then Bishop of London. Such activities led to Bilney's arrest
and questioning by Bishop Tunstall, who persuaded him to recant.

He was imprisoned for a year in the Tower, and subsequently returned to Cambridge full of remorse at having betrayed his beliefs under pressure.

Despite King Henry's desire to be free of the constraints of Rome and the Pope, he was himself no supporter of Martin Luther or of those identified by More as heretics. Though he was influenced by Erasmus and believed the Church to be in need of reform, he was bound to be wary of any movement that threatened to undermine the authority of hierarchies and princes. He was also very devout and heard Mass several times daily, though he was not particularly interested in pilgrimages and was never enamoured of monasteries. He had vigorously defended the Mass in 1521 in a polemic he had written (possibly with the help of Bishop Fisher) against Luther, entitled the *Assertio Septem Sacramentorum* ('Defence of the Seven Sacraments'), for which work Pope Leo X, to whom it was dedicated, rewarded him with the title *Fidei Defensor* ('Defender of the Faith'). In the *Assertio* Henry defended the traditional understanding of the Mass and of transubstantiation, while not insisting on the use of this specific word. 'No one would trouble Luther to believe in transubstantiation,' the King declared, 'as long as he believes that the bread is changed into flesh and the wine into the blood.'

Broadly speaking and for the purposes of understanding what the argument was about, the Catholic doctrine of 'transubstantiation' affirms that the bread and wine really do become the flesh and blood of Christ – the change is one of 'substance' in the Aristotelian sense ('substance' meaning a thing's deepest being, what it is in and of itself, which is not necessarily the same as how a thing appears to the senses). Though after the words of consecration, there may appear to have been no change – the elements still look, taste and feel like bread and wine, as Protestants so frequently pointed out under interrogation – this outward appearance constitutes only the 'accidents' of the elements and not their substance.

Luther's attitude towards this doctrine was not actually as negative as Henry seems to have thought, Luther's principal objection focusing on its being made into a dogma demanding adherence, rather than on the concept in itself – so this particular attack on Henry's part may have been unnecessary, but he also attacked Luther's doctrine of justification by faith alone. This was the doctrine which appeared most to undermine the authority of the Church and to threaten social order – if both priests and 'good works' were unnecessary for salvation, what was to prevent people doing whatever they liked?

To Thomas More, both Martin Luther and William Tyndale were disciples of the Antichrist. There was no time to lose in combating them, and nothing less than complete eradication of heresy was an option. But he made a distinction between the 'simple' man or woman who had been led astray through ignorance, to whom 'little rigor and much mercy' should be shown in setting them right, and the educated man who was defiantly and persistently heretical in his beliefs and, worst of all, determined to persuade others into error. Of heretical books he wrote: 'when they be drunken down [they] infect the reader and corrupt the soul unto everlasting death'. This is why someone like Little Bilney, a university man who had been instrumental in converting other educated men to the evangelical cause, including Robert Barnes, John Lambert and the future Bishop of Worcester Hugh Latimer (all of whom would die for their beliefs), was of such concern to him.

In 1529, More published the first of several works against heresy, entitled *A dyaloge of sir Thomas More knyghte*, in which he set out an imaginary conversation between 'Master Chancellor' (a thinly disguised version of himself) and 'A Messenger', who had been sent by his master to discuss his questions about various doctrinal matters. Not mentioned by name, but present by implication within this conversation, is the case of Little Bilney, whose public trial two years previously had aroused much interest and a fair degree of sympathy, especially in London. The words More puts into the mouth of 'Master Chancellor' stress the danger of the slippery slope involved in listening to, and being influenced by, the initially innocuous-sounding ideas propounded by Bilney. For More, 'every heretic was related to every other heretic, and to oppose one was to oppose all, just as to accept one was to accept all. Thus, to hold even the most minor of heretical opinions risked a total destruction of the edifice of faith.'

London's first heretical community had been that of the so-called Lollards, the name (coming from an old word meaning 'to mumble') their enemies gave to the followers of the teachings of the fourteenth-century John Wycliffe, a philosopher and theologian of some distinction, who had been profoundly concerned by the failings of the contemporary Church. Wycliffe was a committed evangelical reformer who reached two conclusions, both firmly based on the logic of his own philosophy and his reverence for the Bible as 'the mirror of eternal truth': that all human beings are predestined either to salvation or to damnation, and that therefore their own actions, however meritorious they may appear, cannot affect their fate; and that the bread and wine of the Mass are not annihilated and transformed into the body and blood of Christ. Wycliffe did not intend to devalue the Eucharist, but held that its significance had been perverted. By the time he had been condemned as a heretic in 1382, he had attracted many followers. Knowledge of the scriptures, and in English, was the touchstone of the Lollard faith, an attitude shared by the sixteenth-century reformers. 'At the heart of both faiths lay the conviction that Scripture alone enshrined all religious truth, and that to every layman belonged the right to find that truth for himself.' Lollardy had reared its head in England at various times since the death of Wycliffe, and Bishop Tunstall had been closely involved in its repression in the early 1500s in the county of Kent, when he was acting as chief commissary of the Archbishop of Canterbury, William Warham.

Thomas Bilney came to feel such remorse at having been persuaded in 1527 by the same Bishop Tunstall to renounce his dearest beliefs that, four years later, he felt obliged to set off on another unlicensed preaching tour. Thomas More in his *Dyaloge* had characterized the policy of persuasion exercised by Tunstall at Bilney's trial as 'charity'; the implication in what he wrote, however, was that if 'charity' did not work – if, in particular, it did not succeed in silencing the educated (and educating) heretic – then stronger measures would have to be taken, in the interests of protecting others from heresy. Furthermore, certain heretical ideas might lead to disorder in society and, should that be the case, then the civil authorities had not only the right, but the duty, to take action to stamp them out. And if the only way to stamp out heretical ideas was to put to death those who propounded them, then so be it. The justification for the death of one heretic was the stability of society and the salvation of many innocent Christians, who might otherwise have been led astray. In his last extant letter to his friend Erasmus, written around June 1533, More confirmed his attitude towards heretics: 'I find that breed of men absolutely loathsome, so much so that, unless they regain their senses, I want to be as hateful to them as anyone can possibly be; for my increasing experience with those men frightens me with the thought of what the world will suffer at their hands.'

This, briefly, is the theoretical background to the second trial and sentencing of Thomas Bilney who, in 1531, having demonstrated that 'charity' had indeed proved ineffective in silencing him, was convicted of heresy and burnt in Norwich, the first university-educated heretic in England to suffer this fate for propounding the 'new learning'.

Having been inspired to devote himself to that 'new learning' by Bilney and fellow scholars in Cambridge, the priest Richard Bayfield had moved to London where he was sheltered by other sympathizers – for he was still technically a monk, now absent without leave from his monastery. In the meantime his first mentor Robert Barnes had been arrested and was being held in the Fleet prison. It seems likely that Bayfield left England for a time and, on his return, became involved in smuggling prohibited books into the country.

A fundamental element of the dispute surrounding the 'new learning' centred on the act of reading – what was allowed to be read, and by whom. As not everyone could read for themselves, the act of reading was supplemented by that of preaching, with, again, the authorities seeking to control both who might preach and what they might say. While he was in London, in 1527, it was Bayfield's declared intention to preach every day in a City church (St Vedast, Foster Lane, was his chosen venue, very close to St Paul's and known then as 'St Foster's church'), and it was on account of his preaching – and his declaration that a priest should be permitted to preach without having to obtain a licence to do so – that he was arrested for the first time, early in 1528.

At his trial before Bishop Tunstall, Bayfield – like Bilney – was persuaded to abjure (or recant), and for penance was instructed to take part in a procession in the church of St Botolph's Billingsgate, walking in front of the cross and carrying a faggot of wood on his shoulder as a symbol of the fate he had avoided through his recantation. He was also ordered to appear again before the bishop on 25 April, to receive the rest of his penance, but instead he fled abroad for a brief period. He was back before Bishop Tunstall on 20 June, when he was instructed to don his monk's habit again and return to the abbey at Bury St Edmunds. He did so, but only briefly, before again absconding abroad.

In June 1530 a proclamation was promulgated against heretical or 'pestiferous' books, printed abroad in English, and confirming the Bishop of London's order of 1524 that no new books were to be imported without episcopal licence. The banned books included Tyndale's *Wicked Mammon* and *The Obedience of a Christian Man*, the very books which had been among the first to be given to Bayfield and which he was now enthusiastically engaged in helping to distribute. Anyone in possession of these texts was ordered to surrender them to their bishop or parish priest. The proclamation also made clear the authorities' position on access to the scriptures by lay people. The King, according to the proclamation, had considered the question of whether the scriptures should be available in English and had consulted on the matter with the church hierarchy and 'a body of divines from Oxford and Cambridge'. The conclusion reached had been that:

> it is not necessary to have the Scriptures in English in the hands of the common people, but that the permission or denial thereof should depend upon the discretion of the superiors;

and, considering the malignity of the present time, a translation
into English would tend to the increase of error. It is, therefore,
more expedient that the people have the Scripture expounded
to them by preachers in their sermons as heretofore.

But there was no holding back a zealous reformer like Bayfield
who, having discovered what he believed to be an urgent truth
about the need for change, felt compelled to share his discovery
with others. He would not take the easy option of staying in hiding
once out of the country, but instead took it upon himself to become
the main supplier of forbidden books, obtaining them in the Low
Countries and particularly in the major trading city and port of
Antwerp, and getting them shipped back to England. He sent three
major consignments, the first routed via Colchester in 1530, a
second via St Katharine by the Tower in London later that same
year, and a third via Norfolk in 1531. At least one of these consignments was intercepted by Sir Thomas More. In addition to texts
by Luther and copies of Tyndale's New Testament, Bayfield was
intent on supplying English Christians with works by the German
theologian Oecolampadius, John Lambert (later a fellow victim of
burning) and Zwingli, a leader of the Reformation in Switzerland.

Andrew Hope, the compiler of the *Oxford Dictionary of National
Biography*'s entry on Richard Bayfield, remarks that he 'showed
signs of not always appreciating the extreme danger he was in',
being inclined to indulge in indiscreet conversations with people
who did not necessarily share his views. He was arrested at a book-
binder's establishment in London sometime around October 1531,
imprisoned, and interrogated by More. The latter appears to have
believed that Bayfield had two wives, thereby compounding his
guilt (one wife would have been too many for a monk), but there
is no evidence to support this allegation. Bayfield was held before
trial in the Bishop of London's coalhouse (a small, windowless
dwelling which served as the bishop's prison and a frequent place
of confinement for those on their way to Smithfield, as it turned
out) in very unpleasant conditions, forced to remain standing,
shackled to the wall by his neck, waist and legs, in the hope that

he would name people to whom he had delivered his consignments of prohibited books. But he gave nothing and no one away. At his appearance before Bishop Stokesley and a number of other high-ranking officials and clerics in November he was convicted of being a lapsed heretic, and had the 'sentence definitive' declared against him, as detailed earlier in this chapter.

A few weeks after the execution of Richard Bayfield it was the turn of John Tewkesbury to suffer in Smithfield. Tewkesbury was a leatherseller and haberdasher by trade who lived in the City, by the entrance to St Martin's-le-Grand in the parish of St Michael-le-Quern, and he had been found in possession of two banned books: Luther's *Liberty of a Christian Man* and Tyndale's *Wicked Mammon*. Like Bayfield, Tewkesbury had previously abjured but subsequently returned to his heretical ways. Unlike Bayfield, Tewkesbury was a layman, and he told Bishop Tunstall at his trial in 1529 that he had been reading the scriptures in translation for seventeen years. Foxe commented that he was 'in the doctrine of justification and all other articles of his faith . . . very expert, and prompt in his answers, in such sort as Tunstall and all his learned men were ashamed, that a leather seller should so dispute with them'. He was able to hold his own under hostile questioning by the bishop in the presence of a number of senior clerics and professors of divinity, defending *Wicked Mammon* and retorting: 'I pray you reform yourself, and if there be any error in the book, let it be reformed. I think it is good enough.' When the bishop criticized this and the other books Tewkesbury had been reading, Tewkesbury suggested that the bishop should read them for himself and thereby discover that there was nothing wrong with them. He seemed to be attempting to dispute with Bishop Tunstall as with an equal, intellectually and morally, and Tunstall was clearly both annoyed and frustrated by Tewkesbury's stubborn insistence on thinking for himself: 'the Bishop of London declared that he had at divers times exhorted him to recant the errors and heresies, which he held and defended, even as he did then again exhort him, not to trust too much to his own wit and learning, but unto the doctrine of the holy mother the Church'.

Tewkesbury was then questioned on the doctrine of justification by faith alone and the concomitant rejection of 'works' as
necessary for salvation – perceived as a dangerous doctrine for the
preservation of order and authority. His answer was that good
works should be done for the love of God alone, and not in the
hope of attaining a reward in heaven. One can almost see the
church dignitaries spluttering with indignation at some of
Tewkesbury's answers, especially when he expressed the view that
preaching was no more pleasing to God as an activity than was the
washing of dishes. The bishop, declaring himself to be speaking
more in sorrow than in anger, and sounding rather bewildered
before the obstinacy of this self-educated layman, insisted that the
beliefs he was espousing were 'false, erroneous, damnable and
heretical'. He was also at pains to express to all those present that
'he had often and very gently exhorted the said John Tewkesbury,
that he would revoke and renounce his errors, otherwise if he did
intend to persevere in them, he must declare him a heretic, which
he would be very sorry to do'. This was very much in line with
More's expressed belief that 'charity' was the first route to take
with a heretic, but that firmer measures would have to follow if
such charity met with no success.

Eventually, on the occasion of this first series of interrogations,
Tewkesbury, like both Bilney and Bayfield, seems to have been
worn down by the persuasive Bishop Tunstall and abjured on 8
May. He was given the penance of carrying a faggot in the procession at St Paul's Cathedral on the following Sunday morning and
then standing with it at Paul's Cross, the open-air pulpit outside
the cathedral. He was also to appear in public as a penitent at other
places during the week, with faggots embroidered on his sleeve. On
the Wednesday he had to carry the faggot around Newgate market
and Cheapside, the main thoroughfare in the City, and on Friday
at the church of St Peter Cornhill and then in Leadenhall market.

Despite all this public shaming, Tewkesbury's abjuration did not
'stick' and about eighteen months later he was back on trial, this
time the trial taking place at Thomas More's house in Chelsea –
which was an unusual, though not illegal, proceeding. It did,

however, give rise to (unsubstantiated) rumours that the Lord Chancellor was in the habit of torturing heretics in his house. At this second trial, Tewkesbury attempted to deny ever having held the views that he was said to have abjured at his first. Only now did he seem to be coming to the realization that he could not engage in these intellectual and doctrinal arguments with the hierarchy without their leading to the most serious consequences for himself, and he did not know what he could say to get himself out of trouble. He nevertheless admitted that he had continued to read forbidden books since his so-called abjuration, and he refused to accept various Catholic doctrines, including the efficacy of prayer to the saints and the Virgin Mary, and the existence of purgatory. Finally, and most damningly, he declared his belief that 'the sacrament, of the flesh and blood of Christ, is not the very body of Christ, in flesh and blood as it was born of the Virgin Mary'.

Bishop Stokesley pronounced sentence against Tewkesbury in More's house on 16 December 1531, using a similar form of words to that used against Richard Bayfield, minus the degradation of a priest. Tewkesbury was excommunicated, and turned over by the bishop to the 'secular power and to their judgment, beseeching them earnestly in the bowels of Jesus Christ, that such severe punishment and execution as in this behalf is to be done against thee, may be so moderated that no rigorous rigour be used, but to the health and salvation of thy soul, and to the terror, fear, and rooting out of heretics and their conversion to the Catholic faith and unity'. Tewkesbury was burnt four days later, 'terror' and 'fear' playing a rather larger part in his fate than a lack of 'rigorous rigour'. True to his conviction that the death of an obstinate heretic was preferable to his infecting others, Lord Chancellor More commented: 'There was never a wretch . . . better worthy [to be burnt].'

Part of the sentence passed on Tewkesbury at his first trial, when there was still hope on the part of his judges that he would not prove obstinate but would return to the paths of orthodoxy, was that he was to go to the monastery of St Bartholomew's on the eve of Whitsunday and stay there, in the care of the canons, until the bishop told him he could leave. This would have been at the time when the invalid Prior Bolton was nominally in charge; maybe it is even an indication of ineffective leadership in the priory at that time that staying there had little apparent effect on Tewkesbury. Among the clerics assisting the Bishop of London at the trials of both Bayfield and Tewkesbury was Robert Fuller, the Abbot of Waltham Holy Cross, the great Augustinian abbey in Essex, and he had been angling to become the Prior of St Bartholomew's for some time before the long-expected death of William Bolton, which finally occurred on 5 April 1532 (he was buried before the high altar of the Priory Church). A month and a half later, on 22 May, Abbot Fuller wrote to Thomas Cromwell, then the Master of the King's Jewel House, in what appears to have been one in a series of communications concerning his desire to become Bolton's successor: 'Please continue your goodness towards finding this matter for the house of St Bartholomew's, as liberal motions have been set forward. Such matters shall be largely recompensed on my part, not only in reward for your labours, but also for such yearly remembrance as you shall have no cause to be sorry for.' Abbot Fuller referred to himself as 'your assured daily bedesman' (that is, he was telling Cromwell he prayed for him daily) and called Cromwell his 'loving friend'.

Fuller's efforts were not in vain and he was duly elected as the new Prior of St Bartholomew's on 28 June. The election was carried out *per viam compromissi* – that is, by delegates acting in the name of the whole community, and this was done with the expressed intention of 'gratifying his Royal Highness and the bishop'. This meant that, rather than voting directly for Fuller, the canons of St Bartholomew's relinquished their votes, handing over power to choose the prior to the bishop and to Rowland Lee and John Olyver, chaplains of the King. Lee had a reputation as a rough and ruthless man and, by his own admission, was unaccustomed to preaching or the other duties one might expect of a chaplain. But he was good at enforcing the King's desires and was also a friend of Fuller's. Bishop Stokesley, standing in the vestibule of St Paul's Cathedral and in the presence of witnesses, directed that Abbot Fuller should be duly elected, and the nomination was declared later the same day in the priory. Messengers were despatched the following day to Waltham where Fuller, unsurprisingly, accepted, though refusing to do so immediately, insisting that he needed some time to consider as the matter was 'so difficult to agree upon'. In his written assent he declared: 'not wishing further to resist the divine will to the honour of our Lord Jesus Christ and the glorious Virgin Mary His Mother and of Saint Bartholomew, patron of the said priory, and of all saints [I] give my consent and assent expressed in these writings'. As E. A. Webb drily observes: 'It seems to have been the usual custom not to give assent at the first request, even though, as in this case, the appointment had been eagerly sought.'

Soon after his election, on 22 September, the new prior fulfilled the promise he had made to Cromwell by granting him, probably for the King, a lease of the manors of Canonbury and Cutlers in the parish of Islington, part of the possessions of St Bartholomew's, properties for which the King had previously expressed a desire. The King was also desirous of obtaining estates belonging to Waltham Abbey, including Copt Hall park and house; one proposal, which did not ultimately take effect, seems to have been that the Priory of St Bartholomew should be appropriated to Waltham, at the King's cost, in return for the abbot making over the manor of Epping to the King and his heirs. Before becoming Prior of St Bartholomew's, Abbot Fuller had already made a grant to the King (on 1 November 1531) of some of the possessions of Waltham Abbey – namely, the manor of Stansted Abbott, with the lands called Joyses and Isney Parke, Board House, and other lands and tenements in Stansted, Hertfordshire, and Roydon, Essex. All these transactions, or proposed transactions, illustrate the extent to which questions of land and property – and the associated income – were at the heart of decisions surrounding the fate of monastic institutions over the next few years in England.

Right at the centre of that fate, as the first Chancellor of the Court of Augmentations, set up in 1536 to deal with the revenues generated by the dissolution initially of the smaller, and subsequently of the greater, monasteries, we find Richard Rich who, since acquiring an influential patron in Thomas Audley, had been steadily building a successful and lucrative career. A pivotal year for him, as for Abbot Fuller and for several others, including Thomas More, had been 1532, when he secured several significant appointments. On 22 March he was appointed Clerk of Recognizances – a job which entailed recording obligations undertaken by a person before a court or magistrate, whereby the person acknowledges (recognizes) that they owe a personal debt to the state. The obligation would be avoided if the person bound by it performed some specified act, such as appearing in court on a particular day, or keeping the peace; the business of 'recognizances' was therefore not dissimilar from our contemporary practice of 'binding over' to keep the peace. Rich was to be paid 3s 4d for the 'making, writing and enrolment of every such recognizance' and a further 20d when each one was certified.

On 13 May of the same year Rich was also made Attorney General in Wales and the counties palatine of Chester and Flint, a post he held for the next twenty-six years. (Some strong earldoms along the Welsh border had been granted the privileged status of 'county palatine' shortly after the Norman Conquest, but only this one based on Chester survived for a long period.) His other two highlights of 1532 were becoming Deputy Chief Steward of the south parts of the Duchy of Lancaster, and Recorder (or senior judge) of Colchester.

1532 was also a good year for Rich's patron Thomas Audley, who was knighted on 20 May. Four days previously, Sir Thomas More had resigned as Lord Chancellor in the wake of his disagreements with the King, and Audley succeeded him (an appointment overseen by Thomas Cromwell). Rich had chosen his patron well and, as Audley rose, so did he. On 10 October 1533 Rich was appointed Solicitor-General, a post which involved advising the King on the law, and for which he received an annuity of £10; and in recognition of his new appointment, he was also made a knight.

As Solicitor-General, Sir Richard assisted Audley in the House of Lords in the drafting of legislation, and took a leading part with Thomas Cromwell in enforcing compliance with the Act of Succession of 1534, which declared Anne Boleyn's daughter Princess

Elizabeth to be heir to the throne and Katherine of Aragon's marriage to Henry unlawful. Rich was especially active in prosecuting those who refused to subscribe to the Act of Supremacy passed in the same year, and he played significant – and infamous – roles in the trials of Bishop Fisher and Sir Thomas More, at both of which Sir Thomas Audley presided. Fisher and More were both executed in the summer of 1535. Central to More's condemnation was the testimony of Rich, who used the accused man's own words, obtained in private and through a series of mock questions, against him. More's response to Rich at his trial has coloured assessments of the latter's character ever since: 'For we long dwelled both in one parish together,' More recalled, 'where, as your self can tell (I am sorry you compel me so to say) you were esteemed very light of your tongue, a great dicer, and of no commendable fame.'

On 27 July 1535, three weeks after More's execution, Rich was appointed chirographer at the Court of Common Pleas, an office which has been described as a 'wealthy sinecure' and which he held for just under two years. Also known as the Common Bench, this court dealt with actions between subject and subject, not involving the King (in contradistinction to the King's Bench which dealt with any cases concerning the monarch). The court sat in Westminster Hall, in a space marked off by a wooden bar (behind which counsel stood). The court officials sat at a large oak table covered in green cloth, while the Justices sat on a raised platform (or 'bench') at the rear of the court. Many of the cases heard there concerned the recovery of debts or property. The Common Pleas were staffed by a number of Justices (three in the sixteenth century), under one Chief Justice. They were assisted by a staff of over fifty officials, most of whom sat in Westminster Hall but also kept offices at the various Inns of Court. The court chirographer was one of the high-ranking officials, appointed by the Crown, and responsible for noting final concords and filing records of fines. The post does not sound overly arduous, but it does sound fairly lucrative, and the fact that it was a Crown appointment (and the timing of its receipt by Rich) suggest it may have constituted a reward for the part he had played in the conviction of More.

In his capacity of Solicitor-General, Rich travelled to Kimbol-
ton Castle in January 1536 to take the inventory of the goods of
Katherine of Aragon (who had died at the beginning of that
month), and from there he wrote to the King, concerning how the
latter might properly obtain his former wife's possessions. Rich
reminded Henry that the Lady Dowager was a 'woman sole' (by
virtue of the argument that she had never been legally married to
the King, but was merely the widow of his deceased elder brother),
and that therefore she had full authority by law to dispose of her
goods, although she had herself affirmed while she was still alive
that everything she possessed belonged to the King and that she
would give nothing away without his permission. He then prevari-
cated, in typical lawyerly fashion (and demonstrating the uncertainty
that existed among lawyers, since Henry had asserted his control
over the Church, as to precisely what his powers should or could
now be), advising on the one hand that 'the King cannot therefore
seize her goods unless there be some other cause, for the bishop of
the diocese is bound to give administration to her next of kin', but
wondering, on the other, 'whether the King, as Supreme Head of
the Church, may grant administration of her goods, dying intes-
tate'. But ultimately he, Rich, 'dare not say', though he does suggest
a way round the problem, with the idea that 'Henry might seize
her goods by another means, viz., by writing a letter to the bishop
of Lincoln to grant administration to such as he shall name, who
shall hold the goods to his Grace's [i.e. the King's] use'. Having
made this suggestion, the Solicitor-General expressed his willingness to 'execute the King's orders as he thinks fit'.

On 20 April 1536 Rich was appointed Surveyor of Liveries
(which post he held only until autumn of that year), and in the
same month received his appointment as Chancellor of the Court
of Augmentations. His experience to date had made him eminently
prepared for this task, the scale of which was immense:

> The houses [i.e. monasteries, convents and priories] had to be
> suppressed or their surrenders accepted; surveys and valuations
> of their property taken; and the monks disposed of. The lands

accruing to the Crown had to be administered, and their rents collected, expended and accounted for. Disposal by grant, sale or lease had to be arranged and supervised, and the litigation which inevitably accompanied the possession of land had to be coped with. The departing monks had also left obligations behind them that the government was determined to honour, in the form of leases to be carried over and debts to be paid. The monks themselves had to be pensioned, or sent to Chancery to collect their 'capacities' or licences to act as secular priests.

The Court of Augmentations which, like various other courts, met at Westminster, was governed by a council comprising a chancellor, treasurer, attorney and solicitor, supported by ten auditors and seventeen receivers, each of whom was allocated to a specific region of the country. All the 'Augmentations men' primarily owed their positions to the Lord Privy Seal, Thomas Cromwell. Though there may be some truth in the assertion that Sir Richard's 'first care was to augment his own fortune', that he was nevertheless meticulous in his work is evident from the records. One gets the impression from Rich's early career that he was a skilled administrator, demonstrating more 'patient industry' than he has previously been given credit for, with particular talents for the collection and management of revenues and fines, someone who could be relied upon to keep accurate records and chase up payments – as well as being good at making the best of his connections and seizing opportunities as they arose.

The work at Augmentations provided plenty of opportunities for personal enrichment. Cromwell's initial intention was that the former monastic lands, and the income generated by them, should all be retained for the Crown, but as more and more monasteries were dissolved, grants of land and property began to be made to those willing and able to pay, and with an eye for a bargain. The land and property that came Rich's way with the dissolution of the monasteries began to accumulate very soon after his appointment as Chancellor of Augmentations, with a grant dated 25 May 1536 by which he received, in exchange for a rent of 52s 9d, the site of Leighs (or Leez) Priory in Essex, along with various possessions of the priory, including the manors of Little and Great Leighs, Felsted, Fyfield, Leighs Camset, Bernes and Herons – all the possessions, in fact, which had previously been 'enjoyed by Thomas Ellys prior of the said priory'. (The house Sir Richard built on the site, also known as Leez Priory, is now an award-winning wedding venue.)

Thomas Ellys, the last Prior of Leighs, was himself an interesting character. While still prior, he appears to have become interested in alchemy and to have started reading books on the subject. Through a goldsmith of Lombard Street in the City of London, he became acquainted with a priest called 'Sir George' who knew something of alchemy, and this George put him touch with one Thomas Peter, a London clothworker, who asserted that he was as expert in the science of alchemy as any man in England. In order to learn the science himself, Prior Ellys paid 20 nobles (a noble being a coin worth 8s 4d) to Thomas Peter, as well as giving him a bill for 20 marks (a mark being equal to 13s 4d), no inconsiderable sum in those days. With the assistance of a twelve-year-old boy called Edward Freke, who was already a canon of Leighs, the prior set to work, using metals supplied by Thomas Peter, and spent either ten weeks (according to his own account) or eight months (according to that of his assistant) making 'a continual fire night and day, under a furnace, on which he set his silver and quicksilver to boil'. After a time, he reached the conclusion that his occupation was, as he phrased it, 'but a false craft', and, having melted the silver, he sold it, telling Peter that he would pay him no more money.

Several years later Thomas Peter began to take legal steps to get the money owed him by Prior Ellys who, in some distress, confessed the debt he had contracted to the chapter of the priory but then proceeded to get himself further entangled by an involvement with a Richard Lyndsey, who promised to pay off the debt to Thomas Peter in return for a lease of the vicarage of Matching, at that time in the gift of Leighs Priory. It appears that Lyndsey did very well out of this deal, as the lease was worth considerably more than the 20 marks he paid for it, and the prior still found himself in trouble with the law, having to answer for his actions in the Court of Star Chamber (which could deal with actions deemed to be morally reprehensible and not necessarily technically illegal). The outcome is not known, as the decrees and orders of this court are no longer extant, but, as Sir Thomas Ellys ('Sir' was a courtesy title for priests in the sixteenth century, similar to 'the Reverend' now) was presented by Abbot Fuller of Waltham to the vicarage of Blackmore in 1538, it is possible that the matter had been cleared up by then.

The attainments of Sir Richard Rich by the middle of 1536 reflect base metal being turned into gold quite as effectively as any alchemical process. Not only was he Chancellor of the Court of Augmentations and the leaseholder of considerable lands in Essex, he was also married. His wife Elizabeth was two or three years younger than himself and the daughter of William Gynkes or Jenks, a wealthy London spice merchant; in a sketch made of her by Hans Holbein the Younger, she looks plump and matronly, both placid and resilient. And in the parliament of 1536 Rich was selected as a knight of the shire for Essex. Asked to choose a Speaker by the second day of this parliament, the Commons begged for more time before deciding on the third day on Rich himself. John Lord Campbell characterized Rich's election as Speaker as 'an insult . . . put upon the House of Commons, which shows most strikingly the degraded state to which parliament was reduced in the reign of Henry VIII', further describing Rich as 'hardly free from any vice except hypocrisy'. Sir Richard's opening oration, when he was presented as Speaker of the House on 12 June 1536 (among those present to listen to him being the Abbot of Waltham, Robert Fuller), was a model of sycophancy, comparing King Henry to Solomon for prudence and justice, to Samson for strength and bravery, and to Absalom for beauty. Equally extravagant was his concluding address, likening the King's care for his subjects to the sun's influence upon the world.

Chapter Two

FUEL FOR THE FIRE

✠

Let us be thankful for ourselves that we live in a changed world.

James Anthony Froude

THE KING, so extolled by Sir Richard Rich on his appointment as Speaker of the House of Commons, was in fact creating upheaval for his subjects on a grand scale. It is now time to look more closely at what constituted Henry's 'great matter', at what it was over which Thomas More and others disagreed so strongly, and at the horrible fate of Friar John Forest. The events related in this chapter span the years 1532 to 1538, and during the course of those six years much would change in England – particularly in matters of faith, authority and allegiance. Some of what constituted heresy in Henry's realm in 1538 was not considered heretical in 1532, and vice versa. During these years and later, people would react in different ways to the taking of oaths, make different decisions as to whether it was legitimate to say one thing with one's lips while believing another in one's heart, and reach the point at which equivocation was no longer possible at different moments in their lives, if ever. Most people, somehow, accommodated themselves to what was required of them, the instinct for survival proving the strongest of all human instincts. The main protagonists of this chapter were among the exceptions.

First let us turn to the stories of three men burnt in Smithfield in the early 1530s – James Bainham, John Frith and Andrew Huet.

James Bainham, who spent some time in prison with the

leatherseller John Tewkesbury, was, like Richard Rich, a lawyer of the Middle Temple. He came from a higher social class than Rich, being the youngest son of Sir Alexander Bainham and Elizabeth Langley, née Tracy, of Westbury-on-Severn in Gloucestershire, and he was not alone in his family in subscribing to the new ideas emerging in the Church, his uncle Sir William Tracy, a local land-owner, having had his will refused probate on account of its 'heretical' content. It is not known where James received his education as a child, but it is likely that he attended a grammar school as he knew both Latin and Greek. His training and progress as a young lawyer went smoothly, and he was well respected in his profession, until he came to the notice of the authorities for his espousal of reformist ideas.

Suspicion first alighted on Bainham when he married the widow of a man called Simon Fish, who had been a lawyer of Gray's Inn, and whom Thomas More had accused of heresy for having written and published in 1529 a short address to the King, entitled *A Supplication for the Beggars*. (More's response to this work, published later the same year, had been a much longer piece, entitled *The Supplication of Souls*.) *A Supplication for the Beggars* had attacked the behaviour of monks, friars and secular clergy, accusing them of living off the poor through the exaction of tithes and the selling of indulgences (and of having invented the non-scriptural doctrine of purgatory in order to justify the latter).

Fish's short work was dedicated to 'the King, our Sovereign Lord', and it began with a vivid description of the plight of beggars:

> Most lamentably complaineth their woeful misery unto your Highness your poor daily bedesmen the wretched hideous monsters (on whom scarcely for horror any ye dare look) the foul unhappy sort of lepers, and other sore people, needy, impotent, blind, lame, and sick, that live only by alms, how that their number is daily so sore increased that all the alms of all the well disposed people of this your realm is not half enough for to sustain them, but that for very constraint they die for hunger.

He went on to refer to 'Abbots, Priors, Deacons, Archdeacons, Suffragans, Priests, Monks, Canons, Friars, Pardoners and Sumners' as 'ravenous wolves going in [shep]herds' clothing, devouring the flock'. Characterizing this whole catalogue of church dignitaries as 'these greedy sort of sturdy, idle, holy thieves', Fish accused them of extorting money from the poor, with such accusations as:

> Every man and child that is buried must pay somewhat for masses and dirges to be sung for him or else they will accuse the dead's friends and executors of heresy. What money get they by mortuaries, by hearing of confessions (and yet they will keep thereof no counsel), by hallowing of churches, altars, superaltars, chapels and bells, by cursing of men and absolving them again for money?

A particularly interesting accusation by Fish against the varied sorts of clergy, in the light of what was to follow, was that they had 'translate[d] all rule, power, lordship, authority, obedience and dignity from your Grace unto them[selves]'. Such an accusation was also very much in line with what the King had already laid at the clergy's feet in the form of *praemunire* and the fine that had been imposed as a penalty for this alleged offence. So in the words of Fish, the cause of early Protestant reform of the Church and the interests of the King appeared to be going hand in hand.

Fish had escaped being sent to the stake, first by recanting but secondly – and more permanently – by dying of the plague in 1531. Bainham had married his widow Joan only a few months later. She was also committed to the evangelical cause, so this second partnership may have been viewed by herself and James as a way of carrying forward the work of the first (as well as a means of providing material support for the widow).

When Bainham was arrested at his lodgings in the Middle Temple in 1531 by a serjeant-at-arms, he was taken, like John Tewkesbury, to Sir Thomas More's house at Chelsea, where the porter's lodge had become a sort of unofficial prison for the 'sure keeping' of alleged heretics pending their official trials and affording More an opportunity to exercise 'charity' in the form of persuasion. One of

More's persuasive techniques was to try to wear his prisoner down psychologically by telling him of Tewkesbury's recantation at his first trial. When such 'gentle' methods did not succeed in getting Bainham either to renounce his heretical views or to name his Temple colleagues who shared them, he was sent to the Tower to be racked.

Leonard Parry, in *The History of Torture in England*, describes the rack as:

> a large oak frame raised some three feet from the ground. The prisoner was placed under it on his back, with wrists and ankles fixed by cords to two rollers at the end of the frame. By means of levers worked in opposite directions, the body of the prisoner was pulled up level with the frame and left thus suspended by ankles and wrists. If the prisoner did not then give the required information, the levers were moved. The cords pulled on the joints until the bones started from their sockets. There was the danger of the fingers being pulled from the hands, the toes from the feet, the hands from the arms, the feet from the legs, the forearms from the upper arms, the legs from the thighs, and the thighs and upper arms from the trunk. Every ligament was strained, and every joint loosened in its socket, and sometimes even dislocated.

It was later alleged – the most likely source for the allegations being Bainham's wife – that More was present at the racking; it was further alleged that he 'ordered the rack to be worked so violently, that Mr Bainham was lamed by it'. It has been remarked that: 'Given the source, and [Joan Bainham's] considerable animus against More, the stories of his torturing her husband should be treated with caution.' More himself always denied contemporary allegations that accused heretics were beaten in his garden, and there is no evidence that he personally used anything other than psychological and mental force (which he possessed in abundance). Joan Bainham was instructed to hand over the prohibited books her husband had been reading, but she denied that there were any of them in their house; she herself was then sent to the Fleet prison and the couple's goods confiscated.

On 15 December 1531, back at Chancellor More's house, Bainham was brought before the Bishop of London, John Stokesley, and examined about his beliefs. Bainham's responses, as recorded by Foxe, are based on the language of the Bible – of English translations of the Bible, that is. So, for instance, he is quoted as saying: 'If we say we have no sin, we deceive ourselves and the truth is not in us. If we confess our sins, he is faithful and just, and will forgive us our sins, and will purge us from all our iniquities . . .' Most of this is word for word what still appears in the Book of Common Prayer in the opening sentences of Morning and Evening Prayer, quoting in turn English translations of verses from the first chapter of the First Letter of John in the New Testament. Bainham again quotes from the Bible when asked whether the saints are to be honoured and prayed to (that they may pray for us); his answer is: 'My little children, I write this to you, that you sin not. If any man does sin, we have an advocate with the Father, Jesus Christ the just, and he is the propitiation for our sins.' This is a direct quote again from the First Letter of John, this time from the opening of the second chapter. Those who created the records of Bainham's trial may of course have been putting these precise words (which also came to be part of the Book of Common Prayer) into his mouth retrospectively, but if they were doing so they were underlining very specific points – that is, the great value of having the scriptures available, in English, and of the familiarity of Bainham (and other martyrs) with those scriptures, a familiarity greater than the knowledge of the 'learned' men leading the interrogations, who knew the texts only in Latin and Greek, and not very well at that.

In other answers, Bainham denied the necessity of making confession to a priest, saying that it was lawful to confess one's sins to any other Christian, but suggesting that that person did not need to be ordained. Further, he said that God would forgive him if he was moved to repentance by a sermon or the word of God being preached, without the need for any formal confession. He also declared that the truth of the scriptures had been hidden for the last 800 years – because, it was implied, they had not during that time been translated into the vernacular. Only in the last six years (that is, since 1525, the year in which Tyndale had published his first, partial, edition of the New Testament), he asserted, had the word of God been 'plainly and expressly declared to the people'. It was not until such translations had appeared, continued Bainham, that men like 'Mr Crome and Mr Latimer' had come forward to preach the word of God 'sincerely and purely'; previously, people had been told to believe only what the Church believed and, if the Church was mistaken, then the people were instructed to believe the mistakes. But in fact, Bainham argued, the true Church of Christ could not be mistaken and there must therefore be two churches – the true one (to which, implicitly, he and fellow reformers belonged) and the one in error – the 'Church of Antichrist' (to which, implicitly, his questioners belonged). This concept of the opposition of the true and false churches had previously been espoused by the Lollards, and it assisted those accused of heresy to stand firm against their accusers. In doing so, Bainham also aligned himself with the convicted and executed heretic Richard Bayfield, affirming that he believed he had died 'in the true faith of Christ'. When asked for his opinion of Martin Luther's behaviour in marrying a nun, Bainham refused to answer, saying that he 'thought nothing' about it, and could not say whether such an action constituted 'lechery'.

Bainham clearly underwent a psychological struggle during this first trial between, on the one hand, a desire to be true to himself and his new-found beliefs and, on the other, the fear of an imminent and excruciating death. His struggle was exacerbated by the pressure being put on him by the bishop and his other interrogators, on the second day of his examination (16 December), as they endeavoured to persuade him away from his reformist beliefs, offering him either the 'gentle' or the hard way. The 'bosom of his mother [the Church] was open for him', they told him, but otherwise – 'if he would continue stubborn, there was no remedy'. 'Wavering in a doubtful perplexity between life on the one hand and death on the other', he weakened and capitulated, pleading ignorance and agreeing to submit himself to those who knew better – this, of course, after he had already been tortured. He now backtracked on his brave statement about

Richard Bayfield, saying that he 'could not judge' whether he had died in the true faith. He agreed that a priest, having once been vowed to celibacy, could not marry without committing 'deadly sin', and that Luther had been wrong to marry a nun. He also agreed that it was an offence to God to keep books prohibited by 'the Church, the Pope, the Bishop, or the King', and averred that his main fault consisted in not having thought about these matters carefully enough and that 'he pondered those points more now than he did before'.

Bainham officially abjured his beliefs on 8 February 1532, declaring that he held 'the faith of his holy mother the Catholic Church', and he was released from imprisonment nine days later. Nevertheless, he could not bring himself to read out the prepared abjuration in full, unable to assent to the idea that some of his formerly professed beliefs constituted heresy, and he pleaded with the bishop's chancellor, Richard Foxford, to 'be good to him' and not force him to recite the complete abjuration or pronounce sentence against him as a heretic. Bainham's insistence that he did hold the Catholic faith, including assenting to the doctrine of purgatory, seems on this occasion to have been sufficiently persuasive, and Chancellor Foxford stopped midway through reading out the sentence against him and asserted that he would accept Bainham's confession as sufficient, though adding, rather ominously – 'at least for the time being'.

And so Bainham was let go. But almost at once, like both Thomas Bilney and John Tewkesbury before him, he found that the pain of his conscience, the sense of having let down himself, his fellow believers and his God, was stronger than the fear and anticipated pain of being burnt to death. A few weeks later he publicly took back his (incomplete) abjuration, beseeching God and all his fellow believers to forgive him, making this confession in front of a congregation who used to meet in a warehouse in Bow Lane, just off Cheapside in the middle of the City. 'And there he prayed everybody rather to die by and by, than to do as he did; for he would not feel such a hell again as he had felt, for all the world's good.'

More than just confessing to the congregation of his fellow believers, Bainham wrote letters, including to the bishop, renouncing his recantation – which amounted to asking to be rearrested. He was imprisoned first in the bishop's coalhouse 'in the stocks, with irons upon his legs', and then found himself back at the Lord Chancellor's house where, it is alleged, he was 'chained to a post two nights'. Next he spent a week being 'cruelly used' in Fulham (again under the jurisdiction of the Bishop of London), and then he was sent to the Tower – 'where he lay a fortnight, and was scourged with whips, to make him revoke his opinions'. After that he was taken to Barking, and then back again to Thomas More's house in Chelsea where the trial and condemnation took place. Though the stories of Bainham's ill-treatment while imprisoned may be exaggerated, the way in which he was moved around from one place to another does suggest that the authorities, and specifically both Bishop Stokesley and Chancellor More, were still desperately attempting to get him to change his mind and not relapse into his heresies. There is no sense of them wanting to make a martyr of him, no thirst to burn him if it could be avoided; this may have been principally to do with wanting to avoid the scandal of a public execution, desiring instead the potentially more useful spectacle of a prominent member of a reformist congregation renouncing his heretical beliefs. But it is also noticeable that, at this stage, there does not seem to have been an automatic assumption that a relapsed heretic would inevitably burn, and there is a suggestion that the arbiters of his fate still wanted to save him from himself. Alternatively, however, all they were trying to do was to get him to divulge the names of other so-called heretics, particularly within the legal profession. Or perhaps – and this may be the most likely motive of all – they desired him to recant for the sake of his immortal soul, not for the survival of his earthly body.

Whatever the motives of his would-be persuaders, Bainham could not this time be persuaded. On 19 April, he was back before his judges, appearing again before Richard Foxford and a number of senior clergy. As with Bayfield and Tewkesbury, the central point at issue was that of the 'sacrament of the altar'. Did Bainham believe, Foxford asked him, what 'our holy mother, the Catholic Church', determined and taught – 'That in the sacrament of the altar, after the words of consecration, there remains no bread?' Bainham seems by now to have become reconciled to his likely fate (to prefer that fate, in fact, to the torments of his conscience) and, in consequence, he threw caution to the winds. 'The bread is not Jesus Christ,' he replied, 'for Christ's body is not chewed with teeth, therefore it is but bread; yet he is there, very God and man, in the form of bread.'

So what precisely was Bainham saying in the expressions that he chose to use? By declaring that 'Christ's body is not chewed with teeth', he is stating that the bread, after consecration by a priest, remains bread. Of course, the orthodox Catholic leaders with whom he was arguing could not dispute that the bread continued to look, feel and taste like bread. But the point was that these characteristics of bread were only the 'accidents', and that the 'substance' of the bread after the consecration was the body of Christ. Bainham's flippant remark about chewing – though offensive to his hearers, not in itself necessarily heretical – is actually less to the point than his words 'in the *form* of bread'. These were the words that constituted the denial of the bread itself being *transformed*. He was not, however, denying what was (and is) known as the 'real presence' – that Christ is indeed present in the bread and wine of the Eucharist – his words 'yet he is there' making this clear. Bainham's interpretation is very much that espoused by Martin Luther, a fact which would not have escaped his interrogators.

Bainham was further accused of having said that St Thomas Becket was 'a thief and murderer' and he did not deny this, elaborating on his opinion that 'St Thomas of Canterbury was a murderer, and if he did not repent him of his murder, he was rather a devil in hell, than a saint in heaven'. This part of the indictment against Bainham is but one example of how religious policies were suddenly reversed during this period of Henry's reign for, only six years later, far from it being heresy to inveigh against Thomas Becket, the twelfth-century Archbishop of Canterbury who had fallen foul of Henry II and been assassinated for his pains, it would become compulsory to do so. This example of an archbishop who in life had resisted his monarch's authority and in death had continued to triumph over him could hardly be expected to find favour with Henry VIII after his split from Rome (not least because Archbishop Warham, in the stand he was preparing to take against Henry in the weeks before his death, had overtly drawn inspiration from his saintly predecessor). In June 1538 Thomas Becket was posthumously put on trial, judgement being given against him that 'in his life time he disturbed the realm, and his crimes were the cause of his death'. No longer was he to be called a martyr ('although the people hold him' for one), his relics were to be publicly burnt, and 'the treasures of his shrine confiscated to the King'. Now, however, in 1532, Bainham's low opinion of this popular London saint only constituted another nail in his own coffin.

On the following day, 20 April (or, according to some sources, on 26 April), Bainham was condemned as a relapsed heretic, 'damnably fallen into sundry heresies', and therefore deserving of death at the hands of the civil authorities. He was given into the custody of Sir Richard Gresham, one of that year's sheriffs (who was present at the hearing), who committed him to Newgate prison. He remained in Newgate – lodged in one of the dark, damp dungeons reserved for those suspected of serious crimes such as heresy – for only a few days, being burnt in Smithfield on 30 April, at three o'clock in the afternoon.

While in the dungeon at Newgate, Bainham received some visitors; four men – Edward Isaac of Well in Kent, the brothers William and Ralph Morice from Chipping Ongar in Essex, and the Cambridge academic and future bishop Hugh Latimer – came to see him, apparently with the intention of finding out whether his death sentence was inevitable, or whether he could legitimately have avoided it. Wilful martyrdom was not something to be sought; there is a clear sense that Bainham's supporters and detractors alike wished to avoid his burning if possible, but that both equally found it inevitable in the end. His visitors discovered Bainham 'sitting on a couch of straw with a book and a wax candle in his hand'. During this conversation, Latimer asked whether Bainham had a wife (more, perhaps, to test his state of mind than out of concern for his wife – or, at least, a combination of the two) and the latter became distressed, weeping, worrying about what his wife would live on after his death and what her position would be as the widow of an executed heretic. But Latimer rebuked him for this lack of trust in God, asserting that 'if he committed her with a strong faith to the governance of God, he was sure that she would be better provided for than he could do if he were still alive'. Bainham appears to have been comforted by this rather tough advice.

According to the original 1563 edition of Foxe's *Acts and Monuments*, when Bainham was tied to the stake he declared: 'I come hither, good people, accused and condemned for a heretic, Sir Thomas More being my accuser and my judge.' But in later editions Foxe deleted this speech, which would suggest that he doubted its authenticity. Bainham then read aloud the articles of his faith, and the citizens (notable among whom, joining in the abuse with particular vigour, was the Town Clerk of London, William Pavier) cried out: 'Set fire to him and burn him!' to which the condemned man replied, addressing Pavier with his first words: 'God forgive thee, and show thee more mercy than thou showest to me; the Lord forgive Sir Thomas More; and pray for me, all good people.' Then he himself prayed 'till the fire took his bowels, and his head'.

In the second edition of *Acts and Monuments* Foxe adds the edifying detail that, as the flames began to consume his limbs, the victim declared: 'Behold . . . a miracle: for in this fire I feel no more pain than if I were in a bed of down: but it is to me as a bed of roses.' While this sounds like wishful thinking, we cannot rule out the possibility of Bainham being in such a state of exaltation that it affected his perception of pain – or, alternatively, of his nerve endings having been deadened as a result of third-degree burns.

In the summer of the following year, 1533, a further two men were burnt in Smithfield, as briefly recorded by the chronicler and Windsor Herald, Charles Wriothesley: 'This year, in July, on a Friday, one Frith, a serving man, a great clerk in the Greek and Latin tongue, was burnt in Smithfield, and a tailor of London with him, for heresy.' The 'serving man' (a rather inaccurate description) was John Frith, aged thirty, and his fellow sufferer was Andrew Huet, an apprentice tailor, aged only twenty-four.

John Frith had been born in 1503 at Westerham in Kent, his family subsequently moving to Sevenoaks where his father, Richard, became an innkeeper. As a boy John was sent to Eton College (as one of the seventy King's Scholars educated there) and then studied at Cambridge, taking his BA degree at King's College in 1525. His tutor there was Stephen Gardiner, later Bishop of Winchester. Frith was an outstanding scholar and attracted the attention of Cardinal Wolsey, who summoned him to Oxford as one of the junior scholars at his new Cardinal College. This establishment, founded by Wolsey in 1525 on the site of the suppressed Priory of St Frideswide, was, for the brief period of its existence, enormously ambitious, quickly achieving an academic and musical splendour to match its magnificent architecture. The academic body planned by Wolsey, and attracting some of the finest minds in England, consisted of a dean, sixty fellows, forty junior scholars and six public professors. But Frith's promising career here came to an abrupt end in March 1528 when he, along with several of his fellow scholars, was declared to be a heretic and cast into a makeshift prison within the college – in a place where salted fish, rather than prisoners, was usually stored – for having attended an illegal ceremony.

One of the men on the periphery of this outbreak of Lutheranism in Cardinal Wolsey's own college was the composer John Taverner who, like Frith, had been hand-picked by the cardinal to become part of his establishment, taking up the post of choirmaster, or *informator*, there in 1526. His duties involved training the sixteen boy choristers, and preparing and directing the numerous daily choral services (in addition to the boys there were thirteen lay clerks in the choir) in the chapel. Despite this full and demanding schedule, Taverner found the time – and the intellectual curiosity – to become mixed up with the small group of fewer than twenty men whose activities centred on the reading and dissemination of imported heretical books, including Tyndale's recent translation of the New Testament. Taverner, however, escaped serious trouble over his involvement, Cardinal Wolsey taking the view, as expressed in a letter from John Higden, the dean of the college, to one of his chaplains, that Taverner was 'unlearned, and not to be regarded' (in other words, that he was 'just' a musician). He had, it seems, known about some books being hidden and about a letter being sent to Thomas Garrett, another of the miscreants, who had managed to escape, but that was believed to be the extent of Taverner's knowledge. And so he was allowed to continue as choirmaster at Cardinal College – until he resigned shortly after Wolsey's own fall from grace and before the subsequent suppression of the college and its glorious choir.

By midsummer John Frith, along with the other prisoners, had on Wolsey's orders been released from the salted-fish store, on the condition that he stay within a ten-mile radius of Oxford. He realized he would not be safe indefinitely, however (having heard of some fellow reformers being examined and forced to recant and perform penance), so instead he fled to Antwerp, where he put his learning to use by assisting William Tyndale in his translation of the Old Testament. He also spent some time in Amsterdam and was married there. He devoted most of his time while abroad to studying, writing and disseminating reformist literature, including translating theological works by Luther and his fellow German reformer, Philipp Melanchthon.

In 1529 Frith attended the colloquy between Luther and the Swiss reformer and theologian Huldrych Zwingli in Marburg over the nature of the presence of Christ in the sacraments, a colloquy at which no agreement was reached, the leaders of the Reformation proving no more able to tolerate one another's opposing views on this central subject than were the representatives of the officially opposing 'sides' of reformers versus orthodox. Zwingli was in support of viewing the words 'this is my body, this is my blood' as symbolic statements, with 'is' being taken to mean 'signifies', a position labelled 'sacramentarian' and which Luther condemned as blasphemous. John Frith tended towards the Zwinglian position. From a letter William Tyndale wrote to Frith two years later, while the latter was being held prisoner in the Tower of London, it is clear that not only did the various reformers not agree on the interpretation of the sacrament of the altar, but they recognized their lack of agreement as a point of weakness waiting to be exploited by their opponents. Tyndale advised Frith to steer clear of the subject during his interrogations if he could: 'Of the presence of Christ's body in the Sacrament meddle as little as you can, that there appear no division among us.'

In Lent 1531 Frith paid a short visit to England, where he was now more than ever in danger, after the publication in Antwerp during that same year of his *Disputation of Purgatory*, which was an answer to various writings of William Rastell (Sir Thomas More's nephew), More himself and Bishop Fisher; in it, he set out to show the lack of biblical authority for the doctrine of purgatory. More, in particular, was outraged by the presumption of this young scholar in taking on the combined authority of this illustrious trio, complaining about 'good young Father Frith who now suddenly comes forth so sagely that 3 old men, my brother Rastell, the Bishop of Rochester and I, matched with Father Frith alone, be now but very babies'. Always a risk-taker, Frith made a further visit to England a few months later and this time found himself put in the stocks in Reading, on suspicion of being a rogue and a vagabond. He managed to get himself released, despite nearly fainting from hunger, by engaging in lively and learned conversation, in Latin and Greek, with Leonard Cox, a humanist writer who was working as a schoolteacher in the town. Cox went off to the magistrates to plead for his new friend, who was duly released from the stocks. John Frith was clearly a man full of intellectual energy, and of considerable charisma. And he had, as yet, no desire for martyrdom.

On Sir Thomas More's issuing a warrant for his arrest on a charge of heresy, Frith tried to hide and disguise himself, but was seized on the shore at Milton in Essex, near Southend-on-Sea, in October 1532 (by which time More had resigned as Lord Chancellor — but not as a heresy-hunter), while he was on his way to rejoin his wife and family in Antwerp. He was taken to the Tower. Later that month the Lieutenant of the Tower, Edmund Walsingham, wrote to Thomas Cromwell about the conditions of various of the prisoners in his charge, commenting particularly favourably on Frith who once again had managed to exercise his charm and who, Walsingham noted, was not being kept in irons: 'Although he lacks irons, he lacks not wit nor pleasant tongue. His learning passes my judgment. As you said, it were great pity to lose him if he may be reconciled.' It is clear from this that Cromwell also had a high opinion of Frith's abilities and hoped he might be persuaded to come into line. No one, it seems, wanted Frith to die. And yet, caught up in the inexorable, if faulty, logic of their own positions, unable to give an inch without fearing the collapse of a whole edifice of faith, and bound by conscience (at least in the cases of Frith and More), neither side – neither that of officialdom nor that of Frith himself – was able to escape.

The somewhat lenient treatment to which Walsingham alluded did not last, Frith eventually being chained up so extensively that he could neither lie nor stand. And yet all this time he continued to write. Some of what he produced in prison was written down against his better judgement, he having been persuaded to put his incriminating views – 'his faith and opinion in the Sacrament of the body and blood of Christ' – into material form by an incautious friend. This friend was then tricked by a tailor called William Holt, an infiltrator spying on reformist groups on behalf of the authorities, into handing over Frith's writings. Holt then duly passed them on to his masters.

By 9 May 1533, William Tyndale was resigned to the expectation that Frith would be put to death for his faith, and warned him against recanting as Bilney had done at first, thereby only increasing his grief and falling short of the full 'glory' of martyrdom. Tyndale's short, exhortatory sentences sound almost biblical, as though written by St Paul in one of his letters to congregations of the early Church, Tyndale having imbibed the language and style of the apostle in his work of translation: 'The will of God be fulfilled. Commit yourself only to Him. Your cause is Christ's Gospel. Be of good courage. Stick at necessary things. The death of them that come again after they have once denied, though it be accepted of

God, is not glorious. Seek no help from man. Let Bilney be a warning to you.' He seeks to encourage Frith by listing other reformers who have already suffered his likely fate – two in Antwerp, four in Brussels, five in Paris – 'See, you are not alone.' He also assures Frith that his wife (back in Antwerp, where Tyndale was too) is fully supportive of his anticipated martyrdom: 'Sir, your wife is well content with the will of God, and would not for her sake have the glory of God hindered.'

Frith's situation was exacerbated and his death drew closer when one of the royal chaplains, Dr Richard Curwen, was persuaded by Frith's former tutor, Stephen Gardiner, into attacking Frith's views on Christ's body in the sacrament during a sermon preached before the King (further involving Frith in the very subject which Tyndale had warned him to avoid). As a consequence, King Henry ordered Frith to recant or be condemned. This led to an examination before a number of bishops in the market town of Croydon (about nine and a half miles from the centre of London and chosen in order to avoid a large crowd of Londoners turning up). On the way Frith was actually given the opportunity to escape. He was brought by wherry from the Tower to Lambeth, accompanied by one of Archbishop Cranmer's gentlemen and a porter. Cranmer's man attempted to make Frith change his mind about his views (this was presumably the task he had been set), and then they carried on to Croydon on foot. During the walk Cranmer's man (apparently more persuaded by his charge than vice versa, or at least seduced by his personality) and the porter worked out a plan to help Frith escape into the woods on the way and disappear into Kent. They then told Frith what they had worked out. He reacted with some amusement, telling them that if they were to try to carry out their plan and report in Croydon to the expectant bishops that they had lost him en route, it would be a wasted effort as he would only follow them and turn himself in. 'Do you think that I am afraid to declare my opinion to the Bishops of England?' he demanded; in short, Frith refused to run away.

During June, Cranmer himself reported trying three or four times to persuade Frith back to the path of orthodoxy, but having no more success than anyone else. (It is ironic that Archbishop Cranmer would become one of the most famous Protestant martyrs during the reign of Henry's daughter, Mary; at this time, though he was aware of and interested in the religious debates raging in the continent of Europe, and would be favourable towards the doctrine of justification by faith alone, there was nothing to indicate his future path – apart, that is, from his working with the King to extricate the Church in England from the authority of Rome.) As Frith refused to recant in Croydon, he was held for examination by the bishops of London (John Stokesley), Winchester (Stephen Gardiner) and Chichester (Robert Sherborne), which took place on 20 June 1533 at St Paul's. He was questioned about his beliefs concerning the sacrament of the altar and purgatory, and put his name to what he said, confirming that he held reformist opinions. Three days later he wrote his own account: 'The Articles wherefore John Frith died which he wrote in Newgate the 23 day of June the year of Our Lord 1533'. Sentence was pronounced on him as 'guilty of most detestable heresies' and so to be punished 'for the salvation of thy soul'. On 3 July Bishop Stokesley handed him over, along with the apprentice tailor Andrew Huet, to the Lord Mayor (Stephen Peacock) and sheriffs of London as 'obstinate heretics', and both were taken to Smithfield and burnt. They were tied back to back at the stake; Frith's suffering lasted longer than Huet's, the wind driving the flames away from him and towards his companion.

The faggots for this and other fires would have been in a consignment brought into the City, as part of its usual supply of firewood, either by road from, for instance, the manor of Hampstead or by river from further away. The Ward of Castle Baynard, not far from that of Farringdon Without which included Smithfield, had been the centre of the London firewood trade since the twelfth century. Significant numbers of woodmongers lived and worked there, and it was at one of the wharves in Castle Baynard, or in the neighbouring Ward of Queenhithe, that firewood and charcoal would arrive from cultivated woodlands spread over large parts of many of the counties surrounding London. Woodlands closer at hand, such as those at Hornsey (owned by the Bishop of London and originally a portion of the great forest of Middlesex) and Hampstead (belonging to the Abbey of Westminster) could not satisfy all the capital's demand for fuel, though they certainly supplied much of it. Manors employed their own workforces to cut underwood and make the faggots and other types of firewood, such as bavins (small faggots) and talwood (made of beech and oak). Faggots produced one year were often sold in the next, suggesting that the firewood would generally be well dried before use – particularly important when it was being used to set fire to people.

Andrew Huet, Frith's 'fellow that was tied to his back', had earlier been hidden at a house belonging to one John Chapman, in Hosier Lane near Smithfield. Huet, like Frith, was a Kentish man, having been born in Faversham, and was apprenticed to a master tailor in Watling Street in the City. Many of the apprentices working in London came from outside the capital which experienced a vast rise in population in the early sixteenth century, made up partly by an influx of young people in search of their fortunes. Once they had arrived, life was not easy for many of the apprentices, particularly as their increased numbers meant that a smooth career progression to master craftsman could by no means be assured. The restlessness of youth and the hardship of their working lives combined to make apprentices particularly receptive to the currents of new thought. Huet's brief tale has a sad inevitability about it; described in Hall's *Chronicle* as 'a very simple and unlearned young man', he had no resources with which to defend himself – or even, it appears, the desire to do so. Foxe relates that, after his first escape from imprisonment in the bishop's house – an escape engineered by a group of fellow evangelicals – he did not know where to go. Wandering into Smithfield (perhaps drawn there by a premonition of his ultimate fate), he happened to meet 'one Withers, who was a hypocrite as Holt was', and it was Withers who took him to John Chapman's house. By this unlucky meeting, Huet – along with his host, Chapman – was drawn back into the net spread across London by Sir Thomas More's spies – and he soon found himself imprisoned again, this time in the Lollards' Tower, the Bishop of London's prison in the precincts of St Paul's. (There were two prison towers of this name in London, the other being at Lambeth Palace.) The grounds for Huet's arrest were that he had been in possession of heretical books. He was examined by Bishops Stokesley, Gardiner and Longland. According to the account provided by Foxe, the learned bishops derived some amusement from getting the young apprentice tailor to incriminate himself by admitting to more heretical beliefs than the one that got him dubbed a 'sacramentarian'. Though he gave evidence during his interrogation of personal knowledge of the scriptures, quoting from the Gospel according to St Matthew, he also fell back upon the authority of his more educated fellow prisoner, answering the question concerning what he thought 'as touching the Sacrament of the Lord's Supper' with the affirmation: 'Even as John Frith does.' And to this affirmation he held, despite the consequences being made clear to him:

> Then certain of the Bishops smiled at him, and Stokesley, the Bishop of London, said:
>
> 'Why, Frith is a heretic, and already judged to be burned, and unless you revoke your opinion, you shall burn also with him.'
>
> 'Truly,' says he, 'I am content therewithal.'
>
> Then the Bishop asked him if he would forsake his opinions, to which he answered that he would do as Frith did.

Clearly John Frith had been capable of inspiring great loyalty, and it was not only his fellow sufferer Andrew Huet who was devoted to him. He was widely mourned as a young man — he was only thirty when he died — of much talent, wit and charm (the latter a characteristic which could be in short supply among both the reformers and their opponents). Frith's life, though short, was influential, particularly through his writing, the articles he compiled shortly before his execution being adopted almost word for word by the reformed Church under Edward VI for the English prayer book of 1552. He is reported by John Foxe as having foretold as much in his conversation with Cranmer's gentleman who had tried to persuade him to escape:

'I know very well that this doctrine of the Sacrament of the Altar which I hold and have opened contrary to the opinion of this realm is very hard meat to be digested both of the clergy and laity thereof. But this I will say to you,' taking the gentleman by the hand, 'that if you live but twenty years more, whatsoever become of me, you shall see this whole realm of my opinion concerning this Sacrament of the Altar.'

Frith was by no means universally mourned, however, and the burning of these two young men provided an occasion for the profound hostility between the opposing factions around the questions of doctrinal and liturgical reform − and the overriding question of authority and where it was to be placed − to be publicly rehearsed. Many in the crowd who attended the burning were there to support the suffering men, but this display of sympathy aroused the ire of those who believed they had been justly condemned. Among these supporters of the status quo were 'one Doctor Cooke, who was parson of Honey Lane, and one that was the Master of the Temple, [who] willed the people to pray no more for them than they would pray for dogs'. Frith's reaction was to smile and ask God to forgive his abuser. The onlookers reacted less charitably, with anger.

Another vocal supporter of the authorities, both by virtue of his office and by personal conviction, was the Town Clerk of London (the most important paid official of the City Corporation), William Pavier, who had held the post since 1514. He had officiated at the burning of James Bainham and, far from acting as an impassive official carrying out a prescribed duty, he had lambasted the victim, calling him 'thou heretic'.

But Pavier was not present at the burning of Frith and Huet, for he was already dead himself. Highly conservative in his religious beliefs, and Warden of the Guild of the Name of Jesus at St Paul's, he had become horrified at the direction royal policy appeared to be taking soon after the burning of Bainham, and swore that he would cut his own throat if he thought there was any possibility of King Henry having the Gospels printed in

English. He did not in fact cut his throat, but hanged himself in his chamber, before an image of the crucified Christ, in May 1533. His reasons for taking the grave act of committing suicide, thereby depriving himself not only of life on earth but of any possibility of salvation in the life to come (according to the beliefs of the time), are unclear. (As a suicide, his corpse would be buried in unconsecrated ground and his goods confiscated by the state.) He must, however, have realized that Henry – who had indeed held out a promise that an official English translation would eventually be produced, partly to combat the spread of unofficial ones such as that of Tyndale – was proving sympathetic to certain reformist ideas; but also his official position as overseer of the burnings seems to have unhinged him.

The account of Pavier's death by the nineteenth-century historian James Anthony Froude is derived both from Foxe and from Hall's *Chronicle* and he also offers some reflections of his own, suggesting that the Town Clerk was far more conflicted in his attitude towards the punishment of heretics than his public performance attested. On the day of his death, Pavier's servant girl entered his room to find him weeping in front of the large crucifix hanging on his wall. Clearly wanting to be left alone, he told her to go and clean his rusty sword. She took the sword and left; when she returned a little later, she found him hanging from a beam. 'God, into whose hands he threw himself, self-condemned in his wretchedness,' wrote Froude, 'only knows the agony of that hour. Let the secret rest where it lies, and let us be thankful for ourselves that we live in a changed world.'

Pavier's death is not mentioned in the records of the City Corporation which is perhaps not surprising, given the circumstances of his suicide. The only reference to his having ceased to be Town Clerk is the entry recording his successor on 13 May 1533, which reads: 'Item moreover it is agreed at the same Common Council that Master Thomas Ryshton shall be the Common Clerk of the said City of London and was then and there admitted to the same and sworn accordingly.'

Whether or not Pavier was tormented, as Froude suggests, by

the inherent contradiction between worshipping Christ crucified and participating in the execution of men who believed themselves to be his followers, his suicide offers a poignant demonstration of the confusion engendered in many of the King's subjects (and further afield) by his religious policy in the 1530s. Determined to free himself from his marriage to Katherine of Aragon, and having reached the conclusion that the major obstacle to his attaining this goal was Pope Clement VII, Henry was devoting all his energies, and those of his ecclesiastical advisers, to extricating himself – and, by extension, 'his' Church – from the authority of Rome. As this personal and political impulse to sever the connection between Canterbury and Rome happened to coincide with the rise of Protestantism in Europe, and following the adage that 'your enemies' enemies are your friends', Henry and his advisers inevitably found some common cause with the reformers who were also seeking to challenge the authority of Rome – but on very different grounds and with very different ends in view. One of the results was bewilderment all round.

As early as 1524, Henry had given up all hope of Katherine bearing another child (their only surviving offspring being a daughter, Mary), and by the time he became infatuated with Anne Boleyn two years later, he had already begun to convince himself that his wife's failure to give birth to a son who survived infancy was a sign that his marriage to his brother's widow (Katherine having been first married to Henry's elder brother, Arthur) was sinful, in that it had broken the laws concerning affinity laid down in the Old Testament Book of Leviticus: 'And if a man shall take his brother's wife, it is an unclean thing: he hath uncovered his brother's nakedness; they shall be childless.'

In his initial attempts to remedy the situation by obtaining an annulment of his first marriage, Henry was shocked to discover that he could not bend the papacy to his will. His surprise was not at all unreasonable, for this lack of compliancy with the desire of an English monarch was more or less unprecedented – and Rome's refusal to assist had more to do with international politics and the need to keep on good terms with Katherine's nephew, the Holy

Roman Emperor Charles V, than with moral strictures concerning the indissolubility of marriage.

As Henry came to see that he could not solve the dynastic problem of the succession to the throne with the agreement of the papacy, he and his advisers increasingly realized that a solution could be found only by doing without such agreement. Nevertheless, the decision to try to dispense with papal authority was neither sudden nor the first solution to be tested. In the immediate aftermath of Wolsey's fall from power (largely provoked by his failure to deliver the desired outcome), Henry's advisers offered him a range of options on how to obtain the annulment and Henry responded by trying a number of different schemes. Then in 1531 or 1532 (opinions differ as to precisely when) the idea came to predominate, in both Henry's mind and those of his advisers, that there were valid precedents for the English monarch to exercise absolute authority over the English Church and hence altogether dispense with the need for the Pope.

In seeking justification to extricate the Church in England from papal jurisdiction, the King's advisers considered both historical developments – how the role of the papacy had changed over time – and arguments as to the prescribed functions of secular and religious rulers, respectively. As David Loades puts it:

> The functional argument was derived mainly from the *Defensor Pacis* of Marsilius of Padua, and claimed that the task of the clergy in the world was to preach and teach, not to bear rule. Since Christ's Kingdom is not of this world, those who claim to be Christ's vicars and representatives should not exercise jurisdiction over laymen, or hold property, let alone presume to direct the policies of kings. The historical argument was simply that the authority of the papacy had never been recognized in the early church in anything like its high medieval form, and that its development, especially since the days of Gregory VII, was rank usurpation.

The process of gaining – or, arguably, regaining – royal control over the Church began with a process which came to be known as 'the submission of the clergy', by which the Church was forced to give up its right to make church law (canons) without royal assent. This action of the King, which presaged more changes and weakening of ecclesiastical authority to come, was the immediate reason behind the resignation of Sir Thomas More as Lord Chancellor in May 1532. More had been fighting a losing battle for some time in his support of papal authority and opposition to the attempt to annul Henry's marriage to Katherine. He gave ill-health as the official reason for his resignation, but no one was fooled. Opposition to the King's will was further weakened a few months later, in August, with the death of Archbishop Warham.

The elderly Warham, who had been Archbishop of Canterbury since 1504 and also Lord Chancellor from that year until December 1515, had long been one of Henry's trusted advisers in the case of his 'great matter'. He was also a long-term patron of Erasmus, and had succeeded in forming a mutually respectful working relationship with Thomas Wolsey, his successor as Lord Chancellor who, as Archbishop of York and a cardinal, might have been expected to be a rival. Despite Warham presiding over the convocation on 15 May 1532 which surrendered the Church's legislative independence to the Crown and having been one of only three bishops to give apparently unqualified assent to the 'submission of the clergy', he had two months previously publicly rebuked the King in the House of Lords for his conduct in seeking to assert his authority over that of Rome. In consequence he had been accused of misprision of treason on trumped-up charges, and had prepared an eloquent speech in his defence – which he never got to deliver. He was clearly now set on a collision course with Henry and only his death from natural causes on 22 August prevented a showdown. In the event, his death opened the way for the appointment to the see of Canterbury of Thomas Cranmer, who had already been involved in the making of the King's case.

Henry VIII married Anne Boleyn in his private chapel at Westminster on 25 January 1533, although the divorce from Katherine had not yet been obtained. Thomas Cromwell was given the task of making the marriage legitimate – and to do so as soon as possible, as Anne was already pregnant, with what Henry was convinced would be a son. Cromwell 'therefore ensured that the new parliament would be filled with men known to be favourable to the divorce. He also had his confederate, Sir Thomas Audley, appointed Lord Chancellor, which meant he would now officiate over the House of Lords.' Alongside Audley was, as we have seen, Richard Rich.

In the course of 1533, a number of acts were introduced into Parliament which would lead by degrees to the severance of the English Church from Rome. First, in March, Parliament passed the Act in Restraint of Appeals. This prohibited the taking of ecclesiastical appeals outside the jurisdiction of the English courts and so made it possible for Henry's case for a divorce to be tried and concluded by Cranmer in England, with no one, including Katherine of Aragon, having the right to appeal to Rome as a higher authority. Drawn up by Cromwell, the Act contained a preamble setting out the position that England was an empire, with the King in sole charge and subject to no external authority.

Concerning the laws of affinity as set out in Leviticus, which Henry had cited to justify his disquiet over his first marriage, in April the upper house of convocation (that is, the archbishops, bishops and abbots of the English Church) voted by 197 to 19 that the Pope did not have the power to issue a dispensation allowing a man to marry his deceased brother's widow (the implication being that Henry could not have legitimately married Katherine, and hence that their marriage was invalid). Forty-four canon lawyers (experts in ecclesiastical law) were also present at this meeting of convocation and the great majority of them determined that consummation between Katherine and her first husband had been sufficiently proved. (Part of Katherine's line of defence against the assertion that her marriage to Henry was illegitimate was that she had not in fact ever been Arthur's actual wife in the terms implied by Leviticus – that is, that she had never had sex with him, and so Henry could not have been 'uncovering his brother's nakedness' when their own union was consummated.)

Archbishop Cranmer then held a special session of his court to pronounce on the King's first marriage, having previously sought and obtained permission from the King to determine the matter. Katherine was asked to appear before the court but refused to do so. The trial began at Dunstable on 10 May 1533. On 23 May Cranmer gave sentence that the Pope could not license such marriages. This was tantamount to declaring that the marriage between Henry and Katherine had not been a marriage at all, but merely an adulterous liaison – leaving the King free to marry the woman of his choice. Katherine had already been relegated to the status of Princess Dowager of Wales, with the further consequence that her daughter Mary had ceased officially to be a princess and had become, to her great chagrin, merely the Lady Mary.

The theoretical and theological hoops through which Henry's advisers were jumping in order to legitimize the King's desires were noticed by various of his subjects – not least by John Frith who had alluded to them during his interrogation by Thomas More, when the subject under discussion was the infallibility of the Church (upheld by More and questioned by Frith). 'The clergy say,' commented Frith, 'that they be the Church, and cannot err: And this is the ground of all their doctrine. But the truth of this article is now sufficiently known. For if *Queen Katherine* be King Henry's wife, then they do err, and if she be not, then they have erred, to speak no more cruelly.' In other words, if the marriage between Henry and Katherine was valid, the clergy were erring now in supporting the attempt to have it annulled; whereas if it never had been valid, as was now being claimed, they had erred years ago in allowing it to proceed. If they are right now, they were wrong before, and vice versa: so much, implied Frith, for the so-called infallibility of the Church, as represented by her clergy.

The definitive Act of Supremacy was passed in November 1534, confirming the King as supreme head of the Church of England. This was followed by the Treason Act which came into force on 1 February 1535. This latter Act 'extended the definition of that crime to include treason by word, and specifically such speech as might "maliciously" deprive the King of any of his "dignities or titles"'. In consequence of the passing of this Act, anyone who denied, or who even refused to acknowledge, that the King was supreme head on earth of the Church in England, could be charged with high treason. In the spring of 1535, commissioners were appointed to administer an oath upon the Gospels by which subjects were to declare acceptance of the King's headship of the Church. All religious houses were to be visited for this purpose.

In London, it was Bishop John Stokesley, who hoped always for a 'happy day' when the old ways would return, who was expected by Henry and Cromwell to be at the forefront in enforcing the royal supremacy. Stokesley was not in a strong position to object to what Cromwell wanted of him, for he appeared to have a skeleton in his own cupboard, in the shape of the abbess of the Benedictine abbey of Wherwell in Hampshire, who was accused of having been his mistress – and even of being the mother of his child. The abbess was interrogated in 1534: 'was she not too familiar with the bishop when she was a nun; had not the late Bishop Foxe of Winchester prohibited him [Stokesley] from entering her monastery and from her company in order to avoid suspicion; had not the abbess, after she had a baby, come from her house to the bishop's palace at Fulham to be merry with the bishop; was she not lodged in his chamber?' Though these allegations may have helped to ensure Stokesley's obedience to royal policy, the primary target was the abbess herself, as she had not proved compliant to requests over the granting of property to one John Cooke, a confidential servant of the Crown, whose interests were being promoted by both the King and Cromwell. This particular abbess was duly forced out (albeit with a pension and somewhere to live), and was replaced by someone more likely to bend to the political will. The charges of her liaison with Bishop Stokesley were never substantiated.

One result of the King's attempted balancing act – on the one hand, to have the Pope denounced, his own authority asserted, and to promote moderate reform in the Church; on the other, to keep radical reform and doctrinal disputation at bay – was that people at both poles of opinion could fall foul of the law and find themselves in deep trouble. At one pole were the reformers, such as Frith and Huet, who strayed too far from orthodoxy for their own safety. And at the other were the irreproachably orthodox figures of Bishop John Fisher, Thomas More, and the prior and monks of London's Charterhouse, who found themselves unable in conscience to accept the rejection of papal authority over the English Church and who were convinced that such a rejection would open the way for all sorts of pernicious heresy to enter.

The link between Henry's rejection of papal authority and the ideas of the reformers is nowhere clearer than in William Tyndale's *The Obedience of the Christian Man* (published in 1528, with the subtitle *and how Christian rulers ought to govern*), one of the texts which had tempted Richard Bayfield away from the paths of orthodoxy and which had been banned in England in June 1530. Tyndale was ahead of the King's advisers in setting out Henry's position in relation to the Church. In this book, which Anne Boleyn herself was said to have presented to the King, Tyndale wrote 'the first whole-hearted defence of the godly prince'. Setting Henry, as a king approved by God, in a line of descent from the monarchs of the Old Testament, Tyndale maintained that his subjects owed him their entire allegiance, of both body and soul. Early in the text he quoted from the thirteenth chapter of St Paul's Letter to the Romans: 'The powers that be are ordained by God. Whoever therefore resists power, resists God'; he underlined this stricture with the words: 'indeed, even though he is pope, bishop, monk, or friar'.

The London Carthusians, whose monastery the Charterhouse was but a few hundred yards away from St Bartholomew's Priory (the two foundations being situated at two apexes of a triangle, the third being the Priory of St John of Jerusalem), were in the spring of 1534 required, like everyone else, to swear to the first Act of Succession, assent to which implied agreement with the annulling of Henry's marriage to Katherine and the legitimization of Henry's children by Anne Boleyn. They were also instructed not to refer to the Bishop of Rome as Pope, either in public or in private, or to pray for him as Pope. Having initially refused to swear – and the prior (John Houghton) having been imprisoned for a month for his hesitation – they were visited a second time by the commissioners responsible for enforcing submission to the oath, and this time (on 29 May 1534) Houghton and half a dozen of his monks agreed to swear. Clearly anxious to preserve the lives of those entrusted to his care, the prior insisted that the rest of the monks should swear too, which they finally did at a third visit (on 6 June) – encouraged, no doubt, by the presence of men-at-arms. Nevertheless, they succeeded in swearing only conditionally, with the addition of the phrase 'as far as it is lawful'.

After the coming into force of the Treason Act on 1 February 1535, and the further requirement to swear that the King was supreme head on earth of the Church in England, the situation of the Carthusians became more intensely difficult, and the possibility of prevarication ended.

Having learnt that this oath was compulsory, and reaching the conclusion that he and his monks could not deny papal authority without simultaneously denying their faith in 'one holy, catholic, and apostolic Church' – the formula laid down in the ancient creeds of the Church – Prior Houghton arranged three days during which the monks were to confess to one another and be reconciled, in preparation for martyrdom. Cromwell, whom Houghton and two other Carthusian priors had, as a last-ditch attempt to avert disaster, invited to discuss the King's supremacy with them – how could, asked Houghton, a layman be head of the Church? – committed the priors to the Tower as rebels. They were then indicted at Westminster for 'treacherously machinating' to deprive the King of his rightful title. The trial lasted two days, the jury (after some pressure had been applied by Cromwell) returning verdicts of 'guilty'.

On 4 May 1535 Prior Houghton, Richard Reynolds (a Bridgettine monk of the convent of Syon near Isleworth in Middlesex), John Hale (the Vicar of Isleworth) and the priors of two other Carthusian houses, Augustine Webster and Robert Lawrence, were dragged on horse-drawn hurdles three miles through the streets of London, from the Tower to Tyburn. Thomas More, for whom the Charterhouse had been a spiritual home in his youth, watched them setting out on their arduous journey from a window of his own cell in the Tower. According to his biographer and son-in-law William Roper, he asked his daughter who was visiting him at the time: 'Dost thou not see, Meg, that these blessed fathers be now as cheerfully going to their deaths as bridegrooms to their marriage?'

At Tyburn, in front of a large crowd that included many nobles and members of Henry's Privy Council, the five men were hanged, cut down while they were still alive, drawn and quartered. This was the gruesome method of execution especially reserved for traitors – it involved having their hearts cut out, their intestines unwound and pulled out of their bodies (all this while still conscious), and then their limbs, and finally their heads, chopped off. Their dismembered bodies were then parboiled, again in front of the crowd, and their limbs taken away to be displayed in various parts of the city – including Prior Houghton's arm being nailed to the gate of the Charterhouse itself. Three more members of that house, Humphrey Middlemore, William Exmewe and Sebastian Newdigate, were imprisoned for two weeks in the Marshalsea prison in a standing position, bound to stone pillars with iron collars around their necks. They were likewise hanged, drawn and quartered at Tyburn on 19 June.

Three days later, on Tower Hill, John Fisher was beheaded – a concession to his episcopal status and perhaps to his age. On 6 July Thomas More was likewise executed by beheading.

Richard Rich, at this time Solicitor-General, was implicated in the convictions of both Fisher and More, and it is indeed for his alleged part in the condemnation of Thomas More that he has been chiefly remembered. In both cases, his role was to get the accused men to talk with him, with a promise – which he later betrayed – that nothing they said to him would be used against them. He seems to have persuaded Fisher that the King himself wanted to know his true opinion about the changes he was forcing through, without wishing him harm. And so Fisher, trusting in what he believed to be a message from the King (whom he had known well since the latter's boyhood, having at one time been his tutor), declared his opposition to the royal supremacy and, despite denying that he had done so 'maliciously', found himself convicted of treason for what he had said.

The conversation between Rich and the imprisoned More is alleged to have taken place on 12 June 1535, Rich arriving at More's cell in the Tower, with Sir Richard Southwell and two servants, in order to take away all the prisoner's books and writing materials. While Southwell and the servants busied themselves parcelling up the books, Rich engaged More in conversation – the type of sparring conversation two lawyers or students of the law might indulge in together professionally, a form of theoretical disputation and oratory with which they would have been familiar from their training in the Inns of Court, when one young barrister would 'put a case' to the other, in a practice known as 'mooting'. As it has been described by Wilfrid R. Prest, the essence of mooting was the 'formulation and debate of a hypothetical case or set of circumstances involving one or more controversial questions of law'.

On returning from this visit, Rich wrote a report of the conversation for Cromwell, a report which still exists. Rich claimed to have begun by asking More: 'Supposing that it were enacted by Parliament that I should be king, and that it should be treason to deny the same, what would be the offence if you were to say that I was King?' More replied that he would be bound by such an Act of Parliament not to deny that Rich was king, but that this was a 'light case' and he would therefore put a 'higher case' to Rich. 'Suppose it should be enacted by Parliament that God should not be God,' said More – would Rich be committing an offence if he refused to affirm that God was not God? Rich's reply was that this would not be an offence, as it was impossible that God should not be God. And then, claiming to be putting a 'medium case', he came to the crux of the matter. 'You know,' he said to More, 'that our lord the King is constituted Supreme Head on Earth of the Church of England; and why ought not you, Master More, to affirm and accept him so, just as you would in the preceding case, in which you admit that you would be bound to accept me as king?' To this More replied (according to Rich) that the cases were not similar, for a king could legitimately be made and deprived by Parliament, and every person present at Parliament was able to give his assent to such an Act, but that no such power existed in regard to primacy over the Church, and a subject could not be bound by something to which he could not legitimately give his assent in Parliament.

More, however, denied at his trial that any such conversation had taken place, protesting that, given how circumspect he had been throughout the years of his disagreement with the King, never having divulged 'the secrets of his conscience' about the King's supremacy and refusing even to explain his motives in resisting, he was hardly likely to have chosen Rich, of all people, to confide in, even in a hypothetical discussion. More's judgement of Rich's character is preserved in the account of William Roper. 'Neither I nor no man else to my knowledge ever took you to be a man of such credit as in any matter of importance I or any other would at any time vouchsafe to communicate with you,' More is recorded as having said. And he spoke from personal experience: 'I, as you know, of no small while have been acquainted with you and your conversation, who have known you from your youth hitherto.'

The chalk-and-ink sketch of Rich executed by Hans Holbein the Younger sometime between 1532 and 1543 is strikingly similar in composition to the artist's earlier drawing and portrait of More. Did Rich long to be like the man in whose downfall he participated? Did jealousy, and a thwarted desire for approval, constitute part of his (probably unconscious) motivation? The sitters are drawn at exactly the same angle, have the same hairstyle, the same beardlessness but shading of the lower jaw, and Rich attempts the same steady gaze, though his eyelids come down slightly lower over his eyes – as though he cannot maintain such steadfastness of intent, or such candour. Where More is all focus, emanating intelligence and willpower, Rich looks somehow lightweight. Where More's lips are pressed together in determination, Rich's are slightly petulant. Yet, despite these differences and despite Holbein's having produced a number of sketches of Tudor dignitaries in a similar profile pose, the impression remains that Rich is deliberately emulating his fallen idol, this man who refused to take him seriously.

Those who might have overheard the alleged conversation offered no corroboration, one way or the other. One of the servants declared: 'I was so busy about the trussing up of Sir Thomas More's books in a sack, that I took no heed of their talk.' Sir Richard Southwell asserted that he too had been otherwise engaged: 'Because I was appointed only to look unto the conveyance of his books, I gave no ear unto them.'

Either way, Rich does not come well out of this episode: according to one version, he tricked More into uttering opinions that would get him executed and then revealed them to Cromwell; according to the other version, he invented the conversation and committed perjury in helping to ensure More's conviction. The truth probably lies somewhere in the middle – the conversation, as an exercise in mooting, may well have taken place, but in his retelling Rich amended what had been said, particularly as regards the conclusion to the game of putting the case. It has been pointed out that the usual termination of such a game was a so-called moot point – a position that is 'mootable' and consequently open-ended – and, according to Rich's version with its resounding conclusion, this did not happen, making that version even less plausible. But, whatever the truth of the matter, the jury chose to believe Rich and found More guilty of having 'denied the King's supremacy, *maliciously* depriving him of his title'.

Henry's desire both to assert his royal supremacy and to reform aspects of the Church was evident in the first definition of various doctrines and ceremonies to be issued under the new dispensation – the so-called Ten Articles which were drawn up by Archbishop Cranmer on behalf of the Crown and promulgated in 1536. The Ten Articles are brief. They stipulate that the creeds are to be taken as necessary for salvation, and provide explanations of the sacraments of baptism, penance and the altar, followed by an account of justification (insisting that 'good works' were still necessary) and short statements on images, saints, prayers to saints, rites and ceremonies, and purgatory. They were not intended as a full statement of doctrine, but simply dealt with some contentious issues. Their primary purpose, backed up by a royal letter sent to the bishops in

January 1536 regretting the preaching of divisive and extreme views, seems to have been to promote conformity among the King's subjects and to avoid the kinds of ructions being experienced on the continent of Europe. The Ten Articles were succeeded a year later by the first full statement of belief of the Henrician Church, the *Institution of a Christian man* or Bishops' Book, containing an exposition of the Creed, the Seven Sacraments, the Ten Commandments, the Lord's Prayer and the Ave Maria, and a discussion of the disputed doctrines of justification and purgatory, and the human origin of the papacy. The Bishops' Book was uncompromising as to what was expected of faithful subjects: 'whosoever being once taught will not constantly believe [these articles] . . . be very infidels or heretics, and members of the devil, with whom they shall perpetually be damned'. Henry's ecclesiastical policies at this time could certainly not be viewed as endorsing 'Protestantism', except in one fundamental respect – the denial of papal primacy. From July 1536 the Act Against Papal Authority had prohibited the extolling, setting forth, maintaining, or defending of the authority of the Pope, whether by writing, ciphering, printing, preaching or teaching. Furthermore, Cromwell had insisted in his Injunctions to the Clergy that every parish priest was to declare at least four times a year in his sermons 'how the bishop of Rome's usurped power and jurisdiction having no establishment nor ground by the law of God was of most just causes taken away and abolished'.

It was only five years previously that, in succumbing (briefly) to orthodoxy, James Bainham had been forced to agree that it was an offence to God to keep books prohibited by 'the Church, the Pope, the Bishop, or the King', and yet orthodoxy now demanded that the Pope be scrubbed from that list of authority figures. The implications of previous orthodoxies having become heresy, and of heresy having become also a crime of treachery, were played out in the story of the life, and horrific death, of Father John Forest.

John Forest was born in about 1470. Nothing is known of his background or youth, and there are no extant records of his having attended either of the two universities (Oxford and Cambridge), though his contemporaries frequently referred to him as 'doctor'. By 1512 he was a member of the Observant Franciscan community at Greenwich, where Friar William Peto was the guardian. The Observant wings of the old orders were those which adhered rigidly to the letter of their Rules, rejecting the perceived laxity of modern times. Edward IV had set up the first Observant Franciscan house at Greenwich in 1482; Henry VII obtained papal permission to transfer Franciscan friaries at Canterbury and Newcastle upon Tyne to the Observants; and in 1499 an English province of Observant Friars was created, soon joined by two new houses, Richmond, founded in 1500, and Newark, founded in 1507. With their reputation for austerity, and their siting near the royal palaces of Greenwich and Sheen, the Observant Franciscans served the families of both Henry VII and Henry VIII as confessors, preachers and counsellors. The future Henry VIII was actually baptized in the friary church at Greenwich in 1491, and he had his two daughters baptized there too: Mary in February 1516 and Elizabeth in September 1533 (Bishop Stokesley officiating at this latter event).

According to *Lives of the English Martyrs*, John Forest was seventeen years old when he entered the monastery at Greenwich. He may subsequently have been sent to Oxford to study theology in the house of the Franciscans without-Watergate. By the early 1530s he was a senior figure in the community at Greenwich, as well as a regular preacher at Paul's Cross.

Members of the Observant Franciscans, with their close links to the monarchy, were quick to become embroiled in the controversy over the King's 'great matter'. On Easter Day (31 March) 1532, Friar William Peto had denounced King Henry's advisers, referring to them as false prophets, in a sermon he preached at Greenwich in front of the King. Speaking later to the King himself, he told him directly that he was wrong to attempt to divorce Katherine; there were no legitimate grounds for doing so and he was endangering his throne in the process, by fostering opposition from all sections of society. This was not at all what Henry wanted to hear, and there were inevitable consequences for Peto and his fellow preacher, Friar Elston. They were imprisoned and subsequently exiled to Antwerp. From there they continued to militate against the King's attempts to divorce, writing books about it and getting them imported into England. Thomas Cromwell was kept informed about these activities via Stephen Vaughan, who combined in Cromwell's service the roles of merchant, diplomat and spy, and this did not bode well for the future of the Franciscan Observants in England.

There is a tradition that John Forest was Katherine of Aragon's confessor, though there is no reliable evidence to support this. But he, like Peto and a number of fellow Observant Franciscans, was – and was known to be – opposed to the King's divorce and for this he was denounced in a series of letters to Cromwell by two other Observants, John Lawrence (also a priest) and Richard Lyst (a lay brother).

Cromwell had recruited John Lawrence and Richard Lyst as informers in 1532, exploiting the divisions at Greenwich as he would do in many other monastic houses. One of the first letters from Friar Lawrence to Cromwell, written in June of that year, demonstrates how this friar was at odds with his community, and how he wanted to curry favour with the King and his secretary by reporting how he, unlike the rest of his brethren, was prepared to speak in support of 'the King's matter':

> I am not able to hide the ill will that our fathers have conceived against me for favouring the King's part. They invent all the means possible to put me to confusion; and I cannot preach and induce the people to do reverence to their Sovereign, but the friars say I preach the King's matter. Preaching at Kingston yesterday I spoke but a few words, persuading the people to reverence their prince by Scripture and example; and as soon as I entered the convent, divers set upon me with open mouth, saying I had preached the King's matter, and that all our religion should be slandered thereby, and all our benefactors and lovers should, in consequence of my preaching, withdraw both their benefits and devotions.

Richard Lyst, a former grocer and apothecary in Cheapside, and at one time a servant of the late Cardinal Wolsey, did not make contact with Cromwell until November 1532, and may have done so at the instigation of Friar Lawrence, for he writes in support of the latter in his first letter to 'Master Secretary'. He also immediately sets out to denounce John Forest, who has – most unfortunately for him – made an enemy of Friar Lawrence:

> Father Forest, who neither loves nor favours you, has laboured to supplant Father Lawrence, the King's true subject, and bring him out of favour with the King, and our fathers and brethren, and to expel him from the convent of Greenwich . . . If the King knew Lawrence's good qualities, both in learning, preaching, and politic wit, he would not esteem him little; and that he will well know, when he hears him preach, for he has a common custom in his preaching ever to draw the hearts of the King's subjects to favour his Grace. I trust that he will do the King as much honour and pleasure as Fathers Peto, Elston, Forest, and his fellows have done dishonour and displeasure.

As for Forest's preaching, Lyst's opinion was clear: 'I think the chancellor of London should be spoken to no more to assign Father Forest to preach at Paul's Cross. Our fathers have often assigned me to accompany him, supposing me to possess intelligence and learning. Many a time when he has preached, I have sat under the pulpit with a pair of red ears.'

In August 1532 a Chapter of the Order had been held, at which Forest (by now the warden of the community at Greenwich) had warned his brethren that the King was sufficiently annoyed with them to have considered suppressing the Order throughout England but that he, Forest, had managed to dissuade the King from this course of action. Instead, a new Commissary General was to be sent from France to take charge of the English Observant Franciscans. Friar Lawrence seems to have informed Cromwell of when Friar Forest was next going to see the King and what he was likely to say, so that the meeting could be set up to fail – or even be prevented from taking place – as can be seen from a letter

Lawrence wrote to Cromwell in September: 'Today or tomorrow they intend to make suit to the King. It would be well if you would keep them from speaking to him.' Lawrence further informed Cromwell, on 30 November, of what Forest had said to the friars in chapter, and suggested that the expected new Commissary General be told: 'If he do come, in my opinion it will be necessary for you to counsel him to beware of Father Forest, who boasts that he will rule the Commissary at his pleasure. He greatly rejoices that he put the King beside his purpose at our last chapter, saying that if he had not been there, the King would have destroyed our whole religion.'

In February 1533 Richard Lyst wrote with further accusations against Forest to Cromwell, and was keen to be allowed to denounce him in person. However unpleasant and vengeful Lyst may have been, his descriptions do suggest a degree of incautious overconfidence on Forest's part and perhaps a tendency towards self-aggrandizement:

It grieves me sore to see Forest's unkindness and duplicity against the King, considering how good the King has been to him and his poor friends for a long time. I can tell all his behaviour, if you and the King wish to know. On Monday last he was with the King, and he said that he was with his Grace more than half an hour, and was well received; that the King sent him a great piece of beef from his own table, and that my lord of Norfolk took him in his arms and bade him welcome. I understand that he advised the King to send beyond the sea for Father Hey, who was our commissary, but this would not be to the King's honour, for he was ruled by Forest when here last, and so did little good amongst us, neither to the King's honour nor to the profit of the religion. As far as I can perceive, he is on the Queen's part. I understand that Forest is to attend on the King on Saturday to receive writings for Hey. If the King and you were to send for Father Hurlston, a preacher of our house, and me, we could tell the King how Forest has used himself against the King's honour and your worship. I wish we could speak with the King before he sees Forest again.

Lyst also passed on to Cromwell Father Lawrence's willingness to preach 'the King's matter' whenever requested. 'In my judgment,' wrote Lyst, 'he is more able to do the King honour and you worship than three such as Father Forest.' It is unlikely that Cromwell was particularly interested in Lyst's judgement, being more than capable of forming his own. Father Lawrence, no less than Lyst, was clearly an unpleasant, self-seeking character, and he even seems to have managed to fall out with his 'spy master', Cromwell, writing to him:

> I hear you have conceived great displeasure against me, for which I am right sorry. There is, however, no just cause for it. I have always been anxious to do you service. Whatever I have done has been for the King's honour and yours, for which I have incurred great odium. I have informed you I could never be suffered to come to you. If it be your pleasure to admit me to your presence, you will find me at all times pliant and obedient.

It is evident from a letter of 18 February 1533 from Lyst to Cromwell that Father Forest knew denunciations were being made against him. Lyst saw himself as what we might term a 'whistle blower': '[Forest] says that he will labour to the King to get out of your hands all such letters as I and others have written about him, that he may get us punished, though we have written nothing but truth. Our fathers have made a law that whoever shows any act done secretly in the religion, or makes any complaint of any in the religion to secular persons, shall be grievously punished.'

Lyst now takes a superior, self-righteous tone, revealing his own delusions of grandeur, as he tells Cromwell how he means to point out to Forest the error of his ways:

> I wish you to burn all my letters, for I intend to write a long 'epistle' to Father Forest, containing all his faults and transgressions among us, for which he has always avoided punishment. I shall remind him of them, that in this holy time of Lent he may be sorry for them, and make some amends to God and the religion. I shall mention his unfaithful and indiscreet conduct towards the King and you, and will show you a copy of

the letter, if he take it not well *secundum evangelium*, to which,
I think, his perfection will not extend.

Lyst's tone is that of every lay person who has ever written in
indignation to their bishop to complain about the vicar. He
reported that Forest had been unpleasant towards him personally,
which is hardly surprising in the circumstances: 'Since you first
rebuked him for his indiscreet words about you, of which I gave
you knowledge, he will never speak to me, nor show any tokens
outward that he is in charity with me.' There had also recently been
some scandal concerning the Greenwich friary, involving the death
in prison of one 'brother Ravenscroft'. Lyst had made this fact
known to Cromwell and the King, referring to Ravenscroft's death
as 'suspect' and somehow implicating Forest, in the hope that it
would furnish them with an excuse to investigate the Observant
Friars and come down hard on them.

Where Friar Forest was lacking in wisdom was in disregarding
politics – not only the grand-scale politics of the King's 'great
matter', but the internal politics of life in a community. His arrogant dismissal of Lyst may be understandable, but was fatal for his
own position. Lyst wrote in great indignation to Cromwell on
Easter Eve, 12 April 1533:

> I have written my mind to Father Forest, because he will not
> speak to me; but he has not regarded my letter, nor the pains
> I have taken after the form of the Gospel, disdaining both me
> and my writing. Will therefore take a further process with him
> after the Gospel. As he has been extreme in seeking great
> punishment for the small faults of others, I thought it necessary
> to write and remind him of his greater faults, and I send you
> a copy of the letter. You will see how he has misconducted
> himself against God, our religion, the King and you. A
> Frenchman, just come from beyond [the] sea, has been chosen
> our minister, head, and ruler in this province. I hope he will
> do much good, and help to reform Father Forest, and some
> other things among us. It would be well for the King and you
> to speak to him, that he may know how to use himself among

us concerning the King's honour. It would be a meritorious
deed if you had Father Forest removed to Newark or Newcastle.

When the French friar arrived, he was given full power to act and
one of the first things he had to do was deal with Friar Forest, on
account of the repeated accusations of Lawrence and Lyst. And so
Forest was indeed exiled to one of the northern convents in May
1533. Richard Lyst informed Anne Boleyn that year that he was
intending to be ordained as a priest in the near future; the reason
he had been unable to do so before, he claimed, was that he had
been betrothed to a young woman – but she had now died (he did
not sound particularly sorry about this), so he was free to seek
clerical orders. Once ordained, he assured Anne, he would celebrate
100 masses for her 'prosperous state, both spiritual and corporal'.
By October he had set out on this course, having left the Greenwich friary and enrolled as a student at Cambridge, with the
intention of being ordained as a secular priest. He seems to have
been genuinely disenchanted with monasticism, though mainly
because of his own experiences. In the meantime, however, he was
in debt to the tune of 40 shillings and hoped Anne might be able
to help him out.

In 1534 the Observant Friars, like all other friars, monks and
canons, were required to swear acceptance of the Act of Succession
and then of the Royal Supremacy. Their refusal led to the imprisonment of many of them and the suppression of the order in England.
The friars who escaped imprisonment were sent to join various
priories belonging to their rivals, the (non-Observant) Conventual
Franciscans, where most of them eventually succumbed and made
the required oaths. It is at one such house of Conventual Franciscans
– that of the Convent of the Grey Friars in Newgate Street, London
– that Father Forest enters the records again in 1538. By this time he
too had given in and taken the necessary oath, though he would
later declare that 'he took his oath with his outward man, but his
inward man never consented thereunto'. This could be termed
'equivocation' and was considered by some to be a legitimate means
of misleading an unjust interrogator. 'Broadly defined, equivocation

involved making a statement which could bear two meanings, that which the speaker wished the hearer to take, and that which he himself "intended" in a purely technical sense.'

Despite this outward conformity, Forest was again arousing the attention of Cromwell (by now Lord Privy Seal), this time through his conservative teaching in the confessional. One of his penitents that year was John Lord Mordaunt. The Mordaunts had a large house nearby, in the parish of St Sepulchre-without-Newgate, and John, 2nd Baron Mordaunt of Turvey, served at Henry's court and had been created a Knight of the Bath on the occasion of Anne Boleyn's coronation. He maintained his Catholic faith and practice throughout the subsequent reigns of Edward, Mary and Elizabeth, being imprisoned in the Fleet in 1561 as a 'prisoner of the mass'.

Lord Mordaunt had made enquiries in February 1538 as to who was available to hear confessions at the Grey Friars, and Friar Forest was recommended to him. He duly made his confession to Forest, as part of his preparations for Easter, at about nine o'clock in the morning after Forest had celebrated the Lady Mass (celebrated daily in honour of the Virgin Mary) in the monastery. Forest took no fee for hearing the confession, but when Lord Mordaunt offered to make a donation, the friar requested it be used to pay for some coal (which was beginning to take over from firewood as the preferred heating fuel in the City). Mordaunt also gave what we would refer to as a 'tip' to the porter.

When questioned later about his encounter with Friar Forest, Lord Mordaunt insisted that nothing had been said by either of them about the question of the King's supremacy: 'And as for the Bishop of Rome, or any speaking with the said Friar Forest of the said Bishop of Rome, or in any manner further concerning the said Bishop or his authority, or of any matter touching the King's Majesty, or the Bishop of Rome, there was no such matter touched upon or moved by the Friar or by the said Lord or either of them.'

Lord Mordaunt had been questioned as part of an attempt to persuade Forest's penitents to give evidence against him on a capital charge. The Warden of the Grey Friars convent had been instructed by Cromwell to name those who were Forest's friends, including any who had paid him a fee for hearing their confession. In obeying this instruction, the warden also made clear his own intention, and that of those for whom he was responsible, to do as they were bidden, not to stand in the way of the convent being dissolved and to accept their own transition to a secular life: 'Your Lordship spoke to me of changing my coat. We shall be ready to change when commanded.' (This is in contrast to what Forest would stubbornly assert at his trial – that 'he might not lawfully change his habit at the King's commandment, but he might at the bishop of Rome's'.)

Cromwell has a note among his 'remembrances' – or, as we might say, his 'to-do list' – for April 1538: 'To know the King's pleasure touching Lord Mordaunt and such others as Friar Forest named for his principal friends.' Sir John (whose strength of character is clear from his subsequent history) furnished no evidence against his confessor, but another penitent, a man called Waferer, was less resilient. It was Waferer who related that Forest had told him in the confessional that when he had assented to the oath demanded of him in 1534 he had done so 'by his outward man, but not in the inward man'.

By March or early April Forest was under arrest, and a decision was made to try him for heresy. The principal charge against him was that of identifying the Catholic Church of the creed with the Church of Rome. At his trial Forest tried to defend himself by saying that he owed a double obedience: 'first to the King's highness by the law of God and the second to the Bishop of Rome by his rule and profession'. But no such explanation could satisfy the authorities who, while insisting on the inviolability of oaths made to the King, considered oaths made to the Pope to be null and void.

Forest was convicted and ordered to abjure his opinions at Paul's Cross. He appeared initially to accept the judgement, but while incarcerated at Newgate prison with the Carmelite Laurence Cooke and the Carthusian William Horne ('in a fair chamber more like to indurate than to mollify', according to Bishop Latimer), Forest's resistance stiffened. Latimer reported to Cromwell that 'Some think he is rather comforted in his way than discouraged; some think he is allowed both to hear mass and also to receive the Sacrament. If it be so, it is enough to confirm him in his obstinacy.' Latimer also feared that people had been telling Forest that, even if he abjured as a heretic, he would be convicted as a traitor – and so what was the point of abjuration? Whatever his reasons, at Paul's Cross on 12 May Forest refused to read the recantation, laying himself open to the fate of relapsed heretics, death by burning.

The chronicler Wriothesley recorded the events of that day as follows:

This year, the 12th day of May, being the third Sunday after Easter, the Bishop of Worcester, called Dr Latimer, preached at Paul's Cross, at whose sermon should have been present a penitent to have done his penance called John Forest, Friar Observant, Doctor of Divinity, lately abjured for heresy, the eighth day of the said month of May, at Lambeth, before the Most Reverend Father in God Thomas Cranmer, Archbishop of Canterbury, with others, and after his said abjuration, sworn upon the Evangelists, to abide the injunction of the said Most Reverend for his penance; which said Friar Forest, obstinate and forwardly, not like a true penitent performing his said penance, but standing yet stiff and proud in his malicious mind, refused to do; yet this day again, entreated by the Dean of the Arches, called Doctor Quent, with others, like a good Christian to perform his penance, he yet notwithstanding, maliciously by the instigation of the devil, refused to do, although the said Dean opened unto him the indignation of God and damnation of his body and soul perpetually, and also have a temporal death by burning as all heretics should have by the laws of this realm; which said Friar Forest should this day have borne a faggot at Paul's Cross for his penance, and also with a loud voice have declared certain things by his own mouth, after the said sermon enjoined him, for his said penance; all which said things he refusing to do, the said Bishop desiring all the audience then present at the said sermon to pray heartily unto God to convert the said friar

from his said obstinacy and proud mind, that he might have
grace to turn to be a true penitent . . .

Forest's execution took place at Smithfield on 22 May, in the presence of a crowd of thousands, including the Lord Chancellor,
Cromwell, Archbishop Cranmer, the Dukes of Norfolk and Suffolk,
the Earls of Essex and Hertford, the Bishop of London, the Lord
Mayor and the sheriffs. The elderly friar was dragged the short distance from Newgate prison to Smithfield on a hurdle, dressed in his
Franciscan habit which by now was in tatters, and bound hand and
foot. Wriothesley describes how 'the place of execution where the
gallows and fire were made was railed round about; and there was
a scaffold made to set the pulpit on where the preacher stood, and
another against it where the friar stood all the sermon-time, and a
long scaffold next to St Bartholomew's Hospital gate, where the
Lords of the Privy Council sat with the Mayor and Aldermen and
other gentlemen and commons of the City'. At the scene and prior
to the burning, Bishop Hugh Latimer preached a sermon for the
edification of the watching crowds – or, more particularly, for Friar
Forest himself. Latimer does seem to have entertained a genuine
hope that, even at this last moment, Forest might listen to what he
had to say and be converted. He wrote to Cromwell that, if Forest
would again – and genuinely this time – abjure his heresy, he would
'wish his pardon, such is my foolishness'. The sermon lasted for
about an hour, the whole ceremony taking place between eight and
eleven o'clock in the morning. Wriothesley's account continues:

> And being asked by the said Bishop in what state he would
> die, he openly declaring there with a loud voice to the Bishop
> as follows: That if an angel should come down from heaven
> and show him any other thing than that he had believed all
> his lifetime past he would not believe him, and that if his body
> should be cut joint after joint or member after member, burnt,
> hanged, or what pain soever might be done to his body, he
> would never turn from his old sect of this Bishop of Rome;
> and also seven years ago he [Latimer] dare not have made such
> a sermon for his life.

What lends particular credence to this description is that Wriothesley was not himself a supporter of this position, as is clear from his use of such phrases as 'his old sect of this Bishop of Rome'. Forest's remark to Latimer that seven years ago he would never have preached such a reformist sermon is justifiable – it was Latimer, not Forest, who had changed his opinions. If his, Forest's, views were now to be taken as heretical, it should not be forgotten that Latimer (and, by implication, all the other bishops and doctors of the Church) had espoused those same views not so many years ago.

To bring matters to a conclusion, either Latimer or Cromwell cried out (or so it is reported): 'Burn him! Burn him!' There are various versions of Forest's death, during which he appears more or less heroic and saintly or abject and frightened, depending on the viewpoint of the reporter. Possibly he was all of these things at once. According to the Spanish chronicler Garzias, Forest crossed himself and said, 'Gentlemen, deal with my body as you wish.' He was then removed from the platform where he had been standing and led to where he was to be burnt. His habit was pulled off, a chain was tied around his waist, and he was hoisted up, suspended by the middle, pushed into a swinging position by soldiers with halberds. He had asked for his hands to be untied, and they were. Before being heaved into position, he is reported to have said: 'Neither fire, nor faggot, nor scaffold shall separate me from thee, O Lord.'

Extra fuel for the fire was provided by the 'abused image' of Dderfel Gadarn (Derfel the Mighty, a warrior-saint of the sixth century), a great wooden statue from the pilgrimage site of Llanderfel (where the parish church is still dedicated to St Dervel) in north Wales. The claim has often been made that a Welsh prophecy stating that Dderfel Gadarn would one day set a forest on fire prompted the authorities to burn Forest. However, heresy proceedings against Forest had begun before Cromwell knew of the existence of the image, while the earliest reference to any prophecy comes in Edward Hall's *Chronicle*, published in 1548.

Cromwell had been made aware of the image of Dderfel Gadarn from a letter dated 6 April 1538 from Dr Elis Price,

Commissary General of the diocese of St Asaph, who had been busy 'taking away . . . abusions, superstitions and hypocrisies used there'. He reported that there remained this image to which people came in pilgrimage every day, bringing offerings of cows, oxen, horses or money, and that as many as 600 people had done this only the day before. 'There is a belief,' wrote Price, 'that the image has power to fetch persons out of hell that be damned,' and he asked Cromwell for instructions on how to deal with this situation. Cromwell seems to have instructed that the image be brought to London, for by the end of April Dr Price was reporting that it had been taken down and would shortly be conveyed to the Lord Privy Seal himself, despite pleas from the priest and parishioners who were prepared to pay the not inconsiderable sum of £40 to keep it.

Wriothesley describes the image as being a wooden idol 'like a man of arms in his harness, having a little spear in his hand and a casket of iron about his neck hanging with a ribbon'. According to Garzias, the 'great wooden saint' was 'so big that it looked like a giant' and had to be carried by eight men who 'hoisted it on to the platform where Dr Forest was'.

Mocking verses were also on display at the site of execution, linking the fates and the illusions of 'Forest the Friar, that obstinate liar' with the image of Dderfel Gadarn – the latter proved to be a false and useless idol by the fact that it had been brought from Wales to be burnt in Smithfield, and the former 'wilfully' burning on account of his obstinacy. The actual burning was indescribably excruciating, even those chroniclers wishing to emphasize Friar Forest's courage and sanctity unable to disguise the fear and contortions of the old man, his instinctive attempts to avoid the flames. 'Then,' wrote Garzias, 'they began to set fire underneath him, and as it reached his feet he drew them up a little, but directly afterwards let them down again, and he began to burn. The holy man beat his breast with his right hand, and then raised both his hands to heaven and said many prayers in Latin, his last spoken words being '*Domine, miserere mei*' ['Lord, have mercy upon me']: and when the fire reached his breast he spoke no more and gave up his soul to God.'

The great wooden image of the 'giant' had been cast into the flames below the friar as soon as they began to take hold. A strong wind kept blowing the flames to one side, and the fire kept dying down. In the end the chain may have been lowered, so that the poor sufferer fell into the flames along with the idol and finally died.

John Foxe, who was concerned throughout his *Acts and Monuments* to demonstrate the sanctity and courage of the Protestant martyrs, was predictably scornful about the demeanour of this sole Catholic victim of execution by burning, giving the following account of Forest's end (which he took word for word from Hall's *Chronicle*): 'The Friar when he saw the fire come, and that present death was at hand, he caught hold upon the ladder, and would not let it go, but so unpatiently took his death, as never any man that put his trust in God at any time, so ungodly or unquietly ended his life.'

Friar Forest's remains, such as they were, were gathered up and buried somewhere in St Bartholomew's Hospital (perhaps by some of the Augustinian canons who lived at the priory outside which this horrific scene was enacted, and who looked after the hospital). That night, perhaps inflamed by seeing the image of Dderfel Gadarn burn and looking for more 'idols' to attack, unidentified persons damaged the famous rood (or great crucifix) outside the City church of St Margaret Pattens.

A psychological change can be seen developing in all of the characters whose deaths have been recounted in this chapter, a change that took place in them gradually as they began to perceive that death at the hands of executioners – or, in William Pavier's case – by his own hand – was inevitable. William Roper wrote of how, between his father-in-law Thomas More's resignation in 1532 and his imprisonment in April 1534, More 'would talk with his wife and children of the joys of heaven and the pains of hell, of the lives of holy martyrs, of their grievous martyrdoms, of their marvellous patience, and of their passions and deaths that they suffered rather than they would offend God; and what happy and blessed thing it was, for the love of God, to suffer loss of goods, imprisonment, loss of lands and life also'. Nevertheless, More was also firmly of the view that it was wrong to seek martyrdom – which, he considered, would be tantamount to suicide – and his refusal to be drawn into speech and thereby incriminate himself (whatever Rich said to the contrary) is indicative of his desire to avoid execution if possible. Yet such a desire went hand in hand with the acceptance of that fate, if it indeed proved unavoidable. Similar attitudes can be seen in Bishop John Fisher; in the prior and monks of the Charterhouse (who swore, with reservations, to the first oath demanded of them, but resigned themselves to death on realizing the implications of the second); in James Bainham (and in Latimer when he came to visit him in prison); and in John Frith – who initially tried to flee back to Antwerp but later, once he was imprisoned and realized that the only escape would involve renouncing his beliefs, refused to take the chance of running away when it was offered to him. And once the inevitability of death was accepted, then these men embraced their fate and began to seek the 'glory' that could be found in martyrdom.

Not the least ironic aspect of this whole unhappy episode in English history is that the people on opposite 'sides' who met their death – Fisher, More, Forest, the Carthusians on one side, Bainham, Frith, Huet on the other, with Pavier perhaps somewhere in between – all took their inspiration and courage from the same example: that of Jesus Christ in the Garden of Gethsemane, praying, before his arrest and crucifixion, 'Let this cup pass from me – but yet not my will, but thine, be done.' More wrote his *Treatise upon the Passion* during the years he was coming to terms with his likely fate; Pavier contemplated the dying Christ as he prepared to take his own life; Bainham, Frith and Huet – and the struggling Father Forest – commended their souls to him as they burned.

Chapter Three

THE MAKING OF MARTYRS

✠

Crown him, ye martyrs of your God,
who from his altar call;
praise him whose way of pain ye trod,
and crown him Lord of all.

SINGING THE ABOVE VERSE (verse three of the hymn 'All hail the power of Jesu's name') in the Priory Church of St Bartholomew the Great — the former conventual church of the great monastery — on an August Sunday in 2014, I could not help wondering to which particular martyrs the hymn-writer (Edward Perronet, 1726–92) was referring, and which we mean when we sing it now. Perronet, the son of an Anglican priest but himself an early Methodist and later an Independent minister, turns out to have had a connection with St Bartholomew the Great, having been married there (to Duriah Clarke) on 10 September 1748, so he may well have had the men and women burnt at the stake outside its gates in mind when he composed his hymn. Given his aversion to the established Church and his claim that celebrating the sacrament of the Lord's Supper should not be confined to ordained priests (a question over which he fell out with the Wesley brothers, John and Charles), Perronet is very unlikely to have included Thomas More in his list of martyrs — but should we do so, along with the Protestants he pursued, or does awarding the martyr label to one set of those who died for their faith preclude awarding it to another? How does one approach the memory of 'martyrs'? How does one decide who was and who was not a martyr, when over such a short period of time there were so many conflicting beliefs, or conflicting interpretations of fundamental beliefs – for all of which some people would be found who were prepared to stake their lives on them – people from opposing 'sides' each sincerely believing in the causes for which they died, each venerated by their own supporters?

For John Foxe, the hagiographer of Protestants, Friar John Forest was not really a martyr at all, his lack of saintly credentials only underscored by his instinctive attempts to avoid the flames. The opposite view is taken by the Roman Catholic Church, who beatified Father Forest, together with fifty-three other English martyrs, in 1886. Sixteenth- and early seventeenth-century Catholic martyrologists, such as Johannes Molanus (a Flemish theologian of Louvain University), Caesar Baronius (an Italian cardinal and ecclesiastical historian) and Heribert Rosweyde (a professor of philosophy at the Jesuit college at Douai), were as keen to extol 'their' martyrs at the expense of the 'false' Protestant ones as Foxe was to do the reverse. And both Protestants and Catholics denounced the 'Anabaptist' martyrs, the most persecuted Christians of the sixteenth century, regarded as beyond the pale by both major persuasions. First emerging in the 1520s, the Anabaptists believed that true Christians should be re-baptized as adults, were in favour of holding property in common, and were opposed to war and to the swearing of oaths. In the highly ordered society of sixteenth-century Europe, they were bound to be viewed with mistrust, as subversive. Erasmus was not alone in thinking of them as anarchists who were not to be tolerated.

Would it perhaps be best not to call anyone a martyr, and consign the word to history – particularly in view of its having been commandeered in recent years by the suicide bomber? 'We rejoice for him whom God has chosen for martyrdom in the ranks of the people of faith,' writes the al-Qaeda ideologue Abu Bakr Naji in *The Management of Savagery*,* basing his triumphalism on a very

---

* 'This treatise, posted in 2004 and widely cited by jihadists, is both a rationale for violence and a blueprint for the Caliphate. It draws heavily on the writings of Taqi

different interpretation of martyrdom in the twenty-first century from any that would have been recognized in the sixteenth. None of the martyrs whose stories are related in this book set out to terrorize, maim and kill by means of their own immolation.

It is idle, but inviting, to speculate on the heavenly conversations of all those awarded martyrs' crowns when they meet each other after death (assuming they are all let into heaven, where differences dissolve in 'one equal music'). Perhaps some of them will first have to experience the pains of purgatory (if such a place, or state, exists – another point of contention over which opposing martyrs argued), there to learn that killing for the sake of ideas is not the way of Christian love (though some of them sincerely believed it was). There were certainly men and women from all the competing doctrinal positions of the sixteenth century who were prepared to lay down their lives for their beliefs. They did not constitute the majority of believers, but neither did they believe anything different from their fellow believers in each 'camp'; it was the seriousness with which they took their faith, their lack of willingness to compromise, that distinguished them from the majority. And as Brad Gregory has succinctly put it: 'The martyrs died for their fidelity to Christ, but they disagreed about what it meant to be Christian. They died for God's truth, but they disputed what this truth was.'

In determining who could justly be called martyrs, sixteenth-century thinkers considered there was more to it than how the individual bore his or her death (despite Foxe's scorn for Friar Forest's lack of stoicism). Patience under affliction could as easily be demonstrated by a 'false' martyr as by a 'true' one. What was of more importance was the rightness of the cause for which the alleged martyr suffered. St Augustine had presented this point very clearly in his treatise *De Correctione Donatistarum* (A Treatise Concerning the Correction of the Donatists), written in around 400:

---

al-Din ibn Taymiyyah (1263–1328), the medieval theologian who inspired the Arabian Wahhabi movement, and is highly regarded by Islamists for holding rulers to account in the practice of true religion.' Malise Ruthven, 'Inside the Islamic State', the *New York Review*, 9 July 2015.

Accordingly, in the psalm [Psalm 43:1], we must interpret of
the true martyrs, who wish to be distinguished from false
martyrs, the verse in which it is said, 'Judge me, O Lord, and
distinguish my cause from an ungodly nation.' He does not say,
Distinguish my punishment, but 'Distinguish my cause.' For
the punishment of the impious may be the same; but the cause
of the martyrs is always different.

Both Catholic and Protestant apologists expressed the view that it
was perfectly possible to combine a willingness to endure torment
and a horrible death with being deluded. In other words, being
prepared to die for an idea did nothing to lend credence to that
idea (at least in theory; in practice, the stoicism of the martyrs – of
either 'side' – could impress onlookers sufficiently to make new
disciples, or at least to sway opinion). But for the theorists – and
very often for the interrogators and judges – 'death for true
Christianity was steadfastness, death for erroneous beliefs was
stubbornness'. Again and again in the trials of the unorthodox we
see this attitude contributing to their conviction as heretics – their
refusal to recant was interpreted as obstinacy which, according to
Gregory the Great, was the 'daughter of vainglory' (another deroga-
tory term often thrown at heretics) and in itself evidence of a
heretical frame of mind. The Jesuit priest Robert Parsons, the
author of a *Treatise of Three Conversions of England* (1603), drew the
parallels explicitly, arguing that obstinacy was 'so nearly conjoined
in blood and kindred to heresy herself, as they cannot be separated'.
(It is worth noting that heresy is here given a feminine persona –
she is a temptress, a harlot, come to lure the faithful away from the
true path.) It followed that 'dying for opinions in religion, without
other consideration, is not sufficient to make martyrs, for that it
may be pertinacity and not constancy, sin and not virtue, instigation
of the devil, and not inspiration of the spirit of God'. Hugh Latimer
pointed out that even Jesus feared death, so consequently the fear
of death cannot prove that a man is dying for an unjust cause; neither then can the contrary argument be upheld – that if a man does
not fear death, his cause must be righteous. A completely stoical

acceptance of pain was not a prerequisite for martyrdom either, for had not Jesus himself cried out from the cross: 'My God, my God, why hast thou forsaken me?'

Seeking to explain the courage of 'martyrs' deemed to be mistaken, their opponents would identify the devil as the source of both their delusion and their bravery. The Catholic John Christopherson, chaplain and confessor to Mary I, wrote that if someone saw a heretic 'gladly go to the fire, and patiently suffer it', he should 'be right sorry in his heart and lament, that the devil was so great with him that he could make him suffer the hot flames of fire for his wicked opinion, and sold him straight to the fervent flames of everlasting fire'. Both Protestant and Catholic writers 'noted that if Satan could transform himself into an angel of light, then in his envy of God's martyrs, he could inspire heretics to die for false doctrines'.

It is stating the obvious to say that for anyone to become a martyr, somebody else had to be prepared to kill them; for heretics to be executed, enough people had to believe that the appropriate way to deal with heresy was execution. According to Henry C. Lea, author of the magisterial *A History of the Inquisition of the Middle Ages*, a belief in the necessity of dealing unsparingly with heretics, a belief propelled by a sense of duty, was 'universal public opinion from the thirteenth to the seventeenth century'. It was further believed that the Church should not itself shed blood, but that it was appropriate for those whom the Church found guilty of heresy – particularly those who had previously recanted but had lapsed back into their heresy, thereby demonstrating themselves to be both dangerous and irredeemable – to be handed over to the secular authorities for punishment (which generally meant death by burning).*

In England the death penalty for heresy was made official in

---

* It is interesting to note that the modern jihadist attitude towards the fate of heretics – or 'apostates' – also has this two-tier approach, the most reprehensible apostate being the sort who has previously had an opportunity to recant and has not availed himself of it: 'Note . . . that there is no forgiveness for an apostate unless he converts to Islam. When he converts, we have the option of either forgiving him

1401, during the reign of Henry IV, when Parliament enacted a heresy law, known as *De haeretico comburendo* ('On the burning of the heretic'). This statute stipulated that anyone accused of heresy could be arrested by officers of the law or by the diocesan bishop (who also had the right to detain the suspects in his own prison – or, perhaps, his 'coalhouse'), examined by the Church and, if deemed guilty and refusing to abjure, or relapsing after abjuration, handed back to the secular authorities for punishment. That punishment was spelt out: the secular authorities – usually the mayor and sheriffs – should arrange for the convicted heretics 'before the people in an high place . . . to be burnt, that such punishment may strike fear into the minds of others'. *De haeretico comburendo* was used to proceed against heretics in the reigns of the monarchs who succeeded Henry IV, and was not repealed until the reign of Edward VI.

*

Heresy is an opinion chosen by human faculties, contrary to Holy Scripture, openly taught and pertinaciously defended.

Robert Grosseteste (a thirteenth-century English theologian)

The concept of heresy can be seen developing over the early centuries of Christianity, in parallel with the establishment of a body of doctrine which was to be accepted by all members of the Church. The first Christian theologian to refer to doctrinal error as heresy was St Ignatius of Antioch, martyred at the beginning of the second century, who used the word to criticize the so-called docetists, who denied the humanity of Christ. Another writer against heresy was Bishop Irenaeus of Lyon, whose work *Against All Heresies*, written around 180, was widely circulated and was specifically directed against the major heresy of gnosticism. 'As an exponent of the apostolic and Catholic tradition, Irenaeus described heretics as bringers of alien doctrines to the altar of God and as

---

or killing him because he has repented after he had the capacity to do so earlier.' Naji, *The Management of Savagery*, p. 113.

rebels against the truth and church whom God would punish for their separation from the church's unity.' There seems to be no suggestion here, however, that anyone other than God should carry out the punishment. In about the year 200 Tertullian, a rhetorician, lawyer and leading theologian, weighed into the argument with his *Barring of Heretics* or *Prescription Against Heretics*, which included a 'rule of faith' setting out the main tenets of Christian doctrine, in an early version of what would become the official 'Creed' of the Church. He concluded his summary of the accepted faith with the words: 'This rule, as it will be proved, was taught by Christ, and raises among ourselves no other questions than those which heresies introduce, and which make men heretics.' In other words, any questioning of the rule of faith as laid down by Tertullian would in itself be heresy.

Tertullian also explored the nature of heresy as 'choice', heresy being 'a word used in the sense of that *choice* which a man makes when he either teaches them [i.e. false doctrines] (to others) or takes up with them (for himself). For this reason it is that [St Paul] calls the heretic *self-condemned* [in his epistle to Titus], because he has himself chosen that for which he is condemned.' Yet, however much he condemned the self-condemning heretics, Tertullian remained opposed to compulsion in religion.

The passage from St Paul's Letter to Titus (Titus 3:10–11) to which Tertullian refers stipulates that heretics should be 'admonished' once, and for a second time if necessary, but that if they did not mend their ways after the second admonition, they were to be 'rejected'. There is no suggestion from St Paul of doing anything more than 'rejecting' or shunning, but then the early Church was in no position to hand anyone over to the authorities, as Christians were themselves a persecuted minority; they could not have used coercion, even had they wanted to. It was when the Emperor Constantine the Great adopted Christianity and ended the persecution of Christians in the Roman Empire in 313, paving the way for the Edict of Thessalonica in 380, by which the doctrines and structures of what had been defined as orthodox Christianity became established as the state Church of the Empire, that the position fundamentally altered.

The first execution for heresy in the history of the Church was that of Priscillian, a Spanish bishop, and four of his supporters; this took place in 385, under the authority and direction of Magnus Maximus, Western Roman Emperor from 383 to 388. This was by no means greeted with universal acclamation by the Fathers of the Church, both St Martin of Tours and St Ambrose of Milan being horrified by this development. There were further executions in 510 under the auspices of Emperor Anastasius who had some people accused of being Manichaean heretics condemned to death; executions for heresy also took place under Justinian I (527–65). Nevertheless, these remained rare events.

It is sometimes imagined that, in consigning a heretic's body to the fire, the authorities hoped to rescue the heretic's soul from the eternal flames of hell. This is, however, far from the truth. Rather, it was believed – a belief based on particular interpretations of the teachings of St Augustine of Hippo (354–430) and of words attributed to Jesus in the Gospel according to St Matthew ('And these shall go into everlasting pain') – that the soul of an unrepentant heretic would be damned for all eternity. (It is worth noticing, however, that these words attributed to Jesus actually come at the end of his disquisition on the nature of the kingdom of heaven and, though they do refer to a division between 'the sheep and the goats', the 'goats' in question are those who did not give food to the hungry, water to the thirsty, or clothes to the naked, and did not visit those in prison; all this has nothing, ostensibly, to do with heretics – unless heresy is choosing not to love.) For those who held that unrepentant heretics deserved to die, there was no question of an excruciating death somehow earning the heretic mercy in the afterlife; if mercy was to be extended to anyone, so the argument appeared to go, it would be to society for ridding itself of this plague of heresy – by slaying the wolf to save the flock, or cutting away the rotting flesh to save the whole body – and to those people persuaded to return to the true faith through witnessing, or hearing about, the fate of those foolish enough to have deserted it. The purifying fire ensured that nothing at all was left of the pollution of heresy; the wound in the body politic had been cauterized and only ashes remained. The lapsed heretic could still save his soul, even at the last moment, by recanting – as victims were so frequently urged to do at the scaffold or the stake – in which case the punishment was still likely to go ahead, but at least both victim and executioners could have some hope that the eternal flames had been avoided. Watching a recalcitrant heretic burn, on the other hand, was 'like peering through a window into hell'.

In 1525 Johann Eck, a conservative German theologian and opponent of Luther and his followers, published his *Enchiridion locorum communium* or *Handbook of Commonplaces*. The *Enchiridion*, a collection of short Latin essays suitable to be read as homilies, was authorized for use as a preaching aid by Bishop Fisher and also promoted by Bishop Stokesley, who ordered a bookseller in Paul's Churchyard to stock it. In the twenty-seventh chapter, entitled 'On the Burning of Heretics', Eck rehearsed the traditional arguments for the execution of heretics. He quoted from the Old Testament Book of Deuteronomy in support of his hard line:

> If there arise among you a Prophet or a dreamer of dreams, and give thee a sign or a wonder, and that sign or the wonder which he hath said come to pass and then say: let us go after strange Gods which thou hast not known, and let us serve them: hearken not unto the words of the prophet, or dreamer of dreams. For the Lord thy God tempteth you to wit whether ye love the Lord your God with all your hearts and with all your souls . . . And the prophet or dreamer of dreams, shall die for it because he hath spoken to turn you away from the Lord your God . . .

It is important to realize that this was not a one-sided conviction – that is, it was not only the upholders of traditional religion who advocated the use of the death penalty, citing scripture, against the 'dreamers of dreams'. The Protestants could be quite as vociferous against their opponents. Michael Servetus, a Spanish theologian, humanist and polymath, who drew the ire of both Catholics and Protestants with his idiosyncratic, non-Trinitarian version of

Christianity, was convicted of heresy and burnt at the stake in Geneva in October 1553, under the auspices of the Protestant governing council of that city. According to an eyewitness account, Servetus was fastened to the stake with an iron chain, and a thick rope was wound several times tightly round his neck, until he begged the executioners to stop. A crown of straw coated in sulphur was placed on his head, and then the pile of wood stacked up around his feet was ignited. As the flames began to lick his body, Servetus let out a horrifying shriek. He took just under half an hour to die. Defending Servetus's execution, the Protestant leader John Calvin, like the anti-Protestant Johann Eck, quoted verses from Deuteronomy, this time in order to underline the importance of defending God's honour even at the price of executing one's friends or family:

> If thy brother the son of thy mother or thine own son or the daughter of the wife that lieth in thy bosom or thy friend which is as thine own soul unto thee, entice thee secretly saying, let us go and serve strange Gods which thou hast not known nor yet thy fathers of the gods, of the people which are round about thee, whether they be nigh unto thee, or far off from thee, from the one end of the land unto the other. See thou consent not unto him, nor hearken unto him: nor let not thine eye pity him nor have compassion on him nor keep him secret, but cause him to be slain. Thine hand shall be first upon him to kill him, and then the hands of all the people. And thou shalt stone him with stones that he die, because he hath gone about to thrust thee away from the Lord thy God . . .

There were also those, however, who argued that under the Christian dispensation, Christ having redeemed the world, the Old Testament strictures could be disregarded, the uncompromising lack of forgiveness associated with them having been overcome. A central text in this argument was the so-called parable of the wheat and tares, one of the stories told by Jesus to illustrate the nature of the kingdom of heaven and, like all of his parables, open to multiple interpretations – often revealing as much, if not more, about the interpreter as about the teller of the story.

The parable of the wheat and tares (tares being harmful weeds or 'wild oats') is related in the Gospel according to St Matthew:

> Another similitude put [Jesus] forth unto them saying: The kingdom of heaven is like unto a man which sowed good seed in his field. But while men slept there came his foe and sowed tares among the wheat, and went his way. When the blade was sprung up, and had brought forth fruit, then appeared the tares also. The servants came to the householder, and said unto him: Sir, sowedst not thou good seed in thy close? From whence then hath it tared? He said to them: The envious man hath done this. Then the servants said unto him: Wilt thou then that we go and gather them? But he said, nay, lest while ye go about to weed out the tares, ye pluck up also with them the wheat by the roots. Let both grow together till harvest come, and in time of harvest, I will say to the reapers, gather ye first the tares, and bind them in sheaves to be brent [burnt]: but gather the wheat into my barn.

If, in accordance with many of the interpretations of this parable, the 'tares' are taken to be heretics 'sown' by the devil, intent upon destroying the Church, the fundamental question concerning the punishment of heretics hinges on the words 'in time of harvest'. When was the time of harvest to which Jesus referred? Was it to be at some far-off date, such as the Last Judgement or the Second Coming of Christ? – in which case the Church should suspend its own judgement over who was or was not a heretic, and should let 'both grow together', refraining from acting against suspects lest some 'wheat' be accidentally plucked up and burnt along with the 'tares'. Or had the time of harvest already arrived, with the coming into existence of the Church and its ability to distinguish between true faith and heresy? – in which case the injunction was to 'gather ye first the tares, and bind them in sheaves to be burnt' – now, before they could do any more harm to the wheat.

St John Chrysostom (*c.*349–407), in his Homily 46 on this

parable, comes out clearly on the side of the first – 'wait and see' or 'leave it to God' – interpretation:

> What then does the Master? He forbids them, saying, Lest haply ye root up the wheat with them. And this He said, to hinder wars from arising, and blood and slaughter. For it is not right to put a heretic to death, since an implacable war would be brought into the world. By these two reasons then He restrains them; one, that the wheat be not hurt; another, that punishment will surely overtake them [i.e. the tares], if incurably diseased. Wherefore, if you would have them punished, yet without harm to the wheat, I bid you wait for the proper season.

Chrysostom makes the additional point that to execute those convicted of heresy risks killing some who might yet be converted back to the true path – 'in whom there is yet room for change and improvement'. But in arguing against capital punishment of heretics he is certainly not advocating tolerance of heterodox views – there is no prohibition on 'stopping the mouths' of heretics, on 'taking away their freedom of speech' or on 'breaking up their assemblies and confederacies'.

St Augustine dealt with the parable of the tares in his Sermon 23 on the New Testament and he, like Chrysostom, seems to be advocating the 'leave it to God' approach, warning his hearers not to be impatient or to trust their own judgement:

> O you Christians, whose lives are good, you sigh and groan as being few among many, few among very many. The winter will pass away, the summer will come; lo! The harvest will soon be here. The angels will come who can make the separation, and who cannot make mistakes. We in this time present are like those servants of whom it was said, Will You that we go and gather them up? for we were wishing, if it might be so, that no evil ones should remain among the good. But it has been told us, Let both grow together until the harvest. Why? For you are such as may be deceived.

The 'harvest time' is interpreted here by Augustine as being in the future, when 'the angels will come', and he reminds his hearers: 'We are but men, the reapers are the angels. We too indeed, if we finish our course, shall be equal to the angels of God; but now when we chafe against the wicked, we are as yet but men.' His hope is that, while there is still time, all may be saved: 'Let the good tolerate the bad; let the bad change themselves, and imitate the good. Let us all, if it may be so, attain to God.'

These were not, however, the last or only words Augustine wrote on the subject, and his writings were used to bolster the arguments of the 'burn them now' lobby as well as of those who advocated a more cautious approach. Pierre Zagorin claims that Augustine changed his mind to support the idea of violence against heretics, and that we first learn of this change of mind in the treatise Augustine wrote in about 400 in reply to a letter by the Donatist bishop Parmenian (and which has already been referred to for its distinction between 'false' and 'true' martyrs). A key passage in Augustine's treatise is one that can be taken as justifying persecution and in which he quotes from the Psalms (specifically, Psalm 18:37) to support his case:

> Again I ask, if good and holy men never inflict persecution upon any one, but only suffer it, whose words do they think that those are in the psalm where we read, 'I have pursued mine enemies, and overtaken them; neither did I turn again till they were consumed?' If, therefore, we wish either to declare or to recognize the truth, there is a persecution of unrighteousness, which the impious inflict upon the Church of Christ; and there is a righteous persecution, which the Church of Christ inflicts upon the impious.

It is that phrase 'there is a righteous persecution, which the Church of Christ inflicts' that, both for the sake of his own reputation and for the history of the Church, one could wish Augustine had never written. Nevertheless, he did also make clear that the aim of this 'righteous persecution' should not be to kill the impious, but to rescue them and turn them away from their impiety:

> Moreover, she [i.e. the Church] persecutes in the spirit of love,
> they [i.e. the Church's opponents] in the spirit of wrath; she
> that she may correct, they that they may overthrow: she that
> she may recall from error, they that they may drive headlong
> into error. Finally, she persecutes her enemies and arrests them,
> until they become weary in their vain opinions, so that they
> should make advance in the truth . . .

Another hostage to fortune, when taken out of context, in
Augustine's treatise is his question: 'What then is the function of
brotherly love? Does it, because it fears the shortlived fires of the
furnace for a few, therefore abandon all to the eternal fires of
hell?' The context is that he was writing about a heretical sect
– the Donatists – that appeared to have a propensity for suicide,
sometimes by self-immolation. He was not writing about judicial
execution by burning. Rather, his view seems to have been that
if convinced Donatists wanted to set themselves on fire, they
should be allowed to get on with it, while the Church should
busy herself 'persecuting' those not yet convinced enough to go
the same way, so that they could be rescued both from the
Donatists now and from hell hereafter. (The Donatists themselves
were convinced that *they* were the wheat, while the rest of the
Church in Africa – including Augustine – consisted entirely of
tares.)

The crux of St Augustine's argument concerning coercion of
belief and practice is presented in chapter six of his treatise:

> It is indeed better (as no one ever could deny) that men
> should be led to worship God by teaching, than that they
> should be driven to it by fear of punishment or pain; but it
> does not follow that because the former course produces the
> better men, therefore those who do not yield to it should be
> neglected. For many have found advantage (as we have proved,
> and are daily proving by actual experiment), in being first
> compelled by fear or pain, so that they might afterwards be
> influenced by teaching, or might follow out in act what they
> had already learned in word.

In other words, to force people to conform to right doctrine, through the fear or reality of physical pain, when teaching alone had not succeeded, was better than allowing them to carry on in their error – and eventually they would realize this for themselves, and be grateful. One should not forget when reading such arguments that Augustine in the fifth century – as indeed his readers in the sixteenth, and in all the intervening centuries – lived in a society in which corporal punishment, for all but the very privileged, was the norm and assumed to be the right way to correct aberrant behaviour.

An often quoted extract of Augustine's treatise is his comment about St Paul having initially been coerced to believe (when he, as Saul, the persecutor of Christians, was struck down with blindness on the road to Damascus). One can perhaps detect Augustine being rather carried away by his own rhetoric in this passage, careless of its dangerous implications because revelling in its symmetry (fear leading to love, love casting out fear), a favoured device of early Christian theologians who enjoyed reversals such as the redemption of the disobedient Eve ('Eva') through the 'Ave' uttered by the Angel Gabriel to the obedient Virgin Mary:

> Where is what the Donatists were wont to cry: Man is at liberty to believe or not believe? Towards whom did Christ use violence? Whom did He compel? Here they have the Apostle Paul. Let them recognize in his case Christ first compelling, and afterwards teaching; first striking, and afterwards consoling. For it is wonderful how he who entered the service of the gospel in the first instance under the compulsion of bodily punishment, afterwards laboured more in the gospel than all they who were called by word only; and he who was compelled by the greater influence of fear to love, displayed that perfect love which casts out fear.

For Augustine constraint and love were not incompatible, but in later centuries his words were used more to justify constraint than to promote love.

The burning in 1553 of Michael Servetus, referred to above,

gave rise to some protest, most notably on the part of a professor of Greek at Basel, Sebastian Castellio, who compiled a work in favour of toleration, drawing on the writings of earlier thinkers to support his belief that the execution of heretics was both ineffective and unchristian. The work attributed to Castellio (and published anonymously) was entitled *Concerning heretics: whether they are to be persecuted and how they are to be treated; a collection of the opinions of learned men, both ancient and modern.* St Augustine figured among the 'ancient learned men' quoted, as did a number of the other Church Fathers. In his translation and edition of this work, Roland H. Bainton traces the way in which some of Augustine's words came to be used to support policies he would not himself have endorsed:

> The persecutor, said Augustine, is like a kind father who disciplines a wayward son, or like a dutiful son restraining a crazy father from destroying himself. In each case the concern is to save the erring. Such analogies are irrelevant as justification for burning heretics at the stake. But there is another comparison which is susceptible of wider application, namely, that of the physician who amputates a diseased member for the sake of the rest of the body. So long as the death penalty is not admitted, so long as the State is not personified, this simile is innocuous. But the moment the diseased body is identified with the social group, then the individual becomes the rotten member to be destroyed for the sake of the larger good. Then the imagery swiftly shifts; the heretic becomes the wolf, the fox, the serpent, the thief, and the robber, epithets which themselves suggest the proper treatment. All of these terms are found in Augustine, as in his predecessors, waiting to be used as justification for a policy more rigorous than any he would countenance.

In the twelfth century St Augustine's writings on the treatment of heresy – and particular interpretations of them – found their way into Gratian's *Decretum* (c. 1140), a legal compilation which laid the foundation for the body of canon law, the *Corpus iuris canonici.*

Through inclusion in the *Decretum*, the definition of heresy as a crime and the concept of a Christian theory of persecution became part of the law of the Church. In 1179 the third Lateran Council proclaimed anathema against all heretics, along with anyone who defended them, gave them shelter, or engaged in business with them. The Council authorized the confiscation of the possessions of such heretics as the Cathars (translated as 'the Pure Ones' or the 'Albigenses') in southern France. (Catharism was considered by the Church to be a major heresy, or indeed not Christian at all; it was 'dualistic' in that it featured two gods – one of good and one of evil.) In 1184 Pope Lucius III and the Holy Roman Emperor Frederick Barbarossa joined forces to ban a number of heresies, against which Lucius issued a decretal, entitled *Ad abolendam*. This decretal required all archbishops and bishops to conduct regular investigations into heresy in their dioceses, using the evidence of reliable people as to whether there were heretics meeting in their neighbourhoods. In what was to become a familiar process, 'Convicted heretics, unless they abjured their errors, were to be handed over to the secular authority for punishment, and civil officials were required to take an oath to pursue heresy when asked by the bishops.' During the pontificate of Innocent III (1198–1216) the struggle against heresy intensified, with the French nobility being encouraged to join the crusade against the Cathars in the Languedoc (a twenty-year military campaign beginning in 1209, known as the Albigensian Crusade) and much effort being expended on preaching to persuade heretics to return to orthodoxy. In 1215 the Fourth Lateran Council, summoned by Pope Innocent and attended by more than 1,200 prelates as well as representatives of many secular rulers, passed a declaration that stated: 'there is one Universal Church of the Faithful, outside of which there is absolutely no salvation'. Canon 3 of this Council endorsed 'due punishment' for heretics to be carried out by the 'secular arm'.

Church and state were so closely linked in medieval Europe, and culture and everyday life so infused with religion, that the contagion of heresy came to be seen as a danger not only to the health of the Church but to that of society as a whole. It was in large part because of this fear for the stability of society (shared later by, for instance, Thomas More) that the death penalty became so embedded as the usual punishment for heresy, meted out by the secular authorities but with the agreement of the Church.

The process whereby execution as a punishment for heresy became accepted is also traced by G. G. Coulton in his book *The Death Penalty for Heresy from 1184 to 1917*; his argument is particularly valuable in its analysis of the use of the word 'exterminate':

> Abraham did not wish to kill Hagar and Ishmael; but he did find it necessary to get them somehow out of the way; and the medieval churchman was much of the same mind where heretics were concerned. Thus there grew up the habit of using this vague word '*exterminate*', very much as churchmen began soon afterwards to speak of 'handing over to the secular arm' – a euphemistic expression for consequences which were quite well understood.

One churchman prepared to defend 'extermination' in every sense was William of Auvergne, Bishop of Paris from 1228 to 1249, who wrote at some length in defence of capital punishment for heresy, using similar arguments to those adduced by Pope Innocent III. Heretics are traitors to God, he declares, and therefore even more deserving of punishment than other traitors; furthermore, by disseminating their false beliefs, they murder people's souls, and so are more deserving of punishment than simple murderers, who kill only the body. He too uses the parable of the tares in support of his argument, professing the belief that the tares are far more likely to pervert the wheat than the wheat to convert the tares:

> If it be urged that these, who are now tares, might become wheat, since they might be converted to the way of truth, this indeed is true; but there is no certainty that such contumacious folk, pertinacious in their error, would be converted and turn into wheat. On the other side we have the certainty that these tares turn the wheat into tares; for it is incredible with what ease they subvert, by their cunning, the simple and unlearned. Moreover, a few tares easily pervert and choke a

great crop of wheat. For we see how difficult and how very rare is the conversion of heretics; on the other hand, how very easy and frequent is the subversion of the faithful.

In 1233 Pope Gregory IX laid a special responsibility on members of the Dominican order to investigate heresy, and take action against heretics and their supporters. Thus was born the so-called Inquisition, which took over from diocesan bishops the primary responsibility for the discovery and punishment of heretics. The Dominican theologian and philosopher St Thomas Aquinas (1225–74) is cited by Pierre Zagorin as an authoritative voice in support of the belief that obstinate heresy, as a defilement and infection that needed to be removed from society, should be punished by death. Zagorin quotes from Aquinas's great *Summa theologiae* on the subject:

> For it is a much more serious matter to corrupt faith, through which comes the soul's life, than to forge money, through which temporal life is supported. Hence if forgers of money or other malefactors are straightway justly put to death by secular princes, with much more justice can heretics, immediately upon conviction, be not only excommunicated but also put to death.

This quotation is useful in reminding us that the context was a society in which the death penalty was widely used for crimes which we in the twenty-first century Western world would certainly not consider capital offences. It consequently required far less of a leap for the medieval mind to countenance death for heretics – when death for other 'criminals' was far more common – than it does for us.

Zagorin argues that Aquinas afforded the parable of the tares 'the same harsh interpretation as had Saint Augustine: when the tares are recognized and there is no chance of a mistake, then Christ's command against uprooting them no longer applies'. Aquinas's comment in the *Summa* does seem to support this argument; while not appearing to insist on the execution of heretics, he certainly does not condemn it: 'Yet if heretics be altogether uprooted by death, this is not contrary to Our Lord's command, which is to be understood as referring to the case when the cockle [another word for 'tares'] cannot be plucked up without plucking up the wheat, as we explained above . . . when treating of unbelievers in general.' Aquinas also upheld the view that the relapsed heretic should be put to death, even if he or she recanted again; if that were to take place, the individual 'should be admitted to penance but nevertheless sentenced to die'.

Conflicting interpretations of the parable of the tares were still being discussed around the time of the first executions for heresy of supporters of Martin Luther: two Augustinian monks, Hendrik Vos and Johann van den Esschen, who were burnt at the stake in Brussels on 1 July 1523. Their contemporary Erasmus held that the parable indicated that heretics were not to be destroyed, but tolerated, in the hope that they might eventually repent and become 'wheat'. Luther himself preached on the parable in 1525, arguing fiercely and eloquently against the burning of heretics (though later, like Augustine, he changed his mind on the subject):

> Again this Gospel teaches how we should conduct ourselves toward these heretics and false teachers. We are not to uproot nor destroy them. Here [Jesus] says publicly let both grow together. We have to do here with God's Word alone; for in this matter he who errs today may find the truth tomorrow. Who knows when the Word of God may touch his heart? But if he be burned at the stake, or otherwise destroyed, it is thereby assured that he can never find the truth; and thus the Word of God is snatched from him, and he must be lost, who otherwise might have been saved. Hence the Lord says here, that the wheat also will be uprooted if we weed out the tares. That is something awful in the eyes of God and never to be justified.
>
> From this observe what raging and furious people we have been these many years, in that we desired to force others to believe; the Turks with the sword, heretics with fire, the Jews with death, and thus outroot the tares by our own power, as

if we were the ones who could reign over hearts and spirits, and make them pious and right, which God's Word alone must do. But by murder we separate the people from the Word, so that it cannot possibly work upon them and we bring thus, with one stroke a double murder upon ourselves, as far as it lies in our power, namely, in that we murder the body for time and the soul for eternity, and afterwards say we did God a service by our actions, and wish to merit something special in heaven.

The parable also featured, again on the side of not executing heretics, in the Anabaptist theologian Balthasar Hubmaier's *On Heretics and Those Who Burn Them*, published in 1524. Hubmaier contended that heretics should be 'overcome with holy knowledge, not angrily but softly'. He believed it was right for the secular power to execute criminals, but that, as heretics could not injure body or soul – true Christians having the power of the word of God to defend them – they presented an opportunity for good to come out of evil.

But the voices urging toleration were not those that prevailed – certainly not for many centuries – while those who believed that the 'tares' should be identified, uprooted and executed kept the upper hand.

*

For mark, the day cometh, that shall burn as an oven: and all the proud, yea and all such as do wickedness, shall be straw: and the day that is for to come, shall burn them up (saith the Lord of hosts) so that it shall leave them neither root nor branch.

But unto you that fear my name, shall the Sonne of righteousness arise, and health shall be under his wings: ye shall go forth, and multiply as the fat calves.

Ye shall tread down the ungodly: for they shall be like the ashes under the soles of your feet, in the day that I shall make, saith the Lord of hosts.

Malachi 4:1–3 (Matthew Bible)

The next question must be why, having determined that the fate of the obstinate heretic was to be execution, was the chosen method that of burning? A literal interpretation of the parable of the tares must be one reason, along with literal readings of various other texts including, from the Old Testament, the verses from Malachi quoted above, and, from the New, a verse from the Gospel according to St John: 'If a man bide not in me, he is cast forth as a branch, and is withered: and men gather it, and cast it into the fire, and it burneth.'

Leonard A. Parry, in *The History of Torture in England*, notes that burning as a method of punishment dates back a very long time. 'The ancient Britons sacrificed their prisoners to the Gods in this way. The offenders were placed in wicker cages made in the form of some well-known idol, and big enough to hold several persons. The cage was surrounded by wood and was then set on fire and the wretched victims destroyed. This was 1,500 years before the fires of Smithfield.' The exceedingly visible, melodramatic nature of this form of capital punishment has always been a consideration for the authorities interested in exercising social control, as is evident from the words of the early fifteenth-century heresy law *De haeretico comburendo*, referred to earlier: 'that such punishment may strike fear into the minds of others'.

Professors Irene and Yale Rosenberg of the University of Houston Law Center have investigated the methods of execution prescribed in the Jewish scriptures for various crimes, and the rationale behind these prescriptions, publishing their findings in the *Tulane Law Review* in 2004, under the heading 'Of God's Mercy and the Four Biblical Methods of Capital Punishment: Stoning, Burning, Beheading and Strangulation'. They included in their researches not only the Torah (the first five books of the Bible) but also the Jewish Oral Law, known as the Talmud, the two parts of which are the Mishnah and the Gemara. The Mishnah, compiled around the year 200, generally states the law while the Gemara, a much lengthier text compiled some three centuries later, is a commentary on it, consisting largely of rabbinic debates. There is much discussion in the Mishnah and Gemara as to the most severe penalty, and which should be attached to which crime. 'An anonymous Mishnah rule, which usually signifies a majority opinion, lists the penalties in descending order of severity as stoning, burning, beheading and strangulation. There is a dissent by Rabbi Shimon, who argues that the proper sequence is burning, stoning, strangulation and beheading.' In trying to determine whether burning was a more severe punishment than stoning, or vice versa, the rabbinic discussions focused less on the relative physical torment involved than on the nature and seriousness of the crime for which the respective sentences were prescribed in the biblical texts. So some of the rabbis would argue that 'stoning is the most severe because it is the punishment for blasphemy and idol worship, applicable to those who breach the most fundamental tenets of Judaism', while others would contend that 'burning is the most severe because it applies to the daughter of a priest who commits adultery, and that such an act profanes her father. Why is profaning her father a worse offense than profaning God? Because God is not harmed by idolatrous acts or blasphemy, whereas the priest is injured by his daughter's promiscuity.'

Such arguments seem very far removed from sixteenth-century, let alone twenty-first-century, English concerns, but what is of interest is that, whether burning was considered in the Jewish law to be the most severe or only the second-most severe form of execution, it was still designed to be less painful, protracted and shameful than the burning at the stake devised by the Christian persecutors of heretics and specified as the due punishment for heresy in 1231 by Pope Gregory IX in his papal bull *Excommunicamus*. The procedure as described in the Mishnah nevertheless sounds quite horrific enough: 'The defendant is put in manure up to his knees. A coarse scarf is wrapped in a soft scarf, and the witnesses wind them around the defendant's neck, pulling in opposite directions until he opens his mouth. One witness then throws a "lighted wick" [actually a long thin trickle of molten lead] into the defendant's mouth, and it goes down into his stomach and burns his intestines.' The additional discomfort of being made to stand in manure (or mud or dirt, according to some interpretations) has been variously explained as designed to prevent the defendant jumping about and causing the molten lead to spill on to the body or to hide the bodily excretions which occur at death and so aimed at preserving the victim's dignity. Rosenberg and Rosenberg emphasize the differences between this form of execution and that of being burnt alive at the stake. The molten-lead method is 'speedier . . . less painful, and, because the external body is left intact . . . less degrading'.

Incidentally, the Gemara as examined by Rosenberg and Rosenberg also contains a possible explanation as to why a place like Smithfield – outside the walls of the City – should have historically been chosen as a place of execution:

> As the convicted person is being led to the execution site, he is given frankincense and wine 'to dull his senses'. The execution site must be situated 'outside the courthouse' and outside the city. Why? The Gemara gives two answers: that in the absence of sufficient geographic distance from the place of execution, the court itself, having ordered an execution, might be viewed as being comprised of murderers; or, alternatively, that the remoteness of the execution locale gives the condemned person the possibility of rescue.

The type of rescue envisaged here is not an unlawful ambush by supporters, but refers to the possibility of witnesses coming forward, even at this late hour when the accused was on his way to the place of execution, with fresh evidence which could avert the punishment. Those who consigned heretics to burn in Smithfield rarely hoped the condemned might be 'rescued' – at least not in a physical sense – but they were certainly desirous of not being regarded as murderers.

In addition to the biblical and other precedents (or apparent encouragements), for those determined to root out and obliterate not only the heretics but the heresy with which they were infected – and could therefore go on to infect others – the appropriateness of burning was that it removed the problem completely. There was nothing left, only a pile of ashes, some teeth and a few fragments of bone. Such remains may have been almost inseparable from the surrounding material of the burnt wood. The infection was cauterized and could not spread any further. That, at least, was the argument. This desire completely to remove all traces of the heretic is evident in the fate of one of the most renowned religious figures of the fifteenth century, the Dominican friar and preacher, Girolamo Savonarola. On 23 May 1498 Savonarola, in the company of two other friars, was hanged and his body then burnt in Florence's Piazza della Signoria. Officially his crime was heresy; unofficially, in his dominance over the Florentine citizens, he had set himself up in opposition to both secular and ecclesiastical authority and, crucially, he had in recent weeks lost the support of popular opinion. Prior to his execution he had been repeatedly tortured by the *strappado* method – hoisted above the ground by means of a pulley-operated rope tied around his wrists. This torture pulled the arms backwards and upwards, almost inevitably dislocating them. The pain was such that the forty-five-year-old friar, already weakened by his life of austerity, confessed to everything asked of him under torture, retracting what he had said once he regained his composure – and then the process would start again. Death must have come as something of a relief. To ensure that no trace was left of him, the ashes of all three friars were scattered in the Arno.

And what of the process itself? What happened once the victim (usually a living person, rather than one already dead like Savonarola) was securely fastened to the stake, the flaming torch thrust into the wood stacked around his or her legs, the fire crackling and starting to take hold? The first organ of the body to burn is obviously the skin, the layers of the epidermis (the thin waterproof outer layer) and the dermis (the thicker inner layer which contains blood vessels, hair follicles, sweat and oil glands) blistering, tightening and changing colour through red, yellow and brown to black. As the skin continues to tighten, shrink and pull apart, criss-cross and star-shaped patterns form on the surface, where the epidermis and then the dermis are splitting. The thin outer layers are frying at this point and beginning to peel off. After about five minutes the dermis shrinks and begins to split, the yellow fat underneath starting to leak out. Below the dermis is the hypodermis, composed of connective and adipose (fatty) tissues covering muscle and bone. As the fat of the dermis is consumed by the fire, the gaps in the skin widen and the layers beneath – of tendons, ligaments and thick muscle – begin to burn. The depth of the layers of muscular tissue beneath the hypodermis differs over various parts of the body. As these layers of muscular tissue burn away, the underlying bone of areas protected by thinner layers of muscle, such as the ankle joints, is exposed more quickly than, for instance, the bones of the thicker, heavily muscled, thigh. The bone itself will blacken as all soft tissue is consumed, and then it will turn into brittle greyish-white splinters, and feet, hands and limbs may drop off.

As the muscles char and burn away, they also shrink and contract, physically moving joints, and this gives rise to an interesting phenomenon, particularly in relation to the death of martyrs as described by Foxe and others. The muscle shrinkage can lead to the bodies of the victims of burning assuming certain characteristic poses. Dr Elayne Pope, who works with scene-of-crime investigators and specializes in bodies killed by fire, comments: 'If the arms were free to move, you would see flexion of the elbows, fingers, and wrist', and 'For extremities of the arms and legs, rapid dehydration from heat shortens tendons, muscle fibers of the more robust flexors, and produces the universally described and predictable "pugilistic posture".' That is, the arms flex and become raised and drawn away from the body, with the fingers tucked into the palm.

It is easy to imagine that to the onlookers of burnings at the stake, unaware of the shrinking effect on muscles from burning, these involuntary changes in posture – the arms flexing and rising, the fingers curling inwards – could look like the voluntary act of raising the hands in prayer. Likewise with other muscles: 'Smaller muscles of the head, neck, and back also shorten from heat to create a limited range of exaggerated arching of the spine.' The victim would become rigid, back arched, head thrown backwards. When these muscle contractures occurred, it could appear that the sufferer was raising his or her head towards heaven, in supplication or praise. The onlookers would not have realized that, by this time, the sufferer was almost certainly dead.*

When Christopher Wade, a linen weaver from Kent, was seen to be 'still holding his hands up over his head together toward heaven, even when he was dead and altogether roasted', it was interpreted by spectators as a sign from God. It must be God, they concluded, who 'no less wonderfully sustained those hands which he lifted up to him for comfort in his torment'. Another particularly vivid description of this type of phenomenon – a post-mortem reaction interpreted by onlookers as a final act of Protestant defiance – is that given by Foxe in the appendix of the 1563 edition of his *Acts and Monuments*, and believed to have come from an eyewitness, of the burning of one Robert Smith, a priest, at Uxbridge, on 8 August 1555:

> At length he being well nigh half burnt, and all black with fire, clustered together as in a lump like a black coal, all men thinking him for dead, suddenly rose up right before the people, lifting up the stumps of his arms, and clapping the same together, declaring a rejoicing heart unto them, and so bending down again, and hanging over the fire, slept in the Lord, and ended this mortal life.

---

* 'Muscle contractures are common where substantial heat has reached the body. This is almost always a post-mortem occurrence, as deep-heating effects sufficient to cook muscle are incompatible with life.' Saukko and Knight, *Knight's Forensic Pathology*, p. 316.

Chapter Four

RECANTATIONS AND REVERSALS

✠

One of the most perplexing traits in Henry's complex character is the readiness with which he allowed those whom he trusted for the moment – his grandmother and his wife early in the reign, and Wolsey and Cromwell in later years – not only to execute but also to originate and plan high policy . . . It was as if, once convinced of the absolute fidelity and ability of a servant, he allowed him to set the course and hold the wheel through dangerous waters until, without a warning, the captain came on deck to throw the helmsman into the surf.

David Knowles, *The Religious Orders in England*

JOHN LAMBERT, a priest who had been charged with heresy on forty-five counts in 1532, but freed when Thomas Cranmer became Archbishop of Canterbury, met his end 'for great heresy' in Smith-field on 22 November 1538. Lambert, whose family name was Nicholson but who had changed his surname (it is not known why) by the time he received his BA degree in 1519 or 1520, came from Norfolk and was educated at Cambridge. For a brief period, between Michaelmas 1521 and Easter 1522, he was a fellow at Queens' College whose patron was Katherine of Aragon. Around this time he attended the religious discussions held in the White Horse tavern in Cambridge, where he encountered the evangelical teaching of Thomas Bilney.

After leaving Cambridge, Lambert was ordained priest within the diocese of Norwich (according to his own account when later questioned by Archbishop Warham). Soon becoming connected with the reformist cause, he was among those who took refuge in Antwerp, where he became preacher and chaplain to the English House (that is, to the Merchant Adventurers or English merchants in that major trading city); during this period of his life, he became acquainted with other reformers who had (at least temporarily) taken refuge abroad, including John Frith and William Tyndale.

Much is unknown, or uncertain, about Lambert's life at this time, but it is likely that it was as a result of Thomas More's heresy-hunting that he was brought back from Antwerp to London to answer charges relating to the translation of heretical texts. Tom Betteridge in the *Oxford DNB* writes that Lambert was 'probably' examined on a charge of heresy before convocation on 27 March 1531 and was 'certainly' imprisoned during the period 1531 to 1532 and questioned by Archbishop Warham, first at Lambeth and subsequently at Warham's manor house at Otford. Here he was given forty-five 'articles' to answer, to which he wrote the replies without having access to any books.

In his *Acts and Monuments* Foxe reproduces these forty-five articles, along with the responses of the accused, in which Lambert is careful not to give direct answers to questions relating to the central issue of the sacrament of the altar. He, like the vast majority of people interrogated for heresy, had no desire to incriminate himself if he could avoid doing so. By bringing some of his words up to date, using modern language to convey his responses, one can get a real sense of his feistiness and wit.

To begin with, Lambert was asked whether he was suspected of heresy. 'How should I know?' he replied. 'I'm not sure what anyone might have suspected of me, or when. Some may have thought badly of me, some well, for, after all, people had different opinions of all the famous prophets, and of the apostles, and even of Christ himself. And seeing that not everyone thought well of Christ, who is the very author of truth, why should I care if some random person, at some time or other, suspected bad things about me and spoke ill of me? If they did, I took so little notice that I've forgotten all about it, and I'm glad I have. And if I did remember, I'd be a complete idiot if I told you about it, for your own law states that no man is bound to give himself away. But I have certainly never been charged with this crime or asked about it by a judge before now. And considering you haven't managed to prove me guilty, I don't know why you haven't declared me innocent, as I have asked you to. But now you've thought of new things to charge me with, and you've forced me to tell you what I think by keeping me locked up for so long.'

Lambert was then asked whether he owned any books by Martin Luther and, in particular, whether he had kept any since they had been condemned, how long he had had them, and whether he had studied them. 'Yes,' he replied, 'I have had them, both before they were condemned and subsequently, but I neither can nor will tell you how long I had them; but I have certainly studied them, and I thank God for that. For through them God has shown me, and many others, a light that cannot be borne by the deceitful darkness of those who — wrongly — call themselves the holy Church.' He went on to attack the 'over-rich' leaders of that Church who were, he said, 'so drowned in voluptuous living' that they had no time to devote to the study or the preaching of scripture. In Germany, he declared, it was much easier to identify the abuses of the clergy because it was possible to read all sorts of books in the vernacular and, as a result, people could easily follow 'the true light of God's word, refusing the horror of darkness and false doctrine'. Lambert further argued that, as a priest, he must have been considered by the Bishop of Norwich, who ordained him, able to discern good from ill, light from darkness, and therefore his opinion was worth listening to. (This seems a somewhat self-defeating argument, as the clergy he was attacking could reasonably have said the same thing of themselves.)

He was also asked whether he believed in free will — that is, whether 'whatever is done by a man, whether good or ill, is done by necessity'. Lambert treated this as a 'riddle' which he declared himself of insufficient wit or learning to solve (despite all his answers showing he had plenty of both). Behind this question lurked that of 'justification by works' — that is, whether by exercising his will to do good, a person could be deserving of joy.

Lambert's reply is that, as servants of God, it is our duty to do his will, and not to expect thanks or reward for doing so. This is something of a prevarication, with which his hearers could not really disagree, but his answer nevertheless contains a clue as to his true position – that he does indeed support the Lutheran view of 'justification by faith alone'. In other words, it is the grace of God that brings about salvation, not anything that humankind can do through good works – which, being subject to sin, we are unable to fulfil anyway.

The key question, sixth in the list of forty-five, concerned the sacrament of the altar: was it, he was asked, 'a sacrament necessary for salvation' and did the bread and wine become 'the very body and blood of Christ' after they had been consecrated by the priest? To this question Lambert refused to give an answer, while implying that he had answered in the past and adding that he would never have answered at all, had he known as much then as he knew now. Clearly what he knew now was that his fate hinged on his answer to this question.

He was then asked his opinion of baptism, whether he believed it to be a sacrament of the Church and necessary for salvation. Again, Lambert refused to give a complete answer – 'I will say nothing until some men appear to accuse me in the same, unless I know a more reasonable cause than I have yet heard, why I ought to do so' – but he did nevertheless express the opinion that the rite of baptism would be more 'edifying' to the people if it was conducted in English rather than in Latin.

The remaining articles covered just about every other doctrinal and ceremonial issue that could be thought of. Was matrimony a sacrament and carried out correctly by the Church? (Yes, said Lambert, except that some priests charged a fee for it, and there were restrictions on which days it could be performed and when banns could be read.) Did he believe that ordination to the clerical orders of priest, deacon and subdeacon constituted a sacrament, and that priests had a duty to say Mass? (Lambert held, basing his argument on the example of the early Church, that only the orders of priests – which included bishops – and deacons were ordained by God, while 'subdeacons and conjurors otherwise called exorcists and acolytes' were invented by men.) Was the practice of going to confession a sacrament and necessary for salvation, did the confession have to be made to a priest, and could the priest absolve sins? (Such a practice was not biblical, said Lambert, and only Christ can absolve sins.) What about the sacraments of confirmation and extreme unction (that is, deathbed anointing), and do all the sacraments bestow grace on those who receive them? (Lambert's position was that grace was bestowed by God, with or without the sacraments.)

And so to another pivotal question, concerning the authority of the Church to determine doctrine: are all things necessary for salvation contained in holy scripture, Lambert was asked, or are there other things which ought to be believed, that are not written in scripture? Lambert knew he was again on dangerous ground. 'This is the question,' he replied, 'as I have been told by great learned men, whom I count as my friends, since the time I appeared in your chapel at Lambeth, when these questions were first put to me: this, I say, is the question – as they told me – which is the most important and sums up everything of which I am accused.' But despite all the warnings of 'great learned men', this was one question over which Lambert refused to compromise or cavil, declaring that the truth was more important than friendship, and he affirmed that 'all things needful for man's salvation' are indeed to be found in the Bible. He was happy to concede that there were many other things that ought to be observed and believed – such as the law of the land – but that such things were not necessary for salvation. And here, despite the seriousness of his position, he poked fun at his interrogators, remarking that he had, for instance, believed Dr Warham to be Archbishop of Canterbury before he had ever set eyes upon him, and that he believed he knew who his own father and mother were, even though he knew nothing about his conception. And so, while on the one hand he appeared to give a straight answer, on the other he continued to obfuscate.

The questions went on and on. Did Lambert believe in the

existence of purgatory and that departed souls went to be tormented and purged there? ('I say that there is a Purgatory in this world, and that doth the Scripture and also the holy doctors call the fire of tribulation, through which all Christians shall pass . . . Other Purgatory know I none, that you can prove by Scripture . . .') Should holy martyrs, apostles and confessors be prayed to? Do the saints in heaven intercede for us? Should pilgrimages be made to shrines and relics? Should the Lenten fast be kept? Should images be placed in churches to remind people of Christ and his saints? Was it right to pray for the dead? Could people obtain merit through fasting and other deeds of devotion? (another question touching on 'justification by faith alone'). Should priests who had been forbidden by bishops to preach, as they were suspected of heresy, duly desist from preaching until they had been cleared of suspicion? (This presumably applied to Lambert himself.) Was it lawful for all priests to preach? Was it lawful for both laymen and laywomen to celebrate the Mass and to preach? Were all priests bound to say Matins and Evensong every day? Were rulers duty-bound to provide their people with translations of the Bible? Or might they reasonably make the decision that the people should not have the opportunity to read the Bible in their own language? Did excommunication pronounced by the Pope against all heretics bind them before God? (This was a very interesting question, considering when it was posed.) Other questions invoking the Pope included: 'Whether he believed that the Pope could make laws and statutes that would bind all Christian men to observe them, under pain of deadly sin, provided such laws and statutes were not contrary to the law of God'; 'Whether he believed that the Pope and other prelates . . . had the power to excommunicate priests and lay people who were disobedient'; and, most significantly, whether the Pope was the successor of St Peter and consequently, as the vicar of Christ, had 'power upon earth to bind and loose'. These questions, which seemed to demand the answer 'yes', were posed to Lambert in 1532, shortly before Archbishop Warham's death on 22 August; there could be no clearer indication of how far the archbishop was from accepting the changes being foisted upon the English Church by Henry VIII.

Several questions addressed the issue of clerical marriage. Lambert was asked more than once whether he thought it lawful for a priest to marry. He said it was indeed lawful, and even necessary for a man who had not been given the gift of chastity, as St Paul had written. Was a priest who married without papal dispensation (again the assumption that the Pope's authority was valid) and had children by his wife committing a deadly sin? Was a priest who found himself troubled 'with pricking of lust and lechery' right to take a wife as a remedy? (Yes, said Lambert.)

Some of the questions were attempts to get Lambert tainted by association, asking whether he had ever prayed for John Wycliffe, John Hus or Jerome of Prague who had all been condemned as heretics. Did he count any of them as saints, he was asked, and did he believe everything that was affirmed at the Council of Constance (the ecumenical council held from 1414 to 1418, at which these men had been condemned)?

It seems that on this occasion Lambert was saved by Archbishop Warham's death, after which he was released. It is possible that at this point he resigned his priesthood; Foxe records that he began teaching Latin and Greek, living in London by the Stocks Market, and that he considered getting married and also joining the Worshipful Company of Grocers. But it appears that he did neither of these things. Thomas Cranmer having succeeded to the see of Canterbury and being more inclined than his predecessor towards the cause of reform (not to mention being secretly married and the father of a family), it looked for the time being as though Lambert was safe.

But no vocal reformer was safe for long in these years, and Lambert was very vocal (more so than his fellow reformers liked). In the spring of 1536 he was once again in trouble, having been accused of heresy by the Duke of Norfolk. He was questioned by Archbishop Cranmer and Bishops Nicholas Shaxton and Hugh Latimer (all three men generally sympathetic to reform), particularly about intercession to the saints. It seems he was offered a

compromise (to agree that praying to the saints, though not necessary, was not sinful either) by his examiners, who were anxious lest
his extreme views should endanger their more moderate reforms,
but he did not prove tractable. Thomas Dorset, vicar of the City
church of St Margaret Lothbury, writing to the Mayor of Plymouth
about various ecclesiastical matters and events in London in March
1536, included an account of what he had heard about Lambert and
his questioning by the bishops. It is clear from what he writes that
Dorset was himself a reformer:

> One Lambert . . . was 'detected of heresy' to the three bishops
> for saying it was sin to pray to saints. The bishops could not
> say it was necessary, but he might not make sin of it. If he
> would have agreed to this he might have gone; but he refused,
> and was committed to the porter's lodge from that Monday
> till Friday night, when he was set at large. He came back again
> next day, to know the Bishops' pleasure, whether he were all
> free or not, when they opposed him again. He stood firm, and
> they could find by no Scripture that we ought to do it. The
> Bishop of Worcester [Latimer] was most extreme against him,
> and he was sent to ward again. Next morning, Sunday, they
> sent him and his articles to my Lord Chancellor [Thomas
> Audley], and there he remains in prison. My lords of Norfolk
> and Essex, and the Countess of Oxford, wrote to these bishops
> against him; and it is supposed they handled him so to please
> them, which has done great hurt to the truth.

Lambert once again escaped imminent danger, the three bishops
being reluctant to take matters further, and was active in evangelical circles in London for the next two years. He continued to
express uncompromising views, with no regard for politics or the
art of the possible, and in 1538, after hearing the reformer Dr John
Taylor preach at the church of St Peter Cornhill, he challenged his
teaching on the Eucharist. At this point Lambert's fellow reformers
had finally had enough of him, fearing that such an extremist
would jeopardize their own freedom to preach and minister, and it
was another future martyr, Robert Barnes, who reported him to

Archbishop Cranmer as a holder of heretical views on the sacrament of the altar – of being, in short, a 'sacramentarian', who
denied the real presence in the Eucharist. On being imprisoned by
Cranmer, Lambert – never one to shy away from a fight – made
the extraordinary decision to appeal to the King.

In doing so, Lambert played straight into the King's hands, for
Henry was at this time anxious to prove his orthodoxy in doctrinal
terms, in order to demonstrate that the Pope, in excommunicating
him, was doing so for political and malicious, rather than religious,
reasons. He was also trying to avert the possibility of the Holy
Roman Emperor and the King of France joining forces to launch
a crusade against a heretic and schismatic England. Lambert had
chosen the worst possible time to ask Henry to support Protestant
reform or the cause of free speech.

And so the King took Lambert up on his challenge, and
decided to lay on a show trial, at which he himself would play a
leading role. This duly took place on 16 November 1538, with
Henry dressed all in white and accompanied by a number of
bishops including Cranmer (Canterbury), Stokesley (London),
Tunstall (Durham) and Gardiner (Winchester). Lawyers in their
purple robes were also in attendance, as were many peers of the
realm and other nobles, along with the Gentlemen of the King's
Privy Chamber. John Husee wrote an account of the event for his
employer, Lord Lisle:

> This day, in the King's Hall at York Place, certain scaffolds, bars,
> and seats were erected on both sides the hall, and at the high-
> est end a 'haut place' for the King. The hall was richly hung,
> and about noon His Majesty being seated, with the most part
> of the lords temporal and spiritual, bishops, doctors, judges,
> serjeants at law, the mayor and aldermen of London, and
> others, John Nicholson, clerk, *alias* Lambert, sometime chap-
> lain to the English nation in Antwerp, was brought before His
> Grace, and certain articles concerning the Sacrament of the
> Altar objected to him. He held to his opinions, denying the
> very body of God to be in the said Sacrament in corporal

substance, but only to be there spiritually. The King's Majesty reasoned with him in person, sundry times confounding him, so that he alone would have been sufficient to confute a thousand such. It was not a little rejoicing unto all his commons and to all others that saw and heard how His Grace handled the matter; for it shall be a precedent whilst the world stands; and no one will be so bold hereafter to attempt the like cause. After the King had confounded him by Scripture, so that Lambert had nothing to say for himself, the bishops and doctors exhorted him to abandon his opinions, as His Grace did also: but he refused, and will have his deserts. The matter lasted from noon till 5, when he was conveyed to the Marshalsea.

Husee was obviously writing from the point of view of a loyal supporter of the King. The more detailed account of Lambert's trial given by Foxe in his *Acts and Monuments* has as its source the recollections of one A. G., believed to have been Anthon Gilby, a fellow sacramentarian who shared a residence with Foxe in Frankfurt in the mid-1550s. Foxe conveys a sense of the drama of the occasion as he sets the scene: 'When the King was set on his throne, he beheld Lambert with a stern countenance, and then turning himself unto his councillors, he called forth Dr Day, Bishop of Chichester, commanding him to declare unto the people, the causes of this present assembly and judgment.' The opening speech made it clear that the King's intention was to demonstrate that, having abolished the authority of the Pope in his realm, he would himself rule his Church with a firm hand, upholding sound doctrine and not allowing heretics to flourish. He would, in other words, out-pope the Pope. This firm line having been established, the proceedings commenced, with Henry at his most majestic: 'When he had made an end of his oration, the King standing upon his feet leaning upon a cushion of white cloth of tissue, turning himself toward Lambert with his brows bent, as it were threatening some grievous thing unto him, said these words: "How, good fellow, what is thy name?"' Lambert, going down on one knee, replied: 'My name is John Nicolson, though many people call me Lambert.'

'What?' expostulated the King. 'Have you two names? I would not trust someone with two names, even if he was my brother!' After this unpromising beginning, Henry instructed Lambert to explain his views concerning the sacrament of the altar.

Lambert began by thanking God that the King himself was prepared to listen to and understand religious controversies, flattering Henry in the process, but the King was having none of it. 'I didn't come here to hear myself being praised,' he interrupted angrily, and he told Lambert to get on with his explanation. Lambert seemed taken aback by such vehemence, and paused for a moment, trying to work out the best way to reply. Such hesitation only increased the King's anger. 'Why are you just standing there?' he demanded. 'Answer concerning the sacrament of the altar – is it the body of Christ?' And on saying this, the King doffed his cap, indicating his own reverence for the sacrament.

Lambert attempted to prevaricate, stating that he agreed with St Augustine – that it was the body of Christ, 'after a certain manner'. This, unsurprisingly, did not satisfy the King, who snapped: 'Don't tell me what St Augustine or anyone else says, tell me what you say – is it, or is it not, the body of Christ?' The King's bullying manner succeeded where the careful questioning by bishops had not, and Lambert spoke plainly: 'Then I deny it to be the body of Christ.'

One might have thought the matter could have ended there, but the show trial had not been organized for nothing, and the King would make the most of the next few hours to demonstrate both his orthodoxy and his authority. Archbishop Cranmer was now ordered to refute Lambert's assertion, and he set about doing so in a mild manner, addressing the defendant as 'Brother Lambert' and suggesting they defend their relative positions by means of scripture. Lambert knowing his Bible quite as well as did Cranmer, the two men were pretty equally matched in their ability to discuss it, and it began to look as though Lambert might actually get the better of Cranmer – not least because Cranmer may already have been tending towards Lambert's viewpoint, but could not as yet admit it. (One sign of the covert nature of the Archbishop's

The central doctrine propounded by Martin Luther [*left*] was that of 'justification by faith alone', which implied that the whole paraphernalia of the traditional Church, epitomized by men like Cardinal Thomas Wolsey [*below*], was at best unnecessary and at worst a form of idolatry.

A monument in West Smithfield, London EC1, commemorates many of the Protestant martyrs burnt near this spot.

William Warham, Archbishop of Canterbury from 1504 until his death in August 1532, was perhaps fortunate to die of natural causes before his disagreement with Henry VIII had been fully aired.

Tho: Moor L.ᵉChancelour

Hans Holbein the Younger's portrait of Sir Thomas More captures his intensity,
concentration and unwavering focus. For More, any challenge to the traditional
authority of the Church threatened the stability of the entire social order.

The ascetic and saintly Bishop Fisher of Rochester, executed a few days before Thomas More in 1535, chose to die rather than recognize Henry VIII as 'Supreme Head of the Church of England'.

Under Henry VIII, Thomas Cranmer was an advocate of only moderate reform. The Ten Articles he drew up in 1536 were intended to promote conformity among the King's subjects and to avoid the kind of ructions being experienced on the continent of Europe.

Richard Rich, implicated in the conviction of both John Fisher and Thomas More, looks by far the least formidable of the three in this chalk-and-ink sketch by Hans Holbein the Younger, who portrayed them all.

Rich's wife Elizabeth, the daughter of a wealthy London spice merchant, was a couple of years his junior.

Richard Bayfield, a former Benedictine monk, was slowly roasted
to death on 4 December 1531.

The order and manner of the burning of *Anne Askew, John Lacels,*
John Adams, Nicholas Belenian, with certaine of the Councell
sitting in Smithfield.

For the burning of Anne Askew and three others on 16 July 1546, the City of London
Corporation approved the building of 'a substantial stage . . . in Smithfield for the
King's Councillors, the Lord Mayor and the Aldermen to sit in'.

The fifty-nine-year-old John Cardmaker, former Vicar of St Bride's Fleet Street, was burnt alongside a twenty-nine-year-old upholsterer, John Warne, on 30 May 1555. Cardmaker had initially recanted, but later went joyfully to the flames.

Protestantism was his clean-shaven chin; only later, after the death of Henry, did he start to grow the beard favoured by many reformers.) And so the more robust and anti-reformist Stephen Gardiner, Bishop of Winchester, leapt in to take over, despite it not yet being his turn. After Gardiner, Cuthbert Tunstall, Bishop of Durham, made a long speech in defence of the traditional doctrine. By now even Lambert seemed to have realized the extent to which the odds were stacked against him; he was also getting very tired:

> Lambert in the meantime being compassed in with so many and great perplexities, vexed on the one side with checks and taunts, and pressed on the other side, with the authority and threats of the personages, and partly being amazed with the majesty of the place in the presence of the King, and especially being wearied with long standing, which continued no less than five hours, from twelve of the clock, until five at night, being brought in despair that he should nothing profit in this purpose, and seeing no hope at all in speaking, [it] was at this point that he chose rather to hold his peace.

In Foxe's description of the silent Lambert before the powerful bishops and the King himself, one cannot help but discern the pattern of the silent Christ before Pontius Pilate; this can have been no accident, Foxe using the parallel to emphasize the righteousness of 'his' martyrs.

Several more bishops delivered their allotted speeches, but Lambert hardly bothered to argue with them, just making a few further allusions to St Augustine but otherwise choosing to remain silent. The trial ended in as stylized a way as it had begun, the whole event conveying the sense of a set piece, despite the King's words about freedom of choice:

> At last, when the day was past, and torches began to be lit, the King, intending to break up this pretended disputation, said to Lambert as follows: 'What do you say now (he said), after all these great labours which you have taken upon you, and all the reasons and instructions of these learned men, are you not yet satisfied? Will you live or die? What do you say? You still

have free choice.' Lambert answered: 'I yield and submit myself wholly unto the will of Your Majesty.' Then said the King: 'Commit yourself into the hands of God, and not into mine.'

Lambert: 'I commend my soul into the hands of God, but my body I wholly yield and submit to your clemency.' Then said the King, 'If you do commit yourself to my judgment, you must die, for I will not be a patron to heretics', and by and by turning himself to Cromwell, he said: 'Cromwell, read the sentence of condemnation against him.'

That sentence of condemnation was that Lambert should burn.

Not the least mysterious element of Lambert's strange story – that of a reformer persecuted by other reformers for being too radical – is the detour he made en route to his execution. For he was taken, on the day he was to die, to Thomas Cromwell's house in Austin Friars where the two men engaged in a protracted conversation. What they said to one another is not known. On 28 November Cromwell had written to Thomas Wyatt in Spain of Henry having triumphed in disputation over this 'miserable heretic sacramentary' and had extolled the conduct of the King at the trial: 'It was a wonder to see how princely, with how excellent gravity and inestimable majesty his Highness exercised there the very office of a supreme head of his Church of England, how benignly his Grace assayed to convert the miserable man, how strong and manifest reasons his Highness alleged against him.' This was of course the official line which Cromwell would be expected to promote, particularly as he had himself been central to the whole enterprise of establishing Henry as 'supreme head of his Church of England'. But had the Lord Privy Seal, in many ways a supporter of reform, also hoped to be able to save Lambert and, in this last-minute interview, did he seek forgiveness for not having been able to do so? He had been silent throughout the trial, only speaking to read out the sentence against Lambert, on the King's orders. Or did he use these moments to try to persuade Lambert to recant, aware that his death was to be a lingering one, again by express order of the King? Lambert had written to Cromwell from prison before his trial, telling him of a 'rude letter' he had sent to the King expressing his views on the sacrament, and alluding to having previously received much comfort from Cromwell's 'causing the Gospel to be spread'. It is likely that Cromwell was as conflicted as other reformers over the matter of Lambert, who by his radicalism and intransigence threatened to endanger the very cause he supported. It is nevertheless possible that Foxe invented this whole anecdote, in an attempt 'to alleviate the embarrassment caused by Lambert's having been denounced by other evangelicals'. Whatever was – or was not – said between the two men, it made no difference to Lambert's fate, and he resumed his journey to Smithfield.

The eyewitness account of Lambert's execution given by Foxe in the 1570 edition of *Acts and Monuments* suggests that Henry's intention to make an example of this obstinate radical did indeed come to fruition:

> When breakfast was ended, he was taken to Smithfield, where he was very cruelly treated. For after his legs were consumed and burnt up to the stumps, the wretched tormenters withdrew the fire, leaving but very little under him. Then two men, that stood on each side of him, thrust their halberts into his body, and raised him up as high as the chain would permit. Then Lambert, lifting up such hands as he had, his finger ends flaming with fire, cried unto the people in these words 'None but Christ, none but Christ'; and being let down again from their halberts, he fell into the fire, and ended his mortal life.

One of those responsible for the trial and death of John Lambert was Robert Barnes, a character closely allied for much of his life with Thomas Cromwell. Less than two years later, in July 1540, it was his turn to be one of the victims in what was a particularly macabre and intentionally awe-inspiring event:

> And the 30th day of the same month was Doctor Barnes, Jerome and Garrard drawn from the Tower into Smithfield, and there burned for their heresies. And that same day also was drawn from the Tower with them Doctor Powell with two other priests, and there was a gallows set up at St Bartholomew's

gate, and there were hanged, beheaded, and quartered the same day, and their quarters set about the city.

These deaths occurred two days after the execution of Thomas Cromwell, and the events were not unconnected. The fate of all six men – and of Cromwell himself – furnishes the clearest possible illustration that religion and politics could not be separated under Henry VIII, heresy shading into treachery, and vice versa. At the time, Cromwell's downfall was being imputed partly to his alleged complicity in a heretical movement, and the burning of the three heretics Robert Barnes, William Jerome (the Vicar of St Dunstan's, Stepney, the church where Cromwell and his family worshipped) and Thomas Garrett (or Garrard, or occasionally Garratt) could be presented to the people as corroboration of such an allegation – particularly as Barnes had actually been in Cromwell's employment since 1532.

Robert Barnes was born in Bishop's Lynn in Norfolk in about 1495 and entered the house of the Austin Friars in Cambridge while still a boy. He subsequently studied under Erasmus at the University of Louvain, which was at that time a distinguished centre of academic humanism and where Barnes developed humanist sympathies. He returned to Cambridge in the mid-1520s, where he became prior of the Austin Friars and, as a result of his studies at Louvain, initiated a series of educational reforms in the house, including the introduction of various classical Latin authors into the curriculum. One of his pupils was Miles Coverdale, who would go on to produce the first complete translation of the Bible into English. Barnes played a significant role in the meetings of young intellectuals that took place at the White Horse tavern in St Edward's parish in Cambridge – where he, like many other subsequent reformers (including John Lambert), met and was influenced by Thomas Bilney. And in turn, just about everyone who was anyone in the church reform movement seems to have encountered and been influenced by Robert Barnes (we have already seen the effect he had on the life of the former monk, Richard Bayfield). The conservative Stephen Gardiner, who knew Barnes well and had himself been a devotee of Erasmus from an early age, does not seem to have been overly impressed, thinking of him as a typical friar of his period, albeit a very entertaining one – 'a trim minion friar Augustine, one of a merry scoffing wit, friarlike, and as a good fellow in company was beloved of many'.

Barnes received the degree of Bachelor of Theology in 1522 and a doctoral degree a year later. He first attracted adverse attention from the wider authorities towards the end of 1525 when he preached a Christmas Eve sermon in the Cambridge church of St Edward King and Martyr, in which he criticized various aspects of traditional religion, decried the way festivals were observed and condemned the ostentatious splendour of Cardinal Wolsey. The sermon had been planned in advance, Barnes being encouraged to deliver it by Bilney and his other friends. Once in the pulpit, however, he departed from his prepared discourse, based on Luther's sermon on the epistle for the day, and went further than any of his friends had anticipated, particularly in lashing out at the cardinal himself. On this first occasion of his getting into trouble, Barnes was brought to London where he was examined before Bishop Cuthbert Tunstall and Wolsey himself and persuaded, though not without protest, to recant his opinions. He was assisted in his trial by Miles Coverdale, who subsequently abandoned his monastic vows and went abroad.

Barnes's recantation was a public event. It took place at Paul's Cross on Sunday 11 February 1526; Barnes was made to perform public penance by processing around the cathedral bearing a faggot and kneeling while Bishop Fisher preached a sermon. The service was presided over by Cardinal Wolsey himself who, with thirty-six bishops and mitred abbots, sat on a platform specially constructed for the occasion. Bishop Fisher based his sermon on the day's Gospel reading (Luke 18:31–43), concerning the healing of a blind man; he likened the blind man to a heretic and declared: 'Heresy is a perilous weed, it is the seed of the devil, the inspiration of the wicked spirits, the corruption of our hearts, the blinding of our sight, the quenching of our faith, the destruction of all good fruit, and finally the murder of our souls.' And he continued:

My duty is to endeavour me after my poor power, to resist these heretics, the which cease not to subvert the church of Christ. If we shall sit still and let them in every place sow their ungracious heresies, and everywhere destroy souls, which were so dearly bought with that most precious blood of our saviour Christ Jesu, how terribly shall he lay this until our charge, when we shall be called until a reckoning for this matter!

In addition to the performing of Barnes's penance, the service featured a book-burning – which may have been the original point of the ceremony, with Barnes's humiliation thrown in as a last-minute addition for extra effect. Wolsey had recently instituted a commission to round up heretical books, and the members of the commission were the same men who had examined Barnes and persuaded him to recant. The round-up of books had not been entirely successful, a search of the rooms of thirty suspects in Cambridge having yielded nothing (the master of Queens' College having got wind of the search and, being sympathetic to reform himself, having tipped off the scholars involved). The drama of Barnes's recantation saved the ceremony from being a damp squib, with just a little pile of books to be burnt.

Following his recantation Barnes was imprisoned in the Fleet prison for a time, and subsequently placed under what amounted to house arrest in the monastery of the Austin Friars in London. But he did not spend his days in silent contemplation and repentance, as intended; instead he used his time in London to arrange the sale and distribution of William Tyndale's New Testament (one of the books Wolsey had been trying to get hold of to burn). When it became apparent in 1528 what he was up to, Bishop Tunstall had him moved to the Austin Friars' house in Northampton, where he was kept under close guard.

The next stage in Barnes's life reads like a spy drama. Determined to break free from surveillance, he left a suicide note for Cardinal Wolsey, along with a pile of friar's clothes on a river bank. He then disguised himself as a pauper and made his way back to London, from where he managed to sail to Antwerp and then travelled on to Wittenberg. There he became acquainted with Martin Luther, and devoted himself to study and writing in the Protestant cause.

The chief work for which Barnes is remembered is *A Supplication unto King Henry the Eighth*, the original edition of which was printed, probably in Antwerp, in 1531. In all, four editions were published during the sixteenth century. It was written with the intention of its being smuggled into England and – if possible – presented to the King, while Barnes was a fugitive in Germany. Cromwell's confidant and informant, Stephen Vaughan, wrote to his master about the work on 14 November 1531, advising him: 'Look well upon Dr Barnes's book. It is such a piece of work as I have not yet seen any like it. I think he shall seal it with his blood.'

The contents of the book were divided into three sections, the first being the actual 'supplication' to the King, in which Barnes argued why he should be acquitted of the charges of heresy which had been brought against him by Wolsey and Tunstall. The second section, entitled 'Dr Barnes Articles condemned for heresy', gives an account of the twenty-five allegedly heretical propositions which had formed part of his infamous Christmas Eve sermon, and the third section comprised eight theses or commonplaces covering the main points of Protestant doctrine. These eight theses, all of which apart from the fifth had already been summarized in an earlier work by Barnes, entitled *Sententiae ex Doctoribus Collectae*, were:

   i. 'Only faith justifieth before God.'

  ii. 'What is holy church, and who be thereof and whereby men may know her.'

 iii. 'What the keys of the church are and to whom they shall be given.'

 iv. 'Freewill of man, after the fall of Adam, of his natural strength, can do nothing but sin.'

  v. 'It is lawful for all manner of men to read holy scripture.'

 vi. 'Men's constitutions which be not grounded in scripture

bind not the conscience of man under the pain of deadly sin.'

vii. 'All manner of Christian men, both spiritual and temporal, are bounded when they will be housled to receive the sacrament in both kinds under the pain of deadly sin.'

viii. 'It is against scripture to honour images and to pray to saints.'

Being 'housled' meant to receive communion, so in thesis vii Barnes is insisting that all those receiving the sacrament must receive both the bread and the wine, and not just the bread, as was (and still largely is) the Catholic practice.

Notwithstanding Barnes's uncompromising Protestantism, very clearly expressed in *A Supplication*, both his eloquence and his network of contacts led to him being perceived as potentially useful to Cromwell and the King, at a time when Henry was anxious to secure support in Lutheran parts of Europe over his dealings with the Pope. And so, in the summer of 1531, Barnes was asked to find out Luther's opinion about the matter of Henry's divorce from Katherine of Aragon. Luther's attitude was not in fact particularly favourable towards the King, but Barnes nevertheless seems to have profited from this commission, and it paved the way for him to return to at least a limited favour in England, particularly as he was full of praise for Henry and prepared to assert the King's authority against that of the Pope. Barnes was clearly hopeful that, under Henry, the Church of England would be reformed into something approaching fully fledged Protestantism and, in order to support the King in what he imagined to be their shared endeavour, he was prepared to accept a wider remit for royal authority than was Luther.

Towards the end of 1531 Barnes was able to return to England with royal approval, despite the continuing antagonism of the then Lord Chancellor, Sir Thomas More. He did not stay long on this occasion, returning to the Continent in 1532 and going to live in Hamburg, from where he conducted a correspondence with More, defending himself against charges of sacramentarianism. After the execution of More, Barnes became ever more closely associated with Thomas Cromwell, being frequently used by him on diplomatic missions to the Protestant princes and cities of the Holy Roman Empire, particularly in support of the royal supremacy. He nevertheless struggled financially, as he was not paid properly, or on time, for these efforts. As for the King, he never really approved of Barnes, despite appearing to be on the side of such reformers when it was politically expedient.

In November 1534 a second edition of Barnes's *A Supplication* had been published in London. This edition begins, like that of 1531, with a section entitled 'A supplication unto the most gracious prince H. the viii', but most of this section was in fact new material, comprising an attack on the loyalty of the clergy, particularly lambasting the bishops who had previously taken oaths of allegiance to the Pope. Henry was bound to find this useful, whatever his private views of Barnes's religious opinions. In 1535 the latter was appointed as a royal chaplain, but the role brought him little advantage. In May 1536 he requested Cromwell to arrange for him to be appointed master of 'Bedlam', or the Bethlem Hospital for the insane, a post which had recently fallen vacant and which he had heard was worth £40 a year. One benefit of being appointed to the post, Barnes asserted, was that he would then be near Cromwell (Bedlam being located just outside the walls of the City of London and within easy walking distance of Cromwell's home), but he also stressed that he was making the request out of need, as he had 'nothing and nobody to care for him'. He made a further plea to Cromwell in the following month: 'I beg you to remember me with some small living, as you have often promised me.' But no such living ever materialized, and Barnes had to struggle on, scraping together some earnings through his occasional diplomatic forays and his writing.

As the 1530s drew to a close, so Barnes's fortunes declined. He was involved in the negotiations which culminated in Henry's ill-fated fourth marriage, to Anne of Cleves, and he was increasingly finding himself on the wrong side of the religious debate as it began to be clear that the King was no supporter of doctrinal reform. Barnes's betrayal of John Lambert must have come to be a bitter memory to him, once he realized that the attempt to steer Henry towards moderate reform had been in vain. In 1539 the so-called Act of Six Articles was published by the King's authority and passed in Parliament. It confirmed the doctrines of: i) transubstantiation; ii) communion in one kind only; iii) the compulsory celibacy of the clergy (Archbishop Cranmer had to take the step of sending his wife and children to safety out of England in the months leading up to the passing of the Act; until then he had just been keeping them hidden); iv) the perpetual obligation of vows of chastity; v) the use of private masses (masses said for souls in purgatory); vi) auricular confession. Whoever spoke against the first article was to be burnt (without even being given the opportunity to recant), while anyone convicted of speaking for the second time against any of the other articles was to be hanged.

While the Act of Six Articles was making its way through Parliament, Barnes was undertaking a diplomatic mission to the Elector of Saxony and the King of Denmark. Realizing that the passing of the Act spelt failure for his mission, Barnes returned to England where Henry, annoyed that he had not waited to be recalled, refused to see him. In the autumn of the same year, and despite this evidence of the King's displeasure, Cromwell arranged for Barnes to be appointed to the prebend (a type of canonry) of Llanbedye in St David's Cathedral (perhaps hoping to keep him out of harm's way in Wales, now that the tide was turning very much against the reformers in London). If such was Cromwell's motivation, it came far too late. In any event, Barnes did not go to Wales.

Instead, in 1540 he, along with William Jerome and Thomas Garrett, was appointed as a Lenten preacher at Paul's Cross. Such a commission inevitably constituted a test of doctrinal conformity; the occasions would draw large crowds and whatever was said at Paul's Cross would be heard in the highest quarters. The first sermon that Lent was preached (on Sunday 14 February) by Bishop Stephen Gardiner, who used the opportunity to attack the doctrine of justification by faith, arguing that those who said good works were not necessary for salvation were guilty of misinterpreting the scriptures. Barnes rose to the bait, taking issue with Gardiner and accompanying his argument with personal insults in his own sermon, preached a fortnight later. Gardiner complained to the King, who ordered both preachers to be examined before him. Cromwell realized it would be impolitic, and probably useless, to intervene and so did nothing.

The French ambassador, Charles de Marillac, was following – and reporting on – these events with interest, not least because Bishop Gardiner was well known to the French court:

> A private matter, which might become of public consequence, has occurred in the shape of a great contention about religion between the Bishop of Winchester, formerly ambassador in France, and a great doctor of the law, called Barnes, principal preacher of these new doctrines. The Bishop, one of these Sundays in Lent, did marvels of preaching in St Paul's Cathedral against the said doctrines, confirming wisely the old and sharply refuting the new. This Barnes could not endure, so that, some days after, although another was appointed to preach, he mounted the pulpit and, after long insisting on the contrary of what the Bishop had said, angrily threw his glove upon the people, as a defiance to the Bishop, against whom he would maintain what he said to the death. The King, much scandalized by this farce, has ordered both to dispute before him and the Council, in order that it may be seen who is right and who is to suffer punishment.

Gardiner and Barnes both appeared before Henry on 5 March, when the King declared Barnes to have lost the theological argument (there can never have been much doubt as to whose side he would come down on). He ordered him to apologize to Gardiner and preach a recantation sermon, which order Barnes initially complied with, again at Paul's Cross, on 12 March. Eighteen days later, however, unable to live with his conscience, he publicly withdrew his recantation – despite also begging Gardiner for forgiveness – in another sermon, preached at St Mary Spital in the presence of the Lord Mayor and members of the Court of Common Council.

(The 'Spital sermon' is a civic tradition that continues to this day, though it rarely generates such excitement as in 1540.) Barnes seems to have wished to distinguish the personal insults he had made to Gardiner, for which he was sorry, from the statements of his faith, for which he could not apologize. Gardiner, his actions almost as ambiguous as Barnes's words at this point, was slow to respond to the request to indicate his forgiveness and, after hesitating, held up a finger rather than the hand Barnes had asked for. He explained later that he had been taken aback by the request and embarrassed, though also rather put out. His apparent lack of generosity, along with his whole role in the undoing of Barnes – with whom he was reported actually to have been friendly in their younger days in Cambridge – contributed to the reputation for treacherous cruelty he acquired among Protestants as one of their chief persecutors, to be forever remembered (by the name of his see) as 'Wily Winchester'. In the most frequently reproduced portrait of him by an unknown artist, Gardiner looks guardedly out at the viewer, as though himself suspecting treachery. Whatever the personal animosities at play, Henry was furious at Barnes's withdrawal of his recantation – particularly as he felt he had attempted to broker peace between Barnes and Gardiner, and so the refusal of Barnes to comply could be read as a challenge to royal authority. In consequence Barnes, along with Thomas Garrett and William Jerome who had also been preaching dubious sermons, was committed to the Tower on 3 April.

William Jerome had preached at Paul's Cross on 7 March. In his sermon, in which he was perhaps testing the water to see how far he could go, he had denied that magistrates had the power 'to make not indifferent that which was indifferent' (that is, an officer of the law could not determine what was and was not a necessary doctrine for a Christian to believe) and he taught that justification was unconditional (that is, not dependent on 'works'). From his subsequent recantation, it would also appear that he had referred in an earlier sermon to Members of Parliament as 'butterflies, fools [or dissemblers] and knaves'. Jerome, like Barnes, was ordered to appear before the King, who was prepared to forgive him – on condition that he recant and 'make a full and open refusal of these pestilent doctrines'. He agreed to do so, preaching his recantation sermon at St Mary Spital on 29 March, though not without some soul-searching, as recorded in an account given to Cromwell's son Gregory by his former tutor, Henry Dowes, who wrote that though Jerome was 'perplexed, he was not confounded. He was compelled to deny himself, but was not the first that had so done; it was only a form of adversity, and he wished some men would learn to do the same.' And, like Barnes on the following day, he gave a double message, preceding his recantation sermon with another, in which he affirmed the very doctrines he went on to 'recant'.

These various voltes-face, the heartfelt sermons followed by apologies and recantations, succeeded by yet more passionate outbursts in defence of the evangelical position, suggest the confusion these men must have felt when faced with a King who had initially appeared to encourage them, in whose royal supremacy they had believed – or which they had at least wholeheartedly supported – as being a significant step on the road to reform and away from Catholic doctrines, and who now seemed to be backtracking as fast as he could go. It was as though they could not really believe that the King – and his first minister – would allow them to be condemned.

The third member of this trio of passionate preachers was Thomas Garrett, who was forty-two years old at the time of his death. (Robert Barnes was about forty-five when he was executed, and William Jerome presumed to have been around the same age.) At the age of nineteen, Garrett had been admitted to Corpus Christi College in Oxford, two years later becoming a fellow of Magdalen. After obtaining further degrees, he became curate in 1526 of All Hallows, Honey Lane (a City of London church already embracing reform), of which church he eventually, in June 1537, became rector.

Garrett had made use of his contacts in both Oxford and London to participate heavily in a book-smuggling enterprise, involving supplying the universities with Lutheran texts and distributing small (and therefore easily hidden) copies of Tyndale's New Testament. He even sold over sixty books to the prior of the monastery of Reading. In February 1528 he was apprehended in these activities by the commissary of the conservative Bishop John Longland of Lincoln, in whose diocese Oxford then was, probably on a tip-off from Cardinal Wolsey, who knew of the Oxford trade in heretical books. This was part of the same incident that John Frith and John Taverner were involved in at Cardinal College, when Frith was locked up in the fish-store and Taverner was let off. Garrett was locked in a room in Lincoln College, but managed to escape by picking the lock and dressing himself in a friend's coat. (It was a letter sent to Garrett after this escape that Taverner had known about.) He was hoping to be able to reach Wales and sail from there to Germany, but ports were being watched and he was captured at Bedminster near Bristol on the last day of the month. He was examined by Bishops Longland and Tunstall, and agreed to recant.

Like Barnes, Garrett seems to have benefited in the first half of the 1530s from the King's need for supporters of the changes he was making in the Church, and was in fact more successful than Barnes in obtaining church positions. A few years after his arrest and examination he became chaplain to Sir Francis Bigod, a Yorkshire landowner who himself supported the royal supremacy. Bigod obtained a licence for Garrett to preach throughout the country. By June 1536 Garrett had become chaplain to Hugh Latimer, then the Bishop of Worcester, and he soon also became his diocesan chancellor, in which role he assisted Latimer in attempting to implement evangelical reform and in successfully stirring up controversy. This work did not make him very popular, but it certainly kept him busy. John Foxe remarked that he was always 'flying from place to place', preaching throughout the diocese and southern England as well as working directly for Latimer. In his sermons he emphasized Christ's passion as the only means of salvation, and criticized the doctrine of purgatory and the practices of saying masses for the dead, making offerings to saints and going on pilgrimage. The evangelical polemicist John Bale wrote approvingly of him: 'he taught Christ here for an only saviour without the mangy merits of men'.

By the middle of 1539, in addition to being Rector of All Hallows, Honey Lane, Garrett had become chaplain to Archbishop Cranmer, who sent him to preach in Calais. His erstwhile boss, Latimer, was forced to resign his see when he refused to work for the passage of the Act of Six Articles in Parliament. When Garrett was ordered to recant in 1540, his recantation sermon was as sincere as those of his fellows.

The initial imprisonment in the Tower of Barnes, Jerome and Garrett, on 3 April, was only brief, as for a few weeks Cromwell (whom, on 10 April, Ambassador Marillac had described as 'tottering') appeared to be back in control and was able to get them released. But with his own arrest on 10 June, their fates were sealed. The attainder against the three men described them as 'detestable heretics [who] have openly preached erroneous opinions and perverted many texts of Scripture (for which heresies Barnes and Garrard have been before this abjured), and who are to suffer death as heretics by burning or otherwise, and forfeit all possessions'. Yet there was no real evidence that any of them had contravened the first clause of the Act of Six Articles, the only doctrinal offence to carry an automatic death penalty.

The religious radical and member of the Merchant Taylors' Company Richard Hilles wrote to the Zürich reformer Heinrich Bullinger in February 1541, recalling the burning of Barnes, Garrett and Jerome the previous summer: 'They were brought from the Tower on a sledge to Smithfield, tied to one stake and burned . . . They remained in the fire as quiet as if they had felt no pain.' At the stake, the three men maintained that they did not know why they were being burnt, and that they were innocent. With nothing left to lose, they used the moments before the fire was lit to preach their final sermons. Barnes, in particular, played to the crowd and was certainly the ultimate victor as far as public opinion was concerned. He began by asserting his Protestant conviction in the saving power of the death of Christ and went on to mock Catholic teachings, telling the sheriff (waiting to set his torch to the pyre) that, if it were true that the saints in heaven prayed for human beings still on earth, then he, Barnes, would be praying for him in half an hour or so. Declaring his loyalty to the King, he nevertheless went so far as to request he ensure 'that matrimony be had in more reverence than it is; and that men, for every light cause invented, cast not off their wives' (this in the very month that Henry's marriage to Anne of Cleves was dissolved – Richard Rich being one of the officials who witnessed Anne's signature of consent – and Henry married his fifth wife, Katherine Howard). Barnes also had the temerity to insist that the proceeds from the sale of monastic and other church possessions should be used to benefit the poor, rather than to line the pockets of the rich. This was a plea that would have resonated with many of his contemporaries. For his part, Jerome demanded at the stake that 'all Christians put no trust nor confidence in their works, but in the blood of Christ'. According to Foxe, Garrett declared he had never knowingly preached anything 'against God's holy word, or contrary to the true faith'.

The bewilderment this execution caused, the three men never having been formally charged with anything but condemned only by attainder, is eloquently captured in Edward Hall's *Chronicle*. Hall reports that he has attempted to 'search out the truth' but to no avail:

> And as I said before, thus much I find in their attainder, that they were detestable and abominable heretics, and that they had taught many heresies, the number whereof was too great in the attainder to be recited, so that there is not one alleged, which I have often wondered at, that their heresies were so many, and not one there alleged, as special cause of their death. And indeed at their death, they asked the sheriffs why they were condemned, who answered, they could not tell; but if I may say the truth, most men said it was for preaching against the doctrine of Stephen Gardiner, Bishop of Winchester, who chiefly procured this their death, God and he know, but great pity it was, that such learned men should so be cast away,

without examination, neither knowing what was laid to their charge, nor never called to answer.

The burning of these three feisty and determined Protestants, which came at the end of a sultry, pestilence-laden month in which hundreds of Londoners had been arrested on suspicion of having contravened the Act of Six Articles, was carried out alongside the putting to death of three equally uncompromising Catholic priests:

> This year, the thirtieth day of July, 1540, were drawn from the Tower of London into Smithfield these persons following, that is to say: Doctor Barnes, Richard Fetherston, William Jerome, Vicar of Stepney, Doctor Edward Powell, Thomas Garratt, Parson of Honey Lane, and Thomas Abel, priests, of which three of them, that is to say, Barnes, Jerome, and Garratt, were burnt for heresy, condemned by the whole body of Parliament, and Fetherston, Powell and Abel were hanged, their bowels burnt, beheaded and quartered, in the said place of Smithfield, for treason against the King's Majesty, and condemned for the same by the whole Parliament.

There could be no clearer indication than this two-sided wholesale execution that the prime mover in repression was the King, coupled with the King's interests. These were no matters of principle – or else how could these two sets of ideologically opposed people have been executed together, in deliberate display, as though on a stage set? This was the doing of the King, designed to demonstrate his majesty, his omnipotence, his refusal to brook opposition – from whichever direction it came.

Henry had also just agreed to the execution of his own first servant, newly created Earl of Essex and Lord Great Chamberlain, Thomas Cromwell. Charged with heretical opinions and licensing known heretics to preach, as well as with treason, he had been beheaded two days before the deaths of Barnes and his companions.

And, playing his accustomed role of providing damaging testimony if it helped to advance his own position, we find Richard Rich who, having been a protégé of Cromwell's during the latter part of the 1530s, hastily abandoned his former patron in the summer of 1540 (by which time he was himself a member of the Privy Council) and gave 'evidence' against Cromwell. A hint of Rich's treachery can be discerned in Cromwell's desperate letter to the King, written on 12 June:

> Your Grace knows my accusers, God forgive them. If it were in my power to make you live for ever, God knows I would; or to make you so rich that you should enrich all men, or so powerful that all the world should obey you. For your Majesty has been most bountiful to me, and more like a father than a master. I ask you mercy where I have offended. I never spoke with the Chancellor of the Augmentations and Throgmorton together at a time; but if I did, I never spoke of any such matter. Your Grace knows what manner of man Throgmorton has ever been towards you and your proceedings. What Master Chancellor has been to me, God and he know best; what I have been to him your Majesty knows. If I had obeyed your often most gracious counsels, it would not have been with me as now it is.

Is it reading too much into this to wonder whether Henry had at some time warned Cromwell of the danger of trusting in Richard Rich? And, as in the case of Thomas More, here is a man about to be condemned, with part of the evidence appearing to hinge on an alleged conversation with Rich – a conversation the accused denied had ever taken place.

The three Catholics executed at the same time as the three Protestants were Thomas Abel, Richard Fetherston and Edward Powell. All were men who had openly defied the King when he had first set out to rid himself of Katherine of Aragon, and they had never been reconciled to his assumption of authority over the English Church.

Abel (who generally spelt his name Abell) had been educated at the University of Oxford, taking the degree of Master of Arts in 1516 and subsequently becoming a Doctor of Theology. He was also known to be a linguist and to have had some musical training.

He became deeply involved in supporting Katherine of Aragon's cause against the King, being sent by Queen Katherine to Spain in January 1529, ostensibly to deliver a letter from her to Emperor Charles V (a letter which the King had forced her to write) asking for the original of the dispensation issued by the Pope when Katherine married Henry, but at the same time conveying the message that the Emperor should not accede to this request, as the document might be used to injure the Queen's cause. Abel was rewarded by Katherine for the success of his mission by being granted the benefice of Bradwell in Essex in 1530. Some two years later Abel wrote a book against the divorce, entitled *Invicta Veritas, An answer to the determinations of the most famous Universities, that by no manner of law it may be lawful for King Henry to be divorced from the Queen's grace, his lawful and very wife*. This book, though ostensibly produced in Lüneburg, was secretly printed in London. Its uncompromising and defiant tone inevitably infuriated the King, and Abel was thrown into the Tower. He was released on Christmas Eve, on condition that he would not write again or preach until after Easter, and he returned to live in Katherine's household. A few months later he was once more in trouble, this time over what Katherine should be called. She was being required to drop the title of 'Queen', but was refusing to do so, and Abel was implicated in the drawing up of two warrants in which the title had continued to be used. It would seem from the letter that Sir Thomas Audley wrote to Thomas Cromwell about these two warrants that Abel could not rely on the loyalty of his own family, for it was his brother, one of Audley's servants, who had shown the warrants to his master. After the break-up of Katherine's household, Abel was consigned again to the Tower, in December 1534 (just a year after his earlier release), on suspicion of having encouraged her servants to refuse to be sworn to her as princess only (as they had previously been sworn to her as queen).

Richard Fetherston was about fifteen years older than Abel, having received his BA from Cambridge in 1499 or 1500 and his MA from Oxford in 1505. He was Rector of Sulhampstead Abbots in Hampshire until 1519 and then Rector of Newnham, also in

Hampshire. He became Archdeacon of Brecon in April 1523 and seems to have held that post until January 1535. He first attracted Henry's attention when the household of the King's nine-year-old daughter Mary was established in the Welsh Marches in 1525 and Fetherston was appointed as her schoolmaster. In that post he was accountable to Margaret Pole, Countess of Salisbury, who was appointed mistress of Mary's household, numbering over 300 people (and who was herself executed for alleged treason in 1541). Fetherston taught Latin to Princess Mary until at least 1533 and had earlier collaborated with the Spanish humanist Juan Luis Vives in producing an educational work, *De rationis studii puerilis* ('A plan of childish studies') for Mary's use. This set out the texts that Mary should study (according to Vives and Fetherston), which included the New Testament and selected extracts from the Old, along with works by various Fathers of the Church and approved classical authors, such as parts of Plato and selections from Horace. She was also encouraged to read the works of Erasmus and Thomas More.

During the same month that Thomas Abel was committed to the Tower for the second time (December 1534), Fetherston was sent there too. He had been one of the few clerics in the convocation of the province of Canterbury to have signed a protest in 1531 against the King's assumption of the title of supreme head of the Church. He is also believed to have written a treatise against the royal divorce and the break with Rome, unequivocally called *Contra divortium Henrici et Catherinae* ('Against the divorce of Henry and Katherine'), but no copy survives. His imprisonment in the Tower was intended to coerce him into taking the Oath of Supremacy. He continued to refuse, and was in consequence deprived of his benefices in January 1535.

Edward Powell, the third in this trio of priests, was born in Wales in about 1478 and educated at Oxford University where he became a fellow of Oriel College and was awarded his doctorate in theology in 1506. He also spent some time studying in Paris. Ordained priest in 1499, he fulfilled various administrative roles at Oriel, including collector of rents, junior treasurer, chaplain and dean, finally being made commissary to the chancellor of the university in 1508. Two years later he was implicated in an embezzlement scheme involving the university proctors and the Keepers of the University Chests, but the scandal inflicted no lasting damage. Powell was an example of the kind of early sixteenth-century clergyman who managed to hold many offices at once (or 'in plurality'): he was also Rector of Bleadon in Somerset (from 1503), canon of Lincoln (from the same year), canon of Salisbury (from 1507) and provost of St Edmund's College, Salisbury, from 1509 to 1534. He was also Vicar of Powerstock in Dorset from 1522 to 1526, Vicar of Melksham in Wiltshire from 1526 to 1534, and Rector of Radipole in Dorset, again from 1526. So numerous and geographically distant were his livings that in November 1514 he had to be granted a papal dispensation to allow him to hold three incompatible benefices.

After Henry VIII's accession in 1509 Powell was a frequent preacher at court, and in the 1520s he became known for his work in combating Lutheranism, particularly through the publication of a treatise against Luther, in which he defended the seven sacraments and the holiness of the Pope. Like Abel, Powell became involved in Queen Katherine's defence over the question of the proposed divorce, being included among the theologians and canon lawyers appointed to present her case before the papal legates in 1533. In that same year he was one of three priests hired by traditionalists in Bristol to preach against the reformist sermons being delivered there by Hugh Latimer, and in one of his sermons Powell condemned rulers who corrupted their subjects 'with open sinning and ill example of living' – such 'ill example' including the putting away of a first wife and taking of another, without the assent or dispensation of the Church. In 1534 he preached again in Bristol, this time in defence of pilgrimages. While previously Powell's trenchant condemnation of Lutheranism had gained him plaudits, the changed circumstances now meant his outspoken support for the old ways – let alone his hardly veiled criticism of the King – could only land him in trouble.

Powell, like Fetherston, was deprived of all his (many) benefices for refusal to take the required oaths and was committed to the

Tower on 10 June 1534. He spent a brief period in Dorchester jail, in appalling conditions, but was returned to the Tower in 1535. All three men now remained in the Tower until their execution. Thomas Abel left a memorial of himself there, in the form of self-naming graffiti: he etched into a wall his 'rebus', signing himself 'Thomas' above a picture of a bell containing the letter 'A'. In March 1537, the physical conditions of his confinement seem to have brought Abel to a pitch of desperation, for he wrote to Cromwell in the following terms:

> My Lord, I beseech our Saviour Jesus Christ to give your Lordship, after this life, life everlasting in Heaven. Amen. I beseech you to move the King's grace to give me licence to go to church and say Mass here within the Tower, and to lie in some house upon the Green. I have now been in close prison three years and a quarter come Easter, and your Lordship knows that never man in this realm was so unjustly condemned as I am, for I was never, since I came hither, asked or examined of any offence that should be laid to my charge; also Master Barker, my fellow, was commanded hither with me, and both of us for one thing and deed, and he was examined and delivered and I was never spoken to, and yet condemned and lie here still in close prison. What was put in my condemnation is untrue, as I have written to your Lordship largely once before this. I judge and suppose, in your Lordship, such pity and compassion that you would of your own accord have besought the King to give me the liberty I desire, even had I been guilty, after so long imprisonment. I doubt not but that you will do so now, knowing, as you do, that I am innocent and have so great wrong. Therefore I do not rehearse the diseases I have, nor my increasing misery, need, and poverty. I commit to you this little petition of going to church and lying out of close prison.

There is no record of 'this little petition' having received any answer. Three years later, in the aftermath of Cromwell's downfall, and still with no real explanation being offered to the victims,

Abel, Fetherston and Powell were condemned for treason, without trial, by Parliament.

To underline the King's even-handedness in dealing with his rebellious subjects, whether heretics or traitors, the three Protestants to be burnt – Barnes, Jerome and Garrett – were dragged to Smithfield each tied to a hurdle (or 'sledge') shared with one of the Catholics to be hanged, drawn and quartered. Barnes was tied to Powell, one result of which was an anonymous satirical pamphlet, published a few years after their deaths and entitled *The Metynge of Doctor Barons and Doctor Powell at Paradise Gate*. Ambassador Marillac wrote of this whole sorry episode to the French king, Francis I, on 6 July:

> It was wonderful to see adherents to the two opposing parties dying at the same time, and it gave offence to both. And it was no less strange to hear than horrible to see, for the obstinacy and constancy respectively of both parties, and the perversion of justice of which both parties complained, in that they had never been called to judgment, nor knew why they were condemned.

The day after this bloodletting in Smithfield, the heresy quest in the wake of the Act of Six Articles, which had led to so many arrests and given Londoners a chance to settle scores by denouncing one another, was called off, by royal command. The King had realized that such strong-arm tactics to enforce orthodoxy were resulting in considerable social unrest – and he had, in any event, made his point.

Chapter Five

DISSOLUTION AND DISCIPLINE

✠

From all sedition and privy conspiracy, from the tyranny of the Bishop of Rome and all his detestable enormities, from all false doctrine and heresy, from hardness of heart, and contempt of thy word and commandment: Good Lord, deliver us.

From Archbishop Cranmer's *Exhortation and Litany* of 1544,
the first officially sanctioned liturgy in English, and the
only one to be published during the reign of Henry VIII

DURING THE SHORT PERIOD between the burning of Lambert in November 1538 and the six executions in July 1540, much had changed in Smithfield.

To all the faithful in Christ to whom this present charter shall come, Robert by divine permission abbot of the monastery of Waltham in the county of Essex, and prior in commendam of the monastery or priory of St Bartholomew in Smithfield and the convent of the same place, sends greeting. Know ye that we the aforesaid abbot and convent for sure reasons and considerations at present particularly moving us, by our unanimous agreement and consent, and of our spontaneous will, have given granted and by this our present charter confirmed to our most excellent prince and lord, Lord Henry VIII, by God's grace King of England and France, Defender of the Faith, Lord of Ireland, and supreme head on earth of the English Church, all our aforesaid monastery and priory of St Bartholomew and the whole site of our late priory and all our demesnes, manors, churches, chapels, rectories, and vicarages and chantries . . . as well spiritual as temporal, as well in the counties of Middlesex, Hertford, Essex and in the City of London as anywhere else in the kingdom which belong to the monastery . . . and also all and every kind of our church ornaments, jewels and goods which we have in right of the said monastery; to have hold and enjoy all the aforesaid demesnes and manors to our lord the King, his heirs and successors for ever. And we the said abbot and convent and our successors will warrant against all peoples for the lord the King and his successors all the monastery and the demesnes and manors (etc.) with their appurtenances. In testimony of which we have set our common seal to this our present charter.

Dated at our chapter-house the 25th day of October in the 31st year of the reign of our said lord the present king Henry the Eighth.

By the sealing of this charter the last prior of St Bartholomew's, Abbot Robert Fuller, surrendered the great priory, with its extensive lands and all its possessions, to the King, on 25 October 1539, St Bartholomew's being one of the last monastic houses to be dissolved. The very last to go, in the following year, would be Abbot Fuller's own abbey of Waltham.

Over his seven years at the helm of St Bartholomew's, Prior Fuller seems to have worked to prepare the priory, its inhabitants and dependants, for an eventual dissolution. He maintained close connections with Parliament, as an abbot who was also a lord and a bishop (this is what is meant by a 'mitred abbot'), and with the King. He was present, for instance, at the baptism of Prince Edward, the future Edward VI (the son of King Henry and his third wife, Jane Seymour), at Hampton Court on 15 October 1537. And he had long been an acquaintance of Thomas Cromwell, so knew about the likelihood of dissolution – though in the last months before it actually took place, he may have imagined that his own two monasteries would be spared, as the process seemed to have slowed down and almost to have ended. But ever the pragmatic administrator, Fuller had got on with the preparations for change. There are several instances of his making appointments, or formalizing existing informal appointments – such as that of Stephen Fyndley as 'clerk of the church of the monastery' and 'parish clerk of the chapel of All Saints within the church' in 1536 – in order to ensure that the individuals concerned would be eligible to receive a pension after the priory was suppressed. Only eight months before the surrender, he appointed yeoman John Chesewyk and his wife Alyce to the office of launder or washer of all the linen clothes belonging to the church and monastery. Again, the deed of Chesewyk's appointment assured him of a yearly payment when he presented it to the Court of Augmentations after the dissolution.

From the evidence of wills which have survived, the identities of a number of people living in the close (the area immediately surrounding the priory) shortly before its dissolution can be established. One of these was Richard Bellamy, 'gentleman' and friend of John Deane. Bellamy's will, both dated and proved in January 1539 (and witnessed by Deane, then the priest of the parish chapel, as well as by Dr Richard Bartlett and John Burgoyne, fellow dwellers in the close), gives an indication of the kind of ceremonial expected by a parishioner when he died and of the esteem in which the monastery and its canons were held (notwithstanding all the negative propaganda accompanying the dissolution of the monasteries):

I, Richard Bellamy within the precinct of the Close of the monastery of Saint Bartholomew in West Smithfield of London, gentleman, being sick in body and whole in mind . . . to be buried in the body of the church of the said monastery of Saint Bartholomew's between the font set there and the holy image of our Lord Jesus Christ, second person of the Trinity, near unto the place where my children do lie . . . I will that the said canons do bring my body from the house where I shall die if it be within the precinct of the said Close unto the church of the said monastery and there to sing placebo and dirige and mass of Requiem on the morrow after . . . I will my body honestly to be buried without pomp or pride.

Richard Bartlett, one of the witnesses to Bellamy's will, was a physician of considerable eminence, whose services were highly valued by Henry VIII, for when, in the year 1531, the Princess Mary was parted from her devoted mother and her health gave way in consequence, Dr Bartlett was paid the handsome fee of £20 by the King for attending on her. John Burgoyne, another witness to the will, had been appointed by Abbot Fuller in 1533, along with his eldest son Thomas, to be auditor of accounts of rents of the monastery collected in London. Thomas Burgoyne subsequently became auditor to the Court of Augmentations.

As for Prior Fuller, he appeared to have done very well out of the suppression, being amply rewarded for his cooperation by a grant for life of practically all the land and property of the monastery beyond Smithfield itself, comprising holdings in Middlesex (including Little and Great Stanmore), Hertfordshire and Buckinghamshire as well as in other parts of London. On 6 May 1540, the day on which he was granted the possessions of St Bartholomew's, he was also granted a large pension and much of the property of the former Waltham Abbey, which he had surrendered to the King on 23 March. E. A. Webb comments: 'Thus with the surrender of his monasteries did the prior and abbot also surrender his vows of poverty!' But he was to enjoy the fruits of his labours for only a few months, for by October of that year he too was dead (having had the good fortune to die of natural causes).

One of those affected by the dissolution of Waltham Abbey was the composer Thomas Tallis, who had been a very senior member of the extensive musical foundation there since the latter part of 1538. It is likely that he had come to the attention of Abbot Fuller when he was employed as either a singer or the organist at the church of St Mary-at-Hill in the City of London, as the London residence of the abbots of Waltham stood on the south side of that church. At the time of the dissolution of the abbey, Tallis had not been there long enough to be eligible to receive a pension and instead was paid off with 20 shillings in outstanding wages and a further 20 shillings as a 'reward'.

For those, like John Deane and John Burgoyne, still living in the monastic close at St Bartholomew's, the physical impact of the dissolution must have been enormous. They would have seen the church furniture being removed and sold, while six of the priory's bells were taken down and transported along the street to the neighbouring church of St Sepulchre-without-Newgate. The monastic plate and jewels were handed over to the Master of the King's Jewel House and – most overwhelming of all to those for whom it had been the dominant feature of the neighbourhood – the imposing nave of the Priory Church was demolished. By 1544 nothing of it remained (apart from one arched portal at the south-west corner, which is still there and known as the Smithfield Gate, the lone indication of the original size of the great church), all the lead, stone and timber having been carted away and sold for the Crown's profit.

Many of the officials of the Court of Augmentations moved into buildings formerly belonging to the priory, so that Bartholomew Close became a veritable enclave of state officials. And the most obvious beneficiary of the dissolution of St Bartholomew's Priory was the Chancellor of the Augmentations himself, Sir Richard Rich, who, as early as February 1540, converted what had been the prior's house into the town residence of himself and his family. He also benefited financially from his former patron Cromwell's fall, being made chief steward (with fees amounting to £20 a year) of various manors which had previously belonged to Cromwell. Sir Richard ended the year 1540 as a man of substantial means and a considerable landowner; in addition to the property he had acquired at St Bartholomew's, he and his wife Elizabeth had been granted in January, for a fee of £484 6s 10d, the rectory and church of Felsted in Essex, formerly belonging to Syon Monastery in Middlesex, as well as all the land in Fyfield, Essex, and neighbouring villages formerly belonging to Clerkenwell Monastery. His position as Chancellor of Augmentations had meant that there was no one better placed to know what property had become available and to make a bid to purchase it, at favourable terms, before anyone else.

The year 1540 saw a new figure at the helm of the diocese of London, Edmund Bonner being consecrated bishop, in succession to John Stokesley, on 4 April. His episcopacy did not get off to an easy start. It cannot have helped that Bonner seems to have had the kind of facial appearance that easily lent itself to caricature. Clean-shaven, plump and slightly baby-faced with full sensual lips, in the only images that have come down to us, which depict him with either a cartoonish hat or a roll of hair around his tonsured head, he looks somewhat ridiculous, a figure of fun rather than the redoubtable character he certainly was. Like Gardiner, he had been a youthful admirer of Erasmus and had previously – at a time when the King had seemed to favour reform in practice as well as in ecclesiastical structures – been seen by the reformers as friendly to their cause, but changed times called for a different response. And quite apart from the need to follow official policy, he had his own doubts about the results of reform – particularly concerning the liberty of lay people to read the Bible for themselves, since the King had been persuaded by Cromwell in 1538 to take what could be considered the dangerous step of allowing a copy of the so-called Great Bible (a translation prepared by Miles Coverdale and based on the work of John Wycliffe, and produced in a large size for ease of reading) to be placed in every church in the land. At one time Bonner had himself been a proponent of providing English translations of the Bible, but he had become disenchanted when he saw how access to the scriptures was leading to an under-mining of authority, and to arguments among people with no theological training. A month after his enthronement at St Paul's on 16 April 1541, he issued a warning to those who wished to take advantage of the opportunity to read the Great Bible for them-selves, instructing them to read it 'with humility and reverence and not to congregate in multitudes or disturb services or sermons'.

It was during the reign of Mary Tudor that this bishop acquired the sobriquet of 'bloody Bonner' but the seeds of his reputation as a merciless persecutor of heretics were planted in these early years of his episcopacy, as he set out to fulfil the dictates of the Act of Six Articles with a zeal that startled even the King. His handling of the case of Richard Mekins, one of the youngest – and most terri-fied – victims of the Smithfield fires, would always be remembered as particularly brutal. Mekins, while still only a teenager (he was described in Hall's *Chronicle* as a 'child' of no more than fifteen) and without father or mother, was accused of being a 'sacramentary' and a follower of Robert Barnes – even though Barnes himself had never been a sacramentarian. The jury was reluctant to convict, knowing that the only possible outcome of a guilty verdict was death by burning. Quite apart from wanting to spare young Mekins from this fate, there was some uncertainty over whether the boy had called the sacrament a 'ceremony' or a 'signification'; the witnesses were inconsistent in their evidence while Mekins himself was incapable of knowing the difference, having only been repeating what he had heard others talking about. But Bonner, who was himself responding to perceived pressure and experiencing the need to demonstrate both his orthodoxy and his authority – and indeed the authority of the Church as a whole – was determined. Furious, he demanded the jury do as they were told; when they still hesitated, more compliant jurors were drafted in and poor Mekins – who was so frightened by now that he would have confessed to whatever he was asked and, from Hall's account, was desperately trying to think of anything to say that would appease Bonner – went to the stake on 30 July 1541, exactly a year after the deaths of Barnes and his companions. Even the 'anonymous Tractarian' (that is, a supporter of the catholicizing tendency in Anglicanism in the nineteenth century) who wrote a eulogistic account of Bonner's life in 1842 found it hard to justify his hero's behaviour over this episode, particularly as it is recorded of Bonner that he 'cursed and swore at' the jury which, in the words of his anonymous hagiographer, was 'very wrong, even though Bonner was a bishop'. The writer further comments that 'Bonner did not, I can only say, act like any modern Bishop'.

The King and his court had other concerns than those of a young boy being burnt to death for alleged heresy in the summer of 1541, for it was on the last day of June that the King set off on his Great Progress to York, accompanied by his fifth wife Katherine Howard, with the aim both of meeting his nephew James V of Scotland and of demonstrating his power and authority in the north of England, in the wake of the failed popular rising known as the Pilgrimage of Grace, which was partly a protest at the break with Rome and the dissolution of the monasteries. On 15 July when the court was at Grafton, Richard Rich was summoned by other members of the Privy Council (on behalf of the King) to join the Progress at Pipewell or Collyweston. All along the route of the Progress there was much evidence of the destruction of the monasteries; at Pipewell, for instance, the Cistercian abbey had been dissolved in 1538, despite representations against the closure having been made by members of the local nobility, including Sir William Parr, the brother of the woman who would become Henry's sixth and final wife.

The Progress was memorable not only on account of all the places through which it passed and the changes it witnessed in the English landscape, nor for the fact that the Scottish king declined to show up in York, thereby slighting his uncle, but also because it was during this journey that Queen Katherine Howard's alleged pre- and extramarital liaisons came to light. Business transacted by the Privy Council at its meeting back in London on 14 November included the sending of letters to the Deputy of Calais and the ambassadors in Flanders, France and the Holy Roman Empire, declaring 'the story of the Queen's misdemeanour'. On 1 December Rich was appointed as one of the three privy councillors to examine Francis Dereham, William Damport and Joan Bulmer in the case against the Queen, and he was also a member of the special commission appointed to try Thomas Culpeper and Dereham at Guildhall the same day. The indictment against Katherine contained the accusation that she:

> queen of England, formerly called Kath. Howard, late of Lambeth, Surrey, one of the daughters of Lord Edmund Howard, before the marriage between the King and her, led an abominable, base, carnal, voluptuous and vicious life, like a common harlot, with divers persons, as with Francis Dereham . . . maintaining however the outward appearance of chastity and honesty. That she led the King by word and gesture to love

> her and (he believing her to be pure and chaste and free from
> other matrimonial yoke) arrogantly coupled herself with him
> in marriage . . .

Katherine (who had been stripped of her title of Queen on 23
November) was accused of having continued her relations with
Dereham, and of having seduced Culpeper, during the Progress at
Pontefract, among other places. On 6 December Rich was involved,
with other members of the Council, in examining the Dowager
Duchess of Norfolk, suspected of complicity with the accused.
While Rich and other councillors remained in London to deal
with the Howard affair (Culpeper and Dereham were executed
at Tyburn on 10 December, Katherine herself being beheaded on
13 February 1542), the King went away to try to recover his spirits
after this latest marital disaster.

In April 1542 Bishop Bonner, determined to instil discipline
among his clergy in order that they in turn might enforce it on the
laity, issued some 'injunctions' which included the directive that
priests should not:

> rehearse sermons made by other men within these 200 or 300
> years, but shall take the Gospel or Epistle of the day, recite it
> all, desire the people to pray with them for grace after the
> usage of the Church of England, and then declare the same
> Gospel or Epistle according to the mind of some Catholic
> doctor; not affirming anything which cannot be shown in
> some ancient writer, and in no wise rehearsing any opinion
> not allowed, with a view to refute it, but leave that to preach-
> ers admitted by the King or bishop.

So, according to Bonner, it was dangerous for most priests even to
discuss heretical views, let alone to espouse them. He had a point
– more perhaps than he thought – given that an 'opinion not
allowed' today might become accepted doctrine tomorrow, and
vice versa. Happy the man – or woman – who could avoid getting
drawn into controversy in those dangerous days.

One such appeared to be that unassuming priest, Sir John

Deane. In 1544 Richard Rich was granted the right to purchase (at a very low price) the remaining monastic buildings of the former St Bartholomew's Priory, in addition to the prior's house which he already had, this being a right he had anticipated receiving all along. He wished to ensure the provision of a suitable parish church for what was now 'his' domain, and he was instrumental in securing the retention of the monastic quire (the east end of the great church of the priory, beyond the pulpitum or screen) for this purpose, rather than allowing it to be stripped of its valuable lead and fall into ruin. The site of the demolished nave would make an admirable churchyard for his parishioners, and that is what it became. Not only did Sir Richard own the physical property, he was also now patron of the living. He clearly saw no reason why the former parish priest of the monastic close, Sir John Deane, should not continue his ministry at St Bartholomew's under the new dispensation, and so, on 18 June 1544, the twenty-fifth anniversary of his ordination to the priesthood, Deane was duly created first rector of the Priory Church, by order of Sir Richard and in the presence of Alderman and wool merchant Sir Roland Hill, the auditor Thomas Burgoyne and a number of other inhabitants of the close.

Chapter Six

'LO, FAITHLESS MEN AGAINST ME RISE'

✠

> Lo, faithless men against me rise,
> And for thy sake, my death practise.
> My life they seek, with main and might
> Which have not thee, before their sight
> Yet helpest thou me, in this distress,
> Saving my soul, from cruelness.
> I wot thou wilt revenge my wrong,
> And visit them, ere it be long.
>
> Part of a paraphrase of Psalm 54,
> believed to have been
> composed by Anne Askew

SOMETIME IN THE autumn of 1544 Anne Askew arrived in London from Lincolnshire, leaving behind an unhappy marriage and two children. She had been born in about 1521 (so was around twenty-three years old when she came to London), the second daughter of Sir William Askew or Ayscough (who had died in 1540) and his first wife, Elizabeth Wrottesley. The family home was in Stallingborough, near Grimsby in Lincolnshire. She had two brothers, Francis and Edward, and two sisters, Martha and Jane. Her father, an owner of land in Lincolnshire and Nottinghamshire, had participated in the wars against the French and been knighted by Henry VIII in 1513 at Tournai, attended the King at the Field of the Cloth of Gold in 1520 (the occasion of the fortnight-long meeting between Henry and Francis I of France) and been appointed High Sheriff of Lincolnshire in 1521. He had also spent some time as the Member of Parliament for Grimsby. After the death of his first wife he married twice more and had two more sons, Christopher and Thomas. After Sir William's marriage to his second wife, the widow of Sir William Hansard, the family moved to South Kelsey, closer to the county town of Lincoln.

Anne's eldest brother, Francis, followed in his father's footsteps in fighting against the French and was knighted at the siege of Boulogne in 1544. Her other brother, Edward, became a member of Archbishop Cranmer's household and, by the time Anne set off for London, he was a Gentleman Pensioner and Cup-Bearer to the King, while her half-brother Christopher had been appointed a Gentleman of the King's Privy Chamber (though he died a year before Anne arrived in the capital). Her sister Jane was married to George St Paul, steward of the Lincolnshire estates of the Duke and Duchess of Suffolk.

Anne is thought to have received a good education – for a woman of her time – possibly from tutors at home. Her difficulties seem to have begun with the death of her sister Martha, for whom a marriage had been arranged with one Thomas Kyme, the son and heir of a neighbouring farmer. Rather than abandon the match (with all the financial settlements that had been promised) when the original fiancée died, Sir William offered Thomas his second daughter, Anne, as a replacement. The marriage duly went ahead, the couple had two children and, to begin with, Anne behaved as was expected. The change in her came about through personal reading of the Bible, an experience which encouraged her to challenge the authority of both the Church and her husband.

Rather than confine herself to personal Bible study or to meeting with groups of like-minded people, Anne seems to have been quite willing, even determined, to court controversy in a public arena. Having been warned by her friends that, if she travelled to Lincoln, the clergy there – who had clearly heard about her, for she had not been keeping her reformist opinions to herself – would challenge her, she purposely set off for the town, and for the cathedral, in what sounds like an act of deliberate provocation. She related this decision herself, during one of her subsequent interrogations: 'For my friends told me, if I did come to Lincoln, the priests would assault me and put me to great trouble, as thereof they had made their boast. And when I heard it, I went thither indeed, not being afraid, because I knew my matter to be good.' She stayed in Lincoln for about a week, and her whole attitude seems to have been one of scorn for the men who tried to oppose her. As she stood reading the Bible in the cathedral, she was approached by small groups of clerics, who appeared to be about to speak to her but mainly just stared and went away again. Only one priest actually confronted her, and she asserted later that his words were 'of so small effect' that she could not remember what they were. (Throughout her encounters with authority – an authority which is inevitably male – Anne exudes contempt.) What was principally at issue here was not that Anne was reading the Bible per se – as a gentlewoman there was no prohibition on her doing that, *in private* – but the fact that she approached the Great Bible provided, as was now the requirement, in the cathedral, and began to read it out loud. This was expressly forbidden for a woman to do, according to the newly passed Act for the Advancement of True Religion.

The editor and disseminator of Anne's recollections, John Bale, claims that Anne's act of defiance in going to Lincoln and reading the Bible there in public so infuriated her religiously orthodox husband that he drove her out of the house, using violence, and that after this she determined she was quite within her rights to seek a divorce. Having first come to self-awareness through her Bible reading, she turned again to the Bible to justify what was at this period a very unusual, countercultural way for a woman – particularly a woman with two young children – to respond to an unhappy marriage. And her interpretation of the Bible was highly individual – of just the sort to worry the authorities, fearing the anarchy that might be unleashed upon society if every unhappily married woman, reading the scriptures for herself, took it into her head that St Paul was encouraging her to leave her husband. The passage in the New Testament she was relying upon was from chapter 7 of St Paul's first letter to the Corinthians, and specifically verses 13 to 15: 'And the woman, which hath to her husband an infidel, if he consent to dwell with her, let her not put him away. For the unbelieving husband, is sanctified by the wife: and the unbelieving wife, is sanctified by the husband . . . But and if the unbelieving depart, let him depart. A brother or sister is not in subjection to such.' The inference Anne was drawing from these verses, after her husband had allegedly thrown her out, was that he was not 'consenting to dwell' with her; therefore she was free to 'put him away' as she was 'not in subjection' to him. She was further defining him as an 'infidel' and 'unbelieving' because he did not share her new-found evangelical beliefs; according to Bale, she 'could not think him worthy of her marriage which so spitefully hated God the chief author of marriage'. Ultimately, the only true believers in Anne's interpretation of St Paul are those who thought as she did. Such a hard-line attitude on Anne's part inevitably gave rise to opinions of equal vehemence on the part of (male) trad-itionalists, such as the Jesuit Robert Parsons who, writing some fifty years later, characterized Anne's decision to leave her husband as being in order 'to gad up and down the country a-gospelling and gossiping where she might and ought not'.

And so, either having been thrown out or having decided to leave, or maybe both, Anne Askew set off for London. (She had first attempted, unsuccessfully, to obtain a divorce from the ecclesiastical court in Lincoln; the conservative Bishop John Longland, whom we have already encountered as one of the interrogators of Thomas Garrett, would hardly have been sympathetic to an evangelical runaway wife.) Given that she had relatives and contacts already in the capital, and that London was known to be home to a significant number of evangelical believers, there was a certain logic in her decision to go there (though for any young gentlewoman, and a mother, to run away from her husband was in itself a daring and highly unusual act). In London Anne continued to petition for a divorce, this time in the Court of Chancery. Though there is no record of her ever having been successful in this endeavour, she consistently presented herself as either divorced or unmarried. She never, for instance, refers to herself in her writings, including on the statements she signed, as 'Anne Kyme'; she always retains her own identity as 'Anne Askew'.

In addition to her brother Edward who was serving at court, Anne's London contacts included her cousin, Christopher Brittayn, a lawyer of the Middle Temple, and an old friend and neighbour John Lascelles, another lawyer (he had studied at Furnival's Inn – an Inn of Chancery attached to Lincoln's Inn) and also a reformer. Dismissed from service in Sir Francis Bryan's household because of his support for evangelical religion (Bryan was reported to have 'put that man Lascelles from him for that he was so in the new learning, saying that he would have none in his house'), Lascelles had subsequently worked for Thomas Cromwell, acting as a messenger for him in 1538 and 1539, before being given the post of Sewer in the King's Privy Chamber.

Lascelles had been instrumental in the downfall of Katherine Howard, as he had passed on to Cranmer information gleaned from his sister, a lady in the Duchess of Norfolk's household, about Katherine's reputation – that she was known to be 'light both in living and in conditions' and that she had had a series of affairs before her marriage to the King. Other leading figures in the circle of reformers in which Anne moved included Edward Crome, Rector of St Mary Aldermary (referred to with approval by James Bainham at his trial in 1531), Nicholas Shaxton, former Bishop of Salisbury, and Hugh Latimer, former Bishop of Worcester. She did not confine herself to her own level of society, however, but included artisans and apprentices among her evangelical acquaintances. And, at a time when Bishop Bonner was known to be cracking down on dissent in the Church, it appears Anne did little, if anything, to hide her divergence from official doctrine and practice. At the same time, there is no indication that she wanted anything more than to be able to live her own life, and express her own opinions, in peace and without interference. But that was not possible for a lone woman, of outspoken character, in 1540s London.

Anne was arrested on suspicion of heresy on 10 March 1545, being detained by order of the Aldermen of London 'for certain matters concerning the vi Articles'. On the testimony of an unnamed woman, she was brought before a quest (an official commission appointed to hold a hearing into heresy) at Saddlers' Hall in the City. The questioning was led by an official called Christopher Dare, who first asked Anne whether she believed that the sacrament hanging over the altar – that is, the 'reserved' sacrament hanging in a pyx, according to Catholic practice – was 'the very body of Christ really'. Anne addressed the question by asking another: 'why was St Stephen stoned to death?' Dare replied, according to Anne's account, that he did not know (or, at least, that he 'could not tell'). 'No more will I try answering your stupid question,' countered Anne.

It is clear from her answers, or her attempts to evade answering, that Anne had no wish to become a martyr, and intended to get herself out of trouble if she could, while also desiring to remain true to her beliefs: a tricky situation for anyone, particularly for a young woman already under suspicion for having left hearth and home, showing the temerity to claim independence for herself in a world where women were nothing if not dependent.

But Anne was not simply trying to avoid answering Dare's question. Her choice of the martyrdom of St Stephen – the first martyr of the early Church – was deliberate. For one thing, Stephen's martyrdom (as related in the Acts of the Apostles) came about after certain Jews entered into debate with him and, finding they couldn't get the better of him in argument, procured some men to lay false allegations against him. So by introducing Stephen into the discussion, Anne is implicitly accusing her interrogators of acting unfairly towards her. Stephen had also warned his persecutors against idolatry and told them that God does not live in a house made by human hands (referring to Solomon's great temple), and he had accused the Jews, who had benefited by being given the law, of also being the very ones who had not kept it. Again, Anne is implicitly levelling these accusations at her own accusers, as well as actually giving her answer to the question, if only by allusion – for if God does not live in a temple, she is suggesting, he certainly does not live in a box. Nevertheless, technically speaking, she avoided answering the question. The story of Stephen had also arisen as the unnamed woman who had testified against her had accused her of reading aloud that God was not in temples made with hands; Anne's defence was that that was indeed what it said in the Acts of the Apostles, and she showed Dare the relevant passages. In addition to the story of the martyrdom of Stephen, she pointed to the words of St Paul to the Athenians, also from Acts: 'God that made the world, and all that are in it, seeing that he is Lord of heaven and earth, he dwelleth not in temples made with hands . . .'

When she is requested to answer explicitly, rather than in what amount to riddles, she refuses, but again by reference to the scriptures (with which she shows herself to be very familiar). This time she quotes words attributed to Jesus, from Matthew's Gospel, contained in the so-called Sermon on the Mount: 'Give not that which is holy to dogs, neither cast ye your pearls before swine, lest they tread them under their feet, and the other turn again and all to rent you.' Her choice of verse implies both an insult to her questioners, who appear to be equated by her with dogs and swine, and an awareness of the danger she is facing – that her interrogators may use whatever she says to 'rend' her.

Dare also asked her whether it was true that she had said she would rather read five lines in the Bible than hear Mass said five times in church. She admitted that she had indeed said that, for the reason that 'the one did greatly edify me, and the other nothing at all'. He then asked what she thought about 'the King's Book' (the latest formulation of authorized doctrine, which had appeared, with Henry's approval and a preface by him, in 1543; its full title was *A Necessary Doctrine and erudition for any Christian man*). She replied that she could say nothing about it, as she had never seen it. Dare called upon a priest to ask the central question: 'what I said to the Sacrament of the altar?' Though Anne did not know the identity of this priest, she 'perceived him [to be] a papist', and refused to answer.

Anne was then taken to be interrogated by the Lord Mayor, William Laxton, a wealthy merchant and Past Master of the Worshipful Company of Grocers but far from being a sophisticated theologian. He asked similar questions to those already put to her, and she gave him similar replies, but then he asked her something which she claims had never occurred to her to ask herself. 'If a mouse were to eat the host [that is, the consecrated bread],' asked the Lord Mayor, 'would it be receiving God, or not?' Anne said nothing, merely smiling at this strange question. One wonders what the Lord Mayor himself considered to be the correct answer. (Someone who was prepared to address this question, doing so in a sermon delivered around this time, possibly in Lent 1546, was the Dominican Father William Peryn, who would later become head of the small community of Black Friars based for a time at St Bartholomew's in Smithfield. In his defence of transubstantiation, Father Peryn declared that if a mouse should eat the Blessed Sacrament, it would gnaw only on the outward appearance, while the body of Our Lord would remain inviolate.)

When Anne was brought before the bishop's chancellor, he berated her for having the temerity to read out and talk about the scriptures. For St Paul himself, he expostulated, had forbidden women to speak or talk about the word of God. Anne parried his rebuke, telling him she knew what St Paul had said at least as well as he did, and contending that what Paul had actually forbidden women to do was to teach. And this she certainly had not done; neither, she pointed out, had any other woman: 'And then I asked him, how many women he had seen, go into the pulpit and preach. He said, he never saw none.' In which case, declared Anne, he should stop criticizing women who had not broken the law.

After being cross-examined, Anne was imprisoned in one of the two Counters (or 'compters', prisons under the City's jurisdiction and managed by the sheriffs, in some ways not unlike a modern police station) for twelve days. She had asked the Lord Mayor whether she might not be bailed instead, but he had refused. And during those twelve days no friends were allowed to visit her. The bishop did arrange for a priest to be sent to her, but she was clearly not impressed. He had been sent, she said, 'to give me good counsel, which he did not'. The priest also asked her why she had been put in the Counter – 'And I told him I could not tell. Then he said, it was great pity that I should be there without cause, and concluded that he was very sorry for me.' He, like the priest she had dismissed as a 'papist', wanted to ask her about the sacrament of the altar, and the answer she records herself as having given him makes deliberate allusion to the Passion narrative and to the words attributed to Pontius Pilate when he had the inscription 'The King of the Jews' affixed to the cross on which Jesus was crucified. 'What I have written, I have written,' declared Pilate. 'What I have said, I have said,' declared Anne. And about this subject she had so far actually said nothing. Next, the priest asked her whether she had been to confession and received absolution. She said 'no', and he offered to send her another priest for this purpose. But Anne was choosy, and told him she would be pleased to see one of the clergymen she knew and approved of – such as her acquaintance Dr Crome, or one or two others she mentioned – but she would have to reserve judgement about any other priest, as she did not know them. The priest she was talking to seemed rather taken aback at this, and asked why she should think that he, or any other priest sent to her, might not be as good as the ones she had named. 'For if we were not, you may be sure,' he protested, 'the King would not suffer us to preach.' Anne again answered with a biblical text, this time actually a paraphrase of a verse from Proverbs: 'By communing with the wise, I may learn wisdom, but by talking with a fool, I shall take scathe [harm].' All the time she is pushing the boundaries, barely concealing her contempt, while he, one senses, is bewildered at a young woman expressing such independence of thought and setting herself up as an authority. He also tried the Lord Mayor's question on her – 'if the host should fall, and a beast did eat it', did the 'beast' receive God or not? Anne suggested this was some kind of trick question, and requested he answer it himself. He told her that the rules of scholastic debate did not allow for the person who asked a question to answer it, and here she cleverly gave him a reply he could not argue with: 'I told him, I was but a woman, and knew not the course of schools.' Finally the priest asked her whether she intended to take communion at

Easter. 'Of course,' she replied, 'else I were no Christian woman.' And then he left, 'with many fair words'; he seems to have been endeavouring to be friendly, though Anne was unimpressed.

On 23 March Anne's cousin Christopher Brittayn arrived at the Counter, with the intention of getting Anne out on bail. Achieving this took a certain amount of toing and froing. He first set off to see the Lord Mayor (as it was the Lord Mayor who had sent her to prison), who said he would be happy to oblige but could not authorize bail in a heresy case without the consent of the church authorities. So he sent Brittayn off to the bishop's chancellor. The chancellor too declined to make the decision on his own authority, as 'the matter was so heinous', and said he would have to ask the bishop. The latter not being available until the next day, Brittayn was told to come back then. He duly did so, when he met with both the chancellor and the bishop. The decision had been taken that Anne was to appear before the bishop himself on the following day, at three o'clock in the afternoon, and allowed to be accompanied by any 'learned men' she liked, so that they might see she was not being treated badly. Bishop Bonner asked Brittayn to persuade Anne to speak frankly at this hearing – from 'the very bottom of [her] heart' – and he promised that her words would not be used to her own disadvantage. What Bonner hoped to do was convince this misguided young woman, from a well-regarded family and highly respectable background, that she was mistaken in her views, and to guide her gently but firmly back onto the right path. Success for him would be to send Anne back to her husband and children and to a quiet, obedient life in Lincolnshire. He was yet to meet her in person.

The interview on the following day got off to a bad start, as far as Anne was concerned, through the bishop's poor timekeeping. 'On the morrow after,' she noted in her recollections, 'my lord of London sent for me, at one of the clock, his hour being appointed at three.' The friends whom Anne had requested should be present, including Dr Crome, would not be arriving for another two hours, and she did not want to be questioned by the bishop until they were present. He agreed to wait, and arranged for Anne to be spoken to by his archdeacon, John Wymmesley, in the meantime. Wymmesley had not been expecting this, and seemed to know little of what was going on. 'Mistress, what are you accused of?' he demanded. 'Ask my accusers,' Anne replied, 'for I know not as yet.' Anne had been reading and was still holding her book. The archdeacon took it from her, glanced at it, saw – or thought he saw – that it was by John Frith and declared that it was books like this that had got her into trouble. 'Beware,' he said, 'for he that made it was burnt in Smithfield.' Anne scornfully berated him for passing judgement on a book without having read it. She made him look at it again, whereupon he could find nothing wrong with it, and left her.

Anne's cousin Christopher and her other friends having now arrived, the bishop was able to proceed, and again he stressed that he wanted her to feel free to tell him everything that was troubling her. He seemed to imagine that she needed doctrinal guidance, and that he was the man to give it to her (a not unreasonable view for a bishop to take). But Anne could not be so easily won over. 'And therefore he bade me, say my mind without fear. I answered him, that I had nought to say. For my conscience (I thanked God) was burdened with nothing.' Bonner's predominantly kindly manner during his interview with Anne was most probably based on a genuine desire to set her back on what he perceived as the right track, rather than to have to condemn her, his questions and the opportunities he gave her to avoid uttering outright heresies corroborating this, but she was nevertheless wise to be cautious. It is a tried and trusted technique of interrogation, from the Inquisition to the Gestapo and beyond,* and recommended by the fourteenth-century Inquisitor General, the Catalan Nicolau Eymerich, to 'suddenly shift gears, approaching the person being interrogated in a seeming spirit of mercy and compassion, speaking "sweetly" and solicitously, perhaps making arrangements to provide something to

---

* The use of this technique can be seen, for instance, in the interactions between Sophie and her apparently kindly interrogator, the father of a son of around her own age, in the film *Sophie Scholl – The Final Days*.

eat and drink'. The person under interrogation can be thrown off balance by such a change of tone, and before they know where they are they have 'confessed'. But not so Anne: 'I answered, that my conscience was clear in all things. And for to lay a plaster unto the whole skin, it might appear much folly.'

Anne's refusal to confess anything of her own accord meant Bonner next resorted to telling her what she was alleged to have said. One such allegation was that she had contradicted the doctrine that the unworthiness of the minister does not affect the validity of the sacrament – that is, she was alleged to have said that if a priest who was a sinner administered the sacrament, he would be administering the devil rather than God. Anne denied having said this, asserting that she had already told the quest and the Lord Mayor that the wickedness of the priest would not affect her – she would still be receiving the body and blood of Christ, 'in spirit and faith'. Bonner seizes upon these words, knowing they could be used to condemn her – 'what a saying is this? In spirit . . .' But then he backs off – 'I will not take you at that advantage.' It is as though they are playing a game of chess; he has seen the move he could make to checkmate her, but has declined to make it. And she fully understands the game they are playing, and answers his move: 'My lord without faith and spirit, I cannot receive him worthily.' He cannot argue with that, and she has not said one way or the other whether she believes the bread and wine become the body and blood 'really' rather than merely 'in spirit'.

In his manual for interrogators, the *Directorium Inquisitorum*, Inquisitor General Eymerich had listed a number of ways in which heretics were known to 'hide their errors'. These techniques included 'equivocation', 'redirecting the question', 'feigned astonishment', 'twisting the meaning of words', 'changing the subject', 'feigning illness' and 'feigning stupidity', and we can see Anne using all of them – except, it would appear, 'feigning illness'; it seems that she did feel genuinely unwell at various points during her interrogations. One can only conclude that, in addition to reading and study, she had been rehearsing and preparing for such an encounter for some time.

Bonner then revisited another question previously asked by the quest:

> Then he laid unto me, that I should say, that the sacrament remaining in the pyx, was but bread. I answered that I never said so: But indeed the quest asked me such a question, where-unto I would not answer (I said) till such time as they had assailed me this question of mine. Wherefore Steven was stoned to death. They said, they knew not. Then said I again, no more would I tell them what it was.

Bonner attempted to press her on this central question, trying everything he could think of to get her to reply with a yes or a no:

> Then asked he me, what my faith and belief was in that matter? I answered him, I believe as the scripture doth teach me. Then enquired he of me, what if the scripture doth say, that it is the body of Christ? I believe (said I) like as the scrip-ture doth teach me. Then asked he again, what if the scripture doth say, that it is not the body of Christ? My answer was still, I believe as the scripture informeth me. And upon this argu-ment he tarried a great while . . .

One can sense Bonner's frustration at what Eymerich would have termed Anne's 'equivocation'. He next repeats another piece of hearsay against her – that she has declared the Mass to be idolatry. No, she hasn't said that, she replies. But she does admit to having used the word, as part of a question, when asked by the quest about the efficacy of private masses (that is, masses said for souls in pur-gatory). She had implied that it would indeed amount to idolatry if people were to place more faith in private masses for the dead than in the life-giving death of Christ. 'What kind of an answer is that?' expostulated the bishop. 'Good enough for the question,' retorted Anne. Something Eymerich does not include in his list of devices used by heretics is that of poking fun at their interrogators – though it is, perhaps, related to 'feigning astonishment' – but this is something Anne does frequently. When Dr Standish, the Rector of St Andrew Undershaft, interrupts to suggest the bishop ask Anne what she thinks about a particular text of St Paul, she is quick with her riposte: 'I answered, that it was against Saint Paul's learning, that I being a woman, should interpret the scriptures, specially where so many wise learned men were.' Here she is playing back to her interrogators what the bishop's chancellor had earlier tried to rebuke her for – that it would have been contrary both to St Paul's teaching and to the 1543 Act for the Advancement of True Religion, if she had acceded to the request of these 'wise learned men' to speak out loud her interpretation of the scriptures – and, she implies, they should have known better than to have asked her to do so.

Despite this unsatisfactory and inconclusive interrogation, Bishop Bonner was still determined to let this young woman go – but he needed something in writing to justify his leniency. If Anne herself would not comply and recant, when he was giving her the opportunity to do so, without the threat of any penalty (a rare enough event in itself), he would just have to write her recantation for her. So he left the room and went off to write what Anne dismissively referred to as 'a great circumstance'. She claims not to have remembered most of what Bonner wrote, because he refused to give her a copy. She is recalling this a year later, and at least part of the reason for the apparent failure of her normally very retentive memory is that this document had recently been paraded as a genuine recantation, with the intention of discrediting her in the eyes of her fellow Protestants. What she can remember is Bonner reading out:

> Be it known (saith he) to all men, that I Anne Askew, do confess this to be my faith and belief, notwithstanding my reports made before to the contrary. I believe that they which are houseled [i.e. have received communion] at the hands of a priest, whether his conversation [i.e. his behaviour] be good or not, do receive the body and blood of Christ in substance really. Also do I believe it after the consecration, whether it be received or reserved, to be no less than the very body and blood of Christ in substance.

So, in short, the bishop had written down what he considered Anne *ought* to have said in reply to the questions posed by the quest and by himself.

Having read out all he had written, Bishop Bonner asked Anne whether she agreed with it. And still she equivocated, and to the bishop it must have felt as though she were trying to throw his gift of mercy back in his face, for he knew – and surely she knew too – how easily he could have done the opposite and declared her a convinced heretic. She believed as much of it, she declared, as was consistent with holy scripture, so would he kindly add that phrase? His patience, unsurprisingly, was now running out – 'Don't tell me what to write!' was the gist of his reply. He then went into his main reception chamber (so some of this conversation must have taken place in private, despite Anne's friends being in the building) and read out the statement to those who were there. And they, with perhaps more sense of the danger she was in than Anne seemed conscious of herself, encouraged her to sign the statement. The bishop now admitted why he had been taking such pains with her; it was not on account of anything she had said or done herself, he said, but because of the pleas of her influential friends and the fact that she came from a good family. (This underlines the great contrast between Anne's case and that of the poor orphan Richard Mekins, who had no one influential, or of the right social class, to intercede for him.) And so Anne was given the statement to sign, and she finally appeared to have been persuaded to be compliant. But even now she was still determined to keep the upper hand. She took the pen offered to her and wrote: 'I Anne Askew do believe all manner things contained in the faith of the Catholic church.' The bishop took one look at what she had written, seized the paper, and stormed out of the room 'in a great fury'. Anne's cousin Christopher hurried after him. 'Please be kind to her,' he pleaded. 'She's a woman, and she doesn't deceive me,' stormed the bishop. 'Yes, she's just a woman,' agreed her cousin, 'but don't let her weak woman's wit influence your Lordship's great wisdom.' So, with flattering and cajoling, Brittayn calmed the angry prelate down.

Why was Bonner so furious at the seemingly innocuous words Anne had added to the statement he had prepared for her? Again, it is as though interrogator and interrogated are playing a game of chess, and the moves they each make are designed to be understood by the other, if not by the wider audience. By her words, Anne had managed simultaneously to assert her own orthodoxy – 'I . . . do believe all manner things contained in the faith of the Catholic church' – while implying that what he had written and she was being asked to put her name to might not actually be so 'contained'. For she had not merely assented to what he had written, as she would have done with a simple signature. There is also the ambiguity surrounding the word 'catholic'. Was she implying that the church to which she herself gave allegiance – a new reformed church, representing the body of true believers – was the real 'catholic' church, rather than the official one represented by the bishop? Another interpretation, as advanced by Megan L. Hickerson, is that she is merely pretending to recant, 'the addition of a few ambiguous words' somehow invalidating the confession of faith that has been written for her. Whatever her precise meaning, and Bonner's interpretation of her words, he recognized that she was still putting up a challenge both to his authority and to his intended leniency. Principally, it was her continued insistence on maintaining her independence of thought, her own agency and ownership of what she wrote, her refusal to submit as a woman should, that infuriated the Bishop of London. He had all the power in this relationship, and yet Anne seemed somehow immune to it. Her friends and family must certainly have brought a lot of influence to bear, for they also managed to get Dr Hugh Weston, the conservative Rector of St Botolph-without-Bishopsgate, to put in a good word for her with the bishop. There was clearly no appetite whatsoever in the spring of 1545 to let a young gentlewoman get anywhere near the stake, no matter how intransigent and provoking she might be. 'So with much ado,' recalled Anne, 'they persuaded my lord to come out again,' and he agreed to her being granted bail, with her cousin Christopher Brittayn and another lawyer, Francis Spilman, standing as sureties for her. She had hoped to be let out immediately, but there was some further delay. The bishop sent her back to the Counter for that night, ordering her to appear at Guildhall on the following day. She did so, but the City officials still seemed hesitant to release her, and it was not until they were quite certain both of the bishop's intention and of the reliability of her two sureties, that they finally let her go.

Anne was briefly back at Guildhall on 13 June that year, accused with two others of speaking against the sacrament of the altar. But no reliable witnesses came forward, and she was once again released. She seems then to have returned to Lincolnshire, at least temporarily, with her friends, perhaps hoping, as no doubt was the Bishop of London, that that was the end of her (mis)adventures.

It was, however, one of Anne's friends, the famous London preacher Dr Edward Crome, who was responsible, at least in part, for a hardening of the line against heresy and heretics in the following year, for in April 1546, on the fifth Sunday in Lent, he preached a provocative sermon in St Thomas Acons, the chapel of the Mercers' Company, denying the sacrificial nature of the Mass, which went too far to be ignored. Following his sermon, Crome was arrested on the orders of Bishop Bonner and brought before Bishop Stephen Gardiner and other Privy Council members and ordered to recant, several times, in public (the first time to be on the second Sunday after Easter, at Paul's Cross). A number of other prominent evangelicals, including Hugh Latimer, Nicholas Shaxton and John Lascelles, found themselves in trouble too, Crome's arrest leading to the uncovering of the secret network of reformers in the City and the Inns of Court to which they – and, by association, Anne Askew – belonged. There was an atmosphere of nervousness among evangelicals in London, and virtually anyone could suddenly find themselves implicated. It could take just one indiscreet word – or someone alleging an indiscreet word – to set the wheels in motion and (much like the process following an allegation of 'historical' sexual abuse in our own time) it could be very difficult to stop those wheels turning.

The Privy Council issued an order for Anne Askew to be re-arrested in May, rumours having reached them that Anne had been continuing to express her unacceptable views. Anne had enemies – including some who considered her 'wanton' for having gone off to London without her husband – and someone betrayed her. The letter containing the order, dated 24 May, was addressed to her husband, Thomas Kyme, and it required him and his wife to appear before the Council within fourteen days.

Between the issuing of this order and its fulfilment, there took place in the City a celebration of the signing of the treaty of Camp which marked the end of the war with France, the ceremonial demonstrating how the established ecclesiastical traditions continued to thrive:

> Item the 13th day of June after was Whit Sunday, and then was a general procession from Paul's unto St Peter's in Cornhill with all the children of Paul's school, and a cross of every parish church, with a banner and one to bear it in a tenache, all the clerks, all the priests, with parsons and vicars of every church in copes, and the choir of Paul's in the same manner, and the Bishop bearing the sacrament under a canopy with the Mayor in a gown of crimson velvet, the Aldermen in scarlet, with all the crafts in their best apparel; and when the Mayor came between the cross and the standard there was made a proclamation with divers heralds of arms and poursuivants in their coat armours, with the trumpets, and there was proclaimed a universal peace for ever between the Emperor, the King of England, the French King, and all Christian kings for ever.

On 19 June Thomas Kyme and Anne Askew duly appeared before the Privy Council. Here Anne, feisty as ever, denied that Thomas was her husband. The Council did not agree, but nevertheless sent him back to Lincolnshire. Anne, on the other hand, 'for that she was very obstinate and heady in reasoning of matters of religion, wherein she showed herself to be of a naughty opinion', they committed to Newgate prison to await questioning.

The political situation in the country was now very tense, not least because Henry VIII was clearly in the last stages of his life, and there was enormous uncertainty about what would happen after his death, particularly in church circles. Traditionalists, especially those currently exercising power, such as Bishop Stephen Gardiner, were desperately seeking ways to ensure that power would not swing on the King's death towards those of an opposite, reformist and evangelical, persuasion. A central figure in the evangelical camp was the Queen, Katherine Parr, Henry's sixth and final wife, and there were those who suspected that her network might include the alleged heretic now under arrest, Anne Askew. Anne's position and fate had ceased to hinge purely on personal religious beliefs and were now mixed up with politics, though she may not herself have realized this.

Anne was subjected to a two-day interrogation by the Privy Council at Greenwich, her questioners including Sir Thomas Wriothesley (the Lord Chancellor), Stephen Gardiner (the Bishop of Winchester), John Dudley (Viscount Lisle), William Parr (the Earl of Essex) and Sir William Paget (the King's Principal Secretary). Bishop Bonner, who had expended so much effort in getting Anne released the previous year, was not involved this time around, and none of the interrogators in 1546 was prepared to give her any leeway. She was not brought before an official quest, a fact which made her condemnation more likely (though also not entirely lawful). It is noticeable from the list of questioners that this was not a unified group in matters of religion, in that, while Wriothesley and Gardiner were unequivocally on the side of tradition and conservatism, Viscount Lisle and William Parr have always been seen as belonging firmly to the other, more 'Protestant' of the two factions then battling for supremacy at court. Paget, one of the King's closest advisers, was a waverer but ultimately settled for the Protestant side. The hostility towards Anne must therefore have been led by Wriothesley and Gardiner, and they maintained the upper hand throughout. It is possible that Dudley, Parr and Paget viewed this young Protestant woman as an expendable casualty in a larger war being waged; appearing to side with the traditionalist faction now may have been a matter of covering their tracks, helping to give a false sense of security to Gardiner and Wriothesley.

Either that, or they were too frightened to admit that they actually shared many of Anne's views.

Where none of the powerful men ranged against her was likely to agree with Anne was in her attitude to her marriage (even Foxe found this hard to accept and evaded the question in his *Acts and Monuments*), and one of the first questions put to her concerned her relationship with her husband – or, as she refers to him, 'master Kyme'. She replied that the Lord Chancellor already knew what she had to say on that matter. They pressed her, telling her it was the King's wish that she should explain the situation to them. She told them she was quite happy to tell the King, but she wasn't going to tell them. They protested that it was not appropriate for the King to be troubled on her account; she pointed out that even Solomon, believed to have been the wisest king that ever lived, had been prepared to listen to, and resolve, the argument between two 'poor common women'. The councillors gave up questioning her further about her marriage, and turned to the matter of the sacrament of the altar. What was her opinion? asked Lord Chancellor Wriothesley. As in the previous year, she gave an equivocal answer, avoiding mentioning the 'real presence' one way or the other. 'The Bishop of Winchester bade me make a direct answer. I said, I would not sing a new song to the lord in a strange land.' Unsurprisingly, this quotation from the Psalms did not satisfy Gardiner: 'Then the Bishop said, I spake in parables. I answered it was best for him. For if I show the open truth (quoth I) ye will not accept it. Then he said I was a parrot.' Gardiner was suggesting that Anne was just 'parrotting' verses of scripture she had learned off by heart, without understanding them; in fact she was deploying them with great pertinence and with the intention both of saving her life, if she could, and of ridiculing her interrogators. By the end of this session she was exhausted, for it went on for more than five hours. She was then returned to 'my lady Garnish', her term for prison, 'garnish' being slang for the money jailers extorted from new prisoners.

Newgate, where Anne was being held between interrogations, was the main prison of the City of London and the county of Middlesex (it was on the site now occupied by the Central

Criminal Court, better known as the Old Bailey), and often used for holding those considered the most dangerous and hardened of criminals, including rebels, traitors and heretics, before their trials. Other inmates were serving sentences or awaiting execution, while still others were incarcerated for debt. The prison had been reconstructed in the early fifteenth century to include a central hall where meals could be served and where there was a drinking fountain, water for which came through pipes connected to the cistern which served St Bartholomew's hospital. To the north and south of the hall there were groups of rooms that boasted chimneys and privies, and there was a chapel built into the gate, with recreation rooms on either side of it. But such rooms and facilities were for those who could afford to pay for them and who were not suspected of heinous crimes; there were other, less salubrious, spaces and, in the south part of the prison, dark, damp and unventilated basement cells. These were where someone accused of heresy (and bereft of important connections, or having exhausted the patience and efficacy of such connections) could expect to be sent. Even such unpleasant accommodation did not come free, however, particularly if the prisoner wanted anything to eat. Food could either be bought from the jailers, or brought in by the prisoner's friends.

When Anne was brought back before the Council on the following day, she was asked yet again about her views on the sacrament and, yet again, she refused to answer. And she would not give an inch when Gardiner tried to change tack and used a more personal tone: 'Then the Bishop said, he would speak with me familiarly. I said, so did Judas when he unfriendly betrayed Christ. Then desired the Bishop to speak with me alone. But that I refused.' She clearly feared being left on her own with Gardiner, and she was probably right to do so. But her refusal did her no good either: 'Then the Bishop said, I should be burnt. I answered, that I had searched all the scriptures yet could I never find there that either Christ or his Apostles put any creature to death.' And so ended Anne's interrogation by Bishop Gardiner.

Next it was the turn of Sir William Paget. He seemed to do rather better at getting Anne to express an opinion about the sacrament. He asked her how she could ignore the words of Christ – had he not actually said 'Take, eat. This is my body, which shall be broken for you'? What more did she need? Was this not sufficient proof that the consecrated bread was indeed the body of Christ? Anne's answer demonstrated that she took these words to be symbolic only – that when Christ said 'this is my body', he was speaking the same kind of language as when he said 'I am the true vine.' 'Ye may not here (said I) take Christ for the material thing that he is signified by. For then ye will make him a very door, a vine, a lamb, and a stone, clean contrary to the holy Ghost's meaning.' Though at first reading, Anne's argument makes perfect sense here – in fact, it seems 'common sense' – it demonstrated, at least to the theologians present, precisely the problem with allowing untrained lay people to determine their own interpretation of the scriptures. The conversations are going past one another, the discourses operating on different levels. Anne shows no understanding or awareness of the Aristotelian concepts of 'substance' and 'accidents' underlying the Catholic interpretation of the consecrated host as 'the body of Christ'; she thinks she is arguing on the same level as her ecclesiastical interlocutors, but she is not.

Perhaps the only way most of us can understand this kind of argument today is to consider the discussion that might be had between a reasonably well-read member of the public and a trained academic in a discipline such as literary theory. We, the untrained, may believe we understand the discussion – after all, it's conducted in the language we speak and read ourselves, it may concern books we've actually read and thought about. We believe we have a valid contribution to make and we certainly think our opinion is worth listening to. But if, say, the academic gives us her latest article to read or tells us what she is currently working on, we may well start to think such things as: 'But all this is obvious – why do people need to spend years studying something that we could have told them in the first place?' or perhaps 'What rubbish! This is a load of verbiage and the usual incomprehensible quotations from Foucault and Derrida; literary theorists should just read the literature in front of them and stop tying themselves in knots about nothing.' This is very much Anne's attitude – 'If only these old priests and bigwigs would actually read what it says in the Bible, they'd stop making such ridiculous assertions and realize I'm right!' The academic knows there is little point in arguing with someone outside her discipline or 'discourse' – someone who, while appearing to be using language in the same way as herself, is actually not doing so – and will confine her discussions to peer-reviewed journals and scholarly seminars. (What, fortunately, she won't do is suggest her interlocutor be arrested or banned from expressing an opinion at all.)

Be that as it may, Anne, perhaps losing patience with what to her seems a dim-witted discussion, now makes quite clear that she does not view what is contained in the pyx above the altar as something to be revered: 'And though he did say there, Take, eat this in remembrance of me, Yet did he not bid them hang up that bread in a box, and make it a God, or bow to it.' Paget, himself not a theologian, clearly felt he was coming off the worse in this argument (and, indeed, given his later support of the Protestant faction at court, he may even have been in agreement with Anne), and he asked her if she would prefer to talk with 'some wiser man'. She, apparently agreeing that he wasn't very wise himself, consented. Two 'wiser men' later (Drs Coxe and Robinson), Anne was still refusing to give an unequivocal answer about her view of the sacrament, or to sign anything. She asked to speak to Dr Latimer (currently out of favour as a reformist), but this was refused. She was returned to Newgate, exhausted and in pain.

On 28 June Anne Askew was arraigned for heresy at Guildhall, along with Nicholas Shaxton (former Bishop of Salisbury), a 'gentleman' of London called Nicholas White and an Essex tailor called John Hadlam. Their judges (there was no jury) comprised an overwhelming array of 'the great and the good': the Lord Mayor (Sir Martin Bowes), the Duke of Norfolk (Thomas Howard), the Master of the King's Household, the Bishop of London (Bonner), the Bishop of Worcester (Nicholas Heath), the two Chief Justices of the King's Bench and Common Pleas, the Chief Baron of the Exchequer (Sir Roger Cholmley), the Master of the Rolls (Sir

Robert Southwell), the Recorder of London (Sir Robert Broke), and three of Bishop Bonner's officers – the archdeacon (John Wymmesley), the chancellor and the commissary. Though some of the old arguments were rehearsed, this was not so much a trial as the handing down of a predetermined verdict; Nicholas Shaxton abjured, but Askew and Hadlam were condemned to burn. Anne seems to have realized before the sentence was read out that there was no hope for her now, and that assurance gave her the freedom to say what she really thought, without ambiguity. So when she was asked if she denied the sacrament to be Christ's body and blood, she spoke up boldly and said yes, she did deny it – for Christ was in heaven, 'And as for that ye call your God, it is but a piece of bread. For a more proof thereof (mark it when ye list) let it lie in the box but 3 months, and it will be mouldy, and so turn to nothing that is good. Whereupon I am persuaded, that it cannot be God.'

On the next day Anne was removed from Newgate to the Tower. Before she was sent there, Bishop Bonner made one final unsuccessful attempt to turn her back to orthodoxy. Nicholas Shaxton was also sent to try to persuade her to recant as he had done, but she gave him short shrift. According to Anne's recollections, Richard Rich had accompanied the bishop and was also the one to send her to the Tower, where he and 'one of the council' questioned her about whether she knew certain ladies at court. Rich and the other councillor wanted to know who had paid for her upkeep while she was confined in the Counter and at Newgate; she replied that her maid had been free to come and go, and that she had managed to get money from various apprentices – 'But who they were, I never knew.' Her interrogators pressed her for more details:

> Then they said, that there were diverse gentlewomen, that gave me money. But I knew not their names. Then they said that there were diverse ladies, which had sent me money. I answered, that there was a man in a blue coat, which delivered me 10 shillings, and said that my lady of Hertford sent it me.

> And another in a violet coat did give me 8 shillings, and said
> that my lady Denny sent it me. Whether it were true or no, I
> cannot tell.

And now there took place the event that shocked even many who
agreed with Anne's death sentence. Having confessed and been
condemned, there should have been nothing left for Anne to do
but await her punishment, but instead she was tortured in the
Tower on the rack, in an attempt to force her to reveal the names
of aristocratic and courtly ladies, especially those associated with
Queen Katherine Parr, as her associates in heresy. Anne herself
described what happened to her: 'Then they did put me on the
rack, because I confessed no ladies nor gentlewomen to be of
my opinion, and thereon they kept me a long time. And because
I lay still and did not cry, my lord Chancellor and master Rich,
took pains to rack me with their own hands, till I was nigh dead.'

It has generally been accepted, and repeated many times, that it
was these two – Thomas Wriothesley and Richard Rich – named
in Anne's own account, who turned the wheels of the rack (the
Lieutenant of the Tower having refused to go on pulling the young
woman's body apart). But there is nevertheless some doubt, particularly about Rich's participation, for the first two editions of
Foxe's *Acts and Monuments* name Sir John Baker, the Chancellor of
the Exchequer, as Wriothesley's accomplice in the torture, Rich
being substituted for Baker only in the edition of 1583. It is possible that Baker's influential family brought pressure to bear on
Foxe, and that in consequence he replaced his name with that of
Sir Richard Rich.

Rich has always been a convenient figure on whom to pin the
blame for any act of skulduggery in the Tudor court. Having relinquished his post as Chancellor of Augmentations in April 1544, he
had been named treasurer of the recently launched war against the
French and had spent several months across the Channel handling
finances and logistics. After the capture of Boulogne in September
that year, he was one of the commissioners who negotiated peace
(of a sort) with France. But then he resigned. He gave ill health as

the official reason, but his resignation may have been forced, as the King himself had raised questions about his probity and had personally challenged his accounts. Whatever the reasons behind his resignation, Sir Richard had returned to England in November 1544, where he once again set about restoring and consolidating his position, continuing to be an active member of the Privy Council. He undoubtedly 'had form' when it came to betrayal and he always had his own best interests at heart – but his particular treacheries were usually far more circumspect, far more *fastidious* than this act of physical cruelty towards a young woman. These were desperate times, however, and if Anne could be persuaded – or, rather, forced – to name names in the Queen's circle, the resulting shifts in power might be a prize worth fighting, or maiming, for. And what was published as Anne's own account certainly named Rich as one of her torturers.

Chancellor Wriothesley's involvement has never been questioned, and it was he who went on talking to Anne after the torture: 'Then the lieutenant caused me to be loosed from the rack. Incontinently I swooned, and then they recovered me again. After that I sat 2 long hours reasoning with my lord Chancellor upon the bare floor, whereas he with many flattering words, persuaded me to leave my opinion. But my lord God (I thank his everlasting goodness) gave me grace to persevere, and will do (I hope) to the very end.' It is hard to imagine how anyone could address 'many flattering words' to someone he had just tortured, who now lay on the floor, unable to move.

After Anne's condemnation her earlier so-called confession, the statement drawn up by Bishop Bonner to which she had so reluctantly, and ambiguously, appended her signature, was publicized – 'to the intent the world may see what credence is now to be given to the same woman who in so short a time has most damnably altered and changed her opinion and belief and therefore rightfully in open court arraigned and condemned'. These accompanying lines were inaccurate – Anne had been condemned in a closed session of the Privy Council rather than in open court – but the release of the statement was intended not only to justify her treatment as a relapsed heretic, but also to discredit her in the eyes of her supporters. And the latter objective seems to have met with some success, to Anne's great distress, as she had to write to her fellow prisoner John Lascelles to assure him that she had never, as far as she was concerned, actually recanted. 'Oh friend most dearly beloved in God,' she wrote to Lascelles, 'I marvel not a little, what should move you, to judge in me so slender a faith, as to fear death, which is the end of all misery. In the lord I desire you, not to believe of me such wickedness.' Anne also informed Lascelles that she had heard that news of her torture had leaked out, and that the Privy Council (that is, those members who had not been involved in it) were 'not a little displeased' and were anxious that the King should not hear about it.

After her torture Anne was taken away to recover, before being returned to Newgate: 'Then was I brought to a house, and laid in a bed, with as weary and painful bones, as ever had patient Job, I thank my lord God thereof. Then my Lord Chancellor sent me word if I would leave my opinion, I should want nothing. If I would not, I should forth to Newgate, and so be burned. I sent him again word, that I would rather die, than to break my faith.'

It was while she was in prison that Anne compiled the recollections of her two periods of interrogation, which she called her 'examinations': 'by me Anne Askew, that neither wish death, nor yet fear his might; and as merry as one that is bound towards Heaven'. It seems most likely that she wrote them in two separate instalments, before and after her torture; for the second instalment she would certainly have needed assistance in the actual writing, and would have had to dictate most, if not all, of it, for her hands and arms had been rendered virtually useless, and it is also possible her eyesight had been affected by the pressure brought to bear on her entire body. According to the man who edited and published them and provided a commentary (advertised as his 'elucidation'), the exiled reformer John Bale, they were smuggled out of prison and out of the country, and conveyed to him on the continent of Europe. *The First and Latter Examinations* first appeared, respectively, in 1546 and 1547 − very soon after the events they described – and quickly became popular. Versions of them were reprinted in the various editions of Foxe's *Acts and Monuments*.

As she lay awaiting death, Anne ceased all prevarication and wrote plainly what she thought, viewing her writing not only as an account of what had happened to her but also as a testimony of her Protestant beliefs and an encouragement to fellow believers. So now she comes out firmly against the doctrine of transubstantiation: 'But they both say, and also teach it for a necessary article of faith, that after those words be once spoken, there remaineth no bread, but even the selfsame body that hung upon the cross on good Friday, both flesh, blood, and bone. To this belief of theirs, say I nay.' She also confirms her belief that all necessary truth is contained in the Bible: 'Yea, and as St Paul saith, those scriptures are sufficient for our learning and salvation, that Christ hath left here with us. So that I believe, we need no unwritten verities to rule his church with.' She further expresses the view that, if the Eucharist or 'sacrament of thanksgiving' were to be carried out in the way Christ had intended, then it would be a great comfort to believers – 'But as concerning your Mass, as it is now used in our days, I do say and believe it, to be the most abominable idol that is in the world. For my God will not be eaten with teeth, neither yet dieth he again. And upon these words, that I have now spoken, will I suffer death.' This is a very similar formulation to the one uttered by James Bainham, when he was preparing for execution fourteen years previously: 'The bread is not Jesus Christ, for Christ's body is not chewed with teeth, therefore it is but bread; yet he is there, very God and man, in the form of bread.'

On the day before the burning of Anne and three others (her friend John Lascelles, John Hadlam the Essex tailor with whom she had been arraigned at Guildhall, and an apostate Observant friar called John Hemsley), the City Corporation approved the building of 'a substantial stage . . . against tomorrow in Smithfield for the King's Councillors, [the] Lord Mayor and [the] Aldermen to sit in at the execution of Anne Askew and the other heretics which shall then be burned at the costs of this City'. The dignitaries who attended the burning, in addition to the Lord Mayor and Aldermen, included Lord Chancellor Wriothesley, the Duke of Norfolk, other members of the Privy Council and a great number of lords and noblemen. Anne had been so broken on the rack that she was unable to stand or walk, and had to be carried in a chair to the site of her execution. The sermon (a long one, in which the condemned were once again asked to recant, and once again refused) was preached by Nicholas Shaxton, as part of the penance exacted from him following his recantation at Guildhall. Anne was tied to the stake by a chain which held up her body. The deaths were hastened on this occasion by gunpowder having been placed under the victims so that, when the flames reached their bodies, there was an explosion, their bodies blew apart, and all was over. The notables sitting on benches on the stage, just outside St Bartholomew's church, had been anxious they might be injured themselves, but had been assured by Baron Russell that they were at a safe distance from the explosion. As Foxe describes Anne's end, 'Thus she being troubled so many manner of ways, and having passed through so many torments, having now ended the long course of her agonies, being compassed in with flames of fire, as a blessed sacrifice unto God, she slept in the Lord.'

Chapter Seven

DENUNCIATIONS AND NEAR-ESCAPES

✠

Now after this bloody slaughter of God's good saints and servants
thus ended and discoursed, let us proceed to entreat of such as
for the same cause of Religion have been, although not put to
death, yet whipped and scourged by the adversaries of God's
word, first beginning with Richard Wilmot and Thomas Fairfax,
who about the time of Anne Askew, were pitifully rent and tormented with scourges and stripes for their faithful standing to
Christ, and to his truth, as by the story and examination both of
the said Richard Wilmot, and of Thomas Fairfax now following,
may appear.

Foxe, *Acts and Monuments*

THE ATMOSPHERE OF denunciation, fear and reprisal pervading
London in the summer of 1546 cast its shadow over St Bartholomew's in Smithfield, as one of those to fall under suspicion was the
son of Sir John Deane's erstwhile patron, Sir Robert Blagge. This
was George Blagge, who at the time was Member of Parliament
for Bedford; for at least part of his life he lived with his mother in
the parish of St Bartholomew, so it is likely that John Deane knew
him well. In 1546 George was suddenly arrested on a charge of
heresy. He was walking in the area around St Paul's after the
sermon on Sunday, 9 May, when – so he declared – he was tricked
into denying the efficacy of the Mass. He was soon sent for by
Chancellor Wriothesley and on 11 July was committed to Newgate
prison, tried at Guildhall, where Sir Hugh Calverley and Edward
Littleton testified against him, and condemned to be burnt on the

following Wednesday. Blagge did have connections with the evangelical network – as is demonstrated by his spending time while imprisoned sitting with Lascelles by the window of the little parlour at Newgate, entertaining friends from court who were brave enough to visit them.

According to Foxe, Baron Russell, the Lord Privy Seal, then appealed on Blagge's behalf directly to the King who, hearing for the first time of this sentence delivered against one of his own servants – for George Blagge had a position at court as well as being an MP – was 'sore offended' and ordered Wriothesley to draw up a pardon at once. This duly happened, and Blagge was released – after what must have been a highly traumatic few days. Six months later he was appointed Comptroller of the Petty Custom in the port of London, and was never again accused of heresy. He died, possibly of the sweating sickness, in 1551 at Stanmore (having been granted the lease of the manor of Great Stanmore the year before), leaving a two-year-old son as his heir.

Blagge was one of the lucky ones that summer in that no further action was taken against him. The dangers of loose talk, of incitement and consequent denunciation are also illustrated by the story of an eighteen-year-old apprentice, Richard Wilmot, one of the many ardent Bible-reading young men of the City and a godson of Sir Richard Rich. Wilmot worked in a shop in Bow Lane, and was a supporter of Dr Crome who, like other reformist preachers before him, had pleased his Protestant friends by preaching his first 'recantation' sermon in such an ambiguous manner that it served more to emphasize his beliefs than to abjure them. This had not, of course, pleased the bishop, who had ordered him to make a better job of recanting on the following Sunday. And in the meantime he had been sent to prison. It was these matters that were under discussion in the shop in Bow Lane one Tuesday in July. A Welshman called Lewes, a member of the King's Guard, had come into the shop and another customer had taken the opportunity to ask him what news there was at court. Lewes replied that 'the old heretic Dr Crome had recanted now indeed' and that he would be announcing that fact in his next sermon at Paul's Cross.

At this, Wilmot, who had been getting on with work for his master, could not restrain himself from uttering his opinion. He was sorry to hear this, he said, and declared that if Crome were indeed to recant, it would be against both the truth of God's word and his own conscience. Lewes countered with the official line that, as Dr Crome had preached and taught heresy, it was quite right that he should revoke his opinions in public. Wilmot, with all the enthusiasm of a young convert, told him that he was mistaken, that in fact the doctrine Dr Crome preached was entirely in line with what was written in the Bible. Lewes, already rather irritated by the bumptious young man, asked him how he knew that. 'From the Bible,' announced Wilmot. Lewes, now ratcheting up the discussion, announced that 'it was never merry since the Bible was in English' and that the man who had caused it to be translated into English (he meant Thomas Cromwell) had been both a heretic and a traitor and had got what he deserved.

If Wilmot had had any sense, or someone there to warn him, he would have withdrawn from the discussion at this point. But he couldn't resist defending Cromwell, another of his heroes, for having done what 'all the Bishops in the realm yet never did' and making the scriptures available to the people in a language they understood. What's more, he went on, being able to read the Bible means that people don't value bishops and priests so highly any more. Lewes was now clearly leading him on: 'Why's that then?' he asked. 'Because they don't live or believe according to God's word,' said Wilmot. Lewes, a conservative if ever there was one, riposted that bishops and priests are the learned ones, and ordinary people should be instructed by them – that was all right for our fathers, he declared, so it should be all right for us. 'The world has gone to the dogs' was his view. But Wilmot, a very voluble young man, did not agree and now launched into a long speech about how he knew better, from having read the Bible for himself. And he continued unguardedly to criticize 'bishops, priests, and learned men', not by name, but lumping them all together as 'blind leaders of the blind' whom people would do better not to follow. By now Lewes had heard quite enough: 'Marry, sir,' he said, 'you are a holy Doctor indeed. By God's blood, if you were my man, I would set you about your business a little better, and not to look at books: and so would your master, if he were wise.' And, just on cue, Wilmot's master now arrived, accompanied by another young man called Thomas Fairfax, who worked in nearby Watling Street. Lewes expostulated that he had 'a knavish boy here as his servant' and that he would do better to hang him than to keep him in his house. Astonished, Wilmot's master asked his other employees – who had so far kept very quiet – what had been going on. 'They were talking about Dr Crome,' they replied.

On hearing that, and 'swearing a great oath', Wilmot's master demanded the boy tell him what he had said. 'Nothing that could reasonably offend you or Mr Lewes,' answered Wilmot and then, indicating Lewes: 'Why don't you ask him?' So Lewes launched into a summary of what Wilmot had said, in the process exaggerating the most inflammatory parts of it, and emphasizing Wilmot's defence of Cromwell, well aware that to defend a convicted traitor was in itself a treacherous act. Wilmot, now beginning to wake up to the fact that he might be in trouble, protested that Lewes was making what he had said sound worse than it was. His master, infuriated and no doubt very anxious that such dangerous talk had been going on in his shop, lambasted the boy, telling him he was quite likely to be hanged or burnt – or at the very least to have all his books confiscated and destroyed. The other young man, Fairfax, now joined the fray, supporting Wilmot against Lewes; this only stoked the fire and Lewes, furious at being bested in argument by these know-it-all young men, 'went his way in a rage to the Court'.

The next day Wilmot and Fairfax were both summoned to see the Lord Mayor, who this year was Sir Martin Bowes, undertreasurer at the Royal Mint. This was not an official hearing, as they were first of all given dinner and then called into a parlour where they were examined separately by the Lord Mayor himself and Sir Roger Cholmley (or Cholmondeley), formerly the Recorder of London and now the Chief Baron of the Exchequer (and the 'first known eminent resident' of that part of north London known as

Highgate). No church officials were as yet involved, Sir Roger explaining that he and the Lord Mayor had received an instruction from the Privy Council to question the two young men. (And the City authorities, aware of the prevalence of reformist thinking among their young people, were anxious not to be seen as unable to control their own apprentices.) During the questioning, Sir Roger made the rather strange accusation of Wilmot being Dr Crome's son, an assertion Wilmot vigorously denied. They then discussed Crome's anticipated recantation, and whether the content of his previous sermons was heretical. Wilmot, not at all cowed by his surroundings, declared that if Crome was a heretic, then so was St Paul, as Crome's teachings were confirmed in the Epistle to the Hebrews. Sir Roger then raised the pertinent question of the accuracy of English translations of the Bible and the authority to be given to them; how did Wilmot know St Paul actually wrote these things now attributed to him, he asked, when the apostle never wrote in either English or Latin? Wilmot answered that he was sure that the 'learned men of God' who had undertaken this work of translation would not have presumed to alter the meaning of the scriptures. The Lord Mayor now interjected crossly in this rather scholarly discussion, angry at the whole idea that apprentices should be spending their time reading unauthorized texts instead of getting on with the work they were supposed to be doing, and declaring that Wilmot must be punished for having spoken ill of Bishops Gardiner and Bonner. And Sir Roger, presumably intending to frighten Wilmot, referred approvingly to the work Sir Richard Rich had been undertaking in Essex to round up heretics, who were soon to be sent to Bishop Bonner and would then 'all be hanged and burned'. To which the irrepressible Wilmot responded: 'I am sorry to hear that of my Lord Rich, for he was my godfather, and gave me my name at my baptism.' He admitted that he had not, however, spoken to Rich for twelve years. 'If he knew what you'd been getting up to, he'd have arrested you as well,' declared Sir Roger.

Wilmot continuing to defend himself by reference to the Bible, Sir Roger decided it was time to draw the interview to a conclusion.

'Well, sir,' said Cholmondeley, 'because you are so full of your Scripture, and so well learned, we consider you lack a quiet place to study in. Therefore you shall go to a place where you shall be most quiet, and I would wish you to study how you will answer to the Council of those things which they have to charge you with, for else it is like to cost you your best joint.'

And so Wilmot was sent to cool his heels in the Counter at Poultry, while Fairfax was sent to the other Counter in Bread Street. They remained in their respective prisons for eight days. There now began a series of anxious delegations and attempts to get the two boys out of trouble, or at least to mitigate the trouble they were in. The motivation throughout seems to have been to keep the matter as quiet as possible, with as few repercussions for the reputations of City officials and commerce as could be managed. The two apprentices and their masters were connected to the Drapers' Company, one of the most influential of the City's guilds, and so the Wardens of the Drapers were enlisted in the damage limitation exercise and they accompanied the Lord Mayor when he went to report on the case to the Privy Council and Bishop Gardiner. Initially, Gardiner fulminated that the two young men deserved to die, but then agreed to the concession that they should instead be tied to a cart's tail and whipped through the City, on three market days. The Lord Mayor and Wardens of the Drapers' Company came home, thought a bit more, and then went back again the next day. Now they knelt before the bishop and his friend and fellow courtier Sir Anthony Browne and begged the favour that the two apprentices should be punished in the Company's Hall* and in front of some of the members, rather than drag the name of the Drapers through the ignominy of a public whipping. And, finally, this was agreed.

Wilmot and Fairfax were then informed of what had been negotiated on their behalf. 'Then were they sent before the Masters [i.e. the Master and Wardens of the Drapers] the next day to the Hall, both their masters being also present, and there were laid to

---

* Previously, and ironically, the home of Wilmot's hero Thomas Cromwell, forfeit to the Crown on his execution in 1540 and acquired by the Drapers' Company in 1543.

their charges, the heinous offences by them committed, how they were both heretics and traitors, and had deserved death for the same, and this was declared with a long process by the Master of the Company, whose name was Mr Brooke.' The 'long process' delivered by Mr Brooke involved a detailed retelling of all the efforts and humiliation – including having to pay a very large fine of £100 – which their superiors had gone to in order to spare the boys from death or public shame. And following the speech came retribution. 'After these and many other words, he commanded them to address themselves to receive their punishment.' The two young men were stripped to the waist, and each was roped by an ankle to an iron ring in the centre of the Hall. 'Then came two men down, disguised in mummers' apparel, with visors on their faces, and they beat them with great rods until the blood did flow on their bodies.' This savage beating finally put paid to Wilmot's assertiveness. He was so badly injured that he couldn't lie in his bed for a week, and the health of both young men was permanently affected.

A little over six months after Anne Askew's execution and the punishment of Wilmot and Fairfax, on 28 January 1547, King Henry VIII died. He had been seriously ill for months, and from early November had been restlessly moving from place to place, visiting eight houses in Middlesex and Surrey in the space of six weeks. He arrived back in London, at the palace of Whitehall, just before Christmas and, despite his poor health, remained in control until about ten days before his death. The factional struggles at court had resulted in the triumph of those of a Protestant tendency, and Bishop Stephen Gardiner found his power slipping away even before the death of the King. Yet, despite having previously been associated with the traditionalists – even to the extent of being implicated in the torture of Anne Askew, whether or not he actually participated in it – the great survivor, Richard Rich, not only survived but prospered yet again. Henry had arranged in his will for Rich to receive a barony and, on 15 February, the Privy Council ratified the decision that he should be so created, and he took the title of Baron Rich of Leez, in Essex.

Chapter Eight

PROTESTANTISM IN THE ASCENDANT

✠

Where heretofore there hath been great diversity in saying and singing in churches within this realm: some following Salisbury use, some Hereford use, some the use of Bangor, some of York, and some of Lincoln: Now from henceforth, all the whole realm shall have but one use.

From the preface to the 1549 Book of Common Prayer

HENRY'S YOUNG SON Edward was crowned on 20 February 1547, the event accompanied by much pageantry and celebration:

Item the 20th day of the same month the said King Edward the Sixth came from the Tower of London through London, and in divers places pageants, and all the streets hanged richly, with all the crafts standing in Cheap, presenting them as loving subjects unto their King, and so to Paul's; and at the west end of Paul's steeple was tied a cable rope, and the other end beside the Dean's place at an anchor of a ship, and a man running down on the said rope as swift as an arrow out of a bow down with his hands and feet abroad not touching the rope; and when the King had seen the said thing went forth unto the palace of Westminster; and the next day came from thence unto Westminster church, and there was crowned, and kept his feast in Westminster Hall. God of his mercy send him good luck and long life, with prosperity! And this was done in the 9th year of his age and birth.

Among those in charge of the arrangements for the coronation
and accompanying festivities was Lord Rich (a title that by this
time he had enjoyed for five days). On the day of Rich's ennoble-
ment, the corpse of Henry VIII had arrived at Windsor where it
was received by Bishop Stephen Gardiner, who preached at the
Requiem Mass, and at Edward's coronation Archbishop Cranmer
was flanked by both Gardiner and Bishop Cuthbert Tunstall. But
that the tide was turning against such religious conservatives as
Gardiner, Tunstall and Bonner was already evident, Cranmer in his
coronation sermon extolling Edward as a royal iconoclast and
second Josiah. (Josiah, according to the Second Book of Kings,
became King of Judah at the tender age of eight, and was known
for having destroyed the images, idols and other 'abominations'
that had been spreading among the Hebrews.) The nine-year-old
Edward must indeed have appeared a Josiah-like godsend to the
convinced reformers at court and in the Church.

Under the terms of Henry's will, sixteen executors were to act
as Edward's Council until he was eighteen, and these sixteen executors were to be supplemented by twelve other men, who would
assist them. The will had not provided for one of those men to lead
the others or to act as Regent, but on 12 March the young King's
uncle, Edward Seymour, who had recently become first Duke of
Somerset and is therefore usually known merely as 'Somerset', succeeded in getting his nephew to sign letters patent appointing him
as Protector without limitation until the King reached the age of
eighteen.

One of the few people to oppose Somerset was Lord Chancellor Wriothesley (who had been created Earl of Southampton on
the same day that Richard Rich was ennobled). Wriothesley found
himself dismissed and placed under house arrest in Ely Place, in
what was formerly the London townhouse of the bishops of Ely
in Holborn (just outside the City), on a charge of selling off some
of his office to delegates, to which he had laid himself open by
having appointed four persons to take on some of his duties as Lord
Chancellor (not that this was at all unusual, the practice having
been followed by his immediate predecessors and subsequently by

his successors – including Rich). The attack on him, which was part of the power struggle now going on within the Privy Council, was orchestrated by Rich and the man for whom he may have historically taken the rap for the torture of Anne Askew, Sir John Baker. Whoever had actually turned the wheels of Anne's rack, these three – Rich, Wriothesley and Baker – were closely implicated in what had happened to her, and each of them knew what the others had done. Perhaps it is only to be expected that, within this threesome of intrigue and shameful secrets, there should also lurk treachery towards one another.

The replacement Rich had in mind when he set out to topple Wriothesley from his position as Lord Chancellor was – unsurprisingly – himself, but he had to wait a few months for this prize as initially the appointment went to William Paulet. Rich did not complain openly, but he did privately lament the fact that Paulet was not a lawyer and that the Lord Chancellor ought to have been one, and so he got others to complain that the appointment was insulting to the profession and not good for the public. And in fact Paulet does not appear to have been particularly efficient. Rich's campaign to discredit him soon attained its desired outcome with Rich himself being appointed Lord Chancellor of England on 23 October 1547. The Great Seal was delivered to him at Hampton Court in the presence of the child-King, the ceremony being carried out in the King's name by the Lord Protector. Ex-Chancellor Wriothesley was back in the Privy Council fairly soon after his dismissal, but did not regain anything like his former position.

Success in the pursuit of power and influence meant that Rich had to discard, or at least conceal, what had appeared previously to have been his preferences in matters of religion. He was hardly alone in having to perform a volte-face in 1547, with Protestantism now being officially established for the first time in England, after more than a decade of an increasingly conservative doctrinal and liturgical stance under Henry. What had been deemed heresy on the part of Anne Askew and her sympathizers was now being enthusiastically embraced by the church hierarchy and ratified by Parliament. So throughout his time as Lord Chancellor, Rich was responsible, with others, for bringing forward bills to establish the King's power to appoint bishops, to dissolve chantries, to allow priests to marry and to repeal the Act of Six Articles, under which the martyrs of the latter years of Henry's reign had been condemned (with, at the time, Rich's full approval).

Many of those with less elastic consciences went quickly into exile, among them someone we will encounter later at St Bartholomew's, the Dominican Father William Peryn, a staunch conservative in doctrine, who had already been in exile in the 1530s. He had come back to England in the latter years of King Henry's reign, but returned to Louvain in 1547, fleeing before any official changes in doctrine – and accompanying sanctions for deviance – could be introduced. Before departure, he had preached on St George's day (23 April) at St Andrew Undershaft in the City on the spiritual benefits of using pictures of God and the saints in worship. This was in complete opposition to the new approved line, articulated by Nicholas Ridley on Ash Wednesday, 23 February, in a sermon at court deprecating the use of images and holy water. Preferring exile to imprisonment or worse, Peryn had recanted his views, as instructed, on 19 June but then left the country.

Services began to be conducted in English at St Paul's Cathedral as early as Easter 1547, by order of the Dean, William May. In September that year began what was known as the King's visitation at St Paul's and all the images there were pulled down. On 9 September it took place at St Bride's in Fleet Street and after that in various other parish churches. The churches were whitelimed, and the Ten Commandments written on the walls. At the time of the visitation of St Bride's, the vicar there was John Cardmaker, an evangelical, who would have unequivocally approved of the changes being made. All roods – that is, the great crucifixes separating nave and chancel, often affixed to screens – were taken down. The chronicler and Windsor Herald Charles Wriothesley (cousin of ex-Chancellor Thomas Wriothesley) noted that, on the night when the rood with all the images was dismantled in St Paul's, negligence led to some people being hurt and one killed when the great cross fell from the rood loft, 'which the popish priests said was the will of God for the pulling down of the said idols'.

Bishop Edmund Bonner, who had been so active in promoting the Henrician definition of orthodoxy, was called before the Privy Council and sent to the Fleet prison on 18 September 1547 for refusing to observe the Royal Injunctions to have the Epistle and Gospel at High Mass read in English. He was released a few weeks later from this first imprisonment in the Fleet, and actually attended the House of Lords during Edward's first Parliament. In the second session of Parliament, Bonner again regularly attended proceedings in the Lords, opposing the religious changes introduced by the reformers, and encouraging others to follow suit. He neglected to enforce use of the new English prayer book, and this resulted in a remonstrance from the King who wrote to him on 2 August 1549, soon after this first Book of Common Prayer had come into force, taking him to task over the many people in his diocese who were neglecting to attend church and Holy Communion and putting this down to Bonner's own 'evil example and slackness'. Bonner had previously preached a great deal, particularly on all the major feast days, and he was now refusing to do so. The young King told him to reform, and commanded him to preach strongly against rebellion and resistance to temporal authority in his next sermon at St Paul's, and in support of obedience in using the rites established by law to be used in the Church. On 10 August further injunctions were delivered from the King to Bishop Bonner, requiring him to celebrate communion in St Paul's in a few days' time and to declare in his sermon that the present King's authority was no less than that of any of his predecessors, despite his youth, and to preach God's displeasure at rebellion. The Greyfriars chronicler reported that, on 18 August 1549, Bishop Bonner, knowing what was likely to happen to him, 'did the office at Paul's both at the procession and at the communion discreetly and sadly'.

On 1 September Bonner preached at Paul's Cross and was subsequently accused regarding his teaching. His failure to obey the clear instructions from the King was discussed by the Privy Council on 8 September and a commission for his deprivation was appointed. He was made to appear before Archbishop Cranmer and others on 13, 16 and 18 September. On 20 September he was sent at night to the Marshalsea prison and, reported the chronicler, 'he went the same day unto Lambeth in his scarlet habit and his rotchet upon it' (that is, dressed in his episcopal robes). He was deprived of his bishopric at Lambeth on 1 October 1549 by Archbishop Cranmer. He was then sent back to prison, where he was to remain at the King's pleasure.

Bishop Gardiner had also been summoned to appear before the Privy Council early in Edward's reign, on 25 September 1547, and he too was initially incarcerated in the Fleet. At least imprisonment here was not as unpleasant as at Newgate, as it had special privileges on account of being 'the King's own proper prison next in trust to his Tower of London'. Gardiner was held there until January 1548, not being released until after the closure of Edward's first Parliament (it was Gardiner's belief that he was kept locked up expressly to prevent him attending Parliament and being anywhere near the centre of power), and he was then asked to subscribe to a statement on the doctrine of justification. This he refused to do and was subsequently placed under house arrest in his Southwark palace. He then returned to his diocese where he continued in his stubbornness.

The stern treatment meted out to the former bishops who refused to conform was motivated by a desire for conformity and good order; Edward and his advisers had no appetite for open contention in matters of religion – not least because there were many matters over which there was still no firm agreement among the reformers. In the first part of Edward's reign there seems to have been a desire at court and among the church hierarchy to keep the lid on dissent, in the hope of being able to devote some time to working out definitive positions on questions of faith and practice. The first act of Edward's first Parliament was the Act against Revilers of the Sacrament and for Communion in both kinds – so on the one hand setting out the reformed principle that the people were to receive both bread and wine at Holy Communion, while on the other making it an offence punishable by fines and imprisonment to speak disrespectfully of the sacrament of the altar, a measure aimed at those, including some preachers, who had been scoffingly referring to it as a 'jack-in-a-box'.

The chronicler Wriothesley noted in 1548 at Whitsuntide: 'the censing in Paul's clean put down' – that is, no more incense was to be used in St Paul's Cathedral. Many outdoor processions were ended too, including the Worshipful Company of Skinners' procession on Corpus Christi day. Only 'the English procession' – that is, the penitential litany composed by Cranmer (with its repeated refrain of 'have mercy upon us, miserable sinners') – was allowed to take place, inside the churches. There was nevertheless still confusion as to what people could and could not do and, more precisely, what they did and did not do, so for instance the Greyfriars chronicler notes: 'Item the 20th day of June [1549], the which was Corpus Christi day, and as that day in divers places in London was kept holy day, and many kept none, but did work openly, and in some churches service and some none, such was the division.'

When Bishop Gardiner was made to preach in the summer of 1548, as a test of his orthodoxy, he was instructed to comply with the recent ruling that no one was to preach on the theology of the Eucharist until it had been properly determined. As with most other instructions emanating from the Edwardian hierarchy, Gardiner refused to obey. In his sermon, preached on the feast of St Peter and St Paul, 29 June, he spoke of the sacrifice of the Mass and, though he admitted that communion could be received in both kinds and he attacked papal authority, he went on to defend religious ceremonies on the basis that they helped to move men towards God. His insistence on speaking in this way afforded his opponents a pretext for his immediate rearrest and exclusion from the second session of Parliament under Edward, that second Parliament convening in November 1548. A year later, in November 1549, when the third session was convening at Westminster, Gardiner again wrote to the Privy Council, urging them to release him so that he could sit in the Upper House, which he claimed to be his right. But by the time the next session convened, he had been deprived of his see, having been tried on nineteen charges in front of royal commissioners, headed by Cranmer, the trial beginning at Lambeth on 15 December 1550. Though he strongly defended himself, many witnesses spoke against him. The eighth session of the court appointed to try him was held at Lord Rich's house at St Bartholomew's on 20 January 1551. He was deprived of the see of Winchester on 14 February, and spent the rest of Edward's reign in the Tower, the Protestant John Ponet replacing him as bishop. Cuthbert Tunstall, former Bishop of Durham, fared no better, being called before the Privy Council in February 1550, committed to the Tower in 1551, and deprived of his see in October 1552.

The difficulty in controlling what priests said from the pulpit led to restrictions being placed on the parish clergy – who, at Thomas Cromwell's instigation, had been obliged under Henry VIII to preach in their own churches every quarter – so that from April 1548 only a small list of clergy with a royal licence had the right to preach at all. There is no indication that Sir John Deane of St Bartholomew's was ever on this list and no reason why he would have been; a priest who wanted to stay out of trouble in these turbulent years was well advised not to express his opinions from the pulpit, but to administer the sacraments according to the officially sanctioned rite – marrying, burying, baptizing and doing pastoral work – while leaving doctrinal considerations to his superiors. This, as far as we know, was Deane's policy.

Another item up for discussion during Edward's reign was compulsory clerical celibacy, and the desire by the reformers to bring forward legislation to abolish it, but the Lords were not as in favour of this as the Commons, and the bill was not passed early in the reign. Clerical marriage was, though, finally legalized by Parliament in 1549, at which time many clerics either began to marry or brought out into the open the wives they had had for some time. It had clearly been expected that this legalisation would take place, Cranmer himself living openly as a married man from the beginning of Edward's reign, and routine official documents coming from Lambeth Palace soon mentioning clerical wives.

John Deane never married. The bill permitting clergy marriage still maintained that 'it were more commendable for them to live chaste and without marriage, whereby they might better attend to the ministry of the Gospel, and to be less distracted with secular cares'. Whether or not this was John Deane's motivation – that he could better attend to the ministry of the Gospel by keeping to his celibate state – it was a circumstance that certainly aided his survival.

Deane would have been among those who, in May 1550, went to listen to and be examined by Dr Nicholas Ridley, Bishop of London in succession to the disgraced Bonner, as in that month Dr Ridley sat in visitation in St Paul's Cathedral and in various other places within the diocese of London and 'called all the parsons and curates of his diocese with 6 persons of every parish before him, and gave them divers godly injunctions and instructions to be enquired of, and also examining every parson and curate himself in his own house privately of their learning, and gave them four days to make their answer in Whitsun week next'. In addition to fulfilling his role as a priest and demonstrating obedience to his bishop, Deane participated, along with many of his parishioners (so many of whom were officials of the Court of Augmentations), in the redistribution of wealth and property that occurred as a result of the dissolution of the monasteries. Deane was a pragmatist, and he had as his patron the ultra-pragmatist, Lord Rich; he both learnt from him, and benefited from his influence when necessary. The Rector of St Bartholomew's was exceptionally well placed to know what former monastic property was available for purchase and he took advantage of this knowledge – not only, or indeed primarily, for himself, but for his relatives and the people he cared about in his native Northwich, as will be seen subsequently. John Deane made one purchase of monastic property direct from the Crown: in Henry's reign, by a grant dated August 1543, he bought property in Northwich previously belonging to the Cistercian monastery of Basingwerk. For this he paid £54 to the Treasurer of the Court of Augmentations, Sir Edward North (a parishioner, living in Bartholomew Close). The property consisted of two salt pits or 'salinas' (plots of land with buildings on them, one of which had to be occupied by any intending maker of salt before he could be allowed to take brine from the pits). Still in Henry's reign, Deane was involved in litigation to establish his right to part of this, addressing a complaint to the Chancellor of the Court of Augmentations; the exact date of the petition is not known but the Chancellor would have been either Richard Rich or Edward North, both Deane's parishioners. He had further trouble with one of his properties while Rich was Lord Chancellor, addressing a petition to him against Thomas Bromfield and Thomas Newall for withholding the rents and profits of the salthouse from him. Deane asked for a writ of subpoena on Bromfield and Newall, commanding them to surrender the deeds and to pay the rent due at the previous Michaelmas. It is perhaps not surprising that his petition appears to have been successful.

During Rich's period as Lord Chancellor he found himself more exposed than he was accustomed to, and it drew upon all his skills for nimble political footwork and self-preservation. His relations with Lord Protector Somerset, as indeed with anyone else in or out of power, were always ambivalent and dependent on changes in circumstance and alignment. From the start of his Protectorate, Somerset's position was threatened by his own brother, Thomas Seymour. Thomas had been appointed Lord Admiral and given a seat on the Privy Council, in the hope of taming him, but keeping quiet and subservient was not in Thomas's character. In the spring of 1547 he had secretly married Henry VIII's widow, Katherine Parr, who died in childbirth in September 1548, and he was clearly not prepared to work indefinitely under his brother. Steps were therefore taken against him and in January 1549 he was arrested on various charges, including embezzlement at the Bristol Mint. There was no clear evidence against him for treason, so he was not tried but condemned by Act of Attainder. Lord Chancellor Rich was necessarily involved.

Three days after the Bill of Attainder against Thomas Seymour had received the royal assent, the Lord Chancellor called a Council meeting to deliberate about having it carried into effect. The Protector withdrew from the meeting – while knowing it to be very likely that the Council would resolve that his brother be executed – and he himself signed the warrant for the execution later that day. The second signature was that of Archbishop Cranmer, and the third that of Lord Chancellor Rich. It was also Rich who announced to the young Edward VI that his uncle Thomas was to be beheaded, the sentence being carried out on 20 March 1549. Edward betrayed no emotion at this news, accepting the assurances of his councillors that the execution of his ambitious relative was in his own best interests.

A few months after Thomas Seymour's death, Rich found himself having to work out where he stood between opposing rival factions. On the one side there were discontented members of the Privy Council, headed by ex-Chancellor Wriothesley and the Earl of Warwick (formerly Lord Lisle), and they had established a rival government at Ely House (where Wriothesley had not so long before been under house arrest), taking advantage of Somerset's unpopularity and weakness. During 1548 England had experienced much social unrest and, after April 1549, a series of armed revolts had broken out over both religious and agrarian grievances, two serious rebellions occurring in Devon and Cornwall and in Norfolk. These events were taken as evidence of the failure of Somerset's government, a number of members of the Council laying the responsibility at his door. On the other side was Somerset, and at first Rich seemed to be with him.

On 1 October 1549 Somerset had been alerted that his rule faced serious threat, and on that day he issued a proclamation calling for assistance, took possession of the King's person and withdrew with him to the fortified Windsor Castle, in the hope that the King's name might prove a tower of strength. Rich had been with the Protector at Hampton Court and he initially accompanied him and King Edward to Windsor. But when Rich saw that Somerset was being deserted by everybody and was likely to lose, he switched sides and joined forces with the malcontent privy councillors, taking the Great Seal with him as a symbol of authority against the Lord Protector.

On Sunday 6 October Rich made a long and powerful speech

to the Lord Mayor and Aldermen of the City gathered at Ely House, asserting that Somerset had usurped the protectorship against the will of the late King, that he had abused his power, mismanaged foreign affairs by allowing the infant Queen of Scots to be married into the royal family of France, that he had oppressed the nobility and the people at home, and that it was now necessary to rescue the King, who was being held by Somerset at Windsor Castle.

The Lord Mayor and Aldermen were sufficiently receptive to Rich's speech to agree to meet at Guildhall in the afternoon of that day and to consider requests for military assistance from both the Protector and the opposing Council. At that point no decision was taken to offer military assistance to either party, but the Aldermen did agree to strengthen the night watches at the gates of the City. That same day the Earl of Warwick moved the short distance from Holborn into the City and took lodgings with one of the sheriffs, John York. This would suggest that he was expecting the City to declare for his side. On the following day the Common Council met, in the presence of the Lord Mayor, the Recorder and the Aldermen, and heard letters from both Somerset and the Privy Council, deliberated and pondered on them, and agreed to side with the privy councillors, against the Protector, 'for the defence, safeguard, and maintenance of the King's Majesty's person, and for his grace's City of London and to aid the said Lords within the said City according to the tenor of their said letters'. They thereby committed themselves as opposed to Somerset, but agreed to take action only within the City, and not to give money for troops further afield.

On 8 October Common Council convened again and on this occasion the leaders of the Privy Council were present at the meeting at Guildhall. Lord Rich and other lords declared to Common Council 'the great abuses of the said Lord Protector, desiring that all the citizens be aiding and assisting with the lords for the preservation of the King's Majesty's person, which greatly feared being in his adversary's hands'. After the Lord Mayor, Aldermen and Common Council had heard these remarks of Lord Rich and others, they 'promised their aid and help to the uttermost of their lives and goods'. They still had not promised to provide armed forces, however, and it was not until the next day, 9 October, that Common Council agreed to provide armed men, pressure having been put on them by the Aldermen. On 10 October, the Councilmen finally assented to a commitment of 500 men, of whom 100 were to be cavalry. A list was drawn up with numbers of men to be provided by each of the livery companies, and this military force mustered at Moorfields on 11 October, but by that day the Protector's support had dwindled to the point at which troops were no longer required. Somerset was taken into custody by Sir Anthony Wingfield, Captain of the Guard, and the King was brought to Richmond. On 14 October the former Lord Protector was committed to the Tower. Lord Rich 'presided at the examinations of his former patron before the Council, – drew up the articles against him – obtained his confession – and brought in the Bill of Pains and Penalties, by which he was deprived of all his offices, and sentenced to forfeit land to the value of 2,000L a year'.

The overthrow of Somerset occurred only a few days after the deprivation of Bishop Bonner, and the shift of power to Warwick (who became Duke of Northumberland early in 1551 and was subsequently generally referred to as Northumberland) also presaged a strengthening of the reformist position (somewhat to the surprise, and discontent, of the conservatives among the Privy Council who had backed the coup). On Christmas Day 1549 a royal circular to the bishops was issued, reinforcing the message of an earlier proclamation, ordering the destruction of all Latin service books. There were bonfires of books all over England, the bishops being forced to supervise these burnings. The Greyfriars chronicler, sympathetic to Bonner, relates the hard time the former bishop had in prison – how, on 8 January 1550, Bonner had his bed removed by the keeper of the prison and for eight days had only straw and a coverlet to lie on, for refusing to pay his jailer the sum of £10. He appealed against his sentence, and on 6 February he was taken from the Marshalsea to appear before the Privy Council sitting in Star Chamber at Westminster. Here he was informed that his appeal had been considered, and dismissed, by eight privy councillors (among them Lord Rich). It was Rich, as Lord Chancellor, who concluded the proceedings by commanding that Bonner (with whom in the previous reign he had worked closely in the pursuit of heretics) 'be had from thence to the place he came from, from there to remain in perpetual prison at the King's pleasure, and to lose all his spiritual promotions and dignities for ever'.

Lord Rich was also involved in the steps taken against the King's half-sister Princess Mary (now known as 'the Lady Mary', as her father had decreed) in her desire to have Mass said in her house, in defiance of the King's instructions. On 22 July 1550 Sir William Petre and Lord Rich were nominated by the Privy Council to visit Mary to convey the message of the King, insisting that only the authorized English services were to be used in her household. The message was delivered by Rich at Copped Hall in Essex, where Mary was then living. She knelt to receive the King's letter, explaining that she was paying respect to the writer, rather than to the letter's contents.

Though the young Edward expected obedience in religious matters from his half-sister (from whom he did not receive it – though she did eventually agree not to be ostentatious in her observances of traditional worship) and his other subjects (from whom he largely did) and placed a high value on conformity, coercion of belief and practice by means of capital punishment was not, in general, part of his policy. There were nevertheless two people – both Anabaptists – burnt at the stake in his reign. As soon as Edward's first Parliament met, it had repealed the Six Articles and the laws against heresy, but it was subsequently decided, in the cases of Joan Boucher and George van Parris, that the King had the right to punish heretics under the common law, and so these two victims were burnt on the authority of a royal writ. Joan Boucher, also known as Joan Knell and Joan of Kent, came from the area near the Romney Marshes and had been involved in reforming circles in Canterbury in the late 1530s and early 1540s. During Henry's reign she had spoken against the sacrament of the altar, been imprisoned for a while and then released, largely on the initiative of Cranmer's commissary, Christopher Nevinson. Joan was related by blood or marriage to William Knell of Kent, who was executed for speaking in support of the papacy in 1538, and so she was turning against her own family when she embraced Protestantism. Some time after 1543 she became an Anabaptist, or one of those who would be defined as Anabaptists, her views now beginning to part company with even the most radical of Protestant beliefs. She became convinced of a theory concerning Christ's celestial flesh, the belief that Christ did not receive his physical body from his mother Mary, but that it was a divine distillation, views that may have come from exiled Dutch Anabaptists, fleeing persecution in Holland. She was arrested in 1548 and convicted of heresy in April 1549. When she was condemned and her sentence read out, she told the tribunal: 'It is a goodly matter to consider your ignorance. It was not long ago since you burned Anne Askew for a piece of bread, and yet came yourselves soon after to believe and profess the same things for which you burned her. And now, forsooth, you will burn me for a piece of flesh, and in the end you will come to believe this also, when you have read the scriptures and understand them.' She was right about Anne Askew's views on the sacrament now being shared by those in authority, but her own opinions on 'the celestial flesh' remained beyond the pale of Christian orthodoxy.

After her conviction, Joan was imprisoned for more than a year and for some of that time she was held in Lord Rich's house in St Bartholomew's, where both Archbishop Cranmer and Bishop Nicholas Ridley of London made efforts to persuade her back to mainstream Protestantism. But she was adamant in her opinions and would not be moved; as Rich himself (during the trial of a later martyr, John Philpot) described Joan's state of mind when she was his enforced house-guest, 'she was so high in the spirit that they could do nothing with her for all their learning'. These efforts on the part of Cranmer and Ridley (according to Rich, 'my Lord of Canterbury and Bishop Ridley resorted almost daily unto her') suggest considerable reluctance to carry out the sentence of execution but Joan's refusal to compromise left them (they felt) with no alternative.

Joan was burnt in Smithfield on 2 May 1550. After her death, further attempts were made to discredit her, her views being described by Latimer and others as 'Arian' – that is, heretical in denying the divinity of Christ (though in fact she appears to have been doing the opposite and denying his humanity).

John Deane was very close to these events. Not only did the burning take place outside his church, but he would have known about Joan being held in his patron's house in his parish – maybe he even met her – and he would have seen the comings and goings of the prelates in their attempts to dissuade Joan from her heretical beliefs. No wonder if he recognized the value of conformity and of obeying the instructions of the hierarchy, even if the current instructions contradicted those that had been issued previously. Conformity in the month following Joan's burning included replacing the altar in the church with a 'table' for the receiving of Holy Communion. The only City of London church to stand out against this directive was St Nicholas Cole Abbey.

Not long after Joan's burning, in the summer of 1550, came the long-anticipated definitive (for the time being) statement on the Eucharist, with the publication of Archbishop Cranmer's *Defence of the true and Catholic doctrine of the body and blood of our saviour Christ*. Cranmer had been drafting this book as early as the autumn of 1548, and he enlarged upon it in 1551 when he wrote an answer to an attack published by his rival, the incarcerated former bishop Stephen Gardiner. In his *Answer* to Gardiner, Cranmer affirmed that a spiritual eucharistic presence is granted by grace only to the elect believer, not to everyone who receives bread and wine. That would answer the mouse question posed to Anne Askew in her examinations under the previous orthodoxy: if only the elect believer receives the eucharistic presence in spirit (which was very much Anne's view), then a mouse eating the host would not be receiving it. That answer would not have satisfied her interrogators at the time the question was addressed to Anne.

George van Parris, the second person to be burnt by the Edwardian authorities, was a Flemish immigrant to London, about whom little is known. He may have been a surgeon who, after fleeing his native Flanders, settled in France before travelling on to London, where he is thought to have joined the London Strangers' church, founded in 1550. He was arraigned before Cranmer and other commissioners in April 1551, with Miles Coverdale acting as interpreter. He was condemned for Arianism (having declared his belief that God the Father only is God, and that Christ is not very God) on 7 April, and executed at Smithfield just over a fortnight later.

John Foxe, the hagiographer of Protestant saints, had much difficulty in dealing with these two martyrs of the Edwardian reign. As someone who strongly disapproved of execution for religious reasons, he did not wish to acknowledge the fact that Protestants had burnt anyone – let alone that they had burnt people who could also be defined as Protestants, even though their beliefs diverged considerably from the mainstream. In consequence Foxe said very little about the deaths of Joan Boucher and George van Parris in his English editions of *Acts and Monuments*, confining himself to the comment that they had died 'for certain articles not much necessary here to be rehearsed'.

With the views of Anne Askew and fellow Protestants now constituting the new orthodoxy, many reformers were returning from exile, including John Bale, who had edited Anne's examinations. Bale was recorded as living in the Duchess of Richmond's house in London in 1548; on 26 June 1551 he was made Rector of Bishopstoke in Hampshire by John Ponet, Bishop of Winchester, and in the same year he was made Vicar of Swaffham. On 15 August 1552 when he met the King at Southampton, he was promised the Irish bishopric of Ossory, and formally nominated to that see on 22 October. This was connected to Northumberland's plan to convert the Irish to Protestantism.

Another man who made his mark during this period when Protestantism appeared to have triumphed, and whom we will encounter in less happy circumstances under Mary I, was the Mancunian John Bradford, born in about 1510 to parents of gentle birth. He attended Manchester Grammar School as a boy and was next heard of working as paymaster under Sir John Harrington of Exton, Rutlandshire, the vice treasurer of the English army in France, between 1544 and 1547. (In this job Bradford is likely to have encountered the seemingly ubiquitous Richard Rich, as he was Harrington's superior for a few months in 1544.) Bradford served as Harrington's assistant in Boulogne where Harrington's responsibilities included looking after the King's interests and properties there. Bradford's time in Boulogne did not go entirely smoothly; allegations were made of financial irregularity, involving both himself and his employer. Bradford, though alleged to have taken the sum of £140 out of the royal treasury without Harrington's knowledge (a more reliable version of what occurred is that Bradford falsified the army's records, with Harrington's consent, and thereby cheated the government of a considerable sum of money), extricated himself from trouble at the time but his (mis)-adventures in Boulogne seem to have left him with a permanent sense of guilt and the desire to make atonement. Leaving Boulogne in 1547, Bradford enrolled on 8 April of that year at the Inner Temple.

Around the same time he experienced a religious conversion, the crucial roles being played by Thomas Sampson who stimulated his interest in theology and by Bishop Hugh Latimer, whose fiery preaching first woke in him the need to make reparation for his dubious financial activities in France. There does appear to have been some collusion with Harrington at the time of the unauthorized transaction or fraudulent activity, as Bradford spent some considerable effort, between about February 1548 and February 1550, in persuading Harrington to return the money, which eventually he did. Bradford himself sold a number of his valuables and, abandoning the law, devoted himself to the study of the scriptures. In the early summer of 1548, Bradford gained admission to St Catherine's College, Cambridge, was awarded the degree of Master of Arts in October 1549 and by the following month had become a fellow of Pembroke. During his time in Cambridge he became a close associate of a number of Protestant scholars and theologians, including the Strasbourg theologian, Martin Bucer, who came to Cambridge in 1549, having been exiled to England. It was Bucer

who encouraged Bradford to become a preacher, while Bradford
– who never felt worthy of his mission – protested that he still
needed to study. Others disagreed, however, and on 10 August 1550
the Bishop of London, Nicholas Ridley, ordained him deacon, gave
him a preaching licence, and made him one of his own chaplains.
On St Bartholomew's day (24 August) 1551, he became a prebendary of St Paul's Cathedral and by the end of the year he was one
of six chaplains-in-ordinary to the King. Of these six chaplains, two
would at any time be serving at court while the other four travelled
around the country, preaching reformation; the speed at which
Bradford, who had come to theological studies fairly late in life,
was drawn into this elite of Protestant preachers suggests how
gifted an orator he was. He spent some time preaching in Lancashire and Cheshire in 1552, basing much of his ministry in his
native Manchester, but also visiting Liverpool, Bolton, Stockport
and Westchester. He was particularly effective in southern Lancashire, where he made many converts. Foxe describes his physical
appearance as 'somewhat tall and slender, spare of body, of a faint
sanguine colour, with an auburn beard'.

The Reverend John Cardmaker, Vicar of St Bride's Fleet Street
and prebendary of Wells Cathedral, was another larger-than-life
character who flourished under Edward. Cardmaker had been born
in about 1496 in Exeter, and was admitted underage to the Franciscan order. He spent sixteen years studying in Cambridge
and Oxford, receiving the degree of Bachelor of Theology from
Oxford in 1533. By the following year he was Warden of the Franciscans in Exeter, but during that same year he was converted to
the reformist cause after hearing Hugh Latimer preach. He himself
received a preaching licence from Thomas Cromwell in 1536 and
was assigned to preach to the Crutched Friars in London, after the
authorities had been informed that the friars were denying the
royal supremacy. Cardmaker left the Franciscans later that year and
subsequently married a widow, Catherine Testwood, which action
showed how closely he was allied to the reformed cause. From 1537
he received several benefices, while continuing to preach in the
London area. He was one of those quite prepared to speak out,

almost violently, against the Mass. In one sermon, preached at St Bride's in 1540, he declared that it was 'as profitable to hear Mass and see the sacrament as to kiss Judas' mouth'. He was interrogated in 1546, the year of Anne Askew's execution, as a supporter of Edward Crome, the evangelical Rector of St Mary Aldermary, whose sermon had created such a furore that year. During the reign of Edward VI, Cardmaker became one of the most prominent Protestant preachers in London, continuing to be uncompromising in his statements about the Mass, another notable remark being made in a lecture at St Paul's on 20 September 1549, and recorded by the Greyfriars chronicler: 'If God were a man, he was a six or seven foot of length, with the breadth, and if it be so how can it be that he should be in a piece of bread in a round cake on the altar?' (His assertion that if God were a man he would be at least six foot high and wide seems about as ridiculous as the idea that God should be contained in a cake, but perhaps the sense of his remark has been lost in transcription.)

Cardmaker, never one to toe the party line, supported Somerset in October 1549 while the City authorities (St Bride's being within the City) were slowly committing themselves to the other side. He rallied his own congregation to Somerset, in the name of Protestantism, fearing that a coup against Somerset would lead to the repeal of the reforms that had already been made. In this case at least he was proved wrong.

In 1551 the normally cautious Lord Rich came as close as he ever did to catastrophe. Until late November of that year he had presided, as Lord Chancellor, in the Court of Chancery, dealing with all business there without assistance. Though by then he had not been practising at the bar for many years, he had kept up his legal knowledge by attending the mootings in the Middle Temple and by acting as Chancellor of the Court of Augmentations where he had had to hear and decide various legal questions, as he had also done as a privy councillor. But on 26 November a commission was issued to Beaumont, the Master of the Rolls, to hear causes in his absence, an indication that Rich was seeking to make himself less visible. The reason for his anxiety was that he had allowed himself to become entangled in a plot by the former Lord Protector Somerset (who had been released from the Tower in early 1550 and reinstated as a member of the Privy Council) to wrest power back from Northumberland. This plot having failed, Somerset was now to be tried for felony and Rich, as Lord Chancellor, was expected to be created Lord High Steward in order to preside at his trial. But to play such a prominent part could make him vulnerable, or so he seems to have feared, in that his own ambiguous position might be exposed to scrutiny. This was why he organized a commission, authorizing the Master of the Rolls and others to hear causes for him in Chancery, and obtained Northumberland's permission for someone else to be appointed Lord High Steward. He privately informed Somerset that he had withdrawn from the trial out of friendship for his 'ancient friend' (such a loyal action, if it were genuine, would have been a first for Rich), but in reality he had no wish to align himself with either side at this point, as it was too dangerous. His anxiety was considerable, and justified, rumours circulating that the Lord Chancellor himself might be the next to be conveyed to the Tower. One of the stories being told of him was that he had sent a secret message of support to 'the Duke', meaning Somerset, but that the messenger had misunderstood and delivered the incriminating letter to the wrong Duke (Norfolk) who had informed Northumberland of its contents. While such carelessness sounds most unlike Rich, that such a story should be told of him does demonstrate his reputation for treachery and suggests that he was in a precarious position.

And so, like many politicians after him, Rich took refuge in alleged ill-health. He claimed to be very ill indeed, and certainly he must have judged his situation to be life-threatening, for he now voluntarily resigned the post he had been so determined to secure only four years previously, the lord chancellorship. He shut himself up in his house at St Bartholomew's and wrote to tell the King and Northumberland that he was mortally ill and could not even get as far as Whitehall or St James's Palace to deliver up the Great Seal. Northumberland, along with the Marquess of Winchester and others, came in person to collect it on 21 December 1551, Rich declaring that he was now devoting all his thought and energy towards preparations for 'a better world'. The Great Seal was delivered to the King at Westminster. Rich was succeeded as Lord Chancellor by Thomas Goodrich, the Bishop of Ely.

Even after Somerset's execution on 22 January 1552, it was widely rumoured that Rich would be imprisoned, but his lying low had its desired effect and no action was taken against him. He remained a privy councillor but rarely turned up to meetings of the Council for the rest of Edward's reign. He was made Lord Lieutenant of Essex on 16 May 1552 and returned to that county, avoiding being in London. He absented himself from the Parliament of 1552, again claiming sickness, and he was in fact the only privy councillor to absent himself from a session of Parliament during Edward's reign; in an astute political move, he appointed the Duke of Northumberland to act as his proctor.

If Rich furnished John Deane with an example of how to make the most of the opportunities presented by the dissolution of the monasteries, he also showed him that it was possible to survive in these perilous times. Deane never became sufficiently closely involved in politics or controversy to need to emulate Rich's strategic illness (it not being the policy under Edward to purge City clergy who had served under the previous administration, but merely to fill vacancies that occurred with reformers), but he must nevertheless at some point have taken a conscious decision to do his best to survive. In their determination both to stay alive and to play a part in their society (though those parts were very different, Deane's focus being primarily on service rather than on profiting himself), it could be argued that both men were more in tune with their times than those who refused to compromise and who were prepared to kill or be killed for their convictions. If this was a case of the survival of the fittest, then it was men like Deane and Rich who were 'fit', rather than their less adaptable, if more obviously heroic, contemporaries. It is worth remembering that it was not only works of theology that were being written at this period, and a work which encapsulates something of both Rich's and Deane's viewpoint (though it is unlikely that either would have known it at the time) was *Il Galateo* by the Florentine Giovanni Della Casa, published in Venice in 1558 and written between 1551 and 1555. *Il Galateo*, which concerns the rules of polite behaviour, was written in the wake of the collapse of the Italian city states, when the former ruling classes had become employees of the court bureaucracies, and a sort of swashbuckling valour was perhaps becoming less important than the more gentle arts of survival. Della Casa told his readers: 'it is advisable for us to obey not what is the best but what is the modern custom, just as we obey even those laws which are less than good until the state or whoever has the power to do so changes them'. Della Casa stressed the Aristotelian quality of *mediocritas*, the 'golden mean', as necessary for success, and in this sense we can see both Rich and Deane as 'mediocre' in their pursuit of the golden mean as the most appropriate modus vivendi for their time and place. It is also worth considering the question posed by Joseph Lemuel Chester in his 1861 monograph about the martyr John Rogers: 'It is easy enough to say what we would or would not have done, in such a case, at the present day; but the real question is, what should we have said and done, if we had been the actors in those times and under those circumstances?'

The harsh physical punishments meted out in the mid-sixteenth century for even minor infractions of the law – quite apart from the extreme punishment of death by burning – must have provided a very strong incentive for the average person to toe the line. One excruciating example among many is the case of Anthony Fowlkes, 'a gentleman' and merchant who, on 9 December 1552, was 'set on the pillory in Cheap' with his ear 'hard nailed to the pillory' for having swindled his customers and been tried for this offence by the Lord Mayor and Aldermen at Guildhall. After he had stood, attached by his ear, to the pillory all morning, he was allowed to go but was understandably reluctant to tear himself away (literally) as it would have meant leaving part of his ear behind. And so 'one of the beadles slit it upwards with a penknife to loose it'. The fact that the chronicler found this incident of sufficient interest to record it suggests that sometimes the method of release was to be yanked off the pillory, with or without one's ear.

Obedience to the law in 1552 included using the second version of the Book of Common Prayer, which had been revised to remove those survivals of old tradition that were still in the 1549 book. It was complete by the spring of 1552 but was not finally published until the autumn as an annex to the second Act of Uniformity, which declared this revised prayer book to contain the only permissible liturgy in the realm. It was used for the first time in St Paul's Cathedral on All Saints' day, 1 November, in 1552. 'This day all copes and vestments were put down through all England, and the prebendaries of Paul's left off their hoods and the Bishops their crosses, so that all priests and clerks should use no other vestments, at service or communion, but surplices only: as by an Act of Parliament in the Book of Common Prayer more at large is set out.' So John Deane, along with all other obedient clergy, now ceased to wear the eucharistic vestments – chasuble, stole, alb and maniple – that he had worn previously, exchanging them for a simple cassock and surplice to celebrate the Holy Communion. And, for all he knew, this and all the other changes recently introduced were to be permanent. We of a later generation know Edward's reign was brief and that many of his ecclesiastical policies were soon reversed, but there was no particular reason to anticipate this at the time. He was a young king and, though sudden death was a common occurrence, he was in no worse health than most of his subjects until the last few months of his life. His contemporaries could well have imagined that his reign would last as long as that of his father. So decisions to accept – or reject – change were for the long term.

To end this chapter, which has provided something of an interlude between the burnings under Henry VIII and the many burnings under Mary I, it is interesting to consider the reaction to the burning of Joan Boucher on the part of one of the most renowned clergymen to have flourished under Edward VI and of whom we will hear more in the next chapter. This is the Reverend John Rogers and the story is a striking one. Foxe recounts how, after Joan's sentencing, Rogers was approached by an unnamed friend, often assumed to have been Foxe himself. This friend urged

Rogers, who was a prebendary of St Paul's and Vicar of the church of St Sepulchre-without-Newgate, a few hundred yards from St Bartholomew's, to intercede on behalf of Joan, 'exhorting and beseeching him that he would use his utmost influence with the Archbishop of Canterbury, that, her error being as far as possible chastised and restrained, the life at least of the unhappy woman might be spared'. The conversation between the two men is reminiscent of the arguments over the parable of the wheat and tares discussed earlier, the friend suggesting that if Joan were allowed to live, she might in time be cured of her erroneous opinions and would 'corrupt' at most only a few people, whereas her execution might actually promote her opinions. It would therefore be more sensible as well as more merciful to keep Joan in close custody where she could not have access to what the friend termed 'persons of weak mind', while also being given the opportunity to repent. But Rogers, after listening to him, declared that he nevertheless thought Joan deserved to die.

His friend continued to try to persuade him otherwise and then, when he had realized Rogers could not be so persuaded, begged that at least he petition for another method of execution, protesting that Christians should not follow the example of 'the Papists' by consigning someone to 'the horrors of a death so tormenting'. But Rogers disagreed. This form of punishment, 'by which men are burned alive', was, in his opinion, 'the least agonizing of all, and sufficiently gentle'. At this, his friend responded with passion, striking Rogers's hand which he had been holding, and uttering the prophetic words: 'Well, perchance you may yet find that you, yourself, shall have your hands full of this so gentle fire.'

Chapter Nine

'Turn, and turn, and turn again'

✠

No sooner Edward was laid in his tomb,
But England was the slaughter-house of Rome:
Gardner and Bonner were from prison turned,
And whom they pleased were either saved or burned:
Queen Mary, imitating Jezebel,
Advanced again the Ministers of Hell:
Then tyranny began to tyrannise –
Tortures and torments then they did devise:
Then Master Rogers, with a faith most fervent,
Was burned, and died (in Smithfield) God's true servant.

> from the original edition of a poem by John Taylor,
> the 'Water Poet', in the *Book of Martyrs*, London, 1639

*

'Turn, and turn, and turn again, is the very life and property of our popish prelates, and of the whole crown-shaven clergy.'

> from *The confession of John Rogers made and*
> *that should have been made, if I might have been heard,*
> *the 28 & 29 of January, Anno Domini 1555*

EDWARD VI DIED on 6 July 1553 in Greenwich, where his body was embalmed and placed in a lead coffin; he was not buried until over four weeks later. In his will, Edward had named his Protestant cousin and Northumberland's daughter-in-law, Lady Jane Grey, as his successor, overturning the claims of his half-sisters Mary and Elizabeth, and on Sunday 9 July, the day before Jane was officially proclaimed Queen, Bishop Nicholas Ridley, by order of the Privy Council, had preached a sermon at Paul's Cross in which he denounced the Princess Mary as a thoroughgoing papist and declared that, had she become queen, she would have betrayed the kingdom to a foreign power. This outspoken and injudicious language did its speaker no favours in later days. By the next Sunday, when it was the turn of John Rogers to preach at Paul's Cross, Jane's claim to the throne was under threat, with Mary having rallied her supporters and Northumberland having set out from London with his troops in the hope of countering them. Rogers sensibly avoided politics on this occasion, confining himself to speaking about the Gospel text set for the day. Three days after this sermon, on 19 July, the Privy Council having switched sides and Northumberland's support having collapsed, Mary Tudor was proclaimed Queen at the Cross in Cheapside.

The chronicler Wriothesley's account of the proclamation suggests overwhelming support for Mary in the City of London:

> Then [the Privy Council] declaring to the Lord Mayor and his brethren that he must ride with them into Cheap to proclaim a new Queen, which was the Lady Mary's Grace, daughter to King Henry VIII, which was so joyful news that for joy all the people present that heard it wept, and before the Council had ridden up the hill to Paul's Churchyard the people were so great assembled running into Cheap that the Lords could scarce pass by; the Lord Mayor and the Council coming to the Cross in Cheap, where the proclamation should be made, Mr Garter, the King of Arms, in his rich coat of arms, with a trumpeter being ready, and, [when] the trumpet blew, there was such shout of the people with casting up of caps and crying, God save Queen Mary, that the style of the proclamation could not be heard, the people were so joyful, both man, woman, and child. The proclamation there ended, the Lord Mayor and all the Council rode straight to Paul's Church and went up into the quire, where the canticle of Te Deum laudamus was solemnly sung with the organs going, and that done, the Council departed and commanded Mr Garrett the Sheriff,

with the King of Arms and trumpeter, to see the proclamation made immediately in other accustomed places within the City. All the people and citizens of the City of London for such joyful news made great and many fires through all the streets and lanes within the said City, with setting tables in the streets and banqueting also, with all the bells ringing in every parish church in London till 10 of the clock at night, that the inestimable joys and rejoicing of the people cannot be reported.

The threat to the Protestant reforms introduced during Edward's brief reign was apparent almost immediately. Before the end of July, Queen Mary had told the imperial ambassadors that she was unhappy about her half-brother being buried without the benefit of the traditional liturgy and ritual, and asked for their advice. As the newly acceded monarch, she was legally head and governor of the Church of England, however much she did not believe in that concept, and the only legal form of public worship in the realm was the 1552 Book of Common Prayer. The representatives of the Emperor Charles V advised circumspection, both in order to avoid any violent reaction and because Edward had been, in Catholic eyes, a heretic and schismatic, so that it would be inappropriate (as well as illegal) to use the old liturgy for his funeral and burial. On 2 August Ambassador Simon Renard sent a secret memorandum to Mary, suggesting the compromise of Edward being buried according to the Prayer Book ritual but without Mary herself in attendance; she could instead arrange for a traditional Requiem Mass to be said for her half-brother elsewhere.

Despite John Rogers having made no attack on Mary and her attachment to traditional Catholicism, the mere fact of his having succeeded Bishop Ridley in the Paul's Cross pulpit, along with his obvious ability as a reformist preacher which was recognized by supporters and opponents alike, made him a marked man from the outset of Mary's reign. For the public, the first signs that the old ways had returned were the release and reinstatement of the bishops imprisoned under Edward, without their even having to wait for a formal nullification of their deprivations. 'The 5 of August, being Saturday, Doctor Bonner, the old Bishop of London, prisoner in the Marshalsea, and Doctor Tunstall, the old Bishop of Durham, prisoner in the King's Bench, had their pardon sent them by the Queen, under the great seal of England, and were discharged out of prison; the Bishop of London went to his house at Paul's immediately.' 'The 5 of August at 7 o'clock at night came home Edmund Bonner bishop from the Marshalsea like a bishop, that all the people by the way bade him welcome home [both] man and woman, and as many of the women as might kissed him, and so came to Paul's, and knelt on the steps and said his prayers; and then the people rang the bells for joy.' For John Rogers, living at this time with his large family in a clergy house in the precincts of St Paul's, this must have been less an occasion of rejoicing than of anxiety. But, rather than lying low and waiting to see what Bonner's return might mean for his own circumstances, Rogers chose on the very next day to preach a trenchant anti-Catholic sermon at Paul's Cross. According to Foxe, this was 'a most godly and vehement sermon, avowing and confirming such true doctrine as he and others had there taught in King Edward's days, exhorting the people constantly to remain in the same and to beware of all pestilent Popery, idolatry, and superstition'. As a result of this sermon, Rogers was called before the Privy Council but succeeded in defending himself on this occasion, pointing out, quite accurately, that there was as yet nothing illegal in what he had said, the Acts in favour of the Protestant religion enacted under Edward VI having not yet been repealed. This was, however, the last sermon Rogers ever preached.

Despite the compromise suggested by Renard to which Mary had agreed, there was considerably more pomp attending Edward's funeral than might have been expected for a firmly Protestant king. His coffin was transported by river from Greenwich to Whitehall Palace, and on the night of Monday 7 August (the day following Rogers's anti-Catholic sermon) it was carried from there to Westminster Abbey in a traditional procession involving a large number of choirboys and men in surplices, as well as twelve of Henry VIII's 'bedesmen' from the former Observant Franciscan house at Greenwich. There were banners, heralds, and horses decked in black velvet. The coffin itself was draped in blue velvet, borne on a chariot covered in cloth of gold, and topped by an effigy of Edward, carved by the Italian sculptor Niccolò Bellini. In the Abbey on 8 August Archbishop Cranmer reverted to the practice allowed by the 1549, rather than the 1552, Prayer Book by including a Eucharist within the funeral service. The only other reforming bishop present was Hugh Latimer; the sermon was preached by the newly restored Bishop of Chichester, George Day, and it was not laudatory about Edward's achievements. Mary remained in the Tower of London where she duly attended a Requiem Mass for her half-brother, at which the celebrant was Stephen Gardiner, restored to his bishopric of Winchester. After the Mass, Mary moved upriver from the Tower to Richmond Palace, leaving behind as prisoners Lady Jane Grey and the Duke of Northumberland.

There is an indication in the 1563 edition of Foxe's *Acts and Monuments* that the return to the old, Catholic, ways was welcome at John Deane's church for, as early as 11 August, well before any changes were made official, 'did a priest say mass at St Bartholomew's in Smithfield; but before he had half done, he was glad to take him to his legs, for as he was lifting up the bread, there were stones flung at him, and one hit him between the shoulders, as the bread was over his head; so that he would not tarry, to make an end of his mask'. Whether the priest involved in this incident was Deane himself is impossible to say for sure, but the celebration could certainly not have happened without his knowledge and approval. The sharpness of the division in the City of London is well illustrated by this incident, the traditional Mass being celebrated at St Bartholomew's even as, just a few hundred yards away, the vicar of the neighbouring church of St Sepulchre's was inveighing against such practices – though Rogers would also have been the first to condemn stone-throwing, his preferred weapon being always, and only, words.

John Rogers was born in about 1500 in Deritend, then a small village or hamlet in the suburbs of Birmingham but now an area just outside the city centre. He was educated at Pembroke Hall,

Cambridge, where he received the degree of Bachelor of Arts in 1526. He was from the outset a promising scholar, and a man of much energy and application. In the same year that he obtained his degree, he was made a junior canon of Cardinal College, Oxford – as was John Frith, though Rogers does not appear at this time to have been involved with the 'new learning'. Instead he was ordained priest and on 26 December 1532, during the period when some of the early reformers were being burnt in Smithfield, Rogers became Rector of the church of Holy Trinity the Less in the City of London (the church at which the diarist Henry Machyn later became parish clerk) and officiated there for nearly two years. At that time the patrons of the church were the prior and convent of St Mary Overy in Southwark, so Rogers would have been appointed to his rectorship by them (it is one of the ironies of his life that the church of St Mary Overy, which became a parish church after the priory was dissolved, was to be a significant place for him in later, unhappier, days). He resigned as Rector of Holy Trinity the Less towards the end of 1534, moving to the great trading city of Antwerp, where he served as chaplain to the Merchant Adventurers for about three years. By the time he left London, he may already have been entertaining doubts about his future in the established Church, having begun to be influenced by the advocates of reform, but there is no suggestion that he left the country to take up this new post other than through choice. In Antwerp Rogers became acquainted with William Tyndale, who was living there as the guest of an English merchant called Thomas Poyntz and whom we encountered earlier through his friendship with John Frith (see Chapter 2). Rogers would already have known of Tyndale by name through his works, including his translations of the New Testament and his book *The Obedience of a Christian Man* (banned in England in 1530).

More than becoming acquainted with Tyndale, Rogers followed Frith's example by joining him in his work of translating the Bible and, after Tyndale's arrest in 1535 (and subsequent execution on 6 October 1536), he continued that work on his own, rescuing Tyndale's work and bringing to completion what he had begun.

Despite most of Tyndale's property being confiscated on the evening of his arrest, Rogers managed to keep hold of the manuscript of Tyndale's translation of part of the Old Testament. That he was able to do this suggests that he was not yet known to the authorities as a Protestant sympathizer; he had not been in Antwerp for more than a few months, and may have been only a recent convert. Remaining in Antwerp, Rogers began to work on assembling a complete Bible, compiling the Old Testament translation from Tyndale's manuscript supplemented by Miles Coverdale's version which had been printed in 1535, and using Tyndale's 1534 version of the New Testament. More than merely copying what had already been completed and filling in the missing parts, Rogers approached his work as a scholar, using his knowledge of the Church Fathers, including St Ambrose and St Augustine, to gloss his text, and showing evidence of having read widely and with understanding. He must also have worked with extraordinary application and speed, for by the summer of 1537 copies of the complete translation, printed in Antwerp by Edward Whitchurch and Roger Grafton (the latter, a friend of Rogers, being a London grocer and Merchant Adventurer), were being sent to Thomas Cromwell in England. Rogers did not use his own name as translator and editor, but chose instead the pseudonym 'Thomas Matthew', an amalgam of two of Jesus's disciples, and the version became known as 'the Matthew Bible'. Archbishop Cranmer wrote to Cromwell in August about the translation, giving it his general approval – 'I like it better than any other translation heretofore made' – and expressing the view that the bishops appointed to the official task of translation were unlikely to produce a better one 'till a day after doomsday'. A few days later Cranmer wrote again to Cromwell, thanking him for having obtained the King's licence to have this translation published and distributed. It went on to form the basis of the 'Great Bible', from which Anne Askew had made such a point of reading in Lincoln Cathedral in 1544.

The 'Matthew Bible' is a lively translation, many of its verses familiar to anyone acquainted with the later King James 'Authorized' version, but with an earthiness and directness that show this was primarily the work of an orator, gifted in the pulpit, knowing how to deploy his tongue and not only his pen to good effect. It also conveys a sense of urgency, reminding the reader that Rogers, and the translators whose work he built on, were working against time, with a mixture of delight and desperation – this was an unprecedented, joyous task, yet fraught with danger; it had to be completed as quickly as possible, for who knew when they might be interrupted, arrested, even put to death for their endeavours? They were right in perceiving, during Henry's reign and particularly while Cromwell was in power, a 'window of opportunity' when their work might be acceptable and capable of dissemination, but the forces militating against acceptance were also very powerful and there was no knowing how long the opportunity might last. The sense of urgency was compounded by the belief that what they were doing was of enormous significance: those at work on delivering the scriptures in English to an English audience were sure they were doing the work of God, that this was their calling and it could not be ignored; and it must be done to the best of their ability. This sense of urgency gives the work its visceral quality and immediacy, and it is the version I have chosen to use for biblical quotations in this book – both because it would have been familiar to the reformers of the Tudor period, and because it is so alive, so much the vivid language of those who were prepared to die in order to deliver these words to their readers and listeners.

The Matthew Bible is dedicated to 'the most noble and gracious Prince King Henry the Eight, King of England and of France, Lord of Ireland etc. Defender of the faith: and under God the chief and supreme head of the Church of England'. The importance attached to this work of translation is clear from words within that dedication: 'It is no vulgar or common thing which is offered into your grace's protection, but the blessed word of God: which is everlasting and cannot fail, though heaven and earth should perish.' There is also expressed the belief that recent generations of churchmen have prevented this word of God being heard by the people: 'Long and oft was it obscured and darkened, yea and in manner clean abolished in the time of the commonwealth of Israel.

The wily juggling of the priests in persuading the princes and rulers to be conformable to their inventions, and the rash believing people, which thought everything an oracle that the priests breathed into their breasts, did oft and many times fill all full of superstition and Idolatry.' There is also a reference to Josiah, on which Cranmer must have drawn in his sermon on the occasion of the coronation of Edward VI: 'Josiah after he had once read the book of the law found in the temple, let no time slip till he had called all Israel together, put down all kinds of Idolatry, and held the feast of Passover according to the law.' Rogers and his publishers liken Henry to the Old Testament characters to whom his son would also be likened: 'That Hezekiah and Josiah were unto Israel, the same is your grace unto the Realm of England: yea the godly have great hope that your praise shall be far above theirs.'

That in the midst of this frenetic work of translation and scholarship, John Rogers found time to marry and went on to produce a large number of children in a short time testifies to his great energy and zest for life (as well as to the remarkable qualities of his wife). His taking a wife also signalled a path of no return as far as the Catholic Church was concerned. Rogers married a Flemish woman named Adriana de Weyden (or Pratt – both names meaning 'meadow') in 1536 or 1537; Adriana was a relative of Jacob van Meteren who had sponsored Miles Coverdale's Bible of 1535. Rogers stayed in Antwerp for six years, and then left with his young family for Wittenberg where he continued to study, being awarded further degrees in November 1540, and becoming one of four superintendents of the Lutheran Church in the Dietmarsh region, in the north-west of Germany. At about the end of 1543, he became pastor at Meldorf, the capital of the Dietmarsh region, and superintendent of the Meldorf district. Prior to Rogers taking up this post, Philipp Melanchthon had written to the superintendent of one of the other districts to recommend him, writing of him in glowing terms as 'a learned man . . . gifted with great ability, which he sets off with a noble character . . . he will be careful to live in concord with his colleagues . . . his integrity, trustworthiness and constancy in every duty make him worthy of the love and support of all good men'. The only problem, according to Melanchthon, was that Rogers spoke strongly accented German (presumably with a mixture of accents from Birmingham, London and Antwerp), but that would correct itself over time. Rogers and his growing family stayed in Meldorf until the spring of 1548.

By 1 August Rogers was back in England, signing the preface to his translation of Melanchthon's *Weighing of the Interim* with that date and the words: 'at London, in Edward Whitchurch's house'. It is possible that he was staying alone with his publisher, paving the way for bringing his whole family to England (by now he and Adriana had eight children). As noted in the previous chapter, there was no particular reason at the time to suppose that Edward's reign, or the reforms introduced during it, would be short-lived, and hence no reason for a reformist clergyman to imagine that returning to England, complete with wife and children, would turn out to be a life-threatening enterprise. And, if he had had any doubts about his position, he had only to consider the Archbishop of Canterbury, who was now living openly with his (second) wife.

And so on 11 October 1548 Rogers made his return to parochial ministry in the City of London, being inducted into the rectory of St Matthew's, Friday Street, off Cheapside. Eighteen months later, on 10 May 1550, he was also given the rectorship of St Margaret Moyses in the same street and, three days after that, he became vicar of one of the leading London churches, St Sepulchre-without-Newgate, just opposite Newgate prison and a few hundred yards from St Bartholomew's (St Sepulchre's had originally been a possession of the priory). In the following year, on 27 August, he became a prebendary of St Paul's Cathedral, being awarded the prebend of St Pancras by Bishop Nicholas Ridley, and he subsequently surrendered his two livings in Friday Street. He was also appointed lecturer in divinity at the cathedral. In April 1552 his wife and their children who had been born in Germany were naturalized (which indicates how secure he felt in England at that time).

While at St Sepulchre's, Rogers became embroiled in a dispute about clergy dress. It was the custom for the clergy to wear square caps, and sometimes gowns and tippets (ceremonial scarves), when they were out and about. Some of the reforming clergy of Edward's reign refused to wear such garments, Rogers being among the most vociferous, despite these clothes having been prescribed by Parliament; he insisted on wearing no other distinctive garb than his round cap. He seems to have viewed the wearing of any other special clothing for clergy as reminiscent of the practices of the Roman Church; hence his refusal to comply. A 'portrait' which purports to be of Rogers is from a later period and is at best based on a lost sketch, more probably on recollections of him passed down through his numerous descendants. He is shown with a neatly trimmed beard, and not dressed in specifically clerical attire. Apart from this dispute, Rogers's ministry was free of controversy until the untimely death of Edward VI radically altered his position and that of all reformist – and particularly married reformist – clergy in the kingdom.

On Sunday 13 August 1553 the newly reinstated Bishop Bonner was present at Paul's Cross for a sermon given by the leading conservative preacher and one of Queen Mary's chaplains, Gilbert Bourne (who later became Bishop of Bath and Wells). Bourne included in his opening words a prayer for the dead, declared that Bonner had been wrongfully imprisoned, and attacked the preachers of reform, including John Rogers. According to Antonio de Guaras, a Spanish merchant living in London who wrote an account of the events surrounding Mary's accession, Bourne declared that Bishop Bonner had been imprisoned for four years for having preached the truth about the 'Holy Sacrament of the Altar' and other Catholic doctrines. There was a serious commotion at this – it became known as the Paul's Cross riot – and a dagger was thrown at Bourne, missing him but hitting the post of the pulpit. As the chronicler of the Grey Friars recorded the event: 'Item the 13 day of August preached Master Bourne at Paul's Cross at the commandment of the Queen's Grace, and there was pulled out of the pulpit by vagabonds, and one threw his dagger at him.' Machyn, the chronicler and parish clerk of Holy Trinity the Less, who recorded so many of the public events and ceremonies of

Mary I's reign, was even more graphic: 'The 13 day of August did preach at Paul's Cross Doctor Bourn parson of High Ongar, in Essex, the Queen's chaplain, and there was a great uproar and shouting at his sermon, as it were like mad people, what young people and women as ever was heard as hurly-burly, and casting up of caps.' Some among the crowd were also disturbed by what they had heard about a Requiem Mass for the late King having been celebrated in the Tower of London, where Mary was currently staying. The Lord Mayor and Aldermen, who were in attendance, had some difficulty dispersing the crowd, and Bishop Bonner had to be led through St Paul's to safety. Wriothesley's account of this event is also very graphic:

> Sunday the 13 of August Doctor Bourne, one of the Prebendaries of Paul's, preached at Paul's Cross by the Queen's appointment. And in the sermon time, because he prayed for the souls departed, and also in declaring the wrongful imprisonment of Doctor Bonner, late Bishop of London, certain lewd and ill-disposed persons made a hollering and such a crying 'thou liest!', that the audience was so disturbed, that the preacher was so afraid by the commotion of the people, that one Bradford, a preacher, pulled him back, and spoke to the people, desiring them in Christ's name and for the blood of Christ to pacify themselves, which people were so rude that they would not, but one lewd person drew a dagger and cast it at the preacher, which, as God would, hit against one of the posts of the pulpit. My Lord Mayor then and Aldermen rising from the places, went about the churchyard to cause the people to depart away, who were so rude that in a great space they would not depart, but cried 'kill him!'; and so, with great pain and fear the said Bourne was conveyed from the pulpit to the schoolhouse in Paul's Churchyard. The Lord Courtney and the Lady Marquess of Exeter stood above my Lord Mayor, with Doctor Bonner, Bishop of London, who were sore astonished to see the humour of the people, and had as much ado by their means

to see the said Bishop conveyed in safety through the church, the people were so rude.

John Rogers was also present at this sermon and it was he, along with fellow reformer John Bradford, who played the chief role in calming the angry crowd, as the protestors knew and trusted them.

Following these stormy events at Paul's Cross, Rogers was called for a second time before the Privy Council, meeting in the Tower of London, on 16 August 1553. He was not alone in being summoned before the Council, there being much anger against the City authorities too for having allowed matters to get so out of hand. The City was in crisis, as is clear from Wriothesley's account:

This business was so heinously declared to the Queen and her Council, that my Lord Mayor and Aldermen were sent for to the Queen's Council to the Tower the 14 and 15 of August, and it was sore laid to their charge, that the liberties of the City had like to have been taken away from them, and to depose the Lord Mayor, straightly charging the Mayor and Aldermen to make a direct answer to them on Wednesday the 16 of August whether they would rule the City in peace and good order, or else they would set other rulers over them, whereupon my Lord Mayor caused all the Commons of the Livery to be warned to appear at the Guildhall on Tuesday the 15 of August. And, they being assembled, Mr Recorder declared to the Commons the sore words and threatenings of the Queen's Council, praying them to show their minds whether they would stick to my Lord Mayor and his brethren, to see such malefactors and rude people reformed, or else their liberties should be taken away from them; the Commons answering, that by the good help and means of my Lord Mayor and his brethren they would be so aiding and assisting to them, that they trusted the Queen's Highness nor the Council should have no more such cause against the City, but that such malefactors and offenders should be punished; which answer was made by my Lord Mayor and Aldermen to the Queen's Council, at the Tower, on Wednesday the 16 of August, and was well accepted and taken.

Also, my Lord Mayor caused a proclamation to be made in the City, that if any person could bring knowledge who threw the dagger at the preacher on Sunday, at Paul's Cross, should have £5 for his labour.

Rogers was not accused of anything new on 16 August (having already defended himself once), but was being viewed with suspicion on account of the part he and John Bradford had played three days earlier; if, so the argument appeared to go, these two men had had the authority to quell the disturbance at Paul's Cross, they had also had the power to provoke it. After this second appearance before them, the Council instructed that Rogers was to be placed under house arrest. The minute of the meeting reads: 'John Rogers, *alias* Matthew, a seditious preacher, ordered by the Lords of the Council to keep himself as prisoner in his house at Paul's, without conference of any person other than such as are daily with him in [his] household, until such time as he hath contrary commandment.' In other words, Rogers was to become his own jailer, an instruction which he obeyed meticulously. He seems to have made a decision early on that he was not going to run for it, despite being given ample opportunity to do so, for no guards were assigned to him and the cathedral clergy might have been only too glad if he had disappeared. Many other people of his religious persuasion were already packing up their possessions and heading for such Protestant cities as Strasbourg, Frankfurt, Zurich and Geneva, and there is even a suggestion that Stephen Gardiner was encouraging this exodus, while outwardly condemning those who fled. According to the imperial ambassador Simon Renard, Gardiner had sounded pleased with himself as he related how 'When he hears of any preacher, he summons him to appear at his house, and the preacher, fearing he may be put in the Tower, does not appear, but on the contrary absents himself.' But John Rogers chose not to absent himself. His house, henceforth his prison, was in the cathedral close so, while imprisoned, he remained very much at the centre of the scene of action.

Two days after Rogers was placed under house arrest the Queen issued a proclamation on religion in which she affirmed her own Catholic faith, but announced that she was not minded to compel her subjects to adopt it – that is, *not yet*: 'unto such time as further order by common assent may be taken therein'. In the meantime, no one was to stir up trouble over religion or call each other names – neither 'papist' nor 'heretic'. Mary's biographer John Edwards has pointed out that this was more a gagging order than a measure aimed at promoting toleration.

Further restrictions on free speech were issued on 21 August, with a proclamation to the effect that every subject was prohibited from reasoning against or discussing the actions of the Queen and her Council, whatever they might be. Steps were also taken that day (the City authorities demonstrating their zeal) against some of those held responsible for the uproar on 13 August, including another City cleric: 'The 21 day of August were set on the pillory 2 men, one a priest and another a barber, and both their ears nailed to the pillory, the parson of St Ethelburga within Bishopsgate for heinous words and seditious words against the Queen's Majesty Highness at the sermon at Paul's Cross, that was the Sunday the 13 day of August, and for the uproar that was there done.' The Rector of St Ethelburga's was given a further stint on the pillory two days later, his first experience of this painful and embarrassing punishment not having succeeded in silencing him. (The nails were pulled out with a pair of pincers.) It is perhaps not surprising that most of the City clergy complied with the Queen's instructions.

During the period of Rogers's house arrest, full Catholic ceremonial was gradually restored in the cathedral, Bishop Bonner celebrating Mass at the high altar for the first time in four years on 7 October, in his full pontifical vestments. Three days later a successor was appointed to Rogers's prebendal stall, despite his not having been tried or officially deprived of it. And on 1 November, the feast of All Saints, the Protestant practices in language and dress introduced into the cathedral precisely one year earlier were effectively obliterated as 'the sacrament of the body and blood of Christ was hanged up again in Paul's Church over the high altar under a rich canopy of cloth of gold, after the old custom of the Church'. In December, by which time Archbishop Cranmer had been arraigned for high treason in Guildhall and condemned to death, an Act was passed stipulating that no service was to be used in churches other than what had been in use in the last year of Henry VIII's reign (in other words, this made the use of the English services introduced under Edward illegal). Of even more concern to Rogers and many other Protestant clergy, a proclamation issued in the same month announced that no married priest was to be allowed to minister or say Mass.

There was a way back for married priests, but it involved not only repudiation of wife and family and banishment from the dioceses in which they had previously worked, but also the ritual humiliation of public penance. A display of what Rogers could have expected had he been willing to return to the Catholic fold took place on 4 November 1554. This is what happened at Paul's Cross that day to three married priests, one a former canon of the Priory of Elsing Spital, one a Black Friar (or Dominican) and the third an Austin Friar (one has to remember that all these priests would have been dispossessed of their monastic life under Henry and adapted to changed circumstances; now they were being dispossessed again, this time of their family life, as well as of their dignity):

> And this was their penance: first to come out of the vestry with sheets upon their backs, and each of them a rod in their hands with a taper lit, and first came and kneeled before the high altar, and there the suffragan gave them their discipline [i.e. struck them with the rod]; and then went down before the cross: and when the preacher had taken his benediction of the Bishop in the middle of the church, they came down unto the Bishop, and kneeled down in the middle of the church, and there had their disciplines of him, and he kissed them; and so went unto the cross, and stood there all the sermon time, and when he came unto the biddings they turned unto the preacher and kneeled down and asked forgiveness there of him, and then he showed their opinions openly in the pulpit.

The preacher on this occasion was Dr Nicholas Harpsfield, Archdeacon of Canterbury, who played a leading part throughout Mary's reign in the persecution of Protestants.

By the time these three priests underwent their experience of readmission to ministry, Rogers had been incarcerated in Newgate prison for over nine months, having been removed from the relative comfort of his own house on 27 January. Bishop Bonner was partly behind this move; perhaps he had had enough of having a recalcitrant clergyman occupying a house in his cathedral close, and of being reminded of him every time he walked into the cathedral. But the fact that the move occurred only two days after the start of an armed rebellion spearheaded by Sir Thomas Wyatt, the impetus for which was primarily anger and fear at the prospect of the Queen's proposed marriage to a (Catholic) foreigner, Philip II of Spain, the son of Emperor Charles V, would also suggest that the City authorities were anxious to ensure that a Protestant as prominent as Rogers was securely under lock and key during this time of instability and potential danger to the Queen. (The Wyatt rebellion and its failure also had the consequence of Lady Jane Grey being executed in February. She had been tried and condemned towards the end of the previous year, but there had been some hope her life would be spared; the involvement of her father on the side of Wyatt put paid to that hope.) The insecurity suffered by Rogers's wife and ten children (an eleventh was conceived while he was under house arrest) – and his consequent anxiety about them – must have been considerable, as theirs was officially a cathedral house, from which they could have been ousted at any time. He was also receiving no stipend, despite legally being still the incumbent of St Sepulchre's. So both he and his family were in desperate need, the costs of board and lodging in prison being at the prisoner's, or their friends', expense, as we have already seen in the case of Anne Askew.

Newgate was a very unpleasant place to be at this period, the atmosphere being 'fetid and corrupt'. A yeoman of the guard, a fervent Protestant called Edward Underhill, was sent there in 1553 for having written a ballad against the Queen and he left a vivid description of 'the evil savours and great unquietness of the lodgings', emphasizing how hard it was to bear 'so much noise of prisoners, and evil savours'. The smell that came out of the kitchens was one of the worst. Other unpleasant smells were caused by the airlessness of the damp old stone buildings, and the fact that many of the prisoners were kept under ground. One of the greatest hardships for Rogers, apart from now being separated from his wife and children, was that he was also separated from his books. The company of the people who loved him and the freedom to write and study had been of immense support to him during his house imprisonment; now these comforts were withdrawn.

During his subsequent trial Rogers claimed to have had no idea of what was going on in the world outside while he was in Newgate, including the fact that, on the last day of November 1554, St Andrew's day, the Church in England was officially reunited with the Church of Rome, to the great joy of the Queen and the overt (or stage-managed) joy of everyone else. Parliament had met in the days leading up to the 'day of reconciliation' to vote on the matter, though as the preparations must all have been in place by then, the vote could hardly have been expected to be 'no'. Rather, it was intended as a public display of assent, with only two Commons members out of 440 having the courage to vote against reunion with Rome. On the day itself the chapter of the Order of the Garter met at Westminster and a Solemn Mass was celebrated in the Abbey, attended by about 500 other English people and 600 people connected to Philip II of Spain, Mary's husband and King of England since 25 July (for, despite the considerable opposition at court and throughout the country to this marriage, Mary had insisted on going through with it). Later, at the Palace of Westminster, the Queen sat on a dais, flanked by King Philip on her left and her distant relative Cardinal Reginald Pole, fully vested as a papal legate, on her right. Bishop Stephen Gardiner, now Lord Chancellor (he had been in that post since the early days of Mary's reign), read out the resolution of the preceding day of both Houses of Parliament. The climax of the ceremony came when Cardinal Pole pronounced the absolution: 'after a short address in which he once more referred to England's true Christian past, he absolved the kingdom of the sin of schism in the name of the three Persons of the Trinity. There were then "Amens", and Mary is recorded as having wept throughout.'

John Deane would have been involved in the celebrations two days later, on the first Sunday of Advent, when Cardinal Pole and King Philip came to the City and to St Paul's Cathedral, with a great retinue, the cardinal arriving by boat from Lambeth Palace, the King by land from Westminster. The scene was described by Machyn:

> The 2 day of December did come to Paul's all priests and clerks with their copes and crosses, and all the crafts in their livery, and my Lord Mayor and the Aldermen, against my Lord Cardinal's coming; and at the Bishop of London's place my Lord Chancellor and all the bishops tarrying for my Lord Cardinal coming, that was at 9 of the clock, for he landed at Baynard's Castle; and there my Lord Mayor received him, and brought him to Paul's, and so my Lord Chancellor and my Lord Cardinal and all the bishops went up into the quire with their mitres; and at 10 of the clock the King's Grace came to Paul's to hear mass with 400 of guard, 100 English, 100 High Almains, 100 Spaniards, 100 Swissmen, and many lords and knights, and heard mass. Both the Queen's Chapel and the King's and Paul's choir sang.

The music composed for this great occasion included a motet by the Franco-Flemish composer Orlando di Lasso, who was present in London at the time, entitled *Te spectant, Reginalde, poli* ('The heavens observe you, Reginald'). Here the author of the text, probably di Lasso himself, was indulging in wordplay, with the similarity between the word for 'heavens' (*poli*) and the cardinal's surname, Pole. Bishop Gardiner preached to an enormous congregation outside (totalling about 15,000) from Paul's Cross pulpit on the theme of restoration and the end of the nightmare provoked by Henry VIII's split from Rome and, at the conclusion, everyone present knelt to receive absolution.

With the English Church reconciled to Rome, the position of the imprisoned Protestants (for Rogers was only one of several) became more immediately perilous. In January 1555 Parliament re-enacted the heresy laws of Richard II, Henry IV and Henry V, which had been repealed under Edward VI, thereby bringing back the death penalty for heresy. On 22 January, only the second day after the re-enacted laws came into force, Lord Chancellor Gardiner summoned all the Protestant clergy currently imprisoned in London to his house at St Mary Overy to inform them of the Queen's clemency if they would abandon their previous teaching. The officials assembled alongside the Lord Chancellor included the bishops of Durham (Cuthbert Tunstall once again), Worcester (Nicholas Heath, who would succeed Gardiner as Lord Chancellor and whom Rogers referred to as 'my former master', relating to his time as a student at Cambridge) and Ely (Thomas Thirlby), Lord William Paget, Lord William Howard, Secretary Sir John Bourne and Sir Richard Southwell. It is possible that other members of the Privy Council were also present, but these are the names mentioned by Rogers himself in his account of the proceedings. He succeeded in the last days of his life in writing a record of his trial (if it can be called that); he hid the document in his cell, and his wife and one of his sons, Daniel, retrieved it after his death. Whether he had somehow managed to indicate its existence to them or, more likely, let them know that he hoped to be able to write such an account, or whether they were merely searching the cell by chance, looking for any small memento of him, is a matter of conjecture.

Lord Chancellor Gardiner began by asking the prisoner, John Rogers, whether he was aware of the present state of the realm. 'No, my Lord,' replied Rogers, 'I have been kept in close prison, and apart from some general things said at the table, when I was at dinner or supper, I have heard nothing.'

'General things, general things!' replied Gardiner, mockingly. 'You have surely heard of my Lord Cardinal's arrival, sir, and that the *whole* Parliament has received his blessing.' Gardiner went on to tell Rogers of how all but one of the 160 members of the House of Lords had assented to the reunification with Rome and received pardon for the schism. 'How say you?' he then demanded. 'Are you content to unite and knit yourself to the faith of the Catholic Church, with us? Will you do that?'

Rogers, like Anne Askew before him, chose to interpret the word 'catholic' in its wider sense, and replied that he never had and never would dissent from the catholic Church. 'No,' Gardiner said crossly, 'I'm talking about the state of the Catholic Church as it now is in England, having received the Pope as supreme head.'

Rogers was uncompromising in his reply: 'I know no other head but Christ of his catholic Church, neither will I acknowledge the Bishop of Rome to have any more authority than any other Bishop.' (This formulation concerning the Pope was precisely what Henry VIII had demanded his subjects swear to when he had separated the English Church from Rome.) But Gardiner hoped he could now catch him out. 'So why,' he asked, 'did you acknowledge Henry VIII to be supreme head of the Church, if Christ is the only head?' Rogers was ready for this question. 'I never granted him to have supremacy in spiritual things,' he replied, 'such as the forgiveness of sins, or the giving of the Holy Ghost, or authority to be a judge above the word of God . . .'

At this point Cuthbert Tunstall and Nicholas Heath joined Gardiner in laughing. If Rogers had dared to say any such thing at the time, they sniggered, he wouldn't be alive now. (The ability of these men to laugh at the changes in what was required of subjects of the Tudor monarchs suggests they possessed a pragmatism which was entirely beyond the reach of the serious single-minded type of man exemplified by Rogers. Again, like Rich and Deane, perhaps these men, with their lighter approach to belief and vows, were more 'of their time' than those who would rather go to the fire than contradict themselves.) But Rogers had clearly thought all this out before, and probably many times. He wanted to explain to them what precisely was meant, in his view, by the royal supremacy, 'but they looked and laughed one upon another, and made a business of it', so that he was forced to let the matter drop.

The Lord Chancellor now took it upon himself to explain to Lord Howard, who may have been looking mystified at these exchanges, that it was perfectly possible for both Christ and the bishop of Rome to be supreme heads of the Church. Rogers tried to join in the discussion, to demonstrate that Gardiner was, in his view, talking nonsense, but before he could do so, Gardiner demanded again: 'What say you? Make us a direct answer, whether you will or will not be a member of the Catholic Church, with us.' But Rogers still wanted to address the question of the Pope. 'My Lord,' he protested, 'I cannot believe that you yourselves really think in your hearts that he is supreme head in the forgiving of sins, for you and others of this realm have now been preaching and writing the opposite for 20 years, and Parliament also decided this so long ago . . .'

'Tush, man!' Gardiner interrupted him angrily. 'That Parliament was forced, with great cruelty, to abolish and reject the primacy of the Bishop of Rome.'

'With cruelty?' responded Rogers at once. 'Well, in that case, I see you're going the wrong way about this, trying to persuade men's consciences with cruelty, while it appears from the way you're talking now that the cruelty used then did not persuade your consciences. Why then do you think you can use cruelty to persuade ours?'

Gardiner, backed up by Lord Paget, insisted that the difference was that Parliament had now freely, and virtually unanimously, elected to return to the Catholic fold, whereas under Henry's Parliament there had been no possibility of a free choice being exercised. But Rogers was unconvinced, and attempted to continue the discussion. 'Why then, my Lord,' he said, 'what conclusion do you draw from that? That the first Parliament was of lesser authority, because only a few agreed with it, and this last Parliament of great authority, because more agreed with it? That should not be the test, my Lord, whether more or fewer agree, but which is wiser, truer and godlier . . .' He would have gone on, but the Lord

Chancellor interrupted him again with the demand for a straight 'yes' or 'no' to his question. 'We haven't got all day,' he expostulated – 'we've more people to speak to than just you.'

Rogers now asked for pen, ink and books, so that he could set out clearly in writing why he could not agree with the return to Rome, and declared he would be very willing to enter into a written discussion with anyone who disagreed with him. But this suggestion was bluntly rejected. 'No, that shall not be permitted you,' said Gardiner. 'You shall never be offered another chance like this, if you turn it down.' And he added, chillingly: 'There are two things – mercy and justice; if you refuse the Queen's mercy now, then you shall have justice ministered to you.'

Still Rogers would not back down. 'I never offended nor was disobedient to Her Grace,' he declared, 'yet I will not refuse her mercy.' But if they would not engage in serious dialogue with him in writing, then he felt he had to remind them that it was they themselves who had first brought him to understand when he was a young man, twenty years ago, that the Bishop of Rome had only a 'pretended primacy' – 'and will you now,' he protested, 'have me to say and do the contrary? I cannot be so persuaded.'

'If you will not admit the Bishop of Rome to be supreme head of the Catholic Church, then you will never have the Queen's mercy, you may be sure,' responded Gardiner. And then he asserted that he could not possibly engage in serious discussion with Rogers, as he was requesting, because St Paul had instructed in the letter to Titus that heretics should be avoided and not spoken to after one or two warnings. 'First prove that I am a heretic,' retorted Rogers, 'and then quote the text from Titus.'

But 'still the Lord Chancellor played on one string', as Rogers put it, demanding whether Rogers would enter into the one Catholic Church, or not. Rogers insisted that he needed to find the Pope's headship ratified in the scriptures before he would accept it. At this, Bishop Nicholas Heath interjected that the answer was in the creed – '*credo ecclesiam sanctam catholicam*' ('I believe in the holy catholic Church') – but Rogers maintained his original argument: 'I find not the Bishop of Rome there; for catholic does not mean the Church of Rome: it means the consensus of all true teaching churches of all times and of all ages: but how can the Bishop of Rome be one of them, as he teaches so many doctrines that are plainly and directly against the word of God? Should someone who does that be head of the catholic Church? It is not possible.' Gardiner demanded Rogers tell him just one doctrine taught by the Pope that was against the word of God. 'All right, I will,' said Rogers, and he went on to assert that saying, singing and reading everything in their services in Latin was plainly against the instructions given in the fourteenth chapter of the first letter to the Corinthians. 'I deny it,' said Gardiner, 'I deny it is against the word of God. How can you prove that it is?' Rogers quoted the text he had in mind: 'For he that speaketh with tongues speaketh not unto men, but unto God.' Gardiner agreed that in that case a man would be speaking to God. 'Well, then,' said Rogers, 'it is of no use to men.' 'No,' replied the Lord Chancellor, 'for one man speaks in one tongue and another in another, and all well.' 'No,' insisted Rogers, quoting another text from the same chapter – 'when you speak with tongues, unless you speak words that have signification, how shall it be understood what is spoken? For you shall but speak in the air' – and being anxious to prove how these two texts agreed. 'For they must agree,' he said, demonstrating a very Protestant understanding of the scriptures, 'as they are both sayings of the Holy Ghost, spoken by the apostle St Paul – that is, to speak not to men but to God, and to speak to the wind.' And he, like the scholar and biblical exegete he was, wanted to carry on and set out his proof, but the prelates and other men around him all began to talk at once.

'To speak to God, and not to God, is impossible!' cried the Lord Chancellor. 'I will prove it possible,' said Rogers. 'No,' said Lord Howard to Gardiner, 'now I will bear you witness that he's talking rubbish; for first he said that those who speak in a strange language are speaking to God, and now he says the opposite, that they speak neither to God nor to man.' Rogers tried to explain to Howard, who was no theologian: 'I have quoted one text, and now another, and they must agree, and I can make them agree; but as for you, you don't understand what it's about.' 'I understand enough to know it isn't possible,' declared Lord Howard. And now, wanting to break up the discussion, the secretary, Sir John Bourne, whispered to Gardiner: 'This is a point of sophistry.' Then Gardiner began to tell Howard how, in Holland, they had at one time said the whole of their service in Dutch, but then they began to do part in Latin and part in Dutch. 'Yes, it was like that at Wittenberg too,' Nicholas Heath interjected. Rogers tried to explain that this was in a university, where most men understood Latin, and he was still trying to make himself heard, anxious to continue and prove his point, but they were no longer listening to him. 'There is no remedy but to let them alone, and commit the matter to God,' he concluded miserably. His frustration at not being allowed to prove his point almost leaps off the page. He was of course fighting for his life (or would have been, if they had let him) – 'but it was impossible, for one asked one thing, another said another, that I was forced to hold my peace and let them talk: and when I would have taken hold of my proof, my Lord Chancellor bade me go back to prison again'.

'Away, away,' said Gardiner, 'we have other people we need to talk to; if you won't be reformed, away with you.' Rogers, rather indignant at the use of the word 'reformed' in this context, stood up, for he had been kneeling throughout the interview (which must have made it doubly hard for him to be heard). Sir Richard Southwell, who had been standing by the window for the duration of the interview, turned and jeered at him: 'I bet you won't carry on like this when you see the flames.' 'I cannot tell,' responded Rogers quietly, 'but I trust in God.' Then Thomas Thirlby, the Bishop of Ely, 'very gently' explained to Rogers what the Queen had in mind for those who would not conform, so that he could be left in no doubt that he must admit the authority of the Pope, or burn. For the Queen took the view, said Thirlby, that those who would not accept the Bishop of Rome's supremacy were not deserving of her mercy. Rogers repeated that he would not refuse her mercy, and that he had never offended her in all his life, and he beseeched her and all those present to be good to him, while allowing him to remain true to his conscience. This remark seemed to amuse the assembly, and especially Secretary Bourne who scoffed: 'What does he mean, he hasn't offended the law? – he, a married priest?!' Rogers protested that he had not broken any law when he married, for he had done so in a place where such marriages were lawful. His interrogators seemed surprised at this, apparently imagining – or pretending they imagined – that clergy marriage was illegal everywhere. Rogers pressed on, explaining that he had married in Holland, and further, that 'if you had not here in England made an open law that priests might have wives, I would never have come home again: for I brought a wife and 8 children with me, which you can be sure I would not have done, had not the laws of this realm permitted it.' Then all present shouted him down, saying he had come back too soon, and that he would wish he hadn't, with various other such remarks. And, with the argument still raging, Rogers was led out of the room by the serjeant who had brought him there.

On 25 January, the feast day of the Conversion of St Paul, a great church procession was staged in London. It involved all the City clergy (apart, of course, from those Protestants who were awaiting their fate in prison), so Sir John Deane would have been among 'all the clerks, curates, and parsons, and vicars, in copes, with their crosses', accompanied by the choir of St Paul's, all singing '*Salve festa dies*' ('Hail thee, festival day'). Bishop Bonner 'in his pontificals and cope', accompanied by eight other bishops, bore the blessed sacrament under a canopy which was carried by four prebendaries, and the procession, including the Lord Mayor and Aldermen in scarlet gowns and members of the livery companies 'in their best array', wove its way from the cathedral up to Leadenhall and back by a parallel route. When the procession was over, King Philip and Cardinal Pole arrived at the cathedral to hear Mass, and in the evening 'was commandment given to make bonfires through all London for the joy of the people that were converted likewise as St Paul was converted'. All the church bells were also ringing in this demonstration of decidedly non-spontaneous 'joy'. Numbers of their Majesties' subjects were genuinely pleased at this return to the old ways, but joy that has to be commanded cannot easily be measured.

During the night of 27 January Rogers completed writing his account of the questioning he had been subjected to five days previously, having been advised that he would be called back in the morning to be questioned further. He concluded his words with prayer (showing clearly his fear and distress, as well as his earnest desire to acquit himself well in his anticipated torment). He asks that other believers should pray for him, and for his fellow prisoners:

> that the Lord God of all consolation will now be my comfort, aid, strength, buckler, and shield, and also of all my brethren that are in the same case and distress; that I and they all may despise all manner of threats and cruelty, and even the bitter burning fire and dreadful dart of death, and stick like true soldiers to our dear and loving captain Christ, our only redeemer and saviour.

He was also very anxious about the fate of his wife and children, particularly as his wife was a foreigner, and he begged those who would read his words:

> if I die, to be good to my poor wife, being a stranger, and all my little souls, hers and my children; whom, with all the whole faithful and true catholic church of Christ, the Lord of life and death save, keep, and defend, in all the troubles and assaults of this vain world, and bring at the last to everlasting salvation, the true and sure inheritance of all Christians: Amen, Amen.

Beginning on Monday 28 January, Gardiner and a number of other bishops sat in judgement on 'the Protestant preachers' in the church of St Mary Overy, by authority of Cardinal Pole's Legatine Commission. The wardens of the City livery companies had also been instructed to attend as observers (so there must have been quite a crowd). First to appear before them were John Hooper (former chaplain to Lord Protector Somerset, witness for the prosecution at Bishop Bonner's trial in 1549, and former Bishop of Gloucester and then Worcester), John Cardmaker (who on this occasion recanted) and John Rogers.

Rogers made a record of this interrogation too, to which he gave the poignant title: 'The confession of John Rogers made and that should have been made, if I might have been heard, the 28 & 29 of January, Anno Domini 1555'. The questioning began in the same way as it had the previous week, but with Rogers being, if anything, even less willing to compromise than before. He had clearly spent the intervening days coming to terms with his fate – in so far as he had not already done so – and was not expecting anything other than condemnation. So, on being asked once again if he 'would come into one Church with the bishops and the whole realm . . . and so receive the mercy before proffered [him]', he answered boldly that 'before, I could not really tell what his mercy meant, but now I understand: it was a mercy of the antichristian Church of Rome, which I utterly refused'. He then expressed his willingness to prove that all the doctrine he had ever taught was 'true and catholic' and that he would do so 'by the scriptures and the authority of the fathers who lived 400 years after the death of Christ'.

Lord Chancellor Gardiner retorted that he would not, and should not, be allowed to prove any such thing, for he was 'but a private man' and his views should not be allowed to stand against those of the whole realm. Furthermore, he went on, 'when a Parliament has concluded something, does any private person have the authority to discuss whether Parliament has done right or wrong? No, that may not be.' Rogers responded that all the laws of man could not overrule the word of God, and he would have continued, but Gardiner 'began a long tale to a very small purpose' and accused Rogers of exhibiting nothing 'but arrogance, and pride, and vainglory'. Rogers denied he had such qualities, protesting that 'all the world knows well where and on which side pride, arrogance and vainglory is!'

It is noticeable that throughout his interrogation Rogers never speaks ill of, or seems to impute any blame to, the Queen. Rather, he blames Bishop Gardiner for having led her astray – 'The Queen's

Majesty (God save Her Grace!) would have done well enough,' he said, 'if it had not been for your counsel.' Gardiner asserted (truthfully) that the Queen went before him and that what happened as regards the Church represented her desire. 'I neither can nor will ever believe it,' declared Rogers.

The interrogation now turned to another central issue, reminiscent of the question that was unfailingly addressed to those accused of heresy under Henry VIII. 'After many words,' as Rogers put it, Bishop Gardiner asked him what he 'meant concerning the sacrament?' and, on asking the question, he stood up and doffed his cap, as did all the other bishops present. They all wanted to know whether Rogers believed the sacrament 'to be the very body and blood of our saviour Christ, that was born of the Virgin Mary and hanged on the cross, really, substantially, etc.' Rogers insisted that this was a question he had never dwelt upon – 'it was a matter in which I was no meddler' – to the extent that some of his brethren thought he did not agree with them on it. But, he now asserted, seeing 'the falsehood' of his questioners' doctrine 'in all other points', and the fact that they defended it 'only by force and cruelty', he concluded that 'their doctrine in this matter' must be 'as false as the rest'. And now he took the Lord Chancellor to task for the treatment meted out to him. 'My Lord,' he said:

> you have dealt with me most cruelly; for you have sent me to prison without law and against law, and kept me there for almost a year and a half; for I was almost half a year in my own house, where I was obedient to you, God knows, and spoke with no one; and now have been a whole year in Newgate, at great cost and charges, having also a wife and 10 children to support – and I have never received a penny from my livings, neither of the prebend, nor of the residence, neither of the vicarage of St Sepulchre's, against the law.

Gardiner's reply was that Rogers should never have had these livings in the first place, as he had been given them by the former Bishop Ridley, who was a 'usurper' of that role. 'So was the King who gave Dr Ridley the bishopric a usurper too?' asked Rogers, quick as a flash. 'Yes,' said Gardiner, unguardedly, starting to complain about the wrongs King Edward had done to himself and Bonner. Then he remembered himself and retracted the word – 'I misuse my terms to call the King a usurper,' he said hastily. But Rogers detected that he had spoken with genuine resentment about his treatment, and that he was not really sorry for having used that word.

Perhaps taking advantage of Gardiner's momentary discomfiture, Rogers asked him why he had sent him to prison. 'Because you preached against the Queen,' replied Gardiner. Rogers denied he had ever done so, and was prepared to stake his life on being able to defend himself against that charge. 'I preached a sermon at the Cross, after the Queen came to the Tower,' he admitted, 'but nothing was said in it against the Queen.' There were plenty of witnesses to what he had said, and Gardiner himself had initially let him go after examining him about the sermon. 'Yes, but you read your lectures, against the commandment of the Council,' insisted Gardiner.

'No, I did not,' replied Rogers. 'Let that be proved, and let me die for it!' He went on to accuse Gardiner of having held him all this time, illegally, without ever questioning him – 'till now, that you have got a whip to whip me with' – in other words, that he had been held, without charge, until such time as the heresy laws had been re-enacted, so that now they could be used against him. The intention had been, he said, 'to keep me in prison so long, till they might catch a man in the law, and so kill him'. The only mistake Rogers was making about this was to blame Gardiner solely, and not to recognize the Queen's involvement.

Like others before him in a similar position, the more Rogers perceived his case to be hopeless, the bolder he became. 'I was never out of the true catholic Church,' he declared, 'nor ever will be; but by God's grace I will never come into your Church.'

'Well then,' asked Gardiner, ready to seize upon the evidence he needed, 'is our Church false and antichristian?'

'Yes,' said Rogers.

'And what is the doctrine of the sacrament?'

'False!' Rogers replied, throwing up his hands.

The case was closed, and all that remained was the sentencing. 'Come back tomorrow,' said the Lord Chancellor, 'between nine and ten in the morning.'

The hearings being ended by about four o'clock in the afternoon, both Rogers and Hooper were taken for the night to the Counter in Southwark, the crowds pressing around them, so that it was quite hard for the prisoners and their guards to make their way through. On the next morning the two men were returned from the Counter to St Mary Overy. Hooper was condemned first, and then Rogers was summoned. The Lord Chancellor said to him: 'Rogers, you were here yesterday, and we gave you another night to consider your position, whether you would come to the holy Catholic Church of Christ again, or not: tell us now what you have determined – whether you will repent and be sorry, and will return and take mercy again?'

Rogers did not waver, though he was determined yet again to argue his case, taking up Gardiner on the point he had made the day before about Parliament being above the authority of all private persons. 'Yet, my Lord, I am able to show examples,' he declared, 'of one man coming to a general council, and after the whole council had determined and agreed upon an act or article, that one man coming in afterwards has, by the word of God, declared so pithily that the council had erred in decreeing the said article, that he caused the whole council to alter and change the act or article they had previously determined.' He added: 'I could show the authority of a learned lawyer, Panormitanus, who says that more credit ought to be given to a simple layman who brings the word of God with him, than to a whole council gathered together, without the scriptures.'

But Gardiner, tired of listening to Rogers talking, ordered him to sit down, declaring mockingly that it was for him to be instructed by them, and not vice versa. 'My Lord, I stand, and sit not,' responded Rogers defiantly. 'Shall I not be permitted to speak for my life?'

'Shall we permit you to tell a tale, and to prate?' said Gardiner, standing up and, according to Rogers, beginning to abuse him 'after his old arrogant, proud fashion'. Rogers continued to try to speak, but Gardiner had had enough, and he proceeded to excommunicate and condemn Rogers as a heretic, and then to hand him over to the secular power, the sheriffs being at hand to take both Rogers and Hooper away. Before Rogers was removed, however, he had one last plea to make to the bishop – that his wife might come and speak with him before he died, for he wanted to advise her as to what would be best for her and their children.

'No, she is not your wife,' retorted Gardiner.

'Yes, she is, my Lord,' replied Rogers, 'and has been these eighteen years.'

'Should I accept that she is your wife?' asked Gardiner, rhetorically.

'Whether you do or not,' said Rogers, 'she is so, nevertheless.'

'She shall not come to you,' repeated Gardiner.

At this Rogers could barely contain his distress, and he lashed out, exclaiming that while Gardiner and his ilk were 'highly displeased over the matrimony of priests', they allowed non-married clergy to carry on 'in open whoredom' – particularly in Wales 'where every priest has his whore openly dwelling with him, even as your holy father allows in the whole of Holland, and in France, the priests to do the like'. Gardiner made no reply to this furious assault but, according to Rogers, 'looked as it were asquint at it'. Then Rogers was removed from the room.

There was some fear on the part of the authorities of demonstrations in support of Hooper and Rogers – possibly even of an attempt to rescue them – on the evening of their condemnation (an understandable fear, judging from the crowds of the night before), and therefore elaborate precautions surrounded their return journey from St Mary Overy to Newgate. They were first taken to the Clink prison, in Southwark, where they were held until nightfall. In the meantime instructions were given that all the lights in the streets along their route were to be extinguished, including the torches on the costermongers' stalls, with the purpose of ensuring that the two condemned men would not be recognized. When it was deemed safe to set off, the prisoners were led first through the bishop's house and then through the churchyard of St Mary Overy into the streets, then across London Bridge towards Newgate. Despite all the precautions, news had got out and, much to the annoyance of the officers in charge, the streets were lined with supporters of the two men, holding lighted candles and cheering them on with sympathetic words and prayers that they might be given strength to endure what was to come.

Rogers spent much of the time that was left to him – and he would not have been told precisely how long that was to be – writing up the account of his interrogation and of what he had really wanted to say, had he been given the chance. He wrote partly to relieve his feelings, to pour out all his anger, frustration and distress, but he also clearly intended that his written account should be found and read, not only by his wife but by his supporters and fellow believers, whom he addresses as follows: 'But now, dearly beloved, hear what I would have said further, and what I had devised the night before, privately with prayer, and privately by imagining in my mind after what order I would speak, when I came before the aforesaid judges.' What he had hoped to do was to set out some of the contradictions of this and the preceding two reigns, to demonstrate that the voice of Parliament should not be taken as infallible and unchangeable, when so often its deliberations had been occluded by fear of a powerful ruler who wanted his will obeyed – and how that person whose will must now be obeyed was the Lord Chancellor, Bishop Stephen Gardiner. He is insistent that Gardiner's will is not that of the people, and he even makes the political point that it was against the will of the people that Mary should have married a 'foreign prince', Philip of Spain (thereby giving the lie to his earlier assertion that he had no idea of what was going on in the outside world). He thunders against 'the Bishop of Rome', declaring that of 'the rotten head of Rome' there is no mention in the scriptures. He writes with furious oratory, his written style infused with the language, tone and cadences he has imbibed and developed through his work of biblical translation, as he sums up Protestant objections to Catholic ritual:

preaching false lies and men's additions of ashes, candles, palms, water, bread, bells, herbs, dead saints, rotten bones, the Pope's poison and destruction of souls, rocking us all in blindness, with Latin abominable masses, processions and other services, ringing, singing, blessing, yea, and cursing and burning as well (for who can reckon up all their trim toys, foul treachery, false feigned fantasies, loud lies, hypocrisy, and idolatry?) – these, these things will bring the realm to utter ruin.

And then Rogers creates an imaginary scene (following the legal convention of 'putting a case' which we have previously encountered with Sir Thomas More) which would put his persecutors to rout. He imagines Henry VIII 'rising again', and coming to the next Parliament. And there, if Henry were to see how his acts had been overturned, 'there would be no small hurly-burly' and 'what would the Bishop of Winchester say then, and the rest of the rocheted rout, with the whole swarm of deans, archdeacons, prebendaries, and dignities in the convocation house?'* Inevitably, he declares, they would beg the King's pardon and 'change the act again, or repeal the newly passed act, and away with the Pope again, and so on'. And even though 'this merry case' which Rogers puts 'in the midst of his sorrow' is fanciful and Henry will not return from the dead, another monarch of at least equal zeal to Henry's may succeed to the throne, and then the type of bishop who is now sitting in judgement upon him will once again spurn the Bishop of Rome and all his practices. And now Rogers utters his great cry against the current church hierarchy: 'Turn, and turn, and turn again, is the very life and property of our popish prelates, and of the whole crown-shaven clergy!' (He refers here to the practice of Catholic priests being tonsured.) The end result of such 'turning', he argues, is that 'the simple lay people' as well as 'many worldly wise men' now have no idea 'whom they should believe, or whereunto they should trust'.

On Monday 4 February Bishop Bonner went to Newgate,

---

* A rochet was (and is) an item of episcopal dress, so the phrase 'rocheted rout' was directed at all the Catholic bishops.

along with other high-ranking clergy, to carry out the ceremony of degradation against Hooper and Rogers, stripping them of their clerical orders. On the same day, between ten and eleven o'clock in the morning, Rogers was conveyed, in a cart, the short distance from Newgate to Smithfield, passing his old church of St Sepulchre. (Hooper was sent back to Gloucester, where he had formerly been the bishop, and was burnt there on 9 February. The choice of these sites for execution – Hooper in his former diocese, Rogers just a few hundred yards away from the church of which he had been vicar – suggests that the executions were deliberately staged as an example to the people who had been led by these prominent figures of the Edwardian reformation; they were intended as a lesson to bring the rank and file into line.)

Rogers was about fifty-five years old when he died. As the cart rolled along, he prepared himself by reciting psalms, particularly the 'Miserere' which begins: 'Have mercy on me, O God.' Many people lined the route, including members of his own family – his wife and their now eleven children, one of whom was still a baby and being seen by Rogers for the first, and last, time. A path was cleared so that his wife and children could come to say goodbye to him, but one of the sheriffs – Thomas Woodroffe – was furious with the cart driver for stopping to allow this. So it was the briefest of farewells. Among the dignitaries present was the imperial ambassador, Simon Renard, who reported to King Philip: 'Some of the onlookers wept, others prayed to God to give him strength, perseverance and patience to bear the pain and not to recant, others gathered the ashes and bones and wrapped them up in paper to preserve them, yet others threatening the bishops.' There was also 'a great company of the guard' present, to keep the large crowd under control. Not all of the crowd were supporters; some would be there to jeer, or just to watch, drawn by curiosity and the apparently irresistible human urge to witness horror (there had, after all, not been such a spectacle for several years).

Tied to the stake, Rogers was offered one last chance to recant, being offered a pardon if he would do so. He refused, and instead told the onlookers – many of whom must have been his former parishioners – to stand firm in the faith he had taught them. When the fire was lit and the flames took hold of his body, he made no protest or attempt to struggle; it seemed to the spectators that he 'washed his hands in the flame, as though it had been in cold water'. His melting muscles contracting into the characteristic pugilistic pose, he appeared to be 'lifting up his hands to heaven' and he did not move them again 'until they were consumed in the devouring fire'. His prayer that he might endure to the end with steadfastness and faith had been answered. In terms of reputation, he was undoubtedly the victor.

Chapter Ten

DOMINICANS IN SMITHFIELD

✠

Grant me, good Lord, grace earnestly to consider oftentimes from whence I came, what I am, where I am, and whither I go. First from whence I came, plainly I came from vile and sinful flesh, begotten in filthy concupiscence and beastly lust, in the stinking vileness of original sin, fed in my mother's womb with foul menstruous vility. And where thou (most merciful Lord God) created the planets and the stars of the fire, the fishes and fowls of the water, thou hast created me and all other beasts of the foul and vile earth, so that as touching my body I am no better than a beast, created of the earth and unto the earth I shall again. What I am I may soon perceive, I am nought else but dross and dirt, rotten earthworms' meat, and much less perceiving how I shall depart, subject unto many necessities, full of misery, born in sin, living in wretchedness and labour and must die in pain and agony. And if I should earnestly and deeply consider I may perceive and see, that the trees' herbs bring forth leaves, flowers and fruits, and my body brings nothing else, than foul worms, stinking sweat and corruption.

Fr William Peryn,
Spiritual Exercises and Ghostly Meditations, 1557

THE ABOVE WORDS vividly convey a particular sixteenth-century Catholic view of the human body which may go some way towards explaining why bodily torture and execution may have appeared less inimical to the human condition to our sixteenth-century forebears than to ourselves. Their writer, Father William

Peryn, was the head of the community of Dominicans (or Black Friars, so called because of the black *cappa* or cloak they wore over their white habits) established at St Bartholomew's in Smithfield in the reign of Queen Mary. Peryn had readopted the Dominican habit early in that reign, along with at least fifteen other English Dominicans. As a young man he had been associated with the Dominicans at Oxford and had become a zealous member of their order, being ordained in 1531 and soon acquiring a reputation for vigorous preaching against heresy. Following the declaration of the royal supremacy in 1534 he went into exile, but returned in 1543 to undertake further theological studies in Oxford as well as becoming a chantry priest at St Paul's Cathedral. We last encountered him early in the reign of Edward VI, when he had preached about the benefits of praying before images of Christ and the saints, an opinion he had subsequently recanted, declaring that he had been deceived and expressing regret for having taught such doctrines. The insincerity (or Nicodemitism – saying one thing, while meaning another) of his recantation was demonstrated both by his renewed self-imposed exile in Louvain, and by his return to England and engagement in preaching and writing as soon as Edward and his Protestant supporters were no longer in control.

The person who had helped make it possible for the small community of Black Friars to be established at St Bartholomew's was the patron and current owner of the site, Lord Rich, who thereby showed both his probable Catholic sympathies (despite his compliance with the Protestant modus vivendi under Edward) and his unfailing instinct for survival. He did, after all, have some ground to make up with Queen Mary, having been the one to bring her unwelcome instructions during the reign of her half-brother and having initially, along with the other members of the Privy Council, supported her rival for the throne, Lady Jane Grey. Once he had adopted Mary's cause, however, he did so wholeheartedly and she in fact stayed at his (and his wife's) house at Wanstead, prior to her entry into London on 3 August 1553. On 28 August Rich was named as one of Mary's privy councillors. It was an astute political move on his part to continue to demonstrate his support by making the church and what other buildings remained of the priory over to the Crown in December 1555. In addition to the former monastic buildings, Rich also surrendered the rectory, the advowson (the right to appoint clergy to the benefice) and the six tenements which he had previously granted to augment John Deane's stipend. That this move was not purely political but that Rich had a genuine attachment to the old form of religion is also suggested by his marking the death of his eldest son in April 1554 by endowing a chantry to sing masses and dirges for the dead in Felsted parish church. According to the chronicler Wriothesley, the Queen officially revived the monastery at St Bartholomew's at Easter 1556, installing there a number of English, Spanish and Dutch Dominicans, with William Peryn at their head, their own priory formerly located between the River Thames and Ludgate Hill, in the area which still bears the name 'Blackfriars', having been demolished after the dissolution. It is likely that they had taken up residence in Smithfield before the official date of the resuscitation, and possibly even before Rich had completed the paperwork.

Deane was necessarily affected by this change – perhaps personally affected more by the moving in of the Black Friars than by the persecution of Protestants going on around him. There can have been no greater contrast in style between the self-effacing Sir John, quietly going about his pastoral work, spending time with friends and neighbours, and the orotund if ascetic Father Peryn, whose reputation as a flamboyant preacher was considerable. Yet for the space of about two years they shared a building and, as with every 'turn, and turn, and turn again' of this period, they could not have known at the outset that this cohabitation would be fairly short-lived. The Dominicans took over the old monastic quire, which had become the parish church, for their services, and Deane had to accommodate them as best he could, reverting to using part of the old parish chapel for the celebrations of Mass for his lay parishioners. He also suffered a loss in income through the six tenements reverting to the Crown.

William Peryn published three books of his writings, one of

which, entitled *Three Godly and Notable Sermons of the Most Honourable and Blessed Sacrament of the Altar*, sermons that had originally been preached in the Hospital of St Anthony in London in the mid-1540s, was dedicated to Bishop Edmund Bonner. In these sermons Peryn took a very literal approach to the words *Hoc est corpus meum* ('This is my body'), showing himself completely antagonistic to any more 'spiritual' or 'receptionist' interpretations (in which the receiver of the sacrament is the locus for transformation, not the thing in itself) proffered by such as Anne Askew and her successors in the 1550s. His writing and preaching style was very ornate, full of rhetorical flourishes such as word-pairs, alliteration and repetitive devices, as in the following passage from one of his sermons:

> Yet such is the untowardness, of our reckless nature, prone and proclive, unto blind ignorance, that notwithstanding that both, within us, and also without us, there is almost nothing void, of God's singular power and miracles, (the whole world filled full with wonders) yet negligent ignorance, and ignorant negligence, doth grow so fast upon us, that the admirable wonder of the creation, consecration, and administration of all the broad world is almost (as saint Augustine saith) by assiduity and cotidian custom, out of all estimation and marvel, and the power of God herein wiped out of memory.

Another of Peryn's works, *Spiritual Exercises and Ghostly Meditations*, was published during his time in Smithfield, in 1557, and was dedicated to two English nuns, one the abbess of the nuns of Syon at Isleworth (another community revived under Mary) and the other a Poor Clare at Louvain. The book was also aimed at a more general readership, at anyone who desired 'to come to the perfect love of God'. It was based on the work of the Dutch theologian and mystical writer Nicolaus van Esch, and incorporated elements of the spiritual exercises of St Ignatius of Loyola, the founder of the Society of Jesus, or Jesuits. No copy survives of Peryn's third recorded work, *De frequenter celebranda missa*.

When Peryn writes in his *Spiritual Exercises* of fire and of sacrificing one's body to the flames, he does so in a metaphorical sense and also makes a connection to the sacrament of the altar, advising his reader:

> Thou shalt also make a sacrifice and a lively host unto God of thy body, as they did in the Old Testament laying wood upon the altar and put thereon the sacrifice or host and so with fire put thereunder they burnt it upon the altar. In like manner must thou gather together, by contrite remembrance, thy sins upon the altar of thy heart, and thy body must be the sacrifice, for it must be mortified specially from all vices and sinful work and pleasure, and be slain with discreet penance and with the fire of charity. For thou must lament thy sins, for the very love of God, and thou must do penance and punish thy body and mortify it for the pure love of God. And if it be thus consumed and offered unto God with this fire then shall it be a sweet and a savoury sacrifice in the sight of God.

The Dominicans, also known as the Order of Preachers, had been instrumental in pioneering the original Inquisition, having been founded in order to combat heresy. Their presence in Smithfield, at a time when so many 'heretics' were consigned to the flames there, seems almost fateful. There is no record of the Smithfield Dominicans having directly participated in the burnings, or in the trials of heretics, but there is circumstantial evidence that the policy of persecution received support from them, through a connection with the important Spanish Dominican, Fray (friar) Bartolomé Carranza de Miranda.

When Philip II of Spain arrived in England in July 1554 to marry Mary, he brought with him a very large retinue which included a group of Spanish churchmen whose brief was to advise him and the Queen on the reform and 'purification' of the English Church and its eventual resubmission to Rome. One of the central figures in this group was Bartolomé Carranza, who had been specifically commissioned by the head of the Dominicans with restoring the Dominican order in England. He did not, however, limit his activities to the Dominicans, but played a very active role in encouraging the return of Catholic ritual in the Church in general, being particularly keen to restore the outdoor processions that had traditionally accompanied the festival of Corpus Christi. There were liturgical processions on other feast days too, including on the feast of the Annunciation (25 March) in 1555, when a protestor 'delivered a pudding' at one of the prebendaries as he processed. The pudding-thrower was duly whipped at the pillar in Cheap two days later. Carranza was also closely involved with the preparations for Cardinal Pole's arrival in England (he having not set foot in his native country since 1532), and with negotiations over the restitution of monastic property, so is very likely to have worked with Richard Rich in sorting out the arrangements for the Dominicans' installation at St Bartholomew's.

A portrait of Carranza from a later period when he was Archbishop of Toledo shows him in full pontificals, coped and mitred, white-gloved, holding a crozier. Swarthy of complexion, he has a greying beard, but full dark eyebrows over wide-set eyes; he appears sure of himself, and yet slightly wary. Our knowledge of Carranza's activities in England comes mainly from the records of his own trial in Spain many years later for, despite having worked for the Spanish Inquisition since 1539, he himself eventually fell foul of it, being suspected of Lutheran sympathies for which he was tried in 1562. His defence, presented in the form of a hundred questions to be answered by witnesses lined up by Carranza for the purpose, included testimony that he had actively pursued Protestant heretics during his time in London, twenty-three of the hundred questions concerning his stay in England and his activities there. Among the witnesses called was Philip II himself.

One case in which Carranza was involved concerned the stabbing of a priest by a 'sacramentarian' at the church of St Margaret's, Westminster. The offender was Thomas alias William Flower, or Branche, a former monk of Ely, who had become a radical Protestant, and who had worked as both a schoolmaster and a surgeon (as Wriothesley put it, he 'ran about the country using the art of surgery'). The return of the traditional rite of the Mass seemed to have been just too much for him (he may have been mentally disturbed, claiming to hear a 'voice' which told him to attack a minister of what he regarded as the evil idolatry of the Mass) and, on Easter Day (14 April) 1555, while the congregation was receiving communion, he walked into St Margaret's wearing a placard containing the words '*Deum time, Idolum fuge*' ('Fear God, flee from the Idol'). Inside the church he took out a large machete-like wood-knife and started hacking at the head and arms of one of the Abbey clergy assisting with the distribution of communion. According to Machyn, the attacker had first said to the minister: 'What dost thou give them?' and had then drawn his wood-knife, 'and hit the priest on the head and struck him a great blow, and after ran after him and struck him on the hand, and cleft his hand a great way, and after on the arm a great wound'. Blood was everywhere, including all over the consecrated hosts, which, in the eyes of the faithful, made the offence all the more heinous.

Flower was arrested at the scene and conveyed initially to the Tower. Bartolomé Carranza played a part in ensuring he suffered exemplary punishment, personally visiting Philip and Mary at Hampton Court to urge strong action. They needed little encouragement, both Bishop Bonner and the secular authorities being ordered to deal with Flower with the utmost severity. Ten days after the attack, on 24 April, Flower had the hand which had wielded the knife cut off outside the door of the church he had profaned, and he was then burnt, in a slow fire, in the area known as the Sanctuary between St Margaret's and Westminster Abbey. Carranza later arranged for the priest who had been seriously wounded in the attack, a former Dominican, to be taken to the community at St Bartholomew's, readmitted to the order, and there restored to health.

A degree of anti-Spanish feeling was manifest in England from the time of Philip's arrival, and mutual suspicion occasionally spilled over into actual disturbances. The combination of foreignness and traditional religious practices could be a potent mix. In a letter Carranza wrote to Cardinal Pole on 1 September 1554 (a few weeks before Pole returned, as papal legate, to England), he told how he and his fellow Dominicans felt uncomfortable wearing their habits in public as this overt display of restored monasticism sometimes provoked attack in the streets around Westminster Abbey, in the precincts of which they were lodged. The prejudice and bad feeling could operate in both directions, an anonymous Spaniard in Philip's household relaying his view of the English as 'a barbarous and heretical race, with no fear of God or his saints', while another described them as 'white, pink and quarrelsome' and addicted to beer-drinking. When disturbances did break out, both sides could be to blame, as appears to have been the case with the 'great fray' at Charing Cross on 4 November 1554, described by Machyn as taking place 'at 8 of the clock at night between the Spaniards and Englishmen, the which through wisdom there were but a few hurt, and after the next day they were certain taken that began it; one was a blackamoor, and was brought before the head officers by the knight-marshal's servants'.

Queen Mary's husband, King Philip, appears even at this early stage of the burnings not to have been convinced that this was necessarily a wise course of action. Aware that popular opinion in England was already anti-Spanish, he feared that a spate of horrific executions would only exacerbate the ill-feeling and, six days after the burning of John Rogers, he instructed his Franciscan confessor, Alfonso de Castro, to preach a sermon at court in which 'he did earnestly inveigh against the bishops for burning of men, saying plainly that they learned it not in scripture to burn any for his conscience: but the contrary, that they should live and be converted, with many other things more to the same purport'. Castro was in general no opponent of taking the most stringent measures against heretics, but in his book *On the just punishment of heretics*, written in 1549, he did counsel against allowing heretics what we might term 'the oxygen of publicity'. They should be admonished before being punished, but in private, and any public disputation with them should be avoided; it may have been the publicity and public support likely to be engendered by the burning of notorious heretics that both Castro and King Philip deplored, rather than the burnings in themselves. Ambassador Renard also feared the hostility towards the Spanish king and his courtiers that might be provoked by dislike of this policy of persecution. Bartolomé Carranza seems to have suffered no such doubts, one of Philip's courtiers, Luis Venegas, confirming that the friar was 'the main person from whom the Queen sought advice' on matters of heresy and asserting that Carranza was dissatisfied with Cardinal Pole 'because he saw him as being softer than he would have wished in the punishment of such things'. Pole's rather naive and optimistic attitude was that he wanted to be an 'indulgent loving father' to the straying English; he seems to have imagined at the outset of the reign that all they needed was something in the nature of a 'short, sharp shock' to bring them into line, and that after that they would be happy. This, broadly, seems to have been Mary's view too, coupled with her belief that she had a solemn duty to return her people to the Catholic fold and faith. As for the Dominicans in Smithfield, their connection with Carranza would suggest that they too were broadly in support of the burnings, at least in theory and as a matter of politics, even if some individuals among them may have suffered in their conscience through what they knew was going on outside their gates.

Chapter Eleven

CEREMONIES OF MARTYRDOM

✠

> It is very harsh to burn men on account of articles which are not
> only dubious and controversial, but even trivial, and most harsh
> to do so because of propositions which the theologians have just
> made up out of their own heads.
>
> Desiderius Erasmus,
> from '*Adversus Monachos Quosdam Hispanos, Titulus IV,
> Contra Sanctam Haereticorum Inquisitionem*', *Opera Omnia* IX

IN THE ARGUMENTS between authority and dissent in the reign of
Mary I, one can detect a hardening of the battle lines and a more
equal and determined confrontation between two rival religions
– or, arguably, rival interpretations of the same religion – than in
the cases of those who fell foul of the heresy laws in Henry VIII's
reign and earlier. No longer is this a matter of a few reformers
pitched against the orthodox majority; rather, we now encounter
two radically different 'churches', in a realization of the earlier Lollard vision, both convinced of their rightness, both sure that the
other is utterly wrong, blasphemous and evil. As John Philpot put
it in one of his 'examinations' before Bishop Bonner and others,
'You say, you are of the true Church: and we say, we are of the true
Church.' The Protestant opposition to Mary's Catholic England
knew it had the backing of hundreds, if not thousands, of fellow
believers in other parts of Europe; there was a body of doctrine
now in existence (even if not always in internal agreement with
itself) that provided support for their views. The dissenters were
able to perceive themselves less as voices crying in the wilderness,

than as prophetic voices of doom for their opponents and of eventual triumph for themselves (even if this had to be after their own lifetime). They were able to conceptualize the restoration of Roman Catholicism in England as a temporary aberration, believing that they would ultimately be proved right, in this world as well as in the world to come.

The second Protestant to suffer, after John Rogers, was Thomas Tomkins, a weaver from Shoreditch, who was burnt in Smithfield on 16 March 1555, at eight o'clock in the morning. Tomkins had first come to the attention of the authorities at Easter 1554 for refusing to take communion, and he had subsequently been examined by Bishop Bonner and confined in the bishop's palace at Fulham. Here he was made to assist in the hay harvest, as a way of contributing to his keep. He was no shirker, and his hard work impressed the bishop who expressed the hope that he might yet become as good a Catholic as he was a worker. Tomkins was ready with a biblical quotation, citing St Paul's injunction that anyone who did not work did not deserve to eat.

'Ah,' said the bishop, 'St Paul is a great man with you.'

'And so he should be with you,' retorted Tomkins, 'if you were a good bishop.'

Like many of the confirmed evangelical men, Tomkins had a long flowing beard, an accoutrement which such men seemed to associate with their prophetic role (and an affectation which provoked the ire of Bishop Bonner on more than one occasion). Tomkins had a formidable reputation for piety and 'godliness', and was known to begin every encounter with prayer. He was not of a disposition to be moved, whatever attempts at persuasion Bonner might devise. He may also have been very irritating; certainly Bonner found him so – to the extent that on one occasion, during the weaver's imprisonment in his palace, he actually beat him about the face, causing it to swell. The bishop subsequently paid a shilling to have a barber come and shave off Tomkins's beard – because, he said, that would make him look 'like a Catholic', though Tomkins's sympathizers believed the real reason was that removing the beard would disguise the fact that Bonner had, in his rage, already pulled tufts of it out. Whatever the reason for calling the barber, what is clear is that the beard was indeed a source of irritation to Bonner, as a symbol of Tomkins's Protestantism and of his obstinacy, his determination to be different from the clean-shaven, or at least tidily bearded, norm. (A simplistic equation of beard equals Protestant, no beard equals Catholic, is, however, subverted by Cardinal Pole's possession of a magnificent spade-like beard which, in later years, he cultivated into the bifurcated style; whether the bishop found the cardinal's beard irritating is not known.)

Not content with attacking his prisoner's facial hair, Bonner decided to demonstrate to Tomkins what awaited him if he would not recant, grabbing his hand and holding it over a large candle flame – 'till the veins shrank, and the sinews burst, and the water did spurt into Master Harpsfield's face'. Unsurprisingly perhaps, even Archdeacon Harpsfield found this action of Bonner's too much to stomach. If the Bishop had hoped to frighten Tomkins into submission, his action was a complete failure; all it served to do was to enhance his own reputation for brutality. Such stories became widely known, Foxe himself having heard them when compiling successive editions of *Acts and Monuments* from members of Tomkins's parish of Shoreditch.

During an examination by the bishop on 26 September 1554, Tomkins signed a statement of his beliefs which included that 'the body of our Saviour Jesus Christ is not truly and in very deed in the sacrament of the altar, but only in heaven', that the Mass 'is full of superstition, plain idolatry, and unprofitable for my soul' and that 'the sacrament of baptism ought to be only in the vulgar tongue'. That statement ended with a signed refusal to recant: 'I do and will continually stand to my said confession, declaration and belief, in all the premises and every part thereof, and in no wise recant or go from any part of the same.' He was re-examined, along with five other prisoners, on 8 February 1555; like Rogers, he had been held in confinement until such time as the heresy laws had been re-enacted and could be used against him. He was presented with his signed statement and asked to verify his signature, which he did. The bishop then set about trying to persuade him to recant, promising a pardon if he would do so, but to no avail.

Tomkins was back before the bishop and other examiners, including John Feckenham (the Dean of St Paul's) and John Harpsfield (the Archdeacon of London and brother of Nicholas, the Archdeacon of Canterbury), on the following morning. On this occasion he was again asked to 'revoke and deny his said opinions'. Again, he 'utterly refused' to do so, and was ordered to reappear at two o'clock the next afternoon. At this session Tomkins faced the Bishop of Bath and Wells (Gilbert Bourne – he who had earlier been 'rescued' from the pulpit by John Rogers and John Bradford) and the Bishop of St David's (Henry Morgan), as well as Bishop Bonner of London. To Bishop Bourne's exhortation that he should, even at this late stage in the proceedings, 'revoke and leave off' his opinions, Tomkins replied that he had been 'brought up in ignorance' but that now, having discovered 'the truth', he would remain faithful to that truth until death. After resisting further attempts at persuasion by Bishop Bonner, Tomkins himself seems to have wanted the proceedings brought to an end, declaring: 'My Lord, I cannot see but that you would have me forsake the truth, and fall into error and heresy.' Recognizing that Tomkins would never recant, the bishop read out the sentence of condemnation. Tomkins was duly handed over to the sheriffs and conveyed to Newgate. And on 16 March he was burnt.

The Reverend John Cardmaker, former Vicar of St Bride's Fleet Street, had, unlike John Rogers, been persuaded to recant – or, rather, to agree to recant publicly at a later date – when he appeared before Bishop Gardiner on 28 January 1555. As a high-profile Protestant cleric at the time of Mary's accession, he had been deprived of his livings on 18 April 1554 and had been arrested, but subsequently released on bail. In November that year he had made an attempt, along with William Barlow (Bourne's predecessor as Bishop of Bath and Wells under Edward VI, Cardmaker having been made a prebendary of Wells Cathedral in 1550), to flee the country, disguised as merchants, but the attempt had failed, and Cardmaker and Barlow were both rearrested and imprisoned in the

Fleet. The heresy laws having not yet been re-enacted, the two men were charged with trying to leave the country without permission – and kept in prison until such time as they could be charged with heresy.

After Cardmaker had agreed, in fear of his life, to recant, he was remanded to the Bread Street Counter, the intention being that he would shortly give his formal assent to articles of the Catholic faith, whereupon he would be released. His submission – and that of Barlow – was viewed as a considerable propaganda coup by the ecclesiastical authorities and deployed as such, Stephen Gardiner constantly commending the two men's 'soberness, discretion and learning' to others accused of heresy, urging them to follow the example of these well-known evangelicals. The former bishop, Barlow, did indeed recant, was released, and subsequently succeeded in fleeing the country. But in the effort to secure a recantation from Cardmaker, the authorities should have taken more care over where they held him in the interim. Solitary confinement might have kept the fear of fire uppermost in Cardmaker's spirit, but instead the authorities allowed him to come into contact with a fellow prisoner in the Counter, Lawrence Saunders, former Rector of All Hallows Bread Street (only a stone's throw from the prison where the men were being held) and, like Cardmaker, a renowned Protestant preacher. Unlike Cardmaker, however, he had held firm under interrogation and had been condemned to burn. Cardmaker, already troubled by his conscience and deeply disappointed in himself, was immediately receptive to his fellow City cleric's encouragement to renounce his intention to recant. Saunders was burnt only four days after Rogers (on 8 February in Coventry), so his influence on Cardmaker must have been exercised very quickly and been very powerful; the impetuous and usually outspoken Cardmaker was no doubt feeling regretful and ashamed almost as soon as he arrived at the Counter, and Saunders's valour in the face of imminent death had an almost instantaneous effect, increasing both his shame and his determination. Saunders himself had deliberately returned to London from Lichfield, where he held other benefices, on Mary's accession, in order to support his London congregation in resisting the restoration of Catholic practice, so he was well placed to hearten the flagging zeal of his fellow prisoner.

And so Cardmaker refused to recant and was brought back before Bishop Bonner on 25 May. The bishop reminded him that he had formerly been a Franciscan friar, vowed to poverty, chastity and obedience, and charged him with having married 'a widow and with her had carnal copulation', resulting in the birth of a daughter, 'breaking thereby your vow and order'. Cardmaker defended himself by making the valid point that, when the monasteries were dissolved under Henry VIII, so too were his monastic vows. He also insisted, as had Rogers, that he had broken no law by marrying. Moving on from these secondary matters, Bonner came to the central questions: 'Item, that it . . . is the faith of the Catholic church: that the body of Christ is visibly and truly ascended into heaven, and there is in the visible form of his humanity: and yet the same body in substance is invisibly and truly contained in the said sacrament of the altar.' To this article Cardmaker responded that he did not believe any part of it to be true. It was a firm Protestant belief that Christ's body, even in its resurrected state, could only be in one place at a time (as had been expressed by Thomas Tomkins), and hence it made no sense to such believers to claim that it could be both in heaven and materially present in the Eucharist.

Five days later, on 30 May, John Cardmaker was burnt in Smithfield, alongside an upholsterer and member of the Clothworkers' Company called John Warne, whose wife was also a prisoner in Newgate. Warne was only twenty-nine years old (Cardmaker was about fifty-nine) and had been formally condemned as a sacramentarian some nine years previously, but had been saved from execution at that time by a royal pardon. He had found himself in trouble again in September 1553 when his dog – 'a great rough water spaniel' – had been discovered with a tonsured head, thereby making a mockery of Catholic priests, in what turned out to be a series of blasphemous practical jokes played in the City. Warne was not actually the culprit in this instance, though he was known to have been amused by it – and it was, after all, his dog. Nevertheless, he survived for another year, until he and his wife Elizabeth were apprehended while attending a secret Protestant service in a house in Bow churchyard, just off Cheapside, on New Year's Day 1555.

Among the charges made against Warne at his trial on 23 May was that he had refused to attend church, to go to confession or to receive communion since Queen Mary had come to the throne, and that he was not sorry about it, but glad, as to do so would have 'defiled' his conscience. Bonner also recollected that he had encountered this young man before, when he had been arraigned for heresy at Guildhall 'the Thursday after Anne Askew was burned in Smithfield', and then sent to Newgate where Bonner himself went to instruct him 'in the true faith of Christ'. Warne stood firm, both on that earlier occasion and now, and signed a statement assenting to his heretical beliefs. The bishop continued to try to persuade him otherwise and ordered him to reappear for further questioning on the following day. He did so in the morning, carried on refusing to recant, and was ordered to appear again in the afternoon. The same process ensued, and he was called back yet again on 25 May, at one o'clock in the afternoon. At that, his final examination, Bonner recapitulated the accusations, Warne continuing to insist that he held to all his beliefs, adding that he was convinced he was right and saw no reason to repent – 'for all filthiness and idolatry is in the church of Rome'. So Bonner finally abandoned his efforts to get Warne to change his mind, pronounced the definitive sentence of condemnation and handed the prisoner over to the sheriffs. Warne used his final day in Newgate to write down his confession of faith, confirming his Protestant interpretation of all the clauses of the Apostles' Creed and concluding: 'This is my faith: this I do believe, and I am content by God's grace to confirm and seal the truth of the same with my blood.'

A large crowd attended the burnings of Cardmaker and Warne, many of them evangelicals who were nervous lest Cardmaker disgrace himself, and them, by recanting for real when faced with the stake. This nervousness was felt right up until the last moment as, on arrival at the scene of execution, Cardmaker appeared to be delaying, having been called aside by the sheriffs for a long private conversation: could he, wondered the onlookers, be about to recant? – a possibility that had the evangelicals present 'in a marvellous dump and sadness'. Eventually Cardmaker ended his conversation with the sheriffs and approached the stake, to which the young clothworker, Warne, was already chained. He knelt down and began to pray in silence; the tension mounted – could he still be about to recant? But then:

> His prayers being ended, he rose up, put off his clothes as far as his shirt, went with bold courage to the stake, and kissed it sweetly: he took Warne by the hand, and comforted him heartily, and so gave himself to be also bound to the stake most gladly. The people seeing this so suddenly done, contrary to their fearful expectation, as men delivered out of a great doubt, cried out for joy (with so great a shout as had not likely been heard a greater) saying: God be praised, the Lord strengthen thee, Cardmaker, the Lord Jesus receive thy spirit.

The crowd continued to shout and cheer as the executioner set the wood and reeds alight, and the victims were encircled in flame.

John Warne's widow, Elizabeth, followed her husband to the stake, being burnt on 23 August at one of the other major burning sites, Stratford-atte-Bow, to the east of the City of London.

The next of those to suffer in Smithfield was the forty-five-year-old John Bradford who, like Cardmaker, was a very well-known figure in Protestant circles, which adds credence to the idea that the authorities' intention was to come down hard on the leading exponents of the religion of Edward's reign, with the aim of crushing out opposition to the reintroduction of Catholicism. Striking at the heart of the Protestant movement would, the authorities (including Bonner, Gardiner, Pole and the Queen) believed, kill it off quickly, these few high-profile victims being deemed expendable for the sake of the many who would thereby be saved from both their influence and their fate.

We last encountered Bradford assisting John Rogers to quell the disturbances at Paul's Cross on the occasion of Gilbert Bourne's

sermon on 13 August 1553, when 'Mr Bradford at the request of
the preacher's brother, and others then being in the pulpit, stood
forth and spoke so mildly, Christianly, and effectively, that with few
words he appeased all, and afterward he and Mr Rogers conducted
the preacher between them from the pulpit to the grammar school
door, where they left him safe'. Bradford had already issued his own
warning about what might ensue under Mary, having published a
call to national repentance in July which lambasted the people's
ingratitude and lack of real zeal for the Gospel which had resulted,
he opined, in the Lord having taken away the good King Edward,
and now 'a grievous and bitter cup of God's vengeance is ready to
be poured out for us Englishmen to drink of'. A few days after
the Paul's Cross disturbance, Bradford, like Rogers, was summoned
to the Tower to appear before the Privy Council where he was
charged with preaching seditious sermons. The enthusiasm with
which the people had greeted Bradford's intervention on 13 August
is what had unnerved the authorities – it was not the result he had
achieved that troubled them, but the fact that he had been able
to achieve it:

> as soon as the people saw him begin to speak to them, so glad
> were they to hear him, that they cried with a great shout:
> Bradford, Bradford, God save your life, Bradford: well declar-
> ing not only what affection they bore for him, but also what
> regard they gave to his words. For after he had entered a little
> to preach to them, and to exhort them to quiet and patience,
> soon all the raging ceased, and they in the end quietly
> departed, each man to his house.

Here was a powerful man whom it was important either to enlist
on the side of accepted authority or – if, as seemed more likely, he
would not consent to be so enlisted – to silence.

Unlike Rogers, Bradford was not given the comparatively lenient treatment of house arrest, but was immediately incarcerated in
the Tower, initially on his own but subsequently sharing what was
known as the 'Nun's bower' with Edwin Sandys (formerly vice
chancellor of Cambridge University and involved with the sup-

porters of Lady Jane Grey's claim to the throne). On 6 February 1554 Bradford was moved to another room in the Tower, which he shared with Cranmer, Latimer and Ridley, until these three were taken to Oxford in early March. During the month or so they were together, the four men spent their time reading the Bible, praying and discussing theology together, and were each bolstered by this mutual support and encouragement. The authorities had not yet learnt the value to the 'heretics' of such fellowship, and seemed to have no clear strategy of how to deal with their prisoners; the arrangements appear haphazard, it being a matter of accident who ended up sharing a cell with whom.

On Easter Eve, 24 March, Bradford was transferred to the King's Bench prison in Southwark. Here his companions included Robert Ferrar (the former Bishop of St David's), Dr Rowland Taylor (Rector of Hadleigh in Suffolk) and John Philpot. In prison Bradford continued his ministry of preaching (twice a day) and administering communion (according to the second Book of Common Prayer, now outlawed), the keepers (who liked him) admitting many visitors so that they could listen to him and take part in the services he conducted. Like that favourite saint of the Protestant preachers, the Apostle Paul, he also wrote many letters from prison, both to individuals and to congregations throughout the country. He was abstemious in his habits, sleeping for no more than four hours a night, eating only one meal a day, and spending much time in reading and contemplation. Lean-faced, with a neatly trimmed beard, he seems to have been a natural ascetic, unconcerned with such mundane matters as food and drink. But he also showed signs of inner distress: 'In the middle of dinner he used often to muse with himself, having his hat over his eyes, from whence came commonly plenty of tears dropping on his trencher.' He was known for his generosity and his gentleness (even the Jesuit Robert Parsons, no sympathizer with Protestants, admitted that Bradford was 'of a more soft and mild nature than many of his fellows'), and was often in demand for visiting the sick and dying, even being allowed out of the prison by its governor, the knight marshal Sir William Fitzwilliam, a Protestant sympathizer, to make such visits. He never attempted to escape, or even to delay his return. And once a week he would visit the common criminals being kept in the same prison as himself, distributing not only advice but also funds that had been received as donations. He did the same among the prisoners of religion, having been elected by the majority of them as their pastor. These distributions led to some argument, in particular with a splinter group of Protestants called the 'free willers', a large number of whom were imprisoned in the King's Bench, and who accused Bradford of discriminating against them in his sharing-out of alms, a charge which Bradford strenuously denied. The 'free willers' were fiercely opposed to the idea of predestination, espoused by Calvin in Geneva, and a version of which was beginning to be adopted by mainstream Protestantism in England, of which Bradford was a leading exponent. Much of his prison correspondence had to do with this issue, as he was frequently called upon to reassure believers who were fearful that they were not among the 'elect'. The prisons themselves became hothouses of debate over these differing interpretations of their faith, to the distress of many evangelicals and the satisfaction of their opponents. Certainly the fact that even in prison, and faced with the possibility of death, rival groups of Protestants vigorously kept up their doctrinal and other differences can have done little to recommend them to the authorities, despite the acknowledged holiness and sympathetic character of a man like Bradford.

Bradford was examined three times in Southwark, on 22, 29 and 30 January 1555. When he was brought in on the first day to face Lord Chancellor Gardiner, Bishop Bonner and members of the Privy Council, who were sitting behind a table, he fell to his knees but was immediately asked to get to his feet, which he did. Gardiner then attempted to outstare him, but Bradford merely stared back, apart from once raising his eyes in prayer. Next, Gardiner offered him what was becoming the standard line – that the Queen was minded to be merciful, provided Bradford recant and 'return', along with them, to the true Church. Bradford, respectfully but determinedly, insisted there was nothing for which he needed mercy, as he had not, as Gardiner alleged, preached 'seditiously, falsely, or arrogantly' but rather the reverse, in quelling the Paul's Cross disturbance and enjoining 'quietness' on the people. But before he could even finish, Gardiner 'something snuffed', declared this was a lie and brought in Bonner to back him up. Bonner agreed that Bradford had taken it upon himself to 'rule and lead the people malapertly [presumptuously]', and the interpretation he put upon this was that Bradford had incited the very disturbance he then proceeded to quell. Bradford's response was to say that one day God would reveal 'to all the world' that he had spoken the truth; in the meantime, as his judges refused to believe him, he was ready to suffer whatever penalty they imposed. The argument was batted back and forth, Bradford proving at least as eloquent as Bonner and Gardiner, the latter crossly declaring: 'Well, if you make this babbling, rolling in your eloquent tongue, and yet being altogether ignorant and vainglorious, and will not receive mercy offered to you, know for truth that the Queen is minded to make a purgation of all such as you are.' But Bradford was not to be scared into submission, affirming that his only concern was to please God – for 'life in his displeasure is worse than death, and death in his true favour is true life'.

More than merely agreeing to submit to his judges, Bradford wanted them to admit the inconsistency of their own position. Were they questioning him on the authority of the Pope? he wanted to know – and, if so, how could they square this with the fact that he had himself (and, he implied, so had they) 'been six times sworn that I shall in no case consent to the practising of any jurisdiction, or any authority on the Bishop of Rome's behalf within this realm of England'? He could not, he declared, possibly go back on this oath, and could not therefore answer their questions. The secretary of the Council demanded clarification: how had Bradford managed to be sworn six times? 'Forsooth,' replied Bradford, 'I was thrice sworn in Cambridge, when I was admitted Master of Arts, when I was admitted fellow of Pembroke Hall, and when I was there, the Visitors came thither, and swore the University. Again, I was sworn when I entered the ministry, when I had a prebend given me, and when I was sworn to serve the King a little before his death.'

'Tush,' responded Gardiner, and he declared that these were 'Herod's oaths', meaning they were forced or invalid because they demanded the swearer commit some evil act, and as such need not be considered binding. But Bradford disagreed and pointed out that Gardiner had himself affirmed the validity of these oaths in his treatise *De vera obedientia* ('Of true obedience'), which he had written in support of Henry VIII's claim to be supreme head of the Church of England. Backed into a corner by this logic, his interrogators went on the attack, one of them remarking that this just showed what a dangerous man Bradford was and no wonder he had been imprisoned. Another added that he was continuing to do great harm by his letters. To this accusation Bradford responded with the words uttered by Pilate at the crucifixion: 'What I have written, I have written.' This only served to provoke his hearers more, Sir Richard Southwell exclaiming of the forty-five-year-old Bradford: 'Lord God, what an arrogant and stubborn boy is this!' As Bradford continued to defend himself, Gardiner became impatient. 'I see we shall never be done with you,' he complained. 'Be short, be short!'

Showing no inclination to be 'short' himself, Gardiner now embarked on a lengthy discourse about the 'false doctrine' that had been taught under King Edward, and then demanded to know Bradford's response. His view was completely the opposite of Gardiner's, and he was not afraid to say so: 'My Lord, the doctrine taught in King Edward's days was God's pure religion, the which as I then believed, so do I now more believe it than ever I did, and therein I am more confirmed and ready to declare it, by God's grace, to the world than I was when I first came into prison.' And so the first day's questioning ended, as expected, with no concession on either side.

On the following day, 29 January, after John Rogers had been convicted, Bradford was back before the Lord Chancellor and a number of other bishops. Gardiner again opened the proceedings with a declaration of the Queen's mercifulness, encouraging Bradford to recant in order to avail himself of that mercy, and holding up the examples of Barlow and Cardmaker as men who had agreed to recant. But Bradford was not to be moved, much of his strength deriving from a willingness to die. 'I am not afraid of death,' he declared, 'and have looked for nothing else at your hands for a long time.' His fear was not of death itself but of having a troubled conscience at the moment of departing this life; and it was to avoid that possibility that he answered as he did. 'These be gay glorious words,' expostulated Gardiner, 'full of hypocrisy and vainglory!'

As with Rogers, the reason for having held Bradford for so long without trial was that, until early 1555, the laws did not exist to deal with heretics in the way the Queen and her advisers desired, and Bradford was well aware of this. He took his interlocutors to task accordingly. 'I have been now a year and almost three quarters in prison,' he protested, 'and in all this time you never questioned me, when I might have spoken my conscience frankly without peril: but now you have a law to hang up and put to death, if a man answer freely, and not to your appetite . . . Ah, my Lord [addressing Gardiner], Christ used not this way to bring men to faith. No more did the prophets or apostles.' The Lord Chancellor pretended to be appalled at the suggestion that he might be using force, or the threat of force, as a means of persuasion. 'It was not my doing,' he said, 'although some there be that think this to be the best way. I, for my part, have been often challenged for being too gentle.' Bishop Bonner and most of the others present supported Gardiner in his protestations, agreeing that he had been 'ever too mild and too gentle'. To this Bradford retorted: 'My Lord, I pray you stretch out your gentleness, that I may feel it, for hitherto I never have.' And then servants arrived to tell the Lord Chancellor it was time for dinner, so he rose, leaving Bradford mid-sentence, saying the interrogation would continue later in the afternoon. But in fact Bradford had to spend the rest of the day waiting in the vestry; nothing further happened, and at night he was conveyed back to prison.

The final day's examination took place on 30 January. Gardiner began by again exhorting Bradford to abandon his scruples. 'Did I not yesterday tell you plainly,' he said, 'that you made a conscience where none should be? Did I not make it plain that the oath against the Bishop of Rome was an unlawful oath?'

'No indeed, my Lord,' riposted Bradford, 'you said so, but you have not yet proved it, nor can you ever do so.'

Gardiner had had enough of this man holding out against everyone else, including himself, thereby implying that they had all committed perjury by going back on their oaths made to Henry VIII. 'Oh, Lord God, what a fellow are you!' he exclaimed, and went on: 'You would go about to bring into the people's heads that we, all of the Lords of the Parliament house, the knights and burgesses, and all the whole realm be perjured. Oh, what a heresy is this! Here, good people' – turning to his audience – 'you may see what a senseless heretic this fellow is.' And he tried to defend his position that oaths could, and sometimes should, be reneged upon by saying that, if a neighbour were to ask him for help, it would not be an acceptable response to say that he had previously sworn not to help or lend money to anybody, so could not help him now. Bradford was ready to deal with this spurious defence: 'Oh my Lord, discern between oaths that are against charity and faith, and oaths that are according to faith and charity, as this is against the Bishop of Rome.' And again Bradford referred to Gardiner's own treatise, *De vera obedientia*, in support of his argument.

The reference to *De vera obedientia* was repeatedly made by Protestants and it was a severe embarrassment to Gardiner. He had indeed written this attack on papal authority and defence of the royal supremacy in 1535 and, to make matters worse, Edmund Bonner had contributed a preface to it, further lambasting the Bishop of Rome. The work had been written primarily in order for its author to be reinstated in the King's favour, after Gardiner had initially been hesitant about the break with Rome and as a result had fallen out of royal favour. The treatise, written in Latin and intended for international consumption, had had the desired effect, Henry appointing Gardiner as a special ambassador to France in the following year. And now, just at the point when the English Church had resubmitted to papal authority, and Gardiner, as Lord Chancellor, was in charge of prosecuting those who refused to submit to it, an English version of *De vera obedientia*, complete with Bonner's preface, was being eagerly read in Protestant circles, having emerged from a press in Rouen run by a man called Michael Wood, and probably with the involvement of John Bale. It was a public-relations disaster, and all Gardiner could do was bluster and counter-attack.

Still hoping to discredit Bradford in the eyes of his followers, on this last day of questioning Lord Chancellor Gardiner called as a witness a Mr Chamberlayne of Woodstock, who alluded to the time when Bradford had worked for Sir John Harrington and to the suspicions of financial irregularity on his part. Whatever had gone on in the past and had troubled Bradford's conscience for years, Bradford now hotly denied the accusations, demanding justice against those who slandered him with no proof. His anger seemed to take Gardiner aback, and this line of questioning was not pursued. And so the conversation returned to the substantive issues of doctrine and, in particular, the nature of the sacrament of the altar.

'My Lord, I believe Christ is present there to the faith of the due receiver,' affirmed Bradford. 'As for transubstantiation, I plainly and flatly tell you, I believe it not.'

'We were not asking you about transubstantiation,' Gardiner cavilled, 'but about Christ's presence.'

Whatever the precise terms to be used, after all this, there was no genuine reason to delay the conviction of Bradford for heresy, and it was duly pronounced. The Lord Chancellor proceeded to read out the words of excommunication, and appeared surprised in doing so to find Bradford described as a layman, having imagined him to be a priest, whereas in fact he had only ever been ordained deacon (an understandable misapprehension, given that Bradford had been conducting illicit services of Holy Communion while in prison). On his conviction, Bradford – who, of all the martyrs of this period, seemed most willing to embrace his fate – 'fell down on his knees, and heartily thanked God, that he counted him worthy to suffer for his sake'.

After his conviction he was sent first to the Clink and then to the Counter in Poultry, where he was held in solitude in what was known as the Grocers' Hall court. He expected to be executed in short order, as Rogers had been, but was instead held for nearly five more months, while the authorities sought to find ways to diminish his influence, particularly in his native Lancashire – either by arranging to have him executed there or, preferably, by securing his recantation, even at this late stage. If Bradford could be persuaded to recant, it would have a very demoralizing effect indeed on the Protestants. The attempt to persuade him began as early as 4 February, the day of John Rogers's execution, when Bishop Bonner himself spoke to Bradford in the Counter, greeting him by doffing his cap and giving him his hand. He had heard, he said, that Bradford wished to converse with some learned men, so he had brought Archdeacon Harpsfield to talk with him.

'Do like a wise man,' Bonner urged, 'but I pray you, go roundly to work: for the time is but short.'

Bradford denied having requested to speak to anyone, but said he had no objection to doing so.

'What?' said the bishop 'in a fume' to the prison keeper, 'did you not tell me this man wanted to talk?'

'No,' replied the keeper, 'I just said he wouldn't refuse to talk, not that he wanted to.'

Concluding from this that there were people – including the keeper – who cared about Bradford sufficiently to want to help him stay alive, Bonner remarked: 'Well, Mr Bradford, you are well beloved, I pray you consider yourself, and refuse not charity when it is offered.'

On 19 February the writ for Bradford's execution was withdrawn and he was subjected to further attempts to get him to change his mind, a number of eminent churchmen and theologians, including Nicholas Heath (who would be 'translated' from the bishopric of Worcester to the archbishopric of York later that year), the Bishop of Chichester (George Day) and two Spanish divines, being enlisted in the exercise. With the Spaniards, one of whom was Alfonso de Castro, the Franciscan theologian who was highly respected by King Philip and who had recently preached a sermon urging caution over the burning of heretics, Bradford discussed the question of how Christ could be present both in heaven and in the bread on the altar, deliberately poking fun at the Catholic position.

'How does this hang together?' he demanded. 'It is as if you should say because you are here, you must therefore be in Rome. And so you reason that because Christ's body is in heaven, it must therefore be in the sacrament in the form of bread. No wise man will agree with that.'

Alfonso got to the heart of the matter when he asked: 'So will you believe nothing that is not expressly said in the Scriptures?'

'I will believe anything you like,' responded Bradford, 'provided you can demonstrate it through the Scriptures.'

On 21 March it was the turn of Dr Hugh Weston, the Dean of Westminster, to try his luck with Bradford. Weston had been one of the City clergy during Henry's reign, having been made Rector of St Nicholas Olave in 1541 and of St Botolph-without-Bishopsgate in 1544 and, as an orthodox Catholic, he had spent some time in the Fleet prison under Edward. There was unlikely to be much common ground between him and Bradford. But Weston began in conciliatory mood, taking Bradford 'very gently by the hand' and clearing the room of everyone but themselves and a few companions, including the Subdean of Westminster, the keeper of the Counter and the priest in whose parish the Counter was located. Before beginning their conversation, Weston wanted to lay down certain principles for how it should be conducted, including that Bradford should 'put away all vainglory, and not hold anything for the praise of the world'. Bradford responded that, though 'a spice' of vainglory remained in all human beings, he hoped 'by the grace of God' not to yield to it. Weston then asked him to write down and send to him the main points of his views on the sacrament, so that he could return and discuss them with him. And until then, he promised, Bradford could be assured that he was 'without all peril of death'.

As might have been expected, notwithstanding the best efforts of Dr Weston and others, Bradford proved unbending. Yet despite his firmness and resistance to every effort to persuade him to recant and so be spared, it is evident, even from Foxe's at times hagio-graphic account, that he was afraid, even desperately afraid, of the ordeal before him. The waiting, the not knowing when he was to be burnt, contributed to his fear, his wakeful, nightmare-laden nights. On the eve of his being taken to Newgate to await execu-tion, he had particularly disrupted sleep, plagued by many anxious dreams, including one of the chain that was to fasten him to the stake being brought to the gate of the Counter. Such dreams were a frequent occurrence throughout his imprisonment and, unable to sleep, he would often get up to read and pray at about three o'clock in the morning. During the day he was his normal self, even appearing 'very merry'; only those who saw him at night knew of his fear.

In the afternoon after this premonitory dream, the keeper's wife came running into the room where Bradford had been taking what exercise he could by walking up and down with a friend and, upset and out of breath, cried, 'Oh, Mr Bradford, I come to bring you heavy news!' She then told him she had heard he was to be burnt the next day, that the chain for his burning was now being brought, and that he would shortly be transferred to Newgate. The news seems to have come almost as a relief to Bradford, after his having been expecting it, hour by hour, for so many weeks. He went into his own room with his friend to go through his papers and ensure all preparations were made for his death, and later several other friends arrived and they all spent some time in prayer.

On the morning of 30 June, the day he was taken to Newgate, Bradford's preparations included putting on a new shirt or shift (that is, a long white garment underneath his outer clothes; those outer garments would then be removed prior to the victim being chained to the stake), which had been especially made for his burn-ing by a Mrs Marler, one of the wives among the Protestant faithful, who had earlier been the recipient of advice from Bradford – he had written a devotional work for her to help her bear her labour pains. Bradford made a ceremony of donning the shirt: 'when he shifted himself with a clean shirt that was made for his burning . . . he made such a prayer of the wedding garment, that some of those who were present, were in such great admiration, that their eyes were as thoroughly occupied in looking at him, as their ears gave place to hear his prayer'. This clothing with a new white shirt to wear at the stake became a common feature of the burnings, a way of signalling support for and honouring the victim, as though he were being dressed as a bridegroom for his wedding. The white shirt was also a symbol of martyrdom, a deliberate allusion to verses from the Book of Revelation:

> After this I beheld, and lo a great multitude (which no man could number) of all nations and people, and tongues, stood before the seat, and before the lamb, clothed with long white garments, and palms in their hands . . . And one of the elders answered, saying unto me: what are these, which are arrayed in long white garments, and whence came they? . . . And he said unto me; these are they which came out of great tribulation, and made their garments large and made them white, in the blood of the lamb.

It was a reminder of the belief that those who endured martyrdom would be received in heaven by Christ as his faithful servants, for the passage from Revelation concludes: 'They shall hunger no more neither thirst, neither shall the sun light on them, neither any heat: For the lamb, which is in the midst of the seat shall feed them, and shall lead them unto fountains of living water, and God shall wipe away all tears from their eyes.' The ritualized actions which accompanied the clothing with the shirt recalled those of a priest donning his vestments before making the sacrifice of the Mass (for now the victim, like Christ, was himself both priest and sacrificial offering), and so the martyr might pray over and kiss the shirt before putting it on, as a priest kisses the stole before placing it around his neck. The Protestant martyrs, in these preparations they made for their deaths, can be seen as subverting Catholic ritual, adopting and remaking it to serve their own myth and interpretation of what they were doing, underlining their oneness with Christ and the fact that they were choosing to die, embracing their deaths willingly, as a holy sacrifice, becoming themselves the *anamnesis* – the recalling and re-enactment of the sacrificial death of Christ. While rejecting the idea of 'transubstantiation' – of bread being made into the body of Christ – they enact instead their own transformation, of their own flesh and blood becoming Christlike. Finally, and on a very different level, the white shirt served the practical purpose of shortening the time it would take for the flames to reach the body and thus for the sufferer to die.

Having dressed, Bradford emerged from his cell – like a vested priest emerging from the sacristy – said a prayer, and distributed money to the servants and officers who had been with him in the Counter for so many weeks. He then turned to the wall to utter another fervent prayer, all his energy now going into the desire to acquit himself well in the ordeal by fire that lay ahead – like an athlete preparing himself for the most challenging and fearful race of his life. Many people in the Counter wept to see him go.

It was towards midnight when Bradford was conveyed from the Counter to Newgate, the assumption being that there would be no one about on the streets to witness the transfer of the prisoner. But his friends had been busy during the previous few hours, and the authorities were disappointed to find 'a great multitude of people' lining Cheapside and other parts of the short route. A rumour was circulating that he was to be burnt as early as four o'clock in the morning – again with the supposed aim of keeping the event as hushed up as possible – and the crowd consequently grew over the next few hours, Smithfield being packed by the early hours of 1 July.

In fact, Bradford did not appear in Smithfield until nine o'clock, by which time the atmosphere among the crowd must have been electric with tension. The nervousness of the authorities can be detected in the reactions of Sheriff Woodroffe who, on seeing one of Bradford's brothers-in-law, Roger Beswick, among a number of friends taking it in turns to have a 'little secret talk' with Bradford as he was moved along the route, beat Beswick over the head with his staff, inflicting serious injury. No further conversation was permitted, and Bradford was accompanied the rest of the short walk to Smithfield by 'a great company of weaponed men'.

The crowd was so great, with so much pushing and shoving going on to get a glimpse of the condemned man, that at least one woman, a Protestant supporter called Mary Honeywood, lost her shoes in the crush and had to go home barefoot.

Bradford was burnt alongside a young man of nineteen called John Leaf, originally from Yorkshire but now an apprentice tallow chandler who lived and worked in the parish of Christ Church, Newgate. In his working life, Leaf would have been learning how to make candles out of tallow, or animal fats, a more affordable way of illuminating houses, shops and streets than using candles of beeswax, the preserve of the wealthy. In his small amount of free time, he had been listening to sermons and joining in prayers, led by men like Bradford. Leaf was illiterate, and had had two documents read out to him in prison (he had been kept in the Bread Street Counter, having been committed there by the Alderman of his Ward) – one a confession of heresy, the other a recantation that would have set him free. He chose the confession, by (so it was said) sprinkling his blood over it. When examined by Bonner, he had used the words he would have heard in the sermons he had been listening to (including some by John Rogers), denying 'the very true and natural body and blood of Christ in substance' to be in the sacrament of the altar and declaring that sacrament, 'as it is now called, used, and believed in this realm of England' to be 'idolatrous and abominable'. When asked by Bonner whether he was a scholar of Rogers's, he replied in the affirmative and with pride, firmly stating that 'he the same John did believe in the doctrine of the said Rogers, and in the doctrine of Bishop Hooper, Cardmaker, and others of their opinion, which of late were burned for the testimony of Christ, and that he would die in that doctrine that they died for'.

To his interrogators John Leaf embodied the justification for men like Rogers, Cardmaker and Bradford being taken out of circulation; he was – or so he appeared to them – precisely the kind of impressionable, uneducated young man likely to be easy prey for the 'heretics'. They also hoped that setting fire to him now, alongside one of his mentors, would dissuade other impetuous and impressionable apprentices from following his example. He was sentenced on Monday 10 June.

The courage with which Bradford, and others like him, went to their deaths – despite their night-fears – is partly explained by the attitude they took, and which they deliberately cultivated, towards death, and nowhere is this more clearly expressed than in 'A Meditation on Death, and the advantages it brings', composed by Bradford himself. 'What is this life,' he writes:

> but a smoke, a vapour, a shadow, a warfare, a bubble of water, a word, a grass, a flower? *Thou shalt die* is most certain, but the time when no man can tell. The longer thou dost remain in this life, the more thou sinnest, which will turn to thy more pain. By thinking upon death, our minds are often in manner oppressed with darkness, because we do but remember the night of the body, forgetting the light of the mind, and of the resurrection. Thereto remember the good things that shall ensue after this life, and without wavering, in certainty of faith – so shall the passage of death be more desired. It is like sailing over the sea to thy home and country; it is like a medicine to the health of soul and body; it is the best physician; it is like to a woman's travail, for so thy soul, being delivered out of the body, comes into a much more large and fair place, even into heaven!

The ceremonial of martyrdom continued at the site of the burning, with both Bradford and Leaf prostrating themselves on the ground – like a priest at the beginning of the most solemn liturgy of the year, that of Good Friday, and therefore again recalling the sacrifice of Christ – before removing their outer garments and, on being urged to hurry up by one of the sheriffs, approaching the stake. There Bradford, in a further ceremonial act, kissed one of the branches heaped around the stake and the stake itself. He then raised his hands in prayer – Bradford certainly had a highly developed sense of the dramatic, and was performing in the expectation that his words and gestures now would be recorded for posterity – and declaimed: 'Oh England, England, repent of your sins!

Beware of idolatry, beware of false Antichrists, take heed they do not deceive you.' The sheriffs, increasingly restive and wanting the job completed before the crowd got out of control, threatened to bind his hands if he wouldn't be quiet. He spoke some encouraging words to his young companion – 'Be of good comfort, Brother, for we shall have a merry supper with the Lord this night' – and then spoke no more.

Chapter Twelve

'I WILL PAY MY VOWS TO THEE, OH SMITHFIELD'

✠

> The bishop's task is, as far as he may, to teach, correct and cure. What sort of a bishop is he who can do nothing more than constrain, torture and commit to the flames?
>
> Desiderius Erasmus,
> from 'Supputatio Errorum' in 'Censuris Beddae', Opera Omnia IX

NEARLY SIX MONTHS AFTER the burning of Bradford and Leaf, on 18 December 1555, John Philpot, formerly Archdeacon of Winchester, traipsed through a very muddy Smithfield to reach the stake, where he was burnt. In prison, where he had been supplied with food by supporters among the City apprentices, he had signed letters to his friends with the words: 'dead to the world and living to Christ, your own brother, sealed up in the verity of Christ for ever'. Here he and his fellow Protestant prisoners were finally allowed to enjoy freedom of worship, and they made the most of it, spending their time in prayer, psalm-singing and preaching. During his imprisonment Philpot was even more prolific in his writing than Bradford had been, producing and smuggling out to his supporters letters of encouragement, treatises and accounts of his trials and examinations. Philpot, like Bradford, was a very prominent figure among the Protestants and a recantation from him might have been even more influential in quenching the zeal of the rebels, so the authorities believed, than his conviction and execution. As a consequence, immense time and effort went into trying to persuade him to recant, to the annoyance of many hard-liners. Their annoyance was only increased by the fact that there was nothing Philpot liked more than a good argument and, equally, that he was always and entirely convinced he was right.

For a short time after the death of Edward VI, Philpot had remained in post as Archdeacon of Winchester, despite the imme-diate deprivation of the bishop who had appointed him, John Ponet, and the restoration of Stephen Gardiner to the see. But not being one to lie low and see how things would turn out, Philpot had used the opportunity of the Canterbury convocation (the assembly of bishops and clergy of the province of Canterbury), held in London at St Paul's during October 1553, to speak out against the doctrine of the real presence and other matters with which he disagreed. (His performance at the convocation was later described by one of the Queen's commissioners as 'howling and weeping'.) For him there was never any possibility of compromise; he saw himself, and all Protestant believers, as living in the midst of evil, now that the Mass and other Catholic practices had been restored. He was as damning of the 'unreformed' as they of the 'reformed', as convinced of the wickedness of his theological opponents as they were of his; negotiation was impossible.

Philpot was by no means alone in espousing such views. Many people wrote to ask the advice of their Protestant leaders as to how they should behave now that times had changed again: could they, if they succeeded in avoiding the Mass, still attend (as they were officially required to do) the other services of Matins and Even-song? Or could they appear to follow Catholic practice outwardly, while denying it in their hearts (the old method of 'Nicodemitism', which had been pursued in an earlier reign by Friar John Forest and others)? But this generation of Protestant leaders did not incline to half-measures and supported John Calvin, who had coined the term 'Nicodemitism' in 1543, in viewing such dissem-bling as the most heinous of all sins. Bradford, for instance, insisted to one of his correspondents that 'this Latin service is a plain mark of Antichrist's Catholic synagogue' and that to attend would mean being 'cut off from Christ and His Church'. He underlined the point in a letter to Protestant believers in Coventry: 'My dearly beloved, therefore mark the word, hearken to the word; it allows no massing, no such sacrificing nor worshipping of Christ with tapers, candles, copes, canopies, etc. It allows no Latin service, no images in the temples, no praying to dead saints, no praying for the dead. It allows no such dissimulation, as a great many now use outwardly.'

By March 1554 Philpot had been deprived of his archdeaconry, excommunicated and placed in the King's Bench prison (where John Bradford was one of his companions for a time). He now began writing a series of pastoral letters to fellow Protestants, encouraging them to stand firm and accept exile, or even martyrdom if necessary; these letters, numbering twenty in total, were preserved and later printed by John Foxe and Miles Coverdale. He spent eighteen months in the King's Bench, before being transferred in October 1555 to Bishop Bonner's coalhouse prison, just after the start of a lengthy series of examinations. Philpot managed to make a record of these examinations, writing it in sections and getting it smuggled out of prison, a section at a time; this record was published by Foxe in his Latin and English versions of *Acts and Monuments*, supplemented with accounts of the trials both from eyewitnesses and official records.

Philpot's first examination, on 2 October, was conducted by three of the Queen's commissioners – Sir Roger Cholmley, Mr Roper and Dr John Story, chancellor of the diocese of London – with one of the scribes of the Court of Arches in attendance, and took place at Newgate Sessions Hall. Prior to the examination, Dr Story came out into the hall to look over who was there, recognized Philpot, and then commented on how he appeared to have put on weight – that he was 'well fed indeed'. Philpot's response was that it should be no surprise if he had become fat, as he had been 'stalled up' in prison for eighteen months, 'in a close corner'. And he then demanded to know of Story why he had been sent for. 'We hear you are a suspect person,' replied Story, 'and of heretical opinions, and therefore we have sent for you.' Philpot's immediate objection, which he made time and again during the course of his examinations, was that he had already been questioned by his 'ordinary' – that is, by the bishop of his own diocese which in his case was Stephen Gardiner, the Bishop of Winchester – and that those questioning him now had no authority to do so. Story intimated that he would get nowhere with such a defiant attitude, and went into the 'parlour', into which Philpot himself was soon summoned.

The examination began with some sparring between Philpot and Story, Philpot asserting that it was Bishop Gardiner, rather than Ponet, who had originally intended to make him Archdeacon of Winchester, and Story telling his fellow commissioners: 'You may be sure that my Lord Chancellor would not make anyone like him an Archdeacon.' Philpot attempted from the start to set the agenda for this interrogation, demanding that either he be charged with having broken the law in some way or that he be released from his 'long wrongful imprisonment'. And he further insisted: 'I am no heretic.' Story (who would himself be hanged, drawn and quartered for treason, under Elizabeth I, and later adjudged a Catholic martyr) begged to differ: 'I will prove you a heretic,' he said. 'Whoever has held against the blessed Mass is a heretic, and you have held against it – therefore you are a heretic.' Philpot's defence, which he again repeated several times, was that he had indeed spoken against the Mass but that he had done so at the convocation, where everybody had been given liberty, by the will of the Queen and her Council, to speak freely in matters of religion. Therefore, he argued, he should not have been 'molested and imprisoned' for expressing his opinion in that arena, and neither should he be questioned about that incident now. As Philpot continued to stress this point, and to insist that only his 'ordinary' had the right to question him at all, his examiners and their scribe soon began to tire of the conversation. 'This man is full of vainglory,' said the scribe; as has been seen, this was the usual accusation levelled at those accused of heresy who had the temerity to stand up for themselves. Cholmley tried a more conciliatory approach: 'Play the wise gentleman and be conformable,' he said, 'and be not stubborn in your opinions, neither cast yourself away. I would be glad to do you good.' Philpot would not give an inch, continuing to insist that, if they were to keep him in detention, they should charge him with something. Ignoring this, Story asked him the inevitable question: 'How do you say to the sacrament of the altar?' Philpot replied: 'Sir, I am not come now to dispute with your mastership, and the time now does not serve for that, but to answer to that with which I may be lawfully charged.'

Philpot's second examination took place just over three weeks later, on 24 October, again at Newgate Sessions Hall, before the same commissioners but with the addition of a Dr Cooke. Dr Story, who seems to have found Philpot particularly disagreeable, was determined to take a hard line from the outset, announcing to his fellow commissioners that he had spoken to Lord Chancellor Stephen Gardiner (who was now mortally ill and unable to attend the examinations himself), whose will it was that Philpot should be committed to the Bishop of London – 'there to recant, or else burn'. Having made this announcement, he left the room. Philpot refused to acknowledge that he had done anything requiring recantation and continued to assert that the Bishop of London had no jurisdiction over him, and that he should not in any event be re-examined over a matter for which he had already been unjustly imprisoned and suffered the loss of his living.

'There was never poor Archdeacon so handled at your hands as I am,' he complained, 'and that without any just cause you are able to lay against me.'

'You are no Archdeacon,' retorted Dr Cooke.

'I am still an Archdeacon,' insisted Philpot, 'although another is in possession of my living, for I was never deprived by any law.' It was not the loss of the living itself which distressed him, he asserted, but the injustice of the way he was being treated, 'contrary to all law'.

Cooke's response was that of officialdom in every age: 'If we do you wrong, complain about us' – and in the meantime he would be accommodated in the Lollards' Tower at St Paul's, the regimen at the King's Bench having been altogether too lenient.

'Sir, I am a poor gentleman,' protested Philpot. 'Therefore I trust of your gentleness you will not commit me to so vile and straight a place, as I am no heinous criminal.'

'You are no gentleman,' retorted Cooke.

'Oh, yes I am,' said Philpot.

But Cooke declared that a heretic was, by definition, not a gentleman. Philpot responded that a gentleman remained a gentleman, even if he was a traitor – but, he said, he would not insist on his status, given that they placed so little value on it.

At this point Dr Story returned, and was dismayed to find that Philpot had not yet been despatched to the Lollards' Tower. 'What? – will you allow this heretic to prate with you all day?' he asked.

'He says he's a gentleman,' said Cooke.

'A gentleman, he says?' exploded Story. 'He is a vile heretic knave; and a heretic is no gentleman.' So saying, he called in the keeper of the Lollards' Tower and demanded he take Philpot away.

The latter continued to protest vigorously – 'Sir, if I were a dog,' he cried, 'you could not appoint me a worse and more vile place! God give you a more merciful heart – you are very cruel to one who has never offended you.' And he appealed to Sir Roger Cholmley, who had so far played no part in the day's proceedings, to intervene on his behalf. Cholmley appeared to wish to dissociate himself from his colleagues, implying in an undertone to Philpot that he did not understand either the laws they were relying on or their motivation. Philpot's parting shot, as he was being taken away, was to quote, in Latin, the words of Christ to Judas when he was preparing to betray him: 'What you are about to do, do quickly.'

The implication was not lost on Story – 'Do you not hear how he makes us Judases?' he exclaimed.

Philpot, with four other prisoners, was initially taken to the keeper's house in Paternoster Row, next to St Paul's; he was offered a bed for the night by Archdeacon Harpsfield's servant, on the instruction of the archdeacon. Philpot thanked him, but refused, fearing that one night in a comfortable room would only make prison conditions harder to bear. And so after supper Philpot and his fellow prisoners were escorted to the bishop's coalhouse. A married priest called Thomas Whittle, and another man, were already imprisoned there. Whittle had a story to tell of Bonner's brutality, consistent with other episodes related of the irascible beard-hating bishop: having been brought to a state of physical wretchedness through ill-treatment and imprisonment, Whittle had recanted and been set free but then, his conscience proving even more of a torment than his body, he had torn up his recantation – whereupon Bonner sent for him 'and fell upon him like a lion, and like a manly Bishop buffeted him well, so that he made his face black and blue, and plucked away a great piece of his beard'. Bonner's violent tendencies were acknowledged – and viewed as a source of embarrassment – even by his close associates, who, probably with some justification, put them down to his bitter experiences under the previous reign. Dean Feckenham is recorded by Foxe as having said to the Rector of Hadham, after the bishop had lost his temper and hit him, 'Bear with my lord; for truly his long imprisonment in the Marshalsea . . . hath altered him.'

Philpot's own turn to encounter Bishop Bonner came on the second night of his imprisonment in the coalhouse. Bonner began with an attempt to soften him up, by sending to him his registrar, Robert Johnson, 'with a mess of meat and a good pot of drink, and bread', and claiming not to have known that Philpot was being held in his coalhouse and that he was sorry about it. Philpot took the food and drink to share with his fellows, Johnson conveying the message that 'My Lord would know the cause of your being sent here (for he knows nothing thereof) and wonders that he should be troubled with prisoners of other dioceses than his own.' Philpot recounted his view of the case, and the registrar departed to report back to the bishop.

A little later Philpot was himself taken to see the bishop, sitting at a table with several of his chaplains (whom Foxe sometimes refers to as 'Bonnerlings') and the registrar. Bonner was in emollient mood. 'Mr Philpot, you are welcome,' he said, 'give me your hand.' Rather taken aback by this courteous greeting, Philpot responded with equal courtesy. The bishop continued the comedy of having no idea what was going on. 'I am right sorry for your trouble,' he asserted, 'and I promise that until two hours ago I did not know you were here. Please tell me why you have been sent here, for I promise you I know nothing about it as yet, and I

wouldn't want you to think it was my doing.' And he proceeded
to depict himself as a poor put-upon functionary – 'I marvel that
other men trouble me with their matters, but I must be obedient
to my betters: and, I suppose, men speak otherwise of me than I
deserve.' Philpot stated that he had been unjustly detained because
of what he had said at the convocation. The bishop pursued his
tactic of pretending to be a harmless old buffer, perhaps hoping to
trick Philpot into an admission of guilt. 'I marvel that you should
be troubled for that,' he said, 'if there was really no other cause than
this. But perhaps you have maintained the same since – perhaps
some of your friends have asked you recently whether you still
think the same way, and you have said "Yes", and for this you
might have been committed to prison.' Philpot insisted he had
done nothing beyond speaking at the convocation and refusing to
take back what he had said, and that he had only spoken of those
doctrinal matters which it had been agreed might be discussed at
that assembly.

'Why,' said Bonner, persisting with his air of puzzled wonder-
ment, 'may we dispute our faith?'

'Yes, we may,' replied Philpot.

'I don't think so,' said Bonner, 'not according to the law.'

Philpot expressed his belief that, though the civil law forbade
such disputation, God's law encouraged people to be able to give
an account of their faith. Taking up this cue, Bonner asked Philpot
to tell him how he interpreted the sacrament of the altar. But Philpot was not going to be trapped so easily, and gave two reasons for
his refusal to answer: first citing St Ambrose that disputation of the
faith should take place in the congregation and not privately, and
secondly that he knew it would endanger his life to speak his mind
on that subject, so he could not – until such time as he was on trial
and bound by the law to answer, when he would freely do so. 'I
perceive you are learned,' observed Bonner and, trying out another
tactic, declared that he could do with someone like Philpot on his
staff. But for that to happen, he would have to come and 'be of the
Church, for there is but one Church'. Philpot replied that he had
never left it.

'How old are you?' asked Bonner.

'Forty-four,' replied Philpot.

Bonner now asserted that Philpot was no longer of the faith he was baptized into as a child, but that he had been of a different faith for the last twenty years. Philpot responded that he had grown up with no real faith at all, but refused to answer as to whether the current official faith of England was the true one. Bonner agreed not to pursue the question for the time being, and changed the subject. 'I marvel that you are so merry in prison as you are,' he said, 'singing and rejoicing. I think instead you should lament and be sorry.' Philpot defended the singing of hymns and psalms, as commanded by St Paul – particularly as he and his fellow prisoners were in 'a dark comfortless place' and needed to keep themselves cheerful. In ending the conversation, Bonner maintained his kindly demeanour and insisted Philpot be given 'a good cup of wine' – before being returned to the coalhouse.

At the outset of Philpot's next examination, held in the Archdeacon of London's house before the bishops of London, Bath, Worcester and Gloucester, Bonner again seemed in a conciliatory mood, addressing Philpot in a respectful manner, and making it sound as though this was an ad-hoc examination, called just because these other bishops happened to have turned up. The Bishop of Worcester, Richard Pate, suggested Philpot should pray that God would open his heart to the truth, whereupon Philpot, needing no encouragement to engage in extempore prayer at which he was expert, fell to his knees and prayed aloud: 'Almighty God, which art the giver of all wisdom and understanding, I beseech thee of thine infinite goodness and mercy in Jesus Christ, to give me, most vile sinner in thy sight, the spirit of wisdom to speak and make an answer in thy cause, that it may be to the contentation of the hearers before whom I stand and also to my better understanding, if I be deceived in anything.' Bonner, despite his assumption of an avuncular manner, had got the measure of his man more fully than had Pate, and was displeased at Philpot having been given this opportunity for grandstanding. 'No, my Lord of Worcester,' he said, 'you did not well to exhort him to make any prayer. For this is the thing they have a singular pride in, that they can often make their vain prayers in which they glory much.'

'I can't make out what he was praying for anyway,' said Bishop Bourne of Bath. 'Let's hear what he has to say.'

Philpot repeated what he had been saying all along so far – that he had been in prison for the last eighteen months for no just reason, that he had been unlawfully deprived of his living, that he had now been brought into another bishop's jurisdiction instead of that of his ordinary, and that if there was nothing to charge him with, then he should be released. Bonner also repeated what he had said before – that Philpot had been sent to him without his knowledge, and that he only wished to do him good. And he encouraged Philpot to say whatever he wanted 'without any fear'. But Philpot, rightly, continued to be very wary, having learnt enough in his legal training (as a young man and fellow of New College, Oxford, he had spent some time studying law in Italy) to know not to endanger himself by giving a reply before he absolutely had to. And he repeated that, as Bonner was not his ordinary, he was not obliged to answer his questions. Bonner, beginning to lay aside his earlier friendly manner, asserted that Philpot had offended in his diocese by speaking against the sacrament of the altar, and so he did have the right to summon him and proceed against him. No, responded Philpot, he had not offended in Bonner's diocese, but in the convocation house of St Paul's – which, so he understood, was a 'peculiar' jurisdiction belonging to the Dean of St Paul's and not to the bishop.

Bonner professed to be amazed at this – 'Is not Paul's church in my diocese?' he protested. 'It certainly costs me a great deal of money every year!'

A legal opinion was now sought from a Dr Cole who was present (most probably Henry Cole, a cleric with a legal background who, in December 1556, himself became Dean of St Paul's). Cole, predictably, thought that Philpot was making too much fuss about this legal nicety, particularly as Bonner had said he was not trying to hurt but rather help him, and that Philpot should therefore explain what it was that was being held against him. But Philpot said he feared this might prejudice his eventual trial.

The Bishop of Gloucester, James Brooks, approached the nub of the difficulty of the Protestant position that authority lies solely in the scriptures when he asked: 'Why, Mr Philpot, do you think that the universal church has erred, and you only to be in the truth?'

When Philpot responded that, in matters of controversy, the word of God (that is, the Bible) would be the judge, the bishop pressed him further: 'What if you take the word one way, and I another way? – who shall be the judge then?'

'The Primitive Church,' replied Philpot, meaning 'the Doctors' or early Church Fathers.

The bishop did not let up: 'What if you take the Doctors in one sense, and I in another, who shall be the judge then?'

Philpot replied: 'Let that be taken which is most agreeable to God's word.'

The fact that Philpot wrote an account of this conversation after the event suggests that he did not actually realize how circular the argument had become. Dr Cole had had enough of it, however, and interrupted to say that this had nothing to do with why Philpot was being examined, which concerned his error over the sacrament. Bishop Bonner soon brought this examination to an end, with Philpot still complaining that the bishops thought they understood more than they did, and the Bishop of Worcester protesting that he was 'the most arrogant and stoutest fond fellow that I ever knew'.

A large assembly was gathered to hear Philpot's fifth examination, which took place in the gallery of Bishop Bonner's palace. Besides Bonner himself, there were the bishops of Rochester, Coventry and Lichfield, and St Asaph; also Drs Story and Pendleton (one of Bonner's chaplains and Vicar of St Martin Outwich in the City), with various other chaplains and Gentlemen of the Queen's Chamber. Bonner announced that on the following day he would be sitting in judgement on Philpot and so today's conversation was a last chance for him to 'play the wise man' and be ruled by all the learned men who were gathered there. During the ensuing discussion, Philpot was even more insistent than previously that he should not be held to account for what he had said at the convocation, because the convocation house was a member of the Parliament house – 'where all men in matters propounded may frankly speak their minds' – and he appealed for support to one of the Queen's Gentlemen who had been present at the convocation. But this man's opinion was that the most sensible thing Philpot could do would be to take back what he had said on that occasion. The Bishop of St Asaph (Thomas Goldwell) attempted to steer the conversation towards the substantive matter – 'Is not there in the blessed sacrament of the altar [and here everyone, apart from Philpot, raised their caps in reverence] the presence of our Saviour Christ, really and substantially after the words of consecration?' – but as usual Philpot refused to be drawn. As Philpot continued to prevaricate, finding reasons not to answer any questions, Bonner finally lost his patience – 'You are the veriest beast that ever I heard!' he exclaimed. 'I must needs speak it, you compel me to.'

Philpot was sent back, once again, to the coalhouse where he had had neither fire nor candle for a fortnight – and this was now late October, the days getting shorter and the nights colder.

Despite Bonner's assertion that he was to be judged on the day after this last examination, the time of judgement was not yet, and the aim was still to secure a recantation if possible. On 6 November Philpot appeared before a group of laymen, including members of the Privy Council rather than clerics, though Bonner and Dr William Chedsey (another of Bonner's chaplains and the Archdeacon of Middlesex) were there too. The laymen included the Lord Chamberlain (Sir John Gage), the Viscount Hertford (also known as Lord Ferrers), the Lord St John, the Lord Windsor, the Lord Shandoys, Sir John Bridges (the Lieutenant of the Tower) and – someone who played a significant part in the proceedings – the Lord Rich. The importance being attached to persuading Philpot to recant is indicated by Bonner coming up to him privately before the hearing commenced, counselling prudence and to be careful what he said. There is no suggestion that Bonner himself wanted Philpot to burn.

Everyone, apart from Philpot, took their seats, with Bonner

placing himself at the end of the table. Philpot initially knelt, but was commanded to stand, which he did.

Lord Rich intervened early on in the proceedings, instructing Philpot to answer questions of fact – 'Were you imprisoned by my Lord or not? Can you find any fault since with his cruel using of you?' – before going on to other matters. And, when Philpot repeated his assertion that free speech was permissible in the convocation house because it was a member of the Parliament house, it was Lord Rich who put him right: 'You are deceived herein,' he said, 'for the Convocation house is no part of the Parliament house.' Rich was backed up by the Lord Windsor, and Philpot had to admit defeat on that point. Nevertheless, said Rich, they would not want him to be in trouble for anything he had said there, provided he now repented of it.

In the ensuing conversation, Lord Rich showed confidence in discussing theological matters, if only in knowing how to articulate the orthodox position. 'How say you?' he asked of Philpot. 'Will you acknowledge the real presence of the blood and body of Christ, as all the learned men of this realm do in the Mass, and as I do, and will believe as long as I live, I do protest it?' Philpot was evasive, saying he acknowledged 'such a presence, as the word of God allows and teaches me', and Bonner tried to pin him down to a straight answer by providing a definition: 'A sacrament is the sign of a holy thing. So that there is both the sign which is the accident (as the whiteness, roundness, and shape of bread) and there is also the thing itself, as very Christ both God and man. But these heretics will have the sacraments to be but bare signs. How say you? Declare unto my Lords here whether you do allow the thing itself in the sacrament or not?' But Philpot continued to beat about the bush (as Bonner complained), explaining to the assembled lords that he could not speak of these things without endangering his life. 'There is none of us here that seeks your life,' asserted Rich, 'or mean to take any advantage of what you say.' Those who knew Richard Rich also knew that nothing he said should ever be taken at face value, but Philpot seems to have gained the impression that these members of the Privy Council posed less of a danger to him than Bishop Bonner. In fact the reverse was the case; Bonner was still desperate to secure a recantation, while the Privy Council wanted an end to the matter and were not particularly concerned with saving Philpot's life. Nevertheless, in the presence of these lords, Philpot did at last agree to say what he believed: 'And as touching the sacrament, which they term of the altar, I say now as I said in the Convocation house that it is not the sacrament of Christ, neither in the same is there any manner of Christ's presence. Wherefore they deceive the Queen's majesty: and you of the nobility of this realm, in making you to believe that to be a sacrament which is none, and cause you to commit manifest idolatry in worshipping that for God, which is no God.'

It is noticeable that, for Philpot, the real and only culprit is the Roman (and currently the English) Church and the church hierarchy – not the Queen, and not the representatives of temporal power; they have merely been led astray by the likes of Bonner and Gardiner. In fact, he views these church dignitaries in much the same way they view him – as dangerous heretics, who pose a threat to the eternal souls of everyone who comes into contact with them. Once having begun to speak, Philpot went on at some considerable length, and he interpreted Bonner's downcast expression (he was in 'the dumps', Philpot observed) as annoyance that he was talking so much; Bonner may in fact have been depressed at the realization that Philpot was indeed now condemning himself out of his own mouth, and that a recantation was very unlikely indeed.

In giving his opinion of the situation, Lord Rich alluded to an earlier encounter he had had with a heretic. 'All heretics boast of the spirit of God,' he said, 'and every one would have a church by himself – like Joan of Kent and the Anabaptists.' He went on to recall the occasion when Joan Boucher had been held at his house at St Bartholomew's for a week, during which time 'my Lord of Canterbury and Bishop Ridley resorted almost daily unto her: but she was so high in the spirit that they could do nothing with her for all their learning'. Joan 'went wilfully to the fire', declared Rich, and was burnt – 'and so do you now'. Whether anyone present noticed Rich's remarkable slip in what he had just said, no one –

including Philpot – picked up on it. For Rich had just referred, with apparent approval, to 'all the learning' of two men, Thomas Cranmer ('my lord of Canterbury', as he was at the time to which Rich referred) and Nicholas Ridley (the former Bishop of London), who were now judged to be among the foremost heretics of the realm. Cranmer was currently in prison, while Ridley had actually been burnt in Oxford, in horrible, protracted agòny, during the period of Philpot's examinations, on 16 October.

It is of course possible that Rich never made this remark at all, but that it was either misremembered by Philpot or invented by Foxe, who certainly experienced difficulty in justifying the burning of Joan Boucher under a Protestant administration. But Rich's opening phrase – 'All heretics boast of the spirit of God, and every one would have a church by himself' – is in keeping with the general attitude of Philpot's examiners, and there is no reason to think he would not have said this. It is also perfectly believable that Philpot's intransigence reminded Rich of Joan – and that the vividness of that recollection led him to reminisce rather carelessly about this memorable episode in his life at St Bartholomew's, momentarily forgetting that Cranmer and Ridley were the last people he should have mentioned. If the normally circumspect Rich could slip up in this way, it only shows how very difficult it was constantly to censor one's memories and keep a guard on one's tongue. Rich was saved from embarrassment – or worse – on this occasion, by Philpot not taking advantage of his momentary lapse but instead concurring that Joan of Kent was indeed a 'vain woman' and a heretic, and that she had deserved to be burnt. And so what has been remembered from this exchange is that Philpot, like John Rogers, showed no tolerance for Anabaptists or sympathy with Joan.

When Rich next spoke, it was to change the subject. 'Where do you come from?' he asked. 'Are you one of the Hampshire Philpots?'

On Philpot's replying in the affirmative and giving the name of his father, Rich claimed to be closely related to him and all the more sorry for the plight Philpot found himself in – 'In faith I would go a hundred miles on my bare feet to do you good,' he declared.

Returning to theological matters, Rich demanded to know why Philpot insisted on denying Christ's very words, when he had declared of the bread: 'This is my body.' 'Is not God omnipotent?' Rich expostulated. 'And is not he able as well by his omnipotence to make it his body, as he was to make man flesh of a piece of clay? Did he not say: This is my body which shall be betrayed for you? And was not his very body betrayed for us? – therefore it must needs be his body?'

Bonner was impressed – 'My Lord Rich, you have said wonderful well and learnedly,' he declared.

Philpot replied that he did not deny Christ's words, but that he believed they were to be taken 'sacramentally and spiritually' and not 'carnally, as the papists now do'.

Bonner returned to the point about God's omnipotence: 'Is he not able to perform that which he spoke, as my Lord Rich has very well said? I tell you, that God by his omnipotence may make himself to be this carpet, if he will.'

Philpot was well able to deal with this somewhat absurd remark. 'As concerning the omnipotence of God,' he replied, 'I say that God is able to do (as the Prophet David says) whatsoever he wills: but he wills nothing that is not agreeable to his word: as that is blasphemy which my Lord of London has said, that God may become a carpet. For as I have learned of ancient writers: God cannot do what is contrary to his nature, as it is contrary to the nature of God to be a carpet.'

Leaving aside the question of carpets, Bonner tried to get an answer about the sacrament. 'Will you not say that Christ is really present in the sacrament?' he asked. 'Or do you deny it?'

'I deny not that Christ is really in the sacrament to the receiver thereof,' replied Philpot, 'according to Christ's institution.'

'What do you mean by really present?' pressed Bonner.

'I mean by really present, present indeed,' said Philpot, unhelpfully.

'Is God really present everywhere?' asked Bonner.

'He is so,' replied Philpot.

'How do you prove that?' asked Bonner (meaning 'What is your evidence for saying so?').

Philpot quoted the prophet Isaiah – 'that God fills all places' – and the promise contained in Matthew's Gospel, that 'wheresoever there be two or three gathered together in Christ's name, there is he in the midst of them'.

'What? His humanity?' questioned Bonner.

'No, my Lord, I mean the deity,' replied Philpot, 'according to what you asked.'

Rich, perceiving that this line of questioning by Bonner did not seem to be going anywhere, and that Philpot might even be getting the better of Bonner, suggested that Dr Chedsey take over – 'a learned man indeed'. Bonner decided it was time for a pause in the proceedings, and offered the assembled dignitaries something to drink. It was Lord Rich who insisted Philpot be given a drink too, for which he was grateful. And indeed, by the end of this examination, Philpot seemed convinced of Rich's good intentions towards him but that, in agreeing to hear him out fully, he had promised more than he could deliver, as the bishops were the ones in control.

Philpot's seventh examination took place on 19 November (a week after the death, after a protracted illness – possibly dropsy – of Bishop and Lord Chancellor Stephen Gardiner) before Bishops Bonner and Griffith, the chancellor of Lichfield diocese, and Dr Chedsey. By now Bonner was getting very tired of the argumentative Philpot and introduced him tetchily to the chancellor: 'Lo, Master Chancellor, I told you we should have a froward fellow of him: he will answer directly to nothing. I have had him before both spiritual Lords and temporal, and thus he fares still: yet he reckons himself better learned than all the realm. Yes, before the temporal Lords the other day, he was so foolish to challenge the best: he would make himself learned, and is a very ignorant fool indeed.'

'I reckon I answered your Lordship before the Lords plain enough,' retorted Philpot. He had also had enough of Bonner, responding to the bishop's assertion that he was being 'too well handled' with: 'If to lie in a windowless coalhouse may be counted good handling, without either fire or candle, then may it be said, I am well handled. Your Lordship has power to treat my body as you wish.'

'You are a fool, and a very ignorant fool,' responded the bishop. He was also very clear about the choice Philpot had to make; despite the death of Stephen Gardiner (whom he imagined Philpot believed to be the instigator of the burnings), it was not the case that 'we will burn no more'. (In fact, Gardiner, increasingly convinced that the policy of burning was turning out to be a failure, had in recent months become a restraining influence on the Privy Council; with his death, the councillors acquiesced wholeheartedly with the determination of the Queen and Cardinal Pole to continue the persecution.)

'Yes, I warrant you,' Bonner told Philpot, 'I will dispatch you shortly, unless you recant.'

Philpot said he was expecting nothing less. Yet again the discussion turned to whether Bonner had the authority to proceed against his prisoner. 'What? Are you not of my diocese?' asked Bonner crossly. 'Where are you now, I pray you?'

'My Lord, I cannot deny that I am in your coalhouse,' responded Philpot, 'which is your diocese. Yet I am not of your diocese.' And he refused to answer any further questions.

Relations between the bishop and his prisoner now rapidly deteriorated, with Philpot responding offensively to a summons to hear Mass – 'My stomach is too raw to digest such raw meats of flesh, blood and bone this morning' – and Bonner resorting to physical punishment for Philpot's continued refusal to answer the 'articles' he had drawn up. The former archdeacon was now put in the stocks, fastened by his wrists and ankles, and left there for several hours, in solitude, unable to move. And the next day he was forcibly escorted to the bishop by two of his servants. Bonner informed him that his own position was now very difficult, as he was being pressurized to get this case over and done with. There had been complaints from the other bishops, he said, because he had allowed Philpot to speak so much in his examinations – 'they say it is meat and drink to you to speak in an open audience, you glory so of yourself'. And when Philpot still stubbornly tried to insist that Bonner was not his ordinary, the bishop bellowed at him: 'I am your Ordinary and here do pronounce by sentence peremptory, that I am your Ordinary, and that you are of my diocese.'

In between examinations and altercations with his prisoner, Bishop Bonner had other duties to attend to, including officiating at the protracted and elaborate exequies of the late Bishop Gardiner:

> The 21 day of November at noon began the knell for my Lord Chancellor, for then was the body brought to the church of St Mary Overy, with great company of priests and clerks, and all the bishops; and my Lord of London did execute the office, and wore his mitre; and there were 2 goodly white branches burning, and the hearse with arms and tapers burning, and 4 dozen of staves; and all the quire with black, and his arms; and before the corpse the King of heralds with his coat, and with 5 banners of his arms, and 4 of images wrought with fine gold and enamel; and the morrow-mass 3 masses, one of the Trinity, one of Our Lady, and the 3rd of requiem for his soul; and after to dinner; and so he was put in a hearse till a day that he shall be taken up and carried unto Winchester to be buried there.

The onset of winter meant that the removal of Gardiner's body to Winchester did not finally happen until 24 February.

On 24 November Bonner decided to increase the pressure on his prisoner by having him transferred from the coalhouse into solitary confinement in a small room high up in St Paul's, in a turret on the other side of the Lollards' Tower (the earlier threat to accommodate him in the Lollards' Tower itself was never carried out). From here Philpot could 'look over the tops of a great many houses'. On entering the room, the prisoner was searched, and had his pencase, inkhorn, girdle and knife removed. Fortunately, however, he had had an intimation (presumably from someone on the bishop's staff who was sympathetic to him) of what was about to happen before he was removed from the coalhouse, and he had taken the opportunity of going to the latrine to throw away a number of letters – but he had stuffed the latest instalment of his examinations down his hose. The keeper felt the packet, and made an attempt to get it out. 'Let me alone,' said Philpot, 'I'll do that myself,' and he contrived to extract a couple of not very important letters, while manipulating his own written notes into his codpiece. As soon as the keeper had gone out, he hid them near his bed, and by making a great show of tearing up some other letters, he managed to convince the keeper he had nothing further to hide.

Philpot's eighth examination took place before Bishops Bonner and Morgan (the Bishop of St David's), Sir John Mordaunt (a member of the Privy Council, and son of the John Mordaunt who had refused to inform on Friar John Forest in 1538), Archdeacon Harpsfield and a number of others in the bishop's chapel on 25 November. Philpot became very agitated and angry during this brief hearing, again refusing to answer the articles drawn up by Bonner and protesting furiously to him: 'Knock me on the head with a hatchet, or set up a stake, and burn me out of hand without further law: as well you may do so, for all is without order of law. Such tyranny was never seen, as you use nowadays. God of his mercy destroy your cruel kingdom.' Bishop Morgan tried to calm Philpot down, begging him to be quiet, while Bonner gave up and hurriedly left the room. It took three or four men, by his own admission, to get Philpot back to his cell.

A further attempt to cajole Philpot to provide answers to the articles was made the next day. Philpot as usual refused, to Bonner's expressed bewilderment. ('Do you not see all the realm against you?') Archdeacon Harpsfield took a turn at persuasion, privately – but Philpot castigated him as though he, Harpsfield, were the one accused of heresy and not Philpot himself. 'Before God I tell you plainly you are highly deceived, and maintain false religion,' Philpot said to his former schoolfellow (they had been schoolboys together at Winchester College and had even indulged in a late-night Latin verse-writing competition with one another – which Philpot had won), 'and if you do not repent, and leave off your persecuting of Christ's truth, you will go to the devil for it.'

Philpot's formal trial, at which the bishop's registrar (Robert

Johnson) was present alongside the bishop and others, finally began on 27 November. The old argument over Bonner's authority was played out yet again, Philpot asserting that Bonner was not his ordinary, and had no legal grounds on which to deal with him, and Bonner as usual exploding: 'What an obstinate fool is this! I tell you I will be your Ordinary whether you like it or not.' Philpot could certainly not be accused of giving up easily or of a lack of tenacity. 'And because of this your unrighteous force towards me,' he declared, 'I have appealed from you, and I require you, Master Registrar, that my appeal be entered in writing.'

'You are an arrogant fool,' said Bonner. 'And now I have to go to Parliament.'

The trial was resumed on St Andrew's day (30 November) before the bishops of Durham (Cuthbert Tunstall), Chichester (George Day), Bath (Gilbert Bourne) and London (Bonner), the chairman of the lower house of convocation (John Christopherson), Dr William Chedsey, Master Morgan of Oxford, Master Hussey of the Court of Arches, Dr Hugh Weston (Dean of Westminster), Archdeacon Harpsfield and the registrar. Bonner began the proceedings courteously, greeting Philpot at the door and introducing him to the assembled dignitaries: 'My Lords, I shall desire you to take some pains with this man, he is a gentleman, and I would he should do well: but he will wilfully cast himself away.'

The mild-mannered and elderly Cuthbert Tunstall began the examination, asking if, whatever had gone before, Philpot would now agree to 'be a conformable man to the Catholic faith, and leave all new-fangled opinions and heresies'.

'My Lord, I am of the Catholic faith,' replied Philpot, 'and desire to live and die in the same.' The dispute concerned the definition of that faith. Philpot set out his view, held by many on both sides, that two faiths, two churches, were now opposing one another – the true and the false.

The examination quickly became confrontational. One of the questioners, Master Morgan, said he believed that the Protestants who had already been burnt had been drunk when they went to their deaths, and that was why they had appeared brave. This accusation infuriated Philpot, who railed at Morgan, calling him a 'painted wall and hypocrite' and warning him, 'in the name of the living Lord', that 'God shall rain fire and brimstone upon such scorners of his word, and blasphemers of his people as you are'. Philpot had now embraced the role of prophet, seeing himself – and his inevitable fate – as in the tradition and vocation of the prophets of both Old and New Testaments, from Elijah to St Paul. Further calling Morgan a 'blind and blasphemous doctor', he told him: 'I have spoken on God's behalf, and now have I done with you.' Nothing cowed, Morgan traded insult for insult, curse for curse: 'Why, then I tell you, Philpot, that you are a heretic, and shall be burnt for your heresy, and afterwards go to hell fire.' Philpot declared he cared nothing for 'your fire and faggots', and insisted that those heading for hellfire were his adversaries, like Morgan – 'and such hypocrites as you are' – and not himself. Morgan fell back on his original imputation of drunkenness, accusing Philpot of having 'tippled well today'. Philpot justifiably observed that this was precisely what was said by the unbelieving observers of the Apostles on the day of Pentecost, when they were filled with the Holy Spirit. So while he had headed closer to being burnt through this examination, Philpot had also had his sense of righteousness and confidence bolstered by the very accusations flung at him.

Philpot's final examinations, and his condemnation, took place in mid-December. Even now, in this endgame, the accused continued to protest that Bonner was not his 'competent judge'. After examinations on both 13 and 14 December, Philpot was brought before the bishops of London, Bath and Wells, Coventry and Lichfield, and Worcester on the afternoon of 16 December to have 'the definitive sentence of condemnation pronounced against him', if he still refused to recant. Philpot continued to cast himself in the role of prophet, inveighing against the bishops sitting in judgement on him – 'you and all others that be of your generation and sect' – as hypocrites and enemies of Christ. 'And I am sorry to see you sit in the place that you now sit in,' he declaimed, 'pretending to execute justice, and do nothing less but deceive all men in this realm.'

The counterproductive nature of repression as a means of dealing with 'extremism' is clearly demonstrated in the examinations
of Philpot which consistently, and with increasing force as they
neared their climax, bolstered his self-image, his conviction that he
was right and that his adversaries were the enemies not only of
himself and of his fellow believers, but of Christ. 'You profess
Christ and maintain Antichrist,' he asserted boldly. 'You profess the
Gospel, and maintain superstition – and you are able to charge me
with nothing.'

That the condemnation and sentence had already been determined is clear from the arrival at this point of the Lord Mayor,
Sir William Garrard, Alderman Sir Martin Bowes (who had been
Lord Mayor at the time of the trial of Anne Askew) and one of the
sheriffs, Alderman Sir Thomas Leigh. They sat down with the
bishops to await the judgement, and the anticipated handing over
of the condemned man into their charge. Recognizing that the end
was now coming, Philpot ceased any attempt at prevarication
and declared himself not to belong to the 'Babylonical' Church
of Rome, and that the Mass as practised by that Church was
blasphemy, invention and deception. He also 'utterly denied' the
doctrine of transubstantiation, and charged his accusers with being
not only idolaters but traitors – 'for in your pulpits you rail upon
good kings as King Henry, and King Edward his son, who have
stood against the usurped power of the Bishop of Rome'.

Bonner now proceeded to read out the sentence of condemnation, in Latin. Halfway through a sentence the Bishop of Bath
tugged at his sleeve to interrupt him, saying: 'My Lord, my Lord,
first ask him whether or not he will recant.'

'Oh, leave me alone,' snapped Bonner, shrugging off the inter-
ruption and carrying on with his reading. He then handed Philpot
over to the waiting sheriffs. For Bonner, this whole long-drawn-
out procedure had been a failure; he had tried everything he could
think of, from courtesy to bullying, from engaging in argument
himself to enlisting the help of other learned men, from cups of
wine to confinement in the stocks, to get Philpot to recant. Philpot
had never wavered and had proved difficult, stubborn and repetitive

throughout, as well as apparently impervious to fear of the consequences. By the end Bonner had just had enough of the whole
business.

As Philpot was led out into Paternoster Row, his servant was
waiting for him and, seeing that he was now in the custody of the
sheriffs and knowing what that meant, he said: 'Ah, dear master.'
The sheriffs' officers thrust him away, and conveyed Philpot to
Newgate. To begin with, he was treated very badly there, being
shackled to a block with 'as many irons upon his legs as he might
bear'. Only the intercession of one of the sheriffs, John Machil,
along with the gift of his ring, persuaded the keeper of Newgate
to remove the irons.

At least Philpot did not now have long to wait. He was condemned on 16 December, and on the following evening the
message came from the sheriffs that he was to prepare himself for
execution the next day. When the sheriffs duly arrived at eight
o'clock in the morning, Philpot came down to them 'most joyfully'. Outside, the wintry streets had turned to mud. When two of
the sheriffs' officers attempted to lift Philpot above the mud on his
way to the stake, to stop him getting his feet dirty (as if the state
of his feet could really matter at this point), he had the presence of
mind to joke: 'What! Will you make me a pope? I am content to
go to my journey's end on foot.' He, like Bradford and Leaf, made
a ceremony of his final moments, kneeling before the stake and
declaring: 'I will pay my vows to thee, oh Smithfield.' Then, kissing
the stake, he recited three psalms of thanksgiving and gave himself
up to the fire.

Chapter Thirteen

MATTERS OF CONSCIENCE

✠

> The same thing commonly happens in our own day and will
> happen, that many are regarded as heretics and punished, whom
> future generations will revere as saints. Wherefore I fear that
> many good Christians have been numbered among the heretics.
>
> Augustine Eleutherius (Sebastian Franck), 1531

PHILPOT AND CRANMER were the last major clerical leaders to be
burnt under Mary. (The latter was burnt in Oxford in March 1556
and was succeeded as Archbishop by Cardinal Pole.) If the intention
of the authorities had been to showcase a few burnings of major
influencers of opinion, in order to turn their erstwhile followers
away from the path of heresy, the strategy had signally failed. Bishop
and Lord Chancellor Stephen Gardiner had initially expected that
the mere threat of such a terrible death would lead to most if not
all of the Protestant rebels abandoning their convictions, which he
did not believe were held seriously in the first place. He died himself well before the catalogue of burnings was complete, but not
before he had realized the failure of this tactic. The Queen, however,
persisted in believing that the policy of burning was the right one;
she held to the view of the hardliners in the interpretation of the
parable of the tares – that heretics, whoever they were, had to be
rooted up, cast away and burnt, to protect the innocent and maintain the purity of the Church. And so, despite the doubts of many
of her advisers, and of those who had to conduct the heresy trials
– the bishops – the burnings went on.

When John Philpot was searched prior to being confined in the high turret at St Paul's, one of the letters he made a great show of tearing up was addressed to another prisoner of Bonner's, a young lawyer called Bartlet (sometimes referred to as Bartholomew) Green. Bartlet had been born in the City of London, in the parish of St Michael Bassishaw, in 1529 or 1530, into a family who valued education and sent him to Oxford where he took his BA degree in 1547. Being both hard-working and possessed of intellectual curiosity, he found time at Oxford to attend lectures on theology given by the influential Italian Protestant, Peter Martyr Vermigli (often known just as Peter Martyr, the name he had taken on becoming an Augustinian canon), who had been appointed to a professorship during the reign of Edward VI. After some initial resistance and questioning, Bartlet Green was converted to Protestantism. On completing his studies in Oxford, he moved back to London to embark on a legal career at the Inner Temple, associating there with other committed evangelicals and continuing to practise the reformed religion after the accession of Mary, refusing to attend Mass or make confession to a priest. He nevertheless still found time to enjoy some of the lighter-hearted activities available to reasonably affluent students of the law in London – activities such as dressing up, going to banquets and other 'fond follies' – which he later came to regret, as not fitting for a serious follower of the gospel. He was able to afford this sort of lifestyle through the generosity of his grandfather, the eminent physician Dr Richard Bartlett (after whom he was named, his grandfather's surname having been given him as a first name – the two spellings being interchangeable at the time), who lived in Bartholomew Close and was one of Sir John Deane's parishioners.

At Easter of both 1554 and 1555, Bartlet Green received communion according to the outlawed Edwardian rite in the private rooms of the Rector of the City church of St Peter Cornhill, John Pullain, who conducted the services. Such unlawful activities might never have come to the attention of the authorities, had not correspondence been intercepted between Green and one Christopher Goodman, a Protestant in exile and previously one of Green's friends in Oxford, in which Goodman asked whether it was true that the Queen had died. According to Foxe, Green had simply stated in reply that, no, the Queen was not (yet) dead – but the suspicion to which the interception of this correspondence gave rise was that he was more than a mere disseminator of information, and was involved in circulating propaganda, smuggled out of Danzig and into England, denouncing Philip and Mary and advocating her half-sister Elizabeth's claim to the throne. In consequence, Bartlet Green was arrested, initially not for heresy but for treason. He was imprisoned first in the Fleet and subsequently in the Tower. The charges of treason came to nothing, but – as a young man who seems to have had little concern for his own safety, and who must have caused enormous heartache to those who cared for him – he was reckless enough, while in prison, to give voice to his Protestant beliefs, denying the real presence in the Mass. On 10 November 1555, therefore, rather than being released, he was sent by the Privy Council to Bishop Bonner to be examined for heresy.

At first Green was treated well by Bonner, being detained in the bishop's London palace, where he shared a room with John Dee, the mathematician, astrologer and antiquary, who was also at that time in Bonner's custody. (Accused of using magic to plot against Queen Mary's life, Dee had been acquitted of this charge on 29 August 1555 but handed over to Bonner for an inquiry into his religious orthodoxy.) Green got on very well with Dee, as he did with everyone with whom he came into contact; he seems to have been a naturally affable young man, whom people immediately liked. Green himself admitted, in a letter to Philpot, that the bishop and his chaplains were so friendly towards him that he could almost have forgotten he was a prisoner – were it not that 'this great cheer was so often powdered with unsavoury sauces of examinations, exhortations, posings [i.e. posing of questions] and disputations'. As a result of this lenient treatment, rumours spread that Green had recanted and John Philpot wrote him a letter, rebuking him for backsliding. Green responded, in a letter printed by Foxe but never received by Philpot, indignantly denying this, and reproving Philpot for believing 'slanders' made against him.

Foxe mentions, almost as an aside – and a disapproving one – that, during the time of Bartlet Green's imprisonment, his grandfather 'Master Doctor Bartlet' made him 'large offers of great livings', if he would recant and return to the Church of Rome. That this was the Dr Bartlett who was a parishioner of John Deane is evidenced by his will (witnessed by Deane), in which his first bequests are to his niece Anne Grene (the spellings Green and Grene being used interchangeably at the time, and 'niece' also meaning 'granddaughter' until about 1600), to Elizabeth Grene and Margaret Grene. Of the three women, Margaret received the largest bequest (£40), so it is likely that she was Dr Bartlett's daughter, hence Bartlet Green's mother, Anne and Elizabeth being his sisters. That Dr Bartlett's efforts to bring Bartlet back to the 'Church of Rome' were not motivated solely by familial feeling – though he must have been desperate to save the life of his talented young grandson if it could be done – but also by conviction is indicated by other bequests, in particular that of his estate in Edgware to his old college of All Souls, Oxford, on condition that they celebrate a daily Mass for his soul and that of his wife, and by his bequest of £6 to the Black Friars at St Bartholomew's. But however heartfelt, Dr Bartlett's pleas went unheeded by his grandson.

Green's final examination before Bonner took place on 15 January 1556, when he also had a lengthy and ultimately fruitless debate with John Feckenham, Dean of St Paul's and abbot of the restored Abbey of Westminster, and other leading theologians, before being condemned to death and taken to Newgate. Feckenham, like Dr Bartlett, tried to persuade Green not to 'wilfully cast himself away' but to be 'conformable to reason', but the young lawyer was placing his trust in another authority than that of either the ecclesiastical hierarchy or his grandfather.

Bartlet Green not only had a loving family but was also popular among his erstwhile colleagues at the Temple, several of them coming to visit him in prison. Two of his closest friends had intended to offer him some comfort after his condemnation but when they encountered him on his way to Newgate, they broke down in tears, so that he was forced instead to comfort them. His own relief came from the sense that he was being true to his conscience, which gave him a 'most quiet and peaceable mind' and enabled him to be cheerful, even joyful. Some of his friends asked for a token to remember him by, and for one of them, Thomas Hussey, a future Member of Parliament, he inscribed an album with an epitaph popular in the period:

> Behold thyself by me, such one was I, as thou:
> And thou in time shall be, even dust as I am now.

Green's final letter to various of his friends is full of concern for his fellow prisoners, including a number of common criminals he had encountered in Newgate, and requests that his friends help to secure their release. In the case of some other prisoners whose release appears unlikely, or perhaps undeserved, he still asks his friends to provide them with what relief they can. The recipients of his letter share his own religious beliefs, as is clear from his opening injunction: 'if we keep Christ's commandment in loving each other, as he loved us, then should our love be everlasting'. Throughout he is motivated by his reading and understanding of the gospel – that what Christians are called to do is 'help to clothe Christ, visit the afflicted, comfort the sorrowful, and relieve the needy'. His final words are of the hope of eternal life: 'This present Monday, when I look to die, and live for ever.'

Six others were burnt alongside Bartlet Green, on the morning of 27 January 1556, bound in pairs to three stakes: four men, Thomas Whittle, John Tudson, John Went, Thomas Browne; and two women, Isobel Foster and Joan Lashford. The married priest Thomas Whittle was another of those encountered by John Philpot during his imprisonment – he it was who had had part of his beard 'plucked away' by the infuriated bishop. Whittle was from Essex, but had lost his living there on Mary's accession and had subsequently become a wandering preacher – until he was denounced and brought before Stephen Gardiner. By this time, Gardiner was ailing and seems to have had no appetite for dealing with miscreants such as Whittle – particularly when he could see that the person apprehending him (in this case, someone called Edmund

The Martyrdom of Thomas Haukes.

O Lord receive my Spirit

The body cast of a child victim of the eruption of Mount Vesuvius at Pompeii shows the characteristic 'pugilistic posture' caused by the burning and shrinking of muscles. The bodies of people burnt at the stake could assume a similar pose, often interpreted by contemporary onlookers and recorders of the scene as a raising of the hands and arms in prayer.

Right. John Rogers, for whom the reinstatement of Edmund Bonner as Bishop of London in 1553 marked the beginning of the end, was the former Vicar of St Sepulchre-without-Newgate, and the first Protestant martyr to be burnt under Mary I.

Below. The physical appearance of Bishop Bonner seems to have easily lent itself to caricature. He also gained a reputation for violence, his irascibility perhaps exacerbated by his own imprisonment under Edward VI.

Opposite, top. John Philpot, a former Archdeacon of Winchester, was one of the most high-profile churchmen burnt under Mary. He was also one of the most argumentative, and captured the nub of the argument when he declared to Bishop Bonner: 'You say, you are of the true Church: and we say, we are of the true Church.'

Opposite, bottom. John Bradford, another gifted orator, continued his ministry of daily preaching while imprisoned, awaiting execution. His eventual burning was attended by 'a great multitude of people'.

The martyrdome of master Iohn Philpot Archdeacon, with the manner of his kneeling and praying at the stake.

I will pay my vowes in thee O Smithfield.

Filpot

¶ Certaine bishops talking with Maister Bradford in prison.

keper.

Bradfor

Six others, bound in pairs to three stakes, were burnt alongside the idealistic and headstrong young lawyer Bartlet Green on 27 January 1556.

Thomas Cranmer, different both in appearance and conviction from his younger self, was burnt in Oxford on 21 March 1556. He and John Philpot were the last major clerical leaders to be burnt under Mary.

Cranmer was succeeded as Archbishop of Canterbury by Cardinal Reginald Pole, a distant relative of the Queen. Pole hoped to bring the English into line with Rome by acting as an 'indulgent loving father' towards them; the policy of burning heretics did nothing to facilitate this aim.

The effigy of Richard Rich, part of the monument by Epiphanius Evesham erected to him in Felsted church, seems to gaze balefully at the viewer.

The memorial slab marking the approximate burial place in the Priory Church of St Bartholomew the Great of the church's first Rector, Sir John Deane, presented in 1893 by the pupils of the school he founded at Witton, near Northwich.

The interior of St Bartholomew the Great, the surviving conventual church of the once-great Priory of St Bartholomew, witness to the suffering of so many in Smithfield.

Alabaster) had done so in the hope of personal gain – and so Alabaster delivered Whittle to Bishop Bonner instead. As with Philpot, one of the tests Bonner administered to Whittle was to ask him to attend Mass; Whittle refused, which led to Bonner's first physical attack on him – as the hapless priest related it: 'he turned back and beat me with his fist, first on the one cheek, and then on the other'. Ground down by such treatment, Whittle was initially persuaded to recant but, as he had related to Philpot when they first met, his conscience had troubled him so deeply that he had later insisted on withdrawing his recantation – thereby laying himself open to further abuse from the frustrated bishop.

John Tudson, born in Ipswich, and John Went, initially from Langham in Essex, were both twenty-seven years old. Tudson was an apprentice, and Went a shearman. Both had been sent to Bonner by his diocesan chancellor, Dr Story, on suspicion of holding heretical views on the sacrament. Thomas Browne was a married man of thirty-seven, living in the parish of St Bride's Fleet Street, and he had been reported to Bonner by the constables of that parish for non-attendance at church. Initially imprisoned at the bishop's palace in Fulham, he had also been subjected to the test of being summoned to hear Mass on 16 September 1555; refusing, he had gone into the grounds of the palace and knelt to say his prayers among the trees. He remained obdurate throughout his imprisonment and examinations, accusing Bonner of being a 'bloodsucker'.

Isobel Foster was a married woman of fifty-five; her husband was a member of the Worshipful Company of Cutlers and they lived in the parish of St Bride's Fleet Street. She, like Thomas Browne, had initially come to the attention of the authorities through non-attendance at church.

Thomas Whittle's short-lived recantation had been used by Archdeacon Harpsfield to try to persuade Joan Lashford to recant as well, but she had proved resilient, refusing to write or sign anything. Joan, of the parish of Little Hallows in Thames Street, was the daughter of another (deceased) cutler, Robert Lashford, and of his wife Elizabeth who, after the death of Robert, had married the (much younger) upholsterer John Warne – who was burnt in Smithfield along with John Cardmaker on 30 May 1555. Elizabeth herself was burnt in Stratford-atte-Bow on 23 August. Joan was made of as stern stuff as her mother and stepfather (the latter being only about nine years her senior). She had come to the attention of the authorities during the course of visiting her mother and stepfather in prison, suspected of harbouring the same views and beliefs as them, and consequently sent to Bonner, again by Dr Story. She was initially imprisoned for a few weeks in the Counter in Poultry, and then sent to Newgate, where she spent several months.

On the morning of the burnings, a curfew was placed on servants and young people, the beadle of every Ward in the City being ordered to stand guard to prevent any such persons appearing on the City's streets before eleven o'clock. And what of the elderly Dr Bartlett, whom no one would have prevented from venturing out that day? Was he standing in Smithfield, in front of his own parish church, to witness the burning of his beloved grandson in the company of six others, or did he stay away, shutting himself up in his house in Bartholomew Close? Did he perhaps seek solace in the company of his parish priest, John Deane, on that dreadful morning? Were the two men perhaps praying inside the church, or listening to the Dominican friars intoning the psalms, while the fires were being lit beyond the gates of the Priory Church? Could they smell the smoke, the scent of roasting human flesh? It is impossible to know, and we can hardly begin to imagine the pain of having one's gifted, lively, but unbearably stubborn young grandson being publicly executed, in indescribable torment – and for reasons that one considered either incomprehensible or deeply misguided. We may imagine that Dr Bartlett remonstrated with his grandson not only to consider his own position, but also not to inflict such pain on his mother and sisters. Whether or not any of Bartlet Green's family were there to witness the burning, by nine o'clock it was all over.

Within a year Dr Bartlett was also dead – of old age and natural causes, among which must be included grief. His funeral took place at St Bartholomew's, where he was also buried, on 22 January 1557, 'with a dozen of scutcheons of arms, and 2 white branches [of white wax, carried at the head of the procession of acolytes and clergy] and 2 torches, and 4 great tapers'. Dr Bartlett had been the first fellow admitted to the College of Physicians after its foundation in 1518, and had four times been its President – and the whole College, including its then President, John Caius, attended the funeral. Caius described him as 'a good and venerable old man, very famous for his learning, great knowledge, and experience in physic'. In addition to his bequest to the Black Friars of St Bartholomew's, Richard Bartlett left twenty shillings to 'the making of the church wall' and, to John Deane, his worsted gown, furred, on condition that the rector take no money for breaking the ground in the church for his burial, and arranging to have a stone laid over his grave. It was a solemn, impressive and Catholic funeral, a fitting end to a long and distinguished career. But no amount of honour, wealth or learning had been able to deflect Dr Bartlett's grandson from following the dictates of his own conscience to their inevitable conclusion at a stake in Smithfield.

> Item, that you . . . have of late, that is to say, within these past two years, within the City and diocese of London, swerved at the least way from some part of the said Catholic faith and religion: and among other things you have misliked and earnestly spoken against the sacrifice of the Mass, the sacrament of the altar, and the unity of the Church, railing at and maligning the authority of the See of Rome, and the faith observed in the same.

The question which must often have been asked by eminent churchmen such as Bishops Gardiner and Bonner, Archdeacon Harpsfield and Dr Chedsey, as well as by men of great standing in other professions such as medicine and the law, like Dr Bartlett and indeed Lord Rich, was: why will these Protestant zealots not listen to us? It was a question specifically asked of Bartlet Green by one of his examiners, Mr Welch, who took Bartlet into a separate room, clearly wanting to help him get out of the trouble he was in. Welch 'marvelled', Bartlet reported in his letter to Philpot, that 'I being a young man, would stand against all the learned men of the realm, yea, and contrary to the whole determination of the Catholic Church from Christ's time, in a matter in which I could have no great learning. I ought not to think my own wit better than all men's, but should believe those who were learned.' Bartlet's answer to this included the assertion that, to God, it does not matter how learned, or important in a worldly sense, people are: 'There is no respect of persons with God, whether it be old or young, rich, or poor, wise, or foolish, fisher, or basket maker.' Welch still thought it unreasonable that Bartlet should suppose his 'own wit and learning' better than those of all the experts ranged against him, but Bartlet was 'persuaded' and could not be moved. For him it was his conscience that was the final arbiter, as was explicitly stated in a draft of his confession, taken down by the bishop's registrar: 'he cannot be persuaded, in his conscience, that the sacrifice pretended to be in the same [i.e. in the sacrament of the altar], is agreeable to God's word, or maintainable by the same: or that without deadly offence, he cannot worship the body and blood of Christ, that is pretended to be there'.

This sense of the dictates of personal conscience outweighing other, external, considerations is shared by many of the martyrs of the 1550s. The priest Thomas Whittle, for instance, having signed his initial recantation, almost immediately reported that 'Satan in the night-time appeared to him, and said that he was damned, for that he had done against his conscience in subscribing the said submission.' The nightmarish awareness of having violated his own conscience was so strong that Whittle was impelled to tear up his signature, in full awareness of the consequences. Those questioning Whittle and Green found this emphasis on personal conscience perplexing, and it certainly represents a shift – from a patriarchal authoritarian society, where beliefs were expected to be taken on trust, handed down from above, towards a fundamentally different society, one made up of individuals who, whatever their class or educational background, expected to take personal responsibility for their beliefs and actions. At this period of change, the proponents of these very different ways of thinking and perceiving were frequently unable to understand one another; they might as well have been speaking in different languages, while yet appearing to be using the same words. 'In the end I was asked what conscience was,' Green reported to Philpot, 'and I said, the certifying of the truth.'

Even more striking than a man like Thomas Whittle, educated in theology and trained as a priest, or than Bartlet Green, with his experience of having attended lectures in theology at Oxford and coming from a background of intellectual thought, standing up for their own beliefs against accepted authority, are cases of the apprentices, artisans and women who were prepared to take on the might of the Establishment. The twenty-seven-year-old shearman, John Went, told his interrogators that since about the age of twenty he had 'misliked' the way certain things were done in the Church of England, and that this 'misliking' was sufficiently strong for him to reject what his godparents had promised on his behalf when he was baptized as a child. The apprentice John Tudson said much the same thing: once he had begun to think for himself, at the age of about eighteen, he had found he 'did mislike the doctrine and religion then taught and set forth in the Church of England', only being prepared to accept the way things had been done during the reign of King Edward – 'in whose time the Gospel was truly set forth'. Both these young men had come to maturity during Edward's reign, and that is partly why the Protestant ideas they encountered then had such force for them – they were associated with the first time they had begun to think for themselves rather than just doing what their elders had told them to do. And they were able to back up what they had been taught by their Protestant leaders with their own reading of the Bible – something they had not been able to do with the faith they were taught as children, when they had been expected to accept everything they were told on the basis of priestly authority – so that Tudson could now boldly assert that 'the doctrine set forth in the Queen's reign was not agreeable to God's word, nor yet to the true Catholic Church that Christ speaks of'. He challenged Bonner to tell him 'wherein I have offended'.

'In your answers,' replied the bishop.

'No, I have not,' said Tudson, and went on to accuse the bishop of lacking in charity. Both young men also insisted that 'the sacrament of the altar as it is used is an idol and no sacrament at all'. John Went admitted he had accidentally been present at a celebration of the Mass, but was sorry to have been so, believing the Mass to be 'against God's word'.

Isobel Foster, considerably older than these two men, asserted that for most of her adulthood, when she conformed to expectations, she was doing so 'blindly and without knowledge'; everything changed for her when, during Edward's reign, she heard 'the Gospel truly preached and opened to the people'. Whereas previously she had given little thought to what she had been taught about religion, she was convinced by 'the preachers in the time of King Edward' whom she believed 'to have preached the truth'. Whatever else this had done for her, it had completely revolutionized her attitude towards herself, giving her – a middle-aged woman who would previously have been subservient to husband and other (male) authority figures – the confidence to stand up to the mightiest in the land. The importance of having faith as an individual had made her aware for the first time that she actually was an individual – and it was an awareness literally 'to die for'.

The young woman, Joan Lashford, who had been brought up by parents who had themselves been converted to Protestantism, had 'seen the light' much earlier; she announced that, from the age of about eleven, 'she had misliked the sacrifice of the Mass, the sacrament of the altar, and the authority of the See of Rome, with the doctrine thereof, because they are against Christ's Catholic Church, and the right faith of the same'. The bishop, old enough to be her grandfather, could get nowhere with her, whether by flattery or threats; on the contrary, she felt she was able to hold him to account: 'If you will leave off your abomination,' she declared, 'so I will return, and otherwise I will not.' For her, as for her fellow defendants, her own conscience was supreme, and she was sure that she had understood 'Christ's words and institution' and therefore knew that 'confession, absolution, and the Mass, with all their other superfluous sacraments, ceremonies and divine service as then used in this realm of England', were contrary to them. The thirty-seven-year-old Thomas Browne was also quite prepared to contradict Bishop Bonner, to whom he replied, when Bonner told him his opinions were heresies: 'How will you prove it? – for I will not go from my answers, unless you can prove them to be heresies, which you shall never do. For that which you call heresy is no heresy.'

Three months after Bartlet Green and his six fellow sufferers were burnt, it was the turn of six more – Robert Drakes (a minister), William Tyms (a curate), Richard Spurge (a shearman), Thomas Spurge (a fuller), John Cavell (a weaver) and George Ambrose (another fuller) – who were executed in Smithfield on 24 April. These men were all from Essex, and several of them had been apprehended during the previous year on the authority of Lord Rich, who had received complaints about their non-attendance at their parish church and had arranged for them to be sent before Stephen Gardiner, in March 1555. They had afterwards been sent either to the King's Bench or the Marshalsea, where they had spent nearly a year without anything being done about them, the delay exacerbated by the illness and subsequent death of Bishop Gardiner. When Dr Nicholas Heath, Archbishop of York, was appointed to succeed Gardiner as Lord Chancellor, George Ambrose, John Cavell and the two Spurge brothers wrote to him, asking to be brought before him – either to prove their innocence of any charges that might be laid against them or to submit to judgement, if it could be proved they had done anything wrong. Their confinement in the Marshalsea had led, they claimed, to their 'utter undoing', and to that of their wives and children – for while they were there they could not of course work to support their families, but on the contrary incurred expenses which they could not afford. The letter seems to have had the desired effect as not long after it had been sent, Sir Richard Read, one of the officers of the Court of Chancery, was sent to the Marshalsea to examine the four prisoners.

The answers which they made to Read were similar in content and attitude to those given by the group burnt in January. Richard

Spurge said that he had stopped going to church when services in Latin had been resumed, and that he 'misliked' these services and the Mass as they did not, in his opinion, agree with 'God's holy word'. His brother Thomas concurred, adding that the word of God was no longer truly taught in church, nor were the sacraments administered there in the way they ought to be.

A remark made by another of the prisoners, George Ambrose, is illuminating as to why the accused set so little store by what their ecclesiastical judges told them. Ambrose mentioned having read Stephen Gardiner's *De vera obedientia* and its preface by Edmund Bonner – in which both these bishops who were now enforcing obedience to the Pope had, under a different regime, argued against papal authority. This inevitably undermined their credibility with the Protestant rebels, and no amount of sophistry on the part of the bishops could redeem them in the eyes of those who came before them. Inconsistency was also the charge levelled at his parish priest by another of the prisoners, John Cavell, who had given up going to church when 'the parson there had preached two contrary doctrines'. Again, what is noteworthy here and what must have come as a surprise to their questioners is that these men, all craftsmen and manual workers rather than university-educated professional men, felt able to rely on their own judgement in determining whether or not to believe what they had been told.

The other two men in the group who were executed in April were ministers of the Church. Robert Drakes had been the Rector of Thundersley in Essex for three years, having been recommended for ordination by Cranmer, when he was Archbishop of Canterbury. And so, as a relative newcomer, he had been ordained into what was in effect a Protestant church – and he was now being expected to play the role of a Catholic priest. He had been presented to the benefice of Thundersley by Lord Rich – but it was also Rich who had sent him up to Bishop Gardiner when he refused to conform to the changed practice under Mary. (This would suggest that had John Deane, another priest 'presented' by Rich, ever stepped out of line, his patron would have had no compunction about reporting him. But, in any event, both Deane and

Rich appear to have been content with the return to the old ways. Certainly there is no suggestion of anything negative having come to light about the parish of Great St Bartholomew when Bishop Bonner conducted the visitation of his diocese, which commenced in the autumn of 1554. The questions drawn up by him for the inquiries he made of every parish included queries about clerical residence, dress, diligence and morals, as well as wanting assurances that no heretical doctrines were being preached, or lay people being allowed to behave in a less than reverential manner towards the sacraments or showing nonconformity in any way; John Deane came under no suspicion of any kind, under any of these headings.)

The other clerical member of this group, William Tyms, was a deacon and the curate of Hockley, also in Essex. Tyms was allegedly involved in the holding of illegal, Protestant, services in some woods belonging to a Master Tyrrell. (One of these was Beeches Wood, which still exists as part of Hockley Woods, the largest remaining area of the ancient woodland that once covered Essex.) Master Tyrrell had been most put out at hearing that his woods were being 'polluted with sermons' – as well he might be, for fear of blame attaching to him over these unlawful assemblies being held on his land. He conducted inquiries into the matter, which resulted in Tyms being apprehended and sent up to Bishops Bonner and Gardiner, before being remanded in the King's Bench prison.

On 28 March 1556 all six men appeared before Bishop Bonner in the Consistory Court at St Paul's. Bonner held the deacon Tyms responsible for having led many other people into heresy, including his fellow prisoners, but Tyms hotly contested this accusation, pointing out that all the defendants had been active dissenters well before they were arrested and, consequently, before he ever knew them. Tyms also articulated against Bonner and his fellow bishops the charge of inconsistency made by George Ambrose:

> My Lord, I doubt not but I am of the Catholic Church, what-ever you judge of me. But as for your Church, you have before this day renounced it, and by corporal oath promised never to consent to the same. Contrary to the which, you have received

into this realm the Pope's authority, and therefore you are falsely perjured and forsworn, all the sort of you. Besides this, you have both spoken and written very earnestly against that usurped power, and now you burn men who will not acknowledge the Pope to be supreme head.

Bonner appeared surprised at this, and had to be reminded of his preface to Gardiner's treatise. He then gave as his reason for having written such opinions that he had had no choice at the time. 'Thus did we because of the perilous world that then was,' he said. 'For then was it made treason by the laws of this realm to maintain the Pope's authority, and great danger it was to be suspected a favourer of the See of Rome, and therefore fear compelled us to bear with the time, for otherwise there had been no way but one.' The logic of Bonner's position was that the present defendants should now themselves 'bear with the time' and recant their views – particularly as, he implied, they were wrong anyway.

In levelling their charges of hypocrisy against Bonner, the Protestant faithful did tend to ignore the fact that he, and many others of his persuasion, had suffered for their convictions during the reign of Edward VI. These sufferings had, however, amounted to no more than deprivation and imprisonment. These had been bad enough in themselves – and the experience of long months of imprisonment certainly took its toll on Bonner, increasing his unpredictability and violent tendencies – but they did not include torture and death. The implication in Bonner's words was that, had nonconformity during Edward's reign carried a certain death sentence, he would not have considered it his duty to resist. And now, 'Do you also as we have done,' he urged the defendants. But Tyms and his fellows were moved by what they considered a higher authority than that of a turncoat bishop. 'My Lord,' said Tyms, 'that which you have written against the supremacy of the Pope may be well approved by the scriptures. But that which you now do is against the word of God, as I can well prove.'

How that word of God was to be interpreted was another major area of difficulty, with Bonner and his fellow learned divines insisting that these men – including the two clergymen in the group – did not understand what they were reading when they so gleefully quoted from 'the scriptures'. 'You brag much of knowledge, and yet you know nothing,' the bishop accused Tyms; 'you speak much of scripture, and you do not know what scripture is.' He should not approach the Bible so literally, declared Bonner, but instead should rely on the interpretations of 'the old Fathers'. His opponents' view was that, despite the high esteem in which they held the early Church Fathers, particularly those who, like St Augustine, flourished around AD 400, the time after which men like Philpot judged the Church to have taken a wrong turn, they still believed that the Bible could, and should, be allowed to speak directly to believers, without the mediation of any other authority.

In their desire to return to the roots of Christianity and be faithful to the vision of what they believed the Church to have been in its infancy, Catholic ceremonial represented for these 'gospellers' everything that this early, pure Church of their imagination was not. There had been so much accretion, so many things added on that they wanted to strip away, because there was no mention of such things in the Bible. As William Tyms wrote to two female fellow believers:

> Christ . . . never went on procession with a cope, cross or candlestick. He never censed an image, or sang a Latin service. He never sat in confession. He never preached of Purgatory, or of the Pope's pardons. He never honoured saints, or prayed for the dead. He never said Mass, Mattins or Evensong. He never commanded to fast on Friday, or Vigil, Lent, or Advent. He never hallowed church or chalice, ashes, or palms, candles, or bells. He never made holy water or holy bread . . .

This urge to 'get back to basics', to strip away what are perceived as unnecessary occluding practices that always seem to build up around a clear, pure ideal, can be witnessed in the youthful challenge to so many traditions and institutions. The desire to jettison compromise, to cast away practices evolved by generations of elders, is very strong in the young – and that can be the young in faith rather than, or as well as, the young in chronological age. There are many examples from the world of politics, one being the 'neo-Communists' in the Soviet Union of the 1970s, who claimed that they were returning to the ideals of Marxism–Leninism which had, they said, been subverted as early as the late 1920s by a group of Stalin's supporters, representing the interests of the petite bourgeoisie. And of particular resonance in the twenty-first century are the claims of IS to be returning to the roots of Islam, rejecting all innovations in the religion and aiming for the restoration of the caliphate of early Islam. The theological movement in Sunni Islam known as Salafism which is a contrib-uting factor to the ideology of the 'Islamic State' is concerned with purifying the faith: 'Salafism focuses on eliminating idolatry (*shirk*) and affirming God's Oneness (*tawhid*). Salafis view themselves as the only true Muslims, considering those who practice so-called "major idolatry" to be outside the bounds of the Islamic faith. Those worshiping – or perceived to be worshiping – stones, saints, tombs, etc., are considered apostates, deserters of the religion.' And the frustration of authority is as clearly expressed in these words from a letter addressed to 'the fighters and followers of the self-declared "Islamic State"', signed by 126 Islamic scholars and clerics on 19 September 2014, as ever it was in the expostulations of Bishop Bonner and his colleagues:

> Oversimplification: It is not permissible to constantly speak of 'simplifying matters', or to cherry-pick an extract from the Qur'an without understanding it within its full context. It is also not permissible to say: 'Islam is simple, and the Prophet and his noble Companions were simple, why complicate Islam?' This is precisely what Abu Al-Baraa' Al-Hindi did in his online video in July 2014. In it he says: 'Open the Qur'an and read the verses on jihad and everything will become clear . . . all the scholars tell me: "This is a legal obligation (*fard*), or this isn't a legal obligation, and this is not the time for jihad" . . . forget everyone and read the Qur'an and you will know what jihad is.'

The same urge for a return to a hypothetical pure beginning, stripped of 'idolatrous' accretions, can be seen in William Tyms's list of objections to practices that had grown up over centuries in the Church. And for scholars and religious leaders, perceived by outsiders as voices of reason but by those who believe themselves to be embracing pure truth as both compromising and compromised, the task of bringing about 'recantation' and reconciliation is as near-impossible in the twenty-first century as it was in the sixteenth. As Cole Bunzel, a PhD candidate in Near Eastern Studies at Princeton University, points out in an analysis paper written for the Brookings Project on U.S. Relations with the Islamic World, the Islamic State relies on its own scholarly authorities, largely drawn from a younger generation. Chief among these is the thirty-year-old Bahraini Turki al-Bin'ali, for whom the Islamic State is the true keeper of the Salafi-Wahhabi heritage. 'Confident in this role, it will never relinquish its divine mission,' predicts Bunzel. 'Jihadis who fail to support the Islamic State are simply on the wrong side of history.'

A month after the group of men in April 1556, three women, also all from Essex, were burnt in Smithfield – Katherine Hutt from Bocking, Joan Horns from Billericay, and Elizabeth Thackwell from Great Burstead. Margaret Ellis, also from Billericay, was tried and condemned alongside them. Katherine was a widow, the other three all unmarried. Sir John Mordaunt, the son of the Mordaunt who refused to speak against Friar Forest, was instrumental in having these nonconformists 'sent up' to the authorities – 'for that they could not affirm the presence of Christ's body and blood to be truly and really in the sacrament, and for that they came not to their popish parish church'. His aim in doing so was to ensure that the parish of Great Burstead and Billericay should be brought into line; after the removal of these people, he thought, all would be well.

The questions put to the defendants were now beginning to follow a set pattern. They included questions about how many sacraments there were. (The 'correct' answer was seven – baptism, confirmation, Eucharist or Holy Communion, penance, extreme

unction, matrimony and holy orders; the usual Protestant reply
was two – baptism and Holy Communion, or three if matrimony was included, as Katherine Hutt and Elizabeth Thackwell
contended.) These women were less sure of themselves in certain
respects than their male counterparts; a frequent response to the
questions was that they 'could not tell'. Margaret Ellis had heard
that there was 'one sacrament, but what it was she could not tell'.
She was nevertheless convinced that, whatever it was, it was not
what Bishop Bonner and his colleagues were telling her. Margaret
was confident that she now knew more, and better, than had her
godparents when she was baptized, and Katherine Hutt agreed –
'but what her godfather and godmothers did then promise for her
in her name, she could not tell'. They had all learnt to embrace
the faith for themselves during King Edward's reign, and this had
made a strong impression on them – so strong they were not
prepared to relinquish it. Whatever they did or did not know, they
retained a strong sense of identity, which was bolstered by the
refusal to conform. Some of their replies were clearly influenced by
what they had been told by their Protestant leaders, and they did
not necessarily fully understand what their replies meant – but they
were nevertheless sure that there was 'no goodness' in the Mass, and
that 'Christ's natural body is in heaven, and not in the sacrament
of the altar'. Belief in the see of Rome constituted no part of their
experience – 'they acknowledged no such supremacy in that See,
neither have they anything to do with it'.

The courage of these four women was beyond dispute. They
were brought before the bishop for condemnation on 13 April, on
which occasion the widow Katherine Hutt boldly told Bonner that
the sacrament of the altar was not God – 'because it is a dumb god
and made with men's hands'. Joan Horns said the same thing, as
did the other two women. In the end, Margaret Ellis was saved
from the flames by dying in Newgate before she could be executed. The other three were bound to the stake and burnt to death
on 16 May.

Throughout the reign of Philip and Mary, Lord Rich was particularly zealous in dealing with the cases of reported heretics in

Essex, his name appearing often in connection with suspects sent to Bishop Bonner (in whose diocese of London the county of Essex then was) or among the witnesses to an execution. A disproportionate number of heretics condemned in London's diocesan courts came from Essex (at least sixty, as compared with only thirty from London, and one each from Middlesex and Hertfordshire); this suggests how very diligent Rich and his fellow Essex magistrates were being. In addition, from the beginning of the burnings of lay people, Rich was among the local dignitaries whose presence was required by the Privy Council, following directions from the Queen, 'at the burning of such obstinate persons as presently are sent down to be burned in diverse parts of the country'. The presence of local grandees and magistrates was intended to reinforce the policy of religious repression, demonstrating solidarity between monarchy, Church and secular authority. So Rich was heavily implicated, both in the trials and the executions of Protestants.

One of the cases to come before him, as one of the Queen's commissioners in Essex, was that of Thomas Watts, a linen draper from Billericay. Watts was summoned to appear before the Essex Justices sitting at Chelmsford in late April 1555, accused of refusing to go to church and attending illegal evangelical gatherings – or 'conventicles' – instead. Part of his defence was that he had learnt of the new religious teaching – or 'this gear', as it was referred to by Sir Anthony Browne, one of Rich's fellow Justices – from the very people who were now presuming to sit in judgement on him. Sir Anthony himself had, according to Watts, declared during the reign of Edward VI that the Mass was 'abominable' and had also made remarks that could now be construed as critical of the Queen's decision to marry a Spanish prince – that 'whoever should bring in any strange nation to rule here it was treason, and not to be suffered'. Sir Anthony was understandably perturbed at Watts's accusations, and turned to Rich to say: 'He belies me, my Lord. What a knave is this! He will soon belie me behind my back, when he does it before my face.'

'I dare say he does,' responded Rich. Watts continued unwisely to criticize the advent of King Philip, until the assembled Justices decided they had had enough and, muttering 'Treason!' to one another, resolved to send him off to Bonner. At his execution a few weeks later in Chelmsford, Watts specifically accused Rich of having switched religious allegiance with the change of reign. 'My Lord, beware, beware!' he exclaimed. 'For you do against your own conscience herein, and unless you repent, the Lord will avenge it.' As we know well by now, however, Lord Rich's conscience was a flexible organ, and it is unlikely he lost much sleep over Watts's allegation.

Rich's London rector Sir John Deane, meanwhile, carried on with his routine parish ministry, some aspects of which can be traced in the wills of parishioners, including, as we have seen, that of Richard Bartlett. Another parishioner whose will Deane witnessed in 1556 was John Garatt, 'citizen and salter'. Garatt requested to be buried inside the Priory Church between the steps leading to the high altar and the chancel, and left various bequests, including to the Black Friars at St Bartholomew's, requesting them to pray for his soul and for those of his first and second wives, yearly. His third wife, Ursula, was still living, and to her he left his house in Red Cross Street. He also left small sums of money, as many did, to the three main prisons – the King's Bench, the Marshalsea and Newgate.

On 15 August 1557 John Deane would have attended, with all the other City clergy, a service at St Paul's to mark the feast of the Assumption of the Blessed Virgin Mary, specific instructions having been issued for marking this significant day in the Catholic liturgical calendar. All the clergy, vested in copes, were to take part in the procession, which moved from the cathedral along Cheapside, the assembled choirs singing '*Salve festa dies*', and collecting the scarlet-robed Lord Mayor and Aldermen in the return procession to Paul's Cross to hear Archdeacon Harpsfield preach 'a goodly sermon'.

A month after taking part in this festive procession, Deane acquired a second living when he was instituted as Rector of Coulsdon in Surrey (the parish church being that of St John the Evangelist, in what is now known as Old Coulsdon). Before

the dissolution of the monasteries, this living had been in the gift
of Chertsey Abbey, but in 1537 the abbot had conveyed the advowson to the King who subsequently granted it to the courtier and
diplomat Sir Nicholas Carew. Sir Nicholas was executed for treason
shortly afterwards and the advowson reverted to the Crown, with
Archbishop Cranmer exercising it under Edward VI. But Mary
restored the manor of Coulsdon and the advowson to the Carews
– and it was Sir Nicholas's son, Francis Carew, who presented Sir
John Deane to the living, on the death of the previous incumbent.
At first glance, there appears to be no connection between Carew
and Deane, and so Sir John's receipt of this rather lucrative living
(in 1535 it had been valued at almost £22, twice the amount of the
stipend he received from St Bartholomew's) is something of a mystery. But where there is a mystery there is very often a Lord Rich,
and he is indeed the most likely person to have had a hand in the
appointment, his connections and influence spreading far and wide.
Rich was aware that Deane's income had been reduced by his
decision to surrender a number of tenements at St Bartholomew's
to the Crown when the Black Friars took up residence, and he
could well have been looking for a way of making this up to his
protégé.

The particular link between Francis Carew and Lord Rich can
be found in the figure of Carew's brother-in-law, Nicholas Throckmorton (he had married Anne Carew in about 1549), for whom
the year 1557 was also pivotal. In January 1554 Throckmorton,
who had Protestant sympathies (signalled, perhaps, by his luxuri-
ant auburn beard which tapered to two points) and was known to
oppose the idea of the Queen's marriage to Philip of Spain, had
been arrested on suspicion of complicity in the rebellion against
Mary led by Sir Thomas Wyatt. He was tried at Guildhall on 17
April, the indictment alleging that he was 'a principal, deviser, pro-
curer and contriver of the late Rebellion'. But, using all his gifts of
eloquence and learning, as well as appealing to the jury members'
own distaste for the Spanish marriage, Throckmorton, with his
bright piercing eyes and razor-sharp wit, was able to run rings
around the prosecutors and succeeded in persuading the jury of his

innocence – to the fury of the judges. The upshot was that not only the defendant, but also the members of the jury, were imprisoned, Throckmorton being sent to the Tower.

The following year, however, Throckmorton was released and, after initially retiring to his home in Northamptonshire, fled to France in June 1556, fearing accusations of involvement in further conspiracies. But then, despite there being some calls for him to be placed on trial again, he was rather unexpectedly pardoned and recalled by Mary – in May 1557. Is it too far-fetched to detect the hand of Richard Rich in this rehabilitation of Nicholas Throckmorton, with part of the pay-off being the living at Coulsdon for John Deane, which was about to become vacant and was in the gift of Throckmorton's family by marriage? Both men – Rich and Throckmorton – had a reputation for wheeler-dealing, always tending to accomplish their purposes in a roundabout, conspiratorial manner.

In addition to Lord Rich's desire to ensure Deane was in receipt of a healthy income, he had another motive for making Throckmorton beholden to him – Throckmorton knew about certain aspects of his past, including what had happened to Anne Askew between her conviction for heresy and her execution. He had himself been a member of the evangelical circle connected to Queen Katherine Parr, and had visited Anne in prison, as well as being present at her burning. Though people with Anne's views were once again being burnt at the stake, Lord Rich would not have wanted his involvement in the illegal torture of this young woman to become a matter of common currency, so he would always have had his eye on Nicholas Throckmorton, with a view to buying his silence. There was also the matter of the alleged conversation between Rich, Throckmorton (also spelt Throgmorton) and Thomas Cromwell, which had been instrumental in the latter's downfall. However it was accomplished, by the autumn of 1557 both Nicholas Throckmorton and John Deane were in a better position than at the start of that year, and both may have had reason to be grateful to Lord Rich.

As well as acquiring a second living, throughout this period of his life John Deane was increasing his property portfolio and transforming himself into a man of some consequence, particularly in relation to his place of origin in Cheshire. Between 1553 and 1557 he bought a number of properties in Chester, some of which had originally belonged to the great college of St John the Baptist while others had formed part of the estates of the dissolved fraternity of St Anne, and he used some of these properties to endow the grammar school he founded at Witton, close to his home town of Northwich, in late 1557. The statutes drawn up by Deane for his school stipulated that the master was to be a graduate of Oxford or Cambridge, and that the scholars were to be taught 'good literature, both Latin and Greek, and good authors such as have the very Roman eloquence, joined with wisdom especially Christian authors, that wrote their wisdom with clean and chaste Latin, either in verse or in prose for my intent is by founding of this school especially to increase knowledge and worship of God and our Lord Jesus Christ and good life and manners in the children'. Whatever Deane may have felt about the burnings taking place with such frequency outside his church at this period, he was clearly a man who believed in the future and, childless himself, he wanted to be able to influence the young and ensure that boys in his home town were given the opportunity to be both Christian and educated. His statutes and rules for the curriculum were very similar to those drawn up by Dean Colet for St Paul's School, founded in 1518, and themselves based on an Erasmian conception of education, characterized by the combination of virtue with learning.

Other parts of the statutes suggest not only that Deane was by nature attracted to tradition, but also that he rather hankered after the kind of 'great school' he had not himself had the opportunity to attend, for he particularly specified that his school should follow a number of 'old orders and customs', such as the 'barring out' of the schoolmaster in the weeks before Christmas and Easter – 'in such sort as other scholars do in great schools'. This particular custom involved barricading the master out of the school until any offences committed by the boys during that term had been forgiven.

The deed of the statutes of Witton Grammar School also provides us with a visual image, albeit conventional and idealized, of Sir John, the initial letter 'I' containing his illuminated portrait. In this illustration, as in life, he does nothing to offend, while maintaining his office and his calling. He wears a full-sleeved academic gown with a fur tippet, scarf and doctor's cap, and his face bears the suggestion of a short beard. His right hand holds up a closed book, while from his left proceeds a banderole bearing a text from Psalm 51, in Latin, which translated means: 'Have mercy on me, God, and turn thy face from my sins. Amen.' (This is the same psalm his erstwhile neighbour, John Rogers, recited on his way to the stake.)

The aspirations that went into the founding of Witton Grammar School are very much those of someone who wanted the future for Northwich boys to be brighter than it had been in the past. Deane is the opposite of someone who, having achieved a degree of prosperity in his life through a mixture of good luck, good judgement and an ability to stay out of trouble, wants to pull the ladder up after himself; on the contrary, he was determined to leave a legacy that would enable others to improve their circumstances too. And, judging from his actions, he took the view that, whatever was happening in Smithfield, life goes on and must be lived wholeheartedly and with hope.

Chapter Fourteen

CONSTANCY AND CONFLAGRATION

✠

The martyr in his 'shirt of flame' may be looking on the face of
God, but to him who is piling the faggots or loosening the logs
for the blast the whole scene is no more than the slaying of an
ox is to the butcher, or the felling of a tree to the charcoal burner
in the forest, or the fall of a flower to one who is mowing down
the grass with a scythe.

Oscar Wilde, *De Profundis*

DURING THE SECOND HALF of Mary's reign, the burnings rose to
a crescendo. On 12 April 1557, five people – again from Essex –
were burnt in Smithfield: three men (Thomas Loseby, Henry
Ramsey and Thomas Thyrtell) and two women (Margaret Hyde
and Agnes Stanley). Three more men were burnt together on 30
November: William Sparrow, for selling blasphemous ballads and
calling the Mass abominable; John Hallingdale, for christening his
child according to the banned English service, from the time of
King Edward; and Richard Gibson. This last was a gentleman, the
scion of an established City family; his father was a royal serjeant-
at-arms and the bailiff of Southwark, while his grandfather, William
Bayley, had been Lord Mayor for 1524–5 and previously Master of
the Worshipful Company of Drapers. Gibson was learned and witty,
and quite prepared to taunt Bishop Bonner during their encounters. On 22 December John Rough, a beneficed priest at Hull
under Edward VI, and the minister of the 'London congregation',
a group of about twenty Protestants that met secretly in people's
houses and in taverns and included Dutch and French immigrants

as well as native Londoners, was burnt. He was accused of having ministered according to the Edwardian Book of Common Prayer, and of knowing others who used the same book. That the horrors of death by burning were appreciated by the martyrs, and had to be prepared for psychologically, is demonstrated by a comment made by Rough a few months before his own ordeal. Meeting him in the street one day, a fellow Protestant asked him where he had been. 'I have been where I would not for one of my eyes but I had been,' he replied, adding in explanation: 'To Austoo's burning, to learn the way.' (James Austoo and his wife Margery were burnt in Islington about 17 September.) Margaret Mearing, a member of the Islington congregation, died alongside Rough.

Three men were burnt on 28 March 1558, among them Cuthbert Simpson, a wealthy tailor and the deacon of the London congregation. He had been tortured repeatedly on the rack in an attempt to get him to divulge the names of the members. Even Bishop Bonner came to admire his constancy and 'patience', while still abhorring his heresy and supporting his death sentence for 'denial of the Mass'. Alongside Simpson died Hugh Foxe, a hosier, and John Devenish. A further seven were burnt on 27 June: Henry Pond, Reginald Eastland, Robert Southam, Matthew Ricarby, John Floyd, John Holiday and Roger Holland. This turned out to be the final group to suffer this terrible fate under Mary in Smithfield.

Why was the Queen so attached to this policy of burning, even while it appeared to be having little or no success in eradicating the 'contagion' of heresy? We have seen that she was encouraged by Bartolomé Carranza, but he left England in the summer of 1557, when the burnings were at their peak (June that year saw the highest number of burnings in any one month throughout the country – twenty-eight in total), and they did not die down for more than a year. Part of the reason is that, for Mary, the sacrament of the altar, as understood by the Catholic Church, was of fundamental importance; for her to hear of it being traduced and scorned was almost more than she could bear. And she seemed to go on believing, even as others around her changed their minds, that eradication of heretics was the only option and the right thing to do. David Loades, who has devoted much of his scholarly life to trying to fathom this unhappy monarch, perhaps sums her up best with the line: 'For all her humanist education, Mary was a woman whose convictions were stronger than her reason.'

Some of the Essex five who were burnt on 12 April 1557 had been apprehended by Lord Rich, the rest by other magistrates or constables, for the usual misdemeanour of non-attendance at their parish church. They were initially examined by Bishop Bonner's chancellor, Dr Thomas Darbyshire, on 27 January, with the bishop himself questioning them on 6 March. As with Bartlet Green, one of the criticisms directed at them concerned their reliance on their own consciences, instead of on what had been decreed by the Church. None of the accused were learned people, which made their unwillingness to listen to the established authorities seem all the more extraordinary to their judges. They were accused, among other things, of belief in predestination, or in the absence of free will: 'you have thought that all things do chance of an absolute and precise mere necessity, so that whether man does well or evil, he could not choose but so do, and that therefore no man has any free will at all'. They were further charged with rejecting infant baptism, with not believing in purgatory, and with considering the heretics burnt under both King Henry and Queen Mary not to have been heretics at all. While admitting to the bulk of the charges – that they had not attended their parish churches, preferring the English service as it had been under King Edward, or participated in any of the required processions and other ceremonies, and that they did not believe in the necessity of making their confession to a priest – they denied belief in predestination and rejection of infant baptism.

At the beginning of April they were asked if they stood by their earlier answers (they did), and on the morning of 3 April, in the Consistory Court, the bishop asked whether there was any reason why he should not condemn them. Thomas Loseby was the first to reply, declaring: 'God give me grace and strength to stand against you, and your sentence, and also against your law, which is a devouring law, for it devours the flock of Christ. And

I perceive there is no way for me but death, unless I consent to your devouring law, and believe in that idol, the Mass.' Thomas Thyrtell cited the highest possible authority in support of his defiant stance: 'My Lord, I say this, if you make me a heretic, then you make Christ and all the 12 Apostles heretics, for I am in the true faith and right belief, and I will stand in it, for I know full well I shall have eternal life therefore.' Last to reply was one of the women, Agnes Stanley, who was quite as defiant as her male companions. 'I had rather every hair of my head were burned,' she declared, 'than that I should forsake my faith and opinion which is the true faith.'

In the afternoon each was called before the bishop in turn, to go over the articles and answers one last time, and to have the sentence of condemnation read against them. They were then turned over to the sheriffs and, nine days later, burnt together in one great fire.

In view of the illustrious civic connections of Richard Gibson, one of those burnt on 30 November 1557, every effort was made to secure a recantation from him, the carrying out of the death sentence being delayed by twenty-four hours in order to allow Abbot Feckenham of Westminster to make one last attempt. Gibson had appeared before Bishop Bonner, alongside John Hallingdale and William Sparrow, on 5 November, in order to make answer to the usual 'articles'. Hallingdale's particular offence had been to have his new-born son baptized according to the English service, and he was now refusing to have the child confirmed by the bishop. William Sparrow was accused, despite having previously submitted to Bishop Bonner and renounced his heresies, of having lapsed and 'willingly fallen into certain heresies and errors' – and, worse, of having disseminated his 'various unlawful opinions', not only to the 'right great hurt' of his own soul, but also 'to the great hindrance and loss of various others'. His method of dissemination involved the selling of 'heretical, erroneous, and blasphemous ballads'; he had been found in possession of such ballads when he was arrested. Sparrow's response to the charge that he had defaulted on his earlier promise was to admit that he had indeed made such a submission, but that 'I am sorry that ever I made it, and it was the worse deed that ever I did.'

Richard Gibson's travails had begun when he was imprisoned in the Counter in Poultry over a debt; he had been held there for two years, and came under suspicion as a dissenter because he had never gone to confession or Mass during that time. While still in the Counter, he was required in May 1557 to answer to a number of charges. As with Sparrow, one of the most serious aspects of the accusations laid against him was that he had sought to influence others to adopt his beliefs; this was particularly worrying to the authorities when it was someone of their own class of people who was presenting a 'pernicious and evil example' to 'the inhabitants of the City of London, and the prisoners of the prison of the said Counter in the Poultry'. He was also accused of having encouraged other heretics, or those suspected of heresy, to persist in their wrong beliefs. In short, he was a very dangerous young man, apparently as pernicious in prison as out of it. He certainly showed little concern for his own safety, having been not at all discreet about his opinions and intentions, at least if the seventh of the charges laid against him was accurate:

> Seventhly, that the said Gibson has affirmed, that if he may once be out of prison and at liberty, he will not come to any parish church, or ecclesiastical place to hear Mattins, Mass, Evensong, or any divine service now used in this realm of England, nor come to procession upon times and days accustomed, nor carry at any time any taper or candle, nor receive at any time ashes, nor carry at any time palms, nor receive the Pax at Mass time, nor receive holy water, nor holy bread, nor observe the ceremonies or usages of the Catholic Church, here observed or kept commonly in this realm of England.

Gibson's answers to these initial charges having not satisfied the authorities, he continued to be held in the Counter until November, when he was summoned to appear before the bishop. Despite Gibson's outspokenness and determination to witness to the Protestant cause, he did not, as a member of a significant City family, relish the idea of being paraded through the busy City thorough-fares in the obvious and embarrassing guise of someone under arrest. He was, Foxe tells us, 'a very big and tall man, of a person-able and heroical stature'; he also sported the traditional Protestant beard. Whether with the deliberate intention of making him look ridiculous in the City, in the hope that this might bring him to his senses, or through mere absent-mindedness or accident, the authorities had arranged for Gibson to be escorted to the bishop by 'a little and short person', whom Foxe names as Robin Caly, a 'promoter', or one known as a denouncer of heretics. As this mis-matched couple set out from the Poultry, Gibson requested that they take a back route towards St Paul's, avoiding Cheapside, but Caly was having none of it. Not only was he determined to show off his prisoner to as many City dwellers and tradespeople as pos-sible, but he also intended to display his own importance in the process, and so he insisted on grabbing Gibson by the arm and trying to drag him along. Gibson pleaded for him to let go, stating his intention of coming along quietly wherever he was bidden, but requesting to walk merely side by side and not in a way that would draw attention to his invidious position. But Caly, who barely came up to Gibson's shoulder, would not give in, and clung on. 'I will hold you fast, despite your beard,' he bragged, 'whether you like it or not.' Gibson, abandoning Christian forbearance, finally snapped. 'You will, will you?' he said, and told Cary that if he didn't take his hands off him right now, and keep them off, he'd wring his neck. Threats proved more effective than persuasion, and the two walked along separately the rest of the way.

Having arrived before the bishop, Gibson refused to be exam-ined by him. This stalemate persisted for several sessions, until the time came for Gibson to be sentenced in the Consistory Court. Upon being asked if there was any reason why sentence should not be given against him, Gibson replied that he had not done anything for which the bishop could justly condemn him. To the bishop's explanation that 'men said he was an evil man', Gibson retorted that he could say the same thing of the bishop. Like many before him, once the definitive sentence had been passed against him,

Gibson felt free to speak, having previously kept quiet in order not to condemn himself. And so now he told the bishop he was not going to listen to any more of his 'babbling', and he reversed the charge of heresy to turn it against his accusers: 'now heresy is to turn the truth of God's word into lies, and that do you'.

Rather than answer the 'articles' Bonner had put to him, Gibson had chosen to draw up a corresponding set for Bonner to answer – 'by yes, or no, or else to say he cannot tell'. While hardly expecting the bishop to answer his questions, designed to demonstrate episcopal wrong-headedness, inconsistency or ignorance, Gibson had put his finger on some fundamental issues in the war on so-called heresy. Central to the debate was the nature of author-ity. 'What is authority,' asked Gibson's second article, 'and from where does it come, to whom does it appertain, and to what end does it tend?' His sixth article was perhaps even more pertinent than he had himself realized; intended to suggest that those in power in the official Church might be ministers of Satan rather than of Christ, it could equally be turned against those who assumed authority in the unofficial, Protestant, churches:

> By what evident tokens Antichrist in his ministers may be known, seeing it is written that Satan can change himself into the similitude of an angel of light, and his ministers fashion themselves as though they were the ministers of righteousness, and how may it be known to him that is desirous thereof, when he is one of that number or in the danger thereof, or when he is otherwise?

This intellectually gifted and well-built young man was burnt alongside John Hallingdale and William Sparrow: 'being brought thither to the stake, after their prayer made, they were bound to it with chains, and wood set unto them, and after wood, fire'.

An unquestioned assumption made by men in authority on both sides of the Catholic/Protestant divide was that women should be subject to their authority (apart, of course, from the Queen – though she had her own inner conflicts in trying to resolve sovereign rule with womanly obedience). This assumption is by and large shared by Foxe in his accounts of the martyrs, but some female characters nevertheless manage to escape from between his lines, emerging as feisty·and self-defining, even while demonstrating the limitations imposed on them by the society in which they lived. That Protestant leaders wielded quite as much authority over their flock, and particularly over its female members, as did Catholic priests and bishops over theirs, is nowhere clearer than in the story of Margaret Mearing – who also proved those who denigrated her character and misinterpreted her natural warmth and spontaneity to be spectacularly wrong.

Margaret was a member of the congregation led by John Rough, a man whose surname seems to have been rather well-suited to aspects of his personality. Rough, who by his death in 1557 was about fifty years old, was from Scotland and had in his youth entered the Dominican friary in Stirling, possibly after a family argument over property. His first doubts about Catholic practice and doctrine emerged during visits to Rome, when he was taken aback by the adulation afforded the Pope, borne aloft in his *sedia gestatoria* or ceremonial throne, 'to be carried on the shoulders of four men, as though he had been God and no man'. In the 1540s Rough served as chaplain to the Earl of Arran, the governor of Scotland, who was himself inclining towards Protestantism, and Rough showed his own sympathies by requesting, and receiving, a dispensation to cease wearing his Dominican habit while in this role. Not content with making merely sartorial changes, Rough, along with another Dominican called Thomas Williams, began preaching in various parts of Scotland against papal authority, the adoration of images and intercession to the saints. The message of the two men was not received with universal acclaim; there was nearly a riot after they preached in Edinburgh, Arran and the Earl of Angus having to intervene to prevent the preachers being assaulted. Comparing the two zealous Dominicans, the leader of the Scottish Reformation, John Knox, considered Rough to be 'not so learned, yet more simple, and more vehement against impiety'. Rough was later instrumental in developing Knox's own vocation as a preacher, the two men working together to promote the Protestant cause in the town of St Andrews. They had first met while Rough was acting as chaplain to the band of Fife lairds and their families who had seized St Andrews Castle in May 1546 and assassinated the Archbishop and Lord Chancellor of Scotland, Cardinal Beaton (on political rather than purely religious grounds). Cardinal Beaton had been one of Henry VIII's chief opponents in Scotland, and Rough had been in receipt of an annual payment of £20 for acting as one of Henry's agents in the country. After Henry's death, Rough managed to find favour with the Duke of Somerset who continued his pension and sent him to preach at Berwick. He next moved to Newcastle, where he married (in common with many other former friars and monks during Edward's reign), and then to Hull, where he was presented with a benefice by the Archbishop of York, Robert Holgate.

On Mary's accession, the Roughs emigrated to Norden in Friesland, where they engaged in the woollen trade, making a living through knitting caps and hosiery, while associating with other Protestant exiles. Rough returned to England in the autumn of 1557 – hardly a good time to have chosen – ostensibly to purchase yarn for his work, but also (according to the authorities) to smuggle in Protestant literature. The fact that he then became deeply involved with the underground Protestant congregation, succeeding Thomas Foule as its minister, would suggest that this was indeed no mere business trip, nor that his arriving at this time of heightened danger for Protestants was accidental. Like other banned organizations throughout history, the London congregation moved around from one 'safe house' to another, and often made use of taverns, such as the Swan at Limehouse or the King's Head in Stepney.

The vehemence alluded to by John Knox was as evident in the way John Rough led his congregation as in his preaching to the unconverted. His style of leadership involved strict discipline and the use of public shaming, practices witnessed in congregations he had visited while abroad. And like other Protestant authority figures of this time, he would tolerate no compromise with the Catholic Establishment on the part of his followers. So one woman, who had made the mistake of attending Mass (which she was of course obliged to do by law), was instructed by Rough to confess before the congregation (after which she was forgiven and 'received into their fellowship again'), but in the case of Margaret Mearing, who was believed to have spoken incautiously about the meetings of the congregation and whom he suspected of spying on them, he went as far as excommunication, virtually throwing her out of the group altogether. The reason she had fallen under suspicion was that she was by nature a rather talkative woman and very friendly – to the extent that she kept bringing new people with her to the meetings of the congregation. She did not exercise the usual reserve recommended to members of secret societies, and to that extent the nervousness she generated among her fellow believers is understandable, but there is also a sense that she could not – or would not – easily be controlled, and this made her an object of suspicion in a group that was quite as rigid in its ideas of hierarchy and authority as the Church which it was seeking to escape.

And so, on Friday 10 December, Rough took the very serious step of excommunicating Margaret, in public, effectively telling her she was no longer welcome as a member of the congregation. Her initial, furious, reaction served only to make everyone more convinced than ever that she was untrustworthy, indeed a danger to them – for she, 'being moved, did not well take it, nor in good part' and told one of her friends 'in a heat' that it would serve them right if she reported the lot of them.

But when, two days later, on the third Sunday of Advent, a meeting of the congregation was broken up and Rough was arrested, imprisoned in the Westminster Gatehouse and refused visitors, it was Margaret Mearing who showed herself to have a better grasp of Christian charity than many of the eloquent debaters in their opposing camps. Pretending to be Rough's sister, she turned up at the prison and managed to get in to see him, bearing not only words of comfort but a clean shirt. It is to be hoped that he was surprised and comforted, but also mortified, by her arrival, for he had been very harsh in his misjudgement of her.

The meeting at which Rough and others were arrested had

been taking place at a tavern in Islington called the Saracen's Head, and they had let it be thought they were there to watch a play. In fact they had met to hear a lecture and were intending also to hold a communion service, according to the forbidden English rite, but the Vice Chamberlain of the Queen's house, accompanied by officers of the guard, arrived before this could commence. The person who had betrayed the meeting to the authorities was not Margaret Mearing, but a tailor called Roger Sergeant. Upon hearing that this man was the culprit, the forthright Margaret turned up at his house, demanding to know whether Judas lived there. Receiving a negative answer, she persisted: 'No? Dwells not Judas here who betrayed Christ? His name is Sergeant.' Roger Sergeant had nothing to say in reply, and Margaret Mearing 'went her way'.

Margaret was herself soon arrested, an eventuality she embraced as cheerfully and with as much fortitude as she did everything else that happened to her. On the day the bishop's summoner came for her, she was standing gossiping with one of her woman friends at the end of Mark Lane (a street at the eastern end of the City, towards the Tower of London). She saw the summoner, whose name was Cluney, heading towards where she lived. 'Whither goeth yonder fine fellow?' she wondered aloud to her friend. 'I think he's going to my house!' She watched him go in through her door, and then set off to confront him.

'Who are you looking for?' she asked him.

'For you,' replied Cluney. 'You must come with me.'

'Well,' said Margaret. 'Here I am – let's go.' And so she set off uncomplainingly, towards imprisonment, interrogation and death.

Rough was examined by the Privy Council on 15 December and subsequently sent to Newgate, with a report being made to Bonner, describing him as a seditious and heretical person. The bishop examined Rough at his palace, as instructed by the Queen, on 18 and 19 December, putting articles to him which ranged from the usual subjects concerning papal authority and the nature of the sacraments through to his alleged smuggling of books and correspondence. Rough was uncompromising in his replies, insisting that people should pray in a language they understood (so in

English, rather than in Latin), that there were only two sacraments rather than seven, and that there was no need for believers to confess to a priest rather than to anyone else. If Foxe is to be believed, when Rough recounted his youthful impressions of the Pope, declaring that the reverence accorded him proved him to be the Antichrist, Bishop Bonner had another of his beard-plucking tantrums, 'flying upon' Rough to yank out a piece of the offending facial hair. Rough also refused to divulge any of the names of his congregation and maintained that he had been present at the Saracen's Head 'to hear and see a play'.

In the Consistory Court on 20 December, before Bishop Bonner and the Bishop of St David's (Henry Morgan), Abbot Feckenham and others, Rough continued to uphold his Protestant opinions, including that his marriage was lawful and his children legitimate (the youngest, Rachel, was just two years old when her father died), and that the Mass was an abomination. He was in consequence formally degraded from his clerical orders, condemned as a heretic, and committed for punishment to the secular authorities. Margaret Mearing, when asked if she stood by the answers she had given two days previously, declared: 'I will stand to them to the death: for the very angels of heaven do laugh you to scorn, to see your abomination that you use in the Church,' and was also condemned.

Rough reveals his most human, vulnerable side in the letters he wrote to friends and members of his congregation in the forty-eight hours between his condemnation and death. His outward resilience under interrogation, his bold words and forthright manner, had concealed the inward struggle of this fifty-year-old father of young children. 'I have not leisure and time to write the great temptations I have been under,' he tells his friends. 'I speak to God's glory: my care was to have the senses of my soul open, to perceive the voice of God, saying: whosoever denies me before men, him will I deny before my father and his angels. And to save the life corporal, is to lose the life eternal.' Having made the decision to stand firm and face the inevitable punishment, he now feels the worst of the battle – that with himself and with his own desire

for life – is over, though he cannot help but be anxious over
whether he will have the strength to endure what is to come: 'I
have chosen death to confirm the truth by me taught. What can
I do more? Consider with yourselves, that I have done it for the
confirmation of God's truth. Pray that I may continue to the end.
The greatest part of the assault is past, I praise my God.' In a second
letter, addressed to his congregation, he again emphasizes the difficulty of the inner struggle he has been through since his arrest:
'What a journey (by God's power) I have made, these eight days
before this date, it is above flesh and blood to bear: but as Paul says,
I may do all things in him who works in me, Jesus Christ. My
course, brethren, have I run, I have fought a good fight, the crown
of righteousness is laid up for me, my day to receive it is not long
too.' The final paragraph of his letter to his friends calls on them
to be faithful and to pray, believing victory will be theirs in the end
– but his bold rhetoric cannot quite disguise the fear and distress
of a living, feeling human being soon to meet his death by fire:

> It is no time for the loss of one man in the battle, for the camp
> to turn back. Up with men's hearts, blow down the daubed
> walls of heresies: let one take the banner, and the other the
> trumpet, I mean not to make corporal resistance, but pray . . .
> The cause is the Lord's. Now, my brethren, I can write no
> more, time will not allow it, and my heart with pangs of death
> is assaulted: but I am at home with my God yet alive. Pray for
> me, and salute one another with the holy kiss. The peace of
> God rest with you all. From Newgate prison in haste, the day
> of my condemnation.

The farewell to his congregation is more conventional and
restrained than these anguished words to his friends. Here he does
not mention the 'pangs of death', but concludes, like a model
pastor, with a blessing, quoting from the Psalms and the Book of
Revelation; his words are no less genuine for their restraint, for
what he does not say, and his prayer is as much for himself as for
his flock. One can almost hear him weeping as he writes: 'The
Spirit of God guide you in and out, rising and sitting, cover you

with the shadow of his wings, defend you against the tyranny of the wicked, and bring you happily to the port of eternal felicity, where all tears shall be wiped from your eyes, and you shall always abide with the lamb.'

John Rough and Margaret Mearing were burnt together 'most joyfully' on 22 December 1557. One wonders who gave more encouragement to the other.

The secret underground congregation continued, Rough's role as minister and chief pastor being taken on by Augustine Bernher and then by Thomas Bentham, who would later (in the next, and final, reversal of religious policy, under Elizabeth I) become Bishop of Coventry and Lichfield.

Arrested at the same time as John Rough, but held for longer before being condemned, were his second-in-command of the London congregation, Cuthbert Simpson, and two other members – Hugh Foxe (a hosier) and John Devenish. The Friday night before the arrests was a busy one for John Rough, for not only did he excommunicate Margaret Mearing that same evening, he was also plagued by nightmares about Cuthbert Simpson – to the extent that he was moved to get up out of bed. 'Kate, strike a light,' he said to his wife, 'for I am much troubled about my brother Cuthbert this night.' Cuthbert had himself been feeling anxious and unable to sleep – all of which suggests that the leaders of the congregation suspected they were about to be, or had been, betrayed, and goes some way to explain the harsh treatment of Margaret Mearing, amidst nervousness over her lack of discretion – and he arrived, carrying the book in which he maintained the accounts of the congregation (for they were in the habit of collecting donations from the wealthier members to support the less well-off). The accounts book contained names, and it was the thought of this that was giving John Rough – and Cuthbert Simpson – a sleepless night. Cuthbert tried at first to make little of their fears (despite his having turned up in the middle of the night because of them), telling the Roughs (and himself) that dreams were 'but fantasies, and not to be credited'. But then Rough exercised his authority, ordering Cuthbert to stop carrying the accounts book around with him. He obeyed, leaving it with Rough's wife, Kate.

And it was names the authorities wanted, and the hope of getting them the main reason for the delay between Cuthbert Simpson's arrest and his execution. On the day following the arrest, Cuthbert was tortured in the Tower of London, being 'set on a rack of iron' for the space of about three hours. His questioners wanted to know who he had summoned to attend 'the English service' that was to have been held the day before, but he would not tell them. A week later, after he had been given time to recover from his first ordeal, he was brought back to the torture chamber. This time his tormentors began by tying his two index fingers together and then forcing a small arrow between them, ripping his flesh. They racked him again – twice – but still he did not talk. This was no secret, illegal torture, as had happened to Anne Askew in the days of Henry VIII, but officially sanctioned, for Bonner referred to it in the Consistory Court, commending Cuthbert's 'patience' and wishing he were not a heretic – for he was a very 'personable man'. Cuthbert was another of those to enjoy the hospitality of the bishop's coalhouse, from where he wrote to his wife, in words that do indeed demonstrate his patient and accepting spirit: 'For there is nothing that comes to us by fortune or chance, but by our heavenly Father's providence. And therefore pray to our heavenly Father that he will ever give us his grace for to consider it. Let us give him most hearty thanks, for these his fatherly corrections: for as many as he loves, he corrects.' He concluded his letter with sentiments reminiscent of the final words of St John Chrysostom: 'In all things give thanks. At the name of Jesus every knee shall bow. Cuthbert Simpson.'

Another secret congregation or 'conventicle' – this time one that met outside, rather than in houses and taverns – featured in the final mass burning to take place in Smithfield. Again the district concerned was that of Islington, just bordering the City. And again a woman is central to the story – or at least to the history of one of the victims, Roger Holland – in a tale with all the hallmarks of an early romantic novel, in which the feckless hero is redeemed by the virtuous heroine.

Holland was a member of the Merchant Taylors' Company, and had influential friends and relatives. As a young man, apprenticed to a Master Kempton in Watling Street, he had lived a somewhat riotous life, enjoying everything London had to offer the young and irresponsible – 'dancing, fencing, gaming, banquetting, and wanton company'. He was also a committed Catholic – not least because he benefited from having a priest absolve him in between his bouts of sinfulness.

Despite his poor behaviour, his master trusted him with keeping the accounts of the business. One day, Roger received a payment of £30 on his master's behalf – a not inconsiderable sum, the equivalent of about £6,000 in the twenty-first century – and, predictably enough, he fell into bad company and gambled it all away. Overcome with remorse – for our hero came from a good family and had a sense of honour beneath his youthful fecklessness – he resolved to run away, either to France or Flanders, but first he wanted to promise to put things right in the future. And so early in the morning, prior to departing, he spoke to someone he trusted – his master's servant, an unmarried woman called Elizabeth. Foxe describes her as 'an ancient and discreet maid' but she cannot have been as ancient as all that, as the sequel to this story shows. The important thing about Elizabeth, however, is that she was of an evangelical persuasion, and had been trying for some time to turn Roger from his 'licentious living' as well as from his Catholicism. She was also very prudent with money. Roger now confessed to her what had happened, and asked her to give his master – via his master's wife – a note of the debt, with the promise that he would pay it back to him one day. He included the desperate request that his master should tell no one else about it – for the news of his dishonour would, he declared, be the death of his father.

Elizabeth, realizing this was a crisis point for Roger and seeing a way of saving him (in every sense of the word), now made the astonishing assertion that she had enough money put by to meet the debt (she had, it seems, been left a bequest by a relative), and that she would do so – provided Roger amend his way of life and henceforth 'refuse all lewd and wild company, all swearing and ribald talk'. And if ever he spent so much as a shilling again at dice or cards, she would go straight to their master with the note of the debt, and tell him what had happened. Furthermore, Roger was to undergo a crash course in Protestantism (all this took place during Edward's reign), attending a daily lecture at the church of All Hallows and the sermon at Paul's Cross every week, reading the Bible and the English prayer book, and casting away all his 'books of papistry and vain ballads'. He was also to pray for forgiveness, and forget the sins of his youth. The grateful Roger had little choice but to obey.

Whether as a result of the shock of near-ruin, the vigilance of Elizabeth in monitoring his activity, or a genuine interest in and receptiveness to what he heard, in the space of six months Roger Holland had become a convinced Protestant – so much so that when he went home to Lancashire, he took a pile of evangelical literature to distribute among his friends and family. His father, though remaining Catholic, was sufficiently impressed by his son's maturity to give him a substantial amount of money – somewhat in excess of what he had originally lost at gambling – to enable him to make his way in the world.

He returned to London and, like every good fairy-tale prince, to the woman who had rescued him. 'Elizabeth,' he announced, 'here is your money I borrowed from you, and for the friendship, good will, and the good counsel I have received at your hands, to recompense you I am not able, otherwise than to make you my wife.' Perhaps she had been hoping for this outcome all along, for she did not hesitate in accepting. They were married and soon had a child.

The structure of this story rather demands a 'happy-ever-after' ending, but of course that was not to be (unless one counts the happy-ever-after of heaven). For by the time Roger and Elizabeth were man and wife, Mary I had come to the throne, and people with their convictions found themselves in danger. Roger, with all the zeal of a recent convert, could not or would not dissemble or compromise, and he almost immediately did something indiscreet – that is, he arranged for their new baby to be baptized according to the English rite and in his own house. Someone found out, and reported what had taken place to the authorities. Determined to keep the baby safe from the 'anointing hands' of the official clergy, Roger took the child away into the country, presumably to leave it with friends or relatives. But in the meantime his goods were seized and Elizabeth harassed.

They survived this episode, however, and continued to live in the City, while participating in secret congregations and conventicles, including those that met in the open air. About forty people, both men and women, had congregated in a field on the edge of Islington on the morning of 1 May 1558, when they were discovered. The man who first came across them appeared friendly, and told them they could stay there as they looked like 'such persons as intend no harm'. But having reassured them that they were safe, he turned up again fifteen minutes later with the constable of Islington and half a dozen armed men in tow. The constable confiscated their books, and the congregation was escorted, in groups of eight or ten, to the nearest person in authority, who turned out to be Sir Roger Cholmley. Some of the group, particularly the women among them, had the presence of mind to escape, as their guards were not numerous and several of them were armed only with farming implements. But twenty-seven of the original group obediently went along to be questioned, twenty-two of them subsequently being detained and delivered to Newgate, including Roger Holland.

And now Roger's family and City connections mobilized themselves, and exerted all their energy towards saving him from the fires of Smithfield, petitioning Bonner to be merciful. The bishop showed himself prepared to listen to them – as with other young and promising men who had come before him, he would much prefer to receive their submission than have to hand them over to be burnt. 'Since you are now in danger of the law,' he began, when Roger appeared before him, 'I would wish you to play a wise man's part.' Also present at this first encounter were Dr Chedsey, both the Harpsfield brothers (John, the Archdeacon of London and Bonner's chaplain, and his younger brother Nicholas, Archdeacon of Canterbury and Vicar-General of London) and various others. Bonner was explicit about his desire to help Roger. 'So shall you not want any favour I can do or procure for you,' he went on, 'both for your own sake, and also for your friends, who are men of worship and credit, and wish you well, and by my troth, Roger, so do I.' But both the bishop and Roger's well-wishers had reckoned without the determination of the young man himself. His conversion experience had been so profound that he could not conceivably now turn back to the faith of his teenage years, when he used to pay a priest to absolve him for his riotous lifestyle and even perform his penance for him. Rather than accept Bonner's mercy, he lectured him, being particularly critical of the use of Latin in church. 'What are we of the laity the better for it?' he asked, rhetorically. 'I think he that should hear your priests mumble up their service, although he did well understand Latin, yet should he understand few words thereof: the priests do so champ them and chaw them, and post so fast, that neither they understand what they say, nor they that hear them.' He had also done enough reading of history to know the weak points in the Church's armour. 'As for the unity which is in your church,' he expostulated, 'what is it else but treason, murder, poisoning one another, idolatry, superstition, wickedness? What unity was in your church, when there were three Popes at once? Where was your head of unity when you had a woman Pope?' He would have gone on, but the bishop had had enough of this diatribe and interrupted him, telling him his words were 'very blasphemy' and that he was 'over malapert' to try to teach the assembled church dignitaries. And he instructed the keeper of Newgate to 'take him away'.

Roger's next examination proceeded in much the same spirit, his relatives once again there to try to persuade Bonner and his team to be merciful and Roger to be sensible. Dr Chedsey began: 'Roger, I trust you have now better considered of the Church than you did before.'

'I consider this much,' replied Roger – 'that out of the Church there is no salvation, as various ancient Doctors say.'

'That is well said,' commented Bonner. 'But, Roger,' he went on, 'you mean, I trust, the Church of Rome' – while knowing perfectly well that he did not. Nevertheless, by the end of the discussion, and on account of the pressure being exerted by Roger's connections, Bonner still seemed hopeful that Roger might come round – at least sufficiently for a form of words to be agreed that would get him off the hook of being a convicted heretic – and he told the keeper to ensure that the prisoner had anything he needed.

Roger Holland's fellow accused were noticeably reliant in their replies on what they had been taught by their Protestant teachers and pastors. These are the voices of men and women who were not from the privileged classes, who had listened hard to what they had been told, were appreciative of the fact that they were being addressed in English rather than Latin and so could feel properly included, and had read at least parts of their Bibles (again in English). One of them, Henry Pond, when accused of not attending church, replied that 'if he had licence then to go to church, he would', suggesting that he was following the instructions of his leaders, who were unequivocal about attendance at Mass or other Catholic services being forbidden to the faithful. When asked for his views on the sacrament of the altar, Henry could again only fall back on what he had been taught, saying that he did not know about any sacrament by that name, but that he did know about the sacrament of the Lord's Supper which he believed to be 'approved'. Robert Southam declared it was pointless to ask 'a simple man' whether the Latin service was good and lawful – how was he supposed to know, if he couldn't understand it? Reginald Eastland said that he had heard it was not lawful to take an oath at the beginning of a dispute and so, on being asked to swear at the start of his interrogation that he would tell the truth, he refused and would not answer any of the questions. And for this refusal, he declared himself 'content to stand to the order of the law for his punishment, whatever it should be'. When each came to be condemned, a common theme emerging from their response to the bishop before he uttered each sentence was that the heresy was all on the other side. 'We may not know much,' they may be summarized as saying, 'but we do know we aren't heretics – and that you are.'

On the day of judgement, after all Roger's fellow prisoners had been excommunicated, his case was still outstanding, his powerful kinsmen and friends – who included the Earl of Derby, Henry Stanley (known as Lord Strange) and 'various others of worship, both of Cheshire and Lancashire' – still present. The fact that such people could be corralled into offering support and that Bonner was prepared to listen to them suggests that, for those with the right connections, there were ways of escaping death for heresy, provided the accused could be made to see sense. For the majority, whose relatives did not have access to the right strings to pull, this was not an option. Bonner was again in conciliatory mood, telling Roger that his main fault seemed to be that he was somewhat 'overhasty', but admitting that he himself suffered from the same fault – 'For I myself shall now and then be hasty, but my anger is soon past.' And he used the parable of the prodigal son as an entice-ment to Roger to repent: 'As I mean you so well, Roger, play the wise man's part,' he pleaded, 'and come home with the lost son and say: I have run into the church of schismatics and heretics, from the Catholic Church of Rome, and you shall, I warrant you, not only find favour at God's hands, but the Church that has authority shall absolve you and put new garments upon you, and kill the fatling to make you good cheer withal.' Roger's supporters thanked the bishop for his words, but to Roger himself this must have sounded like an invitation to go backwards, to return to his misspent youth with its cycle of sin and absolution, wasting all the efforts he had made at self-improvement over the last few years, letting down himself, his wife and his fellow believers (including those with whom he was standing trial). He did not find the prospect tempt-ing, not even as a way of avoiding death.

And so the bishop came to the crunch question, the test that would show whether Roger was prepared to take the way out being offered him. 'Well, Roger, how say you now?' he asked. 'Do you not believe that after the priest has spoken the words of con-secration, there remains the body of Christ really and corporally under the forms of bread and wine?'

All Roger had to say was: 'I do so believe' and his ordeal would be over. But he had never had any intention of giving in. 'No,' he replied, 'Christ has ascended into heaven, and so is not contained under the forms of bread and wine.'

Bonner had gone as far as he could. There may have been influential people in the room wanting Roger's reprieve, but there were more powerful people outside it – including the Queen – wanting an end to the matter. And there had never been any real doubt that Roger was a committed Protestant and as deserving of condemnation as his fellow defendants. 'Roger, I perceive my pains and good will will not prevail,' he said, 'and if I should argue with you, you are so wilful (as all your fellows are, standing in your own singularity and foolish conceit) that you would still talk to no purpose this seven years, if you might be allowed to.' Where Roger had no argument with the bishop was in his agreement to submit to his authority as an officer of the law. He did not object to being condemned by him, but he would not accept the doctrine propounded by him. Neither would he stop talking, causing Bonner to remark: 'If I were to allow him, he would fall from reasoning to railing, as a frantic heretic.' And finally, having given up the attempt to save the young man from himself, he read out the sentence of condemnation and left the room. The irrepressible Roger immediately began preaching to his friends and acquaintances, who must by now have been both irritated and upset by his intransigence and its inevitable outcome, but he exhorted them to repent and to think well of all those who had been condemned. Realizing what was going on, the bishop angrily returned and instructed the keeper that no one was to speak with the prisoners, on pain of imprisonment themselves.

Of the twenty-two who had been imprisoned after the arrests in the field, thirteen were subsequently burnt: these seven in Smithfield, and a further six at Brentford in Middlesex. The failure of the burning policy – that it had not eradicated heresy or support for heretics – was clearly shown in the atmosphere engendered by these mass burnings. On the day of the Smithfield executions – 27 June 1558 – a proclamation was issued that no one was to speak to any of the victims, or take anything from them (it having become part of the ritual of the burnings for the sufferers to hand out keepsakes on their way to the stake) or touch them, on pain of imprisonment. But the authorities' intentions were subverted by a demonstration of support organized by Thomas Bentham of the London congregation, hundreds of people lining the route and shouting out encouragement in the form of prayers, even if they obeyed the letter of the proclamation by not addressing the prisoners directly. And many of them, despite the prohibition, nevertheless took the victims by the hands as they passed, and comforted them. Such a display of support led Bonner to recommend that burnings should in future be conducted more discreetly and away from what had become a notorious stage-set; it was for this reason that the remaining six victims from the conventicle were taken to Brentford, and despatched there on 14 July.

Though June 1558 marked the end of the Smithfield fires, there were more yet to come in other parts of the country. Five were burnt in Canterbury just a week before the death of Queen Mary, and of Cardinal Pole, on the same day – 17 November 1558 – she predeceasing him by the space of a few hours.

Epilogue

'BY THE LIGHT OF BURNING MARTYRS'

✠

Ô vous, les boutefeux, ô vous, les bons apôtres,
Mourez donc les premiers, nous vous cédons le pas.
Mais, de grâce, morbleu! laissez vivre les autres!
La vie est à peu près leur seul luxe ici-bas;
Car, enfin, la Camarde est assez vigilante,
Elle n'a pas besoin qu'on lui tienne la faux.
Plus de danse macabre autour des échafauds!
Mourons pour des idées, d'accord, mais de mort lente,
D'accord, mais de mort lente.

O all you firebreathers, o all you good apostles,
Go and die first, we'll just stand back and let you through.
But please, I beg you, let the rest of us get on with living,
Life is just about our only luxury down here.
For after all, Death is sufficiently vigilant,
He doesn't need anyone to hold his scythe for him.
Let's have no more macabre dances around the scaffold.
Let's die for ideas, OK, if you want, but just make sure it's
    a slow death,
OK? just a slow death.

Georges Brassens, 'Mourir pour des idées',
translated by Ted Neather*

BY AND LARGE, we – by which I mean the majority of twenty-first-century inhabitants of what we think of as our world, and leaving out the adherents of IS, ISIL, Daesh or whatever acronym

---

* This translation aims to convey meaning and not attempt poetry or song.

the promoters of an Islamic caliphate are currently to be known by – would concur with the French *chansonnier* Georges Brassens that ideas are not really worth dying for, at least not by a premature, chosen death. This may be partly why we are despised by the so-called extremists who are more than willing both to die, and to kill, for ideas. W. B. Yeats captured our current dilemma well in his poem 'The Second Coming': 'The best lack all conviction, while the worst / Are full of passionate intensity.'

Certainly the martyrs of the mid-sixteenth century were full of 'passionate intensity' – but they cannot be defined as 'the worst'. That appellation perhaps belongs to more recent history – characters from our own, and the immediately preceding, centuries. And, perhaps, faced by people whose passionate intensity is unreservedly murderous, we are going to have to find some passion and intensity of our own, some 'idea' for which we are prepared to die if, paradoxically, we want our civilization to stay alive.

What, then, might one be prepared to die for in this post-postmodern age? Not for nuances of definition of the doctrine of transubstantiation, that's for sure (or perhaps it's not as sure as all that). But for the right of people to disagree about it, perhaps? Do we really care that much about freedom of speech and freedom of thought? Certainly we care – but do we care enough to die for it? On the contrary, we seem to care rather less than we used to, given the way we allow our civil liberties to be eroded in the cause of an unattainable, elusive and illusory 'security'.

What if I, as a Christian – and a Catholic (Anglican, not Roman) Christian at that, to whom these things do matter – am one day confronted by a fanatic of another religion (and this is not such a far-fetched possibility as it might once – not so very long ago – have appeared) and told to stamp on the consecrated host, on pain of death? Would I do it? I don't know – I don't know how strong I am, or might be – but I hope I wouldn't. I hope the grace of God would make me strong enough not to deny my faith *in extremis* – less for the thing in itself (whether, or in what sense, the host 'is' the body of Christ) as because I don't want to allow force, bullying or violence to make me be different from how I want to be; I don't want to allow someone else to define who I am and make me do something that contradicts that self-definition. I'm not averse to changing my mind, and my faith has waxed and waned frequently over the years, as has my adherence to particular practices – but it's my mind, and my prerogative to change it. But when (fleetingly) imagining a heroic defiance, it's salutary to reread George Orwell's *1984* and to remember that I think he's right about pain (having seen in my parents dying of cancer how pain can be all-absorbing, when the only thing that matters is that it should end): 'Never, for any reason on earth, could you wish for an increase of pain. Of pain you could wish only one thing: that it should stop. Nothing in the world was so bad as physical pain. In the face of pain there are no heroes, no heroes, [Winston] thought over and over as he writhed on the floor, clutching uselessly at his disabled left arm.'

So I have no idea whether I could really hold firm in the face of a violent challenge to what I want to stay true to, but it interests me that I can contemplate – even if it never gets beyond contemplation (and I earnestly hope my strength will never be tested in this way) – dying for something that's not that far removed from the kind of thing the martyrs died for: dying *pour des idées*, in fact. Perhaps what has really changed is the weight society as a whole attaches to the importance of conformity. We still, as human beings, carry within us the potential to be martyrs, but if our society as a whole doesn't really care what its individual components believe, then there's no real opportunity for martyrdom; if I want to hang onto some weird outmoded idea about a piece of wafer being somehow holy, then the strongest penalty I'm likely to encounter in twenty-first-century Britain is derision. To state the obvious, however, when belief becomes a matter of life and death, individuals may have to choose one or the other. And in some parts of the world this is a very present reality. A media headline in February 2016 read: 'Saudi Arabia sentences a man to 10 years in prison and 2,000 lashes for expressing his atheism on Twitter.' (The message from sixteenth-century England to the twenty-first-century Saudis is that such methods won't work.)

Maybe it always has been, and always will be, a minority who care enough not to choose life over conscience. And maybe it's insane, or at least evidence of hubris, not to do so, particularly in matters of faith. Why do we think ultimate reality, if there is such a thing, is affected by what we say and do? So what if we deny God, or what we take to be God? – it won't affect God's existence one way or the other.

It does affect how we feel about ourselves, though, and perhaps that's the real point. The martyrs couldn't save themselves in this world because they would have been lost to themselves if they had. We see that in the torments of conscience suffered by those who did recant and then took back the recantation; they couldn't live with themselves after they had uttered what seemed to them a denial of their faith – because it was a denial of their very selves. So the 'luxury' that is life, according to Georges Brassens, proved not to be worth as much as the integrity that meant embracing death.

Dying for an idea is one thing; killing for ideological reasons quite another. There have been people throughout history who have been prepared to kill in defence of their beliefs – it's an easy win for scorners of Christianity to point to the Crusades (Pope Urban II in 1095 having implied that the killing of 'infidels' in a 'crusade' to recapture the Holy Land was a work of Christian piety), and then there are the original 'assassins', the medieval Nizari Ismailis and their leader Hassan-i Sabbah – but it seems particularly urgent to try to understand the psychology of present-day jihadists, if only because they may be the current most significant threat to our society, even to civilization itself. I am writing this a few months after the murderous attacks on people just enjoying themselves during an evening out in Paris, scores of young people being shot down while doing nothing more harmful than attending a rock concert. What did the attackers think they were doing? What was (and is, because it's not going to go away any time soon) the point? Knowing, as they must have done, that theirs was also a suicidal mission, did the motivation of the gunmen have any similarities with that of the sixteenth-century martyrs? Or with that of their persecutors?

The most obvious answer to the first question must be 'no'. The Smithfield martyrs did not anticipate their executions leading to the deaths of others, and they would certainly not have wished harm on an indiscriminate gathering of people whose views and beliefs they could not know; if encountering a group of young people eating, drinking and party-going, some of the martyrs might well have set about trying to convert them, but they certainly wouldn't have thought of killing them. The answer is perhaps slightly less obvious when we consider those – both Catholic and Protestant – who believed the correct course of action to deal with an obstinate heretic was to kill him or her (and several of the martyrs themselves also fall into this category). They too would have been horrified at the idea of indiscriminate killing – they would have needed proof that each individual was irredeemably lost to heresy and consequently a danger to other Christian souls, and they would have wanted some legal formulation to help justify a death sentence before handing anyone over to die – but, nevertheless, the preparedness to accept judicial execution as an appropriate sanction for 'wrong belief' is somewhere on the spectrum that reaches its darkest point in the mass murder of people of a different, or no, religion. There is a kind of awful purity, an intransigence, a refusal to live with compromise or to accept and make allowance for human imperfection, that can be detected as much in the austere figure of Thomas More as in some of those drawn towards a world-denying version of Islam that wants to smash everything – and everyone – that stands in the way of a particular vision of the absolute.

It must be underlined that there are many voices of 'mainstream' Islam anxious to stress that an approach to non-Muslims that involves killing them is not sanctioned by a right understanding of Islamic law, one of these voices being Shaykh Abdallah bin Bayyah, a Mauritanian professor of Islamic studies and President of the Forum for Promoting Peace in Muslim Societies. Addressing himself to young people tempted to go off and fight for IS, he writes:

All forms of oppression and aggression against religious minorities are in direct contradiction to the values of our religion. In fact, Islam calls us to do well by religious minorities, to place them under our protection, and threatens those who harm them with punishment in the afterlife. This is evidenced by the track record of the Muslim world, which has no peer in history when it pertains to people living harmoniously with religious minorities, beyond what basic humanity demands of equal rights and responsibilities. Hence, any aggression of any kind or coercion to convert is unacceptable. Coerced conversion is invalid in Islamic law. Islam has nothing to do with this, as the Qur'an states, 'There is no compulsion in religion' (Qur'an, 2:256).

One must also not forget about politics or be tempted to draw too easy a parallel between situations that may appear similar only on a very superficial level. The political element which is such a potent feature of current 'Islamist extremism' has no parallel with the sixteenth-century martyrs' experience; they were not interested, and nor by and large were their accusers, in exercising political power and certainly not in forming a new 'state' – loyalty to the monarch was important to everyone involved (except, perhaps, to a few of the radical Anabaptists), even if that loyalty was interpreted and expressed in conflicting ways. What does remain the same, however, is the great difficulty in turning back a young 'extremist' from his (or her) path once it has been embarked upon. The old authority figures – be they Bishop Bonner or Shaykh bin Bayyah – find themselves frustrated at their lack of power to convince, while to the youthful 'protestant' the words and actions of their elders seem not only out of date, but contaminated – by compromise with error and by departure from a perceived original 'pure' source.

Where there may also be a similarity between the martyrs of four and a half centuries ago and the suicidal 'martyrs' of today is in the firm belief in an afterlife, a conviction that heaven, or paradise, exists and that they are destined to reach it very soon, possibly immediately after death. Those who believe that they are martyrs (*shahid*) dying in battle for the sake of Allah – which is how they interpret what they are doing when they take part in terrorist attacks against those they perceive to be enemies of Islam – also believe that they will be rewarded with the pleasures of paradise, including food, drink and beautiful women, and that they will not have to wait for their reward.

> The distinction of martyrs, compared to other Muslims, lies primarily in the fact that they are guaranteed the privilege of Paradise: the act of falling in battle for the sake of Allah washes away every violation or sin they have committed during their lives. The shahid enters Paradise immediately, without enduring the 'torments of the grave', whereas an ordinary Muslim who does not have the privilege of dying as a martyr must wait for the Day of Judgment.

A. J. Caschetta, a senior lecturer in English at the Rochester Institute of Technology and a fellow of the Middle East Forum, asserts in his article 'Does Islam Have a Role in Suicide Bombings?': 'The "vast reward" offered to the martyr is the single most important incentive for suicide bombers', alluding specifically to the following verse from the Qur'an: 'Let those fight in the way of Allah who sell the life of this world for the other. Whoso fighteth in the way of Allah, be he slain or be he victorious, on him We shall bestow a vast reward.'

While the heaven awaited by the Smithfield martyrs was of a different order from the paradise envisaged by a twenty-first-century jihadist (beautiful women in particular playing little part in Christian views of the afterlife), an expectation that they were soon to arrive and be welcomed there is evident in the words reported to have been uttered at the stake by more than one of the victims. Nicholas Ridley encapsulated this view in his farewell letter from prison: 'Let us not then fear death, which can do us no harm, otherwise than for a moment to make the flesh to smart; for that our faith, which is surely fastened and fixed unto the word of God, telleth us that we shall be anon after death in peace in the hands of God, in joy, in solace, and that from death we shall go straight unto life.' A willingness to accept that the physical body was of far less importance than the immortal soul was shared by those, including Queen Mary, who consigned the martyrs to the flames and was one of the reasons that made the action possible. And such a belief contributed in no small part to the courage of many of the martyrs; indeed, without that belief – not only in the existence of an afterlife but in the granting of a greater significance to it than to our mortal, transient, earthly life – the willingness to give up that earthly life for the sake of holding firm to a particular doctrine or set of doctrines, 'to die for ideas', would surely have been less. People who are prepared to die for ideas are giving ultimate value to those ideas; they must be seen to transcend death, if the individual's death is to have any meaning. If the ideas die with the person, what is the point in dying for them?

With the accession of Queen Elizabeth I in November 1558 those characters in our story who had so far succeeded in not dying for ideas had to decide yet again what position to adopt, as what constituted orthodoxy was again subject to revision.

In the first year of the new Queen's reign, the church of St Bartholomew was restored to its use as a parish church and Sir John Deane to his official title of rector (he had signed himself as 'curate' during the period of the Black Friars' residence). In 1559, under the terms of Elizabeth's Act of Supremacy, the clergy were required to take an oath recognizing the Queen's supremacy in the Church, and Deane duly did so, signing his name at a ceremony in the church of St Lawrence Jewry. He would also now have had to return to celebrating Holy Communion in English, wearing only surplice and cope rather than full eucharistic vestments, and once again eschewing most processions, prayers to the saints and any sacred images that had been brought back into use under Mary.

The Black Friars officially departed on 14 July; the majority of them were Spanish or Dutch and they left the country. Friar Richard Hargrave, a priest from Dartford who had been elected Prior of Smithfield shortly before Mary's death, refused to take the oath and escorted a group of Dominican nuns to exile in Seland, near

Antwerp. About half of Deane's fellow City clergy felt unable to embrace this latest reversal of ecclesiastical policy and resigned, or were removed. It must have been particularly difficult for those appointed during Mary's reign who had been out of favour under Edward, while for those who had already proved their ability to adapt to change – such as John Deane and Alan Percy, the latter having served as priest at St Mary-at-Hill continuously from 1521 – the requirement to change yet again may have felt tiresome, but not unendurable.

The beginning of the new reign was marked for Richard Rich by bereavement, his wife Elizabeth dying at their house in Bartholomew Close in December 1558. Her body was 'carried in a chariot from St Bartholomew the Great unto Essex to be buried, with banners and banner-rolls about her', and the funeral at Rochford in Essex, as recorded by Machyn, was accompanied with much pomp and markedly Catholic accoutrements: 'The 18 day of December was buried my Lady Rich, the wife of Lord Rich, with a hearse of 5 principals and a 8 dozen pensells* and a 8 dozen escutcheons and a great banner of my Lord's and my Lady's arms and 4 banner-rolls, and 4 banners of saints; and great white branches and 6 dozen of torches; and 24 poor men had gowns; and the morrow mass and a great dinner, and 2 heralds and many mourners.' Lord Rich actually turned out to be less flexible in his religion than John Deane, and in April 1559 he voted in the House of Lords with the Roman Catholic minority against the Act of Uniformity (which reintroduced the Book of Common Prayer and established the Church of England along broadly Protestant lines). Perhaps his participation in so many heresy trials under Mary had left their mark on him; he had not been merely playing a part when upholding Catholic doctrine and, after all he had witnessed and the zeal he had put into bringing people to condemnation – as well as on occasion trying to encourage them to avoid it – he could not in the end 'turn, turn and turn again', or not full circle, at least. The strength of his convictions was never unduly tested –

---

* Very small heraldic banners.

and he did support the restoration of the royal supremacy, as might indeed be expected of someone who had played such a large part in bringing the Church in England under the monarch's control, particularly as Chancellor of Augmentations. He was not appointed to Elizabeth's Privy Council and he retired to Essex, but his services were still sought on occasion, as when he was summoned in 1566 to join a delegation of members of both Houses of Parliament who addressed the Queen on the delicate question of her marriage (or lack of one).

Lord Rich died at Rochford in Essex on 12 June 1567. He had spent his last years as a local magnate and magistrate, also becoming involved in education, converting the endowment he had used to set up a chantry at Felsted in 1554 to establish the 'Free School of Richard Lord Rich' there in May 1564. (The motto of Felsted School remains that of Richard Rich – 'Garde Ta Foy' or 'Keep thy faith' – an injunction which perhaps he finally embraced in the last years of his life. It nevertheless seems an ironic, even cynical, label to be attached, and in perpetuity, to this great survivor of an age in which many people who genuinely 'kept their faith' paid the ultimate price for doing so. But maybe another way of interpreting it, more fitting to Rich and suggesting one of the secrets of his survival, would be: 'Keep your faith to yourself.') Rich also founded almshouses at Felsted and funded the building of the tower of Rochford church.

He was buried at Felsted on 8 July. His eldest son Robert succeeded him in the peerage and received his estates, and his nine surviving daughters and illegitimate son all received legacies. Rich's descendants were patrons of the church of St Bartholomew the Great until the nineteenth century.

In about 1620 his great-grandson had a monument erected to him in Felsted church, by the sculptor Epiphanius Evesham, celebrating Rich's achievements as Speaker of the House of Commons and Lord Chancellor. He lies in effigy, in what seems now a rather lonely corner of the church, infrequently visited and little remembered – except for his role in the trial of Sir Thomas More and as the villain in several fictional accounts of the period – gazing rather balefully at anyone who cares to meet his eye.

John Deane died in October 1563, and was buried on the south side of the sanctuary in the church he had served for so long. He was about seventy years old when he died and, like the diarist Henry Machyn who died in the following month, he may well have succumbed to the plague which was ravaging London at that time. Nearly a quarter of the city's population died in this major outbreak of bubonic plague which lasted from June to October, a more serious and deadly outbreak, with a higher percentage of the population killed, than the better-known one of 1665. Whether or not Sir John himself died of the plague, he must have spent much of the last few months of his life engaged in burying the dead of his parish and consoling the bereaved. According to one of Machyn's final diary entries, the inhabitants of any house stricken by the plague were not to come to church for an allotted period, and so the parish priest would have to go to them, the house indicated by a blue cross painted on its door.

Deane's approximate burial place is marked by a memorial slab inlaid with brass, presented to St Bartholomew's by the pupils of Witton Grammar School in 1893. The school is now a sixth-form college, and it bears his name: Sir John Deane's College, or simply 'SJD'.

Throughout his ministry in London Deane had remained in touch with his family and acquaintances – and with the school he had founded – in Northwich, and had also made occasional visits there. He had many nephews and nieces, to several of whom he was also godfather. He died as a fairly wealthy man, having been judicious in his property dealings and not given to personal extravagance. He left money to his relatives and made numerous charitable legacies, including to the poor householders both in the parish of St Bartholomew and in Northwich, to those in need in St Bartholomew's Hospital, and to prisoners in Newgate, the King's Bench and the Marshalsea. One beneficiary under his will was instructed to distribute, every Christmas Eve, ten shillings' worth of coal, wood or money among the poor householders of St Bartholomew's, according to the advice of the churchwardens. In a time of mutability, John Deane must have been one of the few 'still points in a turning world' in the lives of the people who knew and depended on him, whatever the turns he had to make in his own head in order to preserve a sense of stability for his flock.

Most of the bishops who had served under Mary were dismissed by the Elizabethan regime, and many spent years in prison; none of them, however, was executed and neither was any priest. (Executions of 'recusant' Catholic priests, on the grounds of treason, would come later in the reign, particularly after 1570, when the Pope excommunicated the Queen and authorized her subjects to depose her.) Most of the lower clergy agreed to take the Oath of Supremacy, only about three hundred being deprived of their livings for refusing to do so; seventy or eighty chose to go into exile, while just over one hundred were imprisoned. Bishop Edmund Bonner was still being used on diplomatic business at the start of Elizabeth's reign, hosting the French ambassadors at his palace in late May 1559. Two days after they left, he was asked to swear the Oath of Supremacy; he refused, and was deprived of his bishopric, though not yet arrested.

On 20 April 1560 Bonner found himself back in the Marshalsea, where he had spent most of Edward's reign. Though the conditions of his imprisonment were less unpleasant than they had been ten years previously, it is unlikely they afforded him much comfort. He stayed in prison for the rest of his life, dying in the Marshalsea on 5 September 1569. His burial in the churchyard of St George's, Southwark, took place at midnight, on the order of the then Bishop of London, Edmund Grindal, for fear of disturbances – much as the burnings at Smithfield, so many of which were the result of Bonner's condemnations, were held at 'unsocial hours' to try to avoid drawing crowds of onlookers. His body was later moved to Copford church, near Colchester, where it was rediscovered in 1810 when a grave was being dug for another priest.

*

By the light of burning martyrs,
Christ, thy bleeding feet we track,
Toiling up new Calvaries ever
With the Cross that turns not back.
New occasions teach new duties;
Time makes ancient good uncouth;
They must upward still and onward
Who would keep abreast of truth.

J. Russell Lowell, 1819–91

Though the mass burnings of heretics came to an end with Mary's death, burning for the 'crime' of heresy continued sporadically, the last such burning to take place in England occurring in 1612, when Elizabeth's successor, James I, had two Antitrinitarians burnt at the stake. During Elizabeth's reign this form of execution was the fate of six Anabaptists and Antitrinitarians. Elizabeth is often (mis)-quoted as having declared that she did not wish to 'make windows into men's souls' and, while this should not really be taken as an embracing of religious tolerance in any way that we would recognize today, what it does imply is a greater interest in outward conformity than inner conviction. What the Queen did demand was strict adherence to the concept of royal supremacy over the Church, so that conformity in religious observance was equated more strongly than ever with loyalty to the Crown – and the opposite, of course, was also true.

In considering this period in our history, and in trying to understand the motivations both of those who died and of those who brought about their deaths, and how Western culture succeeded in moving from religious hatreds to religious toleration (in so far as it has), it is important to remember what might appear to be an obvious point made by Brad Gregory in his book *Salvation at Stake*: 'The act of martyrdom makes no sense whatsoever unless we take religion seriously, on the terms of people who were willing to die for their convictions.' It is likely that, for anyone who refuses to take religion seriously at all, or at least to accept that other people might legitimately take it seriously, the kinds of arguments waged between the proponents of different beliefs – the various 'articles' set out to the accused and their responses, as discussed in this book – are at best incomprehensible and very probably preposterous. Viewing the martyrs from the outside, so to speak, not just from the vantage point of the twenty-first century but even at the time, the fact that people of contradictory beliefs were prepared respectively to die, or kill, to defend them inevitably has the unintended consequence of calling the whole nature of religious truth, and its knowability, into question. The sixteenth-century defenders and critics of the real presence, or of papal authority, or of seven sacraments as opposed to two, could not – presumably – both be right, yet there were people on both sides of the argument sufficiently convinced of their rightness to make it a matter of life and death. This has done little to recommend institutional religion to many, as it appears to demand adherence to beliefs that are not only incomprehensible in themselves but which other people, who also call themselves Christians, declare to be false. The mixture becomes even more toxic when the state is involved, and belief becomes a matter of the law. And the answer to the question of how we became a more tolerant society must appear obvious: because we gave up believing such ridiculous things. Religion is the source of all the inhumanity and suffering of 'the burning time' and the only sensible, enlightened option is to abandon it altogether. How can it even merit discussion?

Well, that is one line to take. I don't think it gets us very far, if only because religion and wars of religion have never gone away, even if they appear to die down in some parts of the world for quite lengthy periods. Now they are once again centre stage and, not least because of our own history, we cannot merely dismiss religious conviction and the willingness to die and kill for competing convictions as belonging to the 'other', something removed from our own civilization. This is a part of the human experience, and we have to grapple with it. I also find I don't want to dismiss the feisty, principled and complex characters who have emerged in this book as merely 'backward', deluded or ignorant – and yet I cannot deny that some of the disagreements that were so fundamental to them appear like splitting doctrinal hairs to us, even when we are prepared to take religion seriously.

It is the attitude to religion, rather than religion itself, that can lead to inhumanity – when adherence to a particular set of doctrines and practices acquires an ultimate significance that overcomes every other consideration, when I am so sure that I am right, and that there is an absolute, eternal meaning attached to the maintenance of my position, that I can hear or see or feel nothing else. There can then be no compromise, no backing down, no possibility that I might be wrong (or, even, that it might not matter all that much whether I am right or wrong). A very important factor in the move from intolerance to acceptance of diversity, in religion as in anything else, is doubt – the realization that I might, after all, not have all the answers. Sebastian Castellio, the sixteenth-century professor of Greek whose work on toleration we encountered in Chapter Three, named his final treatise *De arte dubitandi* ('The Art of Doubting') and in it he tackled the subjects of doubt, belief, ignorance and knowledge. It was left unfinished at the time of his death in 1563, surviving only in manuscript, and was finally published in 1981. It is a defence of both toleration and reason in religion and sets out to demonstrate how to distinguish between those things that should be believed and those that can reasonably be doubted. It is essential, according to Castellio, to exercise the 'art' of doubting 'because men often sin owing to the fact that they believe where they should doubt, doubt where they should believe, are ignorant of what they should know, and think they know what is unknown'. Though Castellio, being a Western European of his time, assumed as givens that God exists and that Christianity is the best of all religions, he nevertheless emphasized the value of fair and open discussion of religious differences and severely criticized the intellectual rigidity that dismisses opposing views without a hearing.

Alongside doubt on the path towards tolerance goes indifference; it is when we start to take religion less seriously, yet without dismissing it as a complete aberration, that there is more room for multiple discourses and far less inclination either to coerce others

or to sacrifice oneself. Yet those who first promoted the values of
tolerance, such as Castellio, were themselves profoundly religious,
if unorthodox, so there is also evidence that religion can itself
tolerate toleration. Here perhaps we return to the question of
the parable of the wheat and the tares, looked at from a slightly
different perspective: is the 'truth' of religion – which may be
unknowable – really affected by allowing other versions, even contradictions, of itself to grow alongside it? There is a difference in
the discussion as soon as we depersonalize it. When we see 'wheat'
and 'tares' as code names for other human beings, we paradoxically
dehumanize those 'others', the tares (we, of course, are always the
wheat), and can begin to envisage them being uprooted and
destroyed. When we see the wheat and tares as ideas or different
systems of thought, then the most important thing becomes the
necessity to articulate one's own understanding of the truth, to
persuade by spoken and written argument, rather than to coerce
by physical force. The spread of education and of literacy, while
initially causing disquiet and fear on the part of the authorities and
violently repressive measures, may actually have opened the way to
toleration, simply by virtue of more people being able to join in
the debate, to persuade and be persuaded on an intellectual level.

One cannot, however, work backwards and attempt to impose
twenty-first-century Western values on a very different world and
on people who would be utterly horrified by the levity with which
we treat many of their most deeply held beliefs today. Brad Gregory offers a very clear and convincing summary as to why religious
toleration would have been impossible as a solution to the characters caught up in the tragic turmoil of the burning time:

> For *ecclesiastical and secular authorities* to have forsaken alto-
> gether the willingness to kill, they would have had to abandon
> their profound paternalism in a culture saturated with a sense
> of hierarchy and responsibility of the higher for the lower.
> They would have had to renounce several centuries of legal
> precedent in a culture horrified by the notion of innovation.
> And they would have had to decriminalize heresy sufficiently

to permit obstinate heretics to go free, even as they thought that doing so would have imperiled others' eternal salvation.

For *martyrs* to have been unwilling to die for their beliefs, they would have had to consider ambiguous the many biblical passages that stipulated steadfastness in suffering. Or they would have had to believe that the Bible was not God's word . . . Or they would have had to reckon that the particular Christian group to which they belonged was merely one among others and that they might as well have belonged to another group. That is, they would have had to think that God's teachings were not really so important after all.

Gregory concludes: 'To suggest that the course and character of early modern Christianity might have been completely different – with the divergences and intensity, but without the disagreements, conflict, and violence – is to imagine early modern Christians who never existed in a world that never was.'

*

The Thirty-Nine Articles of Religion, first established in 1563, finalized in 1571 and still to be found at the back of the Book of Common Prayer, represented an attempt to define once and for all what members of the Church of England, under the authority of the sovereign, were supposed to believe, especially in all those areas of contention that had so dominated the reigns of Henry, Edward and Mary. It is interesting to look at them to see how the Anglican Church sought, and largely managed, to enshrine a degree of ambiguity in its doctrinal formulations, enabling the continuance of a 'broad church' in which, although there may be – and are – disagreements, different traditions by and large manage to rub along together. This is sometimes characterized as Anglicans having no idea what they believe, or not believing very much at all, and there may be some truth in both those flippant accusations. It used to be the case that all clergy of the Church of England were required to affirm their loyalty to the Thirty-Nine Articles; now the formula used at ordination does not use those actual words, though it does imply them. The archdeacon or registrar has to confirm to the bishop that those to be ordained 'have affirmed and declared their belief in the faith which is revealed in the Holy Scriptures and set forth in the catholic creeds and to which the historic formularies of the Church of England bear witness'.

Article VI of those 'historic formularies' is entitled *Of the Sufficiency of the holy Scriptures for salvation* and it begins: 'Holy Scripture containeth all things necessary to salvation: so that whatsoever is not read therein, nor may be proved thereby, is not to be required of any man, that it should be believed as an article of the Faith, or be thought requisite or necessary to salvation.' One can almost imagine John Lambert cheering at this clear statement of an attitude that had landed him in trouble when on trial before Henry VIII. To be set alongside this is Article XX, *Of the Authority of the Church*, which declares: 'The Church hath power to decree Rites or Ceremonies, and authority in Controversies of Faith: And yet it is not lawful for the Church to ordain any thing that is contrary to God's Word written.' That is also a dig at 'the Church of Rome' which, it is declared in the previous Article, has 'erred', not only in its 'manner of Ceremonies, but also in matters of Faith'. Furthermore, General Councils of the Church are also to be approached with caution: 'when they be gathered together, (forasmuch as they be an assembly of men, whereof all be not governed with the Spirit and Word of God,) they may err, and sometimes have erred, even in things pertaining unto God. Wherefore things ordained by them as necessary to salvation have neither strength nor authority, unless it may be declared that they be taken out of holy Scripture.'

Article X, *Of Free-Will*, is an example of an attempt to hold opposing views in balance: 'The condition of Man after the fall of *Adam* is such, that he cannot turn and prepare himself, by his own natural strength and good works, to faith, and calling upon God: Wherefore we have no power to do good works pleasant and acceptable to God, without the grace of God by Christ preventing us, that we may have a good will, and working with us, when we have that good will.' So we do not of ourselves have free will, but when we have the grace of God bestowed on us by Christ ('preventing' meaning 'going before' rather than having its modern meaning of 'hindering') then we do have free will to do good. It is an elegant answer to a question constantly argued over in the mid-sixteenth century.

Article XI, *Of the Justification of Man*, affirms the Protestant doctrine of justification by faith alone, so central to Luther's teaching, defended by Tyndale and preached by Little Bilney: 'We are accounted righteous before God, only for the merit of our Lord and Saviour Jesus Christ by Faith, and not for our own works or deservings: Wherefore, that we are justified by Faith only is a most wholesome Doctrine, and very full of comfort.' But then, in the following Article, good works are commended too, as stemming from faith and pleasing to God, even though they 'cannot put away our sins'. Article XIII, *Of Works before Justification*, makes it clear that 'works' can only really be good if they follow from grace and faith. These three articles together, along with the next one which condemns the idea that people can reap virtue by allegedly doing more good works than they are called to do, neatly resolves the difficulty of affirming that good works do not of themselves 'justify' while avoiding the anarchy of saying there is no need to perform them.

One of the most contentious doctrinal disputes of the Reformation concerned so-called Predestination and Election, and it is these with which Article XVII deals. This is one of the longer articles, and it largely consists of setting out the problem: while 'godly persons' who 'feel in themselves the working of the Spirit of Christ' may be comforted by the idea that they have been 'chosen', others – particularly 'curious and carnal persons' – may find this doctrine drives them either to desperation or to the pursuit of 'most unclean living', because there is no point in trying to do anything else. The Anglican answer does seem to be something of an evasion in this case; the Article concludes with the injunction to perform 'the Will of God' as 'expressly declared unto us in the Word of God'; the implication is that we shouldn't worry too much about whether or not all is 'predestined', but accept the promises of God 'as they be generally set forth to us in holy Scripture'.

The doctrine of purgatory and all practices associated with it are roundly condemned in Article XXII: 'The Romish Doctrine concerning Purgatory, Pardons, Worshipping, and Adoration, as well of Images as of Relics, and also invocation of Saints, is a fond thing vainly invented, and grounded upon no warranty of Scripture, but rather repugnant to the Word of God.' Despite its unequivocal tone, this is an Article regularly disregarded by the current Catholic, or 'High Church', wing of Anglicanism.

Those martyrs, such as John Rogers and John Bradford, who made such a point of condemning the use of Latin in church are fully vindicated by Article XXIV: 'It is a thing plainly repugnant to the Word of God, and the custom of the Primitive Church, to have public Prayer in the Church, or to minister the Sacraments in a tongue not understanded of the people.'

Article XXV, *Of the Sacraments*, comes down firmly in favour of there being 'two Sacraments ordained of Christ our Lord in the Gospel, that is to say, Baptism, and the Supper of the Lord'. There are another five 'commonly called Sacraments' – that is, 'Confirmation, Penance, Orders, Matrimony, and extreme Unction' – but, though these are not in any way forbidden, they are 'not to be counted for Sacraments of the Gospel'. One thing, however, is definitely frowned upon: 'The Sacraments were not ordained of Christ to be gazed upon, or to be carried about.' Although such a clear stricture would have delighted Anne Askew, who had declared to William Paget in 1546: 'though he did say there, Take, eat this in remembrance of me. Yet did he not bid them hang up that bread in a box, and make it a God, or bow to it', it is another which is regularly ignored by Catholic Anglicans.

There is the hint of an allusion to the parable of the wheat and tares in the opening words of Article XXVI, *Of the Unworthiness of the Ministers which hinders not the effect of the Sacrament*: 'Although in the visible Church the evil be ever mingled with the good . . .', and this perhaps suggests that the Anglican interpretation of the parable is that the tares are to be left there, to be dealt with by Christ on the Day of Judgement, and not before.

Article XXVIII deals with the central question of what Bishops Bonner and Gardiner termed 'the sacrament of the altar', though that term is resolutely not used here, and the emphasis is on the action, the sharing of the bread and wine by the people, and not on the nature of the elements themselves: 'insomuch that to such as rightly, worthily, and with faith, receive the same, the Bread which we break is a partaking of the Body of Christ; and likewise the Cup of Blessing is a partaking of the Blood of Christ'. The doctrine of transubstantiation is explicitly rejected: 'Transubstantiation (or the change of the substance of Bread and Wine) in the Supper of the Lord, cannot be proved by holy Writ; but is repugnant to the plain words of Scripture, overthroweth the nature of a Sacrament, and hath given occasion to many superstitions.' The description of what does occur is entirely in line with what Anne Askew and other Protestants insisted during their interrogations: 'The Body of Christ is given, taken, and eaten, in the Supper, only after an heavenly and spiritual manner. And the mean whereby the Body of Christ is received and eaten in the Supper is Faith.' So important is the rejection of the sacrament of the altar as an object of veneration in itself that the stricture already uttered in Article XXV is repeated here: 'The Sacrament of the Lord's Supper was not by Christ's ordinance reserved, carried about, lifted up, or worshipped.' Game, set and match to the Protestant martyrs, you might think – and yet . . . neither this Article nor Article XXV expressly forbids the reservation, carrying about, lifting up or worshipping of the sacrament – they just state such things were 'not by Christ's ordinance'. This opens the way to a very Anglican compromise, perhaps, or to the turning of a blind eye towards those who like that sort of thing, even if no such compromise was envisaged by the members of the convocation who compiled the Articles, under the direction of Archbishop Matthew Parker, in 1563.

Article XXXI, *Of the one Oblation of Christ finished upon the Cross*, rejects the Catholic idea of the Eucharist being offered as a sacrifice rather than a commemoration, while Article XXXII, *Of the Marriage of Priests*, leaves the decision of whether or not to marry up to the individual bishop, priest or deacon, just as with 'all other Christian men'.

One of the most interesting of the Articles in the light of all the bitter controversies that preceded the Elizabethan Settlement is Article XXXIV, *Of the Traditions of the Church*, which begins with an apparent embracing of difference: 'It is not necessary that Traditions and Ceremonies be in all places one, and utterly like; for at all times they have been diverse, and may be changed according to the diversities of countries, times, and men's manners, so that [i.e. 'provided that'] nothing be ordained against God's Word.' Nevertheless, such apparent latitude comes with a stern caveat; the individual is not thereby empowered to do what he pleases: 'Whosoever through his private judgement, willingly and purposely, doth openly break the traditions and ceremonies of the Church, which be not repugnant to the Word of God, and be ordained and approved by common authority, ought to be rebuked openly, (that others may fear to do the like,) as he that offendeth against the common order of the Church, and hurteth the authority of the Magistrate, and woundeth the consciences of the weak brethren.' It is offending against 'the common order' and the undermining of authority that constitute the most serious threats, according to the compilers of the Articles, to the Church and, it is implied, to society as a whole. The privileging of personal conscience over collective authority is never, almost by definition, acceptable to the Establishment.

Article XXXVII affirms the rule of law, repeats that 'The Bishop of Rome hath no jurisdiction in this Realm of England' and affirms the lawfulness of capital punishment 'for heinous and grievous offences'. (I would imagine that many Anglicans who think they accept the Thirty-Nine Articles have a) not read them recently, if ever, and b) are unaware they contain this endorsement of capital punishment.) This same Article also states that Christians (or, rather, 'Christian men') may fight in wars, if so commanded by 'the Magistrate'. Article XXXVIII refutes the Anabaptists' claim that property should be held in common: 'The Riches and Goods of Christians are not common, as touching the right, title, and possession of the same, as certain Anabaptists do falsely boast. Notwithstanding, every man ought, of such things as he possesseth, liberally to give alms to the poor, according to his ability.' The final

Article deals with the question of whether or not Christians may swear oaths (an uncertainty which had led Reginald Eastland to refuse to answer during his interrogation), and concludes that they may indeed do so, when required to by a magistrate.

*

Despite these religious questions being allegedly 'settled' for the Church of England under Elizabeth I, from time to time the old enmities emerge, even in the City of London, with evangelical Protestants and liberal Catholics (both of the Anglican variety) holding apparently irreconcilable views and, if not actually setting fire to one another, trying to incinerate with words. When one of Sir John Deane's successors as Rector of St Bartholomew's blessed the civil partnership of two gay priests in 2008, for instance, the reaction from some of the evangelical clergy and laity of the City Deanery was fierce and uncompromising. In an 'open statement', they declared 'with great sadness' that they could not recognize the Rector of St Bartholomew's as 'a teacher of the same gospel as ours'. In his response, Deane's successor alluded to the parable of the wheat and tares, and to the Donatist heresy: 'To the represent-atives from St Helen Bishopsgate, St Peter-upon-Cornhill, and St Botolph-without-Aldersgate, I say this: We become Donatists if we doubt the faithfulness and promises of God. We do it if we think the Gospel is ours and not the Gospel of Jesus Christ. We do it if we think we, and we alone, are the good seed and everyone who does not agree with us is no better than weeds.' And he asks the old question of how this parable is to be interpreted, in words that would not have been out of place in any of the 'examinations' of the sixteenth-century martyrs: 'Is this City of London the world? Is this present time the harvest? Are the representatives of these City churches the reapers?' He even makes a direct reference to the burning time in pointing out the dangers of such disputations in the Church: 'Perhaps we do have one claim to superiority in Smithfield: experience tells us that it is dangerous to judge others, to pronounce them unchristian, to declare fellowship fractured, to rend the Body of Christ – it leads to the fires that consume the martyrs. We know that because it is a shameful part of our history.'

The Bishop of London, Dr Richard Chartres, while perhaps longing to emulate his predecessor Bishop Bonner by depositing all concerned in a coalhouse to cool off, restricted himself to writing a cross letter, which he made public (in fact it appeared in a national newspaper before the intended recipient had actually read it himself) and in which he asserts: 'The point at issue is not Civil Partnerships themselves or the relation of biblical teaching to homosexual practice. There is of course a range of opinion on these matters in the Church and, as you know, homophobia is not tolerated in the Diocese of London. The real issue is whether you wilfully defied the discipline of the Church and broke your oath of canonical obedience to your Bishop.' Bishop Chartres concluded his letter: 'I have already asked the Archdeacon of London to commence the investigation and I shall be referring the matter to the Chancellor of the Diocese. Before I do this, I am giving you an opportunity to make representations to me direct.' Rather like Bishop Bonner when faced with a recalcitrant heretic whom he nevertheless hoped to be able to pardon rather than burn, Bishop Chartres seemed to be trying to offer a way to the Rector of St Bartholomew's to dig himself out of a hole. The rector duly 'recanted' – in so far as he promised not to conduct such a service again, at least as long as it remains contrary to Anglican teaching, and further confrontation between the City Deanery's liberal and evangelical factions was averted through a tacit agreement to say nothing. In the meantime, shifts in public opinion and an increased emphasis on equalities of all kinds continue to have an effect on attitudes in the Church as in the rest of society, and what was considered anathema in 2008 may well be common practice by 2020, even if some people leave the Church of England as a result. This particular controversy could not possibly have occurred in the sixteenth century – everyone would have been on the same side – but it does serve to illustrate, particularly in the references to the parable of the wheat and tares, that some of the old fault lines are still there and occasionally give rise to tremors. (And, as I write,

I read that an old acquaintance of mine from my student days, Canon Jeremy Davies, formerly precentor of Salisbury Cathedral, has just been refused permission to officiate in the diocese of Winchester because he has married his male partner of thirty years; this, then, is the present-day equivalent of all those clergy who had taken wives during the reign of Edward VI and who were deprived of their livings under Mary.)

If a 'gay wedding' can start to provoke language that would not have been out of place in sixteenth-century ecclesiastical disputes, allegations of 'abuse' of various kinds can sound even more like accusations of heresy, and inquiries into such abuse appear to take on the attributes of a heresy quest. We may not now be able to comprehend how a misplaced word about the 'sacrament of the altar' could lead to being on trial for one's life, but it requires no leap of the imagination to think of the possible consequences of, for instance, admitting to curiosity about child pornography or wondering, out loud and in the wrong company, whether we have got it right to construe any sexual relation between an adult and someone under the age of sixteen as abuse. We no longer burn people, but we do attempt to silence them – and ourselves.

Anglicanism has continued to evolve since the days of Elizabeth I and, particularly since the mid-nineteenth century, when the so-called Oxford Movement sought to re-emphasize an awareness of the Church of England as part of the 'one Catholic and Apostolic Church', many 'Catholic' practices have become an accepted part of the liturgy of a significant minority of Anglican churches. And so, on the evening of Sunday 6 December 2015, as on many Sunday evenings in the last fifteen or so years, I kneel in the sanctuary at St Bartholomew the Great, amid clouds of incense, at Benediction, when the 'most holy sacrament of the altar' is placed in a monstrance to be gazed at in adoration by priest and people, and then lifted up by the priest in blessing. Somewhere below my feet (or, rather, knees) is buried Fr William Peryn, prior of the Dominicans at St Bartholomew's from 1556 until his death in 1558, and a firm defender of the kind of ritual in which I am participating. Also somewhere below me, close to Fr Peryn but his exact location not known, is Prior William Bolton, the last prior but one, who died just a few years before his beloved monastery was dissolved and the Church in England torn apart by political and doctrinal dissension. Over towards my right, just outside the sanctuary, again his precise location not known but the approximate place marked by his memorial slab, lies Sir John Deane – to whom this ceremony would also have been familiar, though by the end of his ministry it had, as far as anyone could tell, been abandoned forever. Others buried in the Priory Church, in long-unidentified locations, their coffins probably several feet below the ground and indeed below other coffins, include Sir Robert Blagge, Deane's patron and the father of George who came under suspicion of heresy in 1546, and Richard Bartlett, eminent physician and grandfather of the Protestant martyr, Bartlet Green, whom he tried so hard to persuade to return to the Catholic fold. And outside the church is the memorial to many of the martyrs, while opposite the entrance is the place of their execution where, in 1849, during the excavation of a drain, workmen are reputed to have found a heap of unhewn stones, 'blackened as if by fire and covered with ashes and human bones charred and partially consumed'.

To these people on two opposing 'sides' in the sixteenth century reconciliation appeared impossible, the practices and doctrines of each side anathema to the other. And yet now, within the ancient walls of St Bartholomew's, well known to most of the characters in this history, the traditions meet and coalesce, and it seems possible to twenty-first-century believers, semi-believers and doubters, to pick and choose in our religion, to take the parts that suit us, temperamentally, intellectually, aesthetically, politically, and discard the aspects we like less, and no one seems to worry very much about it. Benediction works well in this building; some congregants love it, others find it a little hard to take – but this is the City of London, and if you prefer another tradition, it's easy enough to find it.

So what does it mean to me, when I participate in Benediction and repeat the 'Divine Praises' which include the explicit affirmation: 'Blessed be Jesus in the most holy sacrament of the altar'? Words that come to my mind when I gaze at the sacrament are grace, forgiveness, reconciliation. I think of the words of Julian of Norwich – 'All shall be well, and all manner of thing shall be well' – and, when the monstrance is lifted high in blessing, also of the words of Jesus, which may well have given courage to the martyrs (though they would have shunned this ritual that reminds me of them): 'For in the world shall ye have tribulation: but be of good cheer. I have overcome the world.'

When gazing at the sacrament, I approach in my mind the image of an absolute love, impossible to express in words. An attempt at words would be: white-hot, molten but solid, solid but yielding to the touch, golden, utterly itself, immovable yet fluid, open, uncompromising in its selfhood, far beyond all definitions yet encompassing them all, entirely sweet graciousness, and gracious sweetness, undefeatable yet not insisting on itself, taking everything into itself, all-embracing, unchanging (or where mutability and constancy are the same), not contingent, non-negotiable and yet at the same time utterly accepting.

John Donne, poet and Dean of St Paul's from 1621 until his death in 1631, comes the closest to expressing what I occasionally catch a glimpse of at Benediction:

> Bring us, O Lord God, at our last awakening into
> 　　the house and gate of heaven,
> to enter into that gate and dwell in that house,
> 　　where there shall be
> no darkness nor dazzling, but one equal light;
> no noise nor silence, but one equal music;
> no fears nor hopes, but one equal possession;
> no ends nor beginnings, but one equal eternity:
> in the habitations of thy glory and dominion,
> world without end. Amen.

Nothing else really matters. And all the arguments, imperfections, misunderstandings, foolishnesses, hatreds and cruelties are gathered up into the one equal light and transformed.

All this – whatever 'this' is – is beyond definition, beyond grasping at to extract the meaning – and that is how it should be. It's the defining, the attempt to trap the absolute in language, in doctrinal formulations, in particular translations, that has given us so much trouble – that has paved the way for hatreds and made the very concept of heresy possible. Accepting a degree of ignorance and of incomprehension on all our parts, with no one laying claim to absolute truth, makes heresy evaporate. Where there is no orthodoxy, there can by definition be no heresy.

In the Priory Church of St Bartholomew where, on a dark evening, in the flickering light thrown against the stout Norman pillars by the many candles, and in a mist of incense, it is easy to imagine the ghosts of former priors and rectors kneeling in prayer or processing from cloister to apse, we feel we take the best of our history – of its music, liturgy, preaching and architecture – to combine it into a living present. And the screams (or silence – how can we know for sure?) of the martyrs burning outside our walls are part of that history, adding both to the darkness and to the wonder of what it means to be human and made in the image of God.

> Sing praise, then, for all who here sought and here found him,
> whose journey is ended, whose perils have past:
> they believed in the light, and its glory is round them
> where the clouds of earth's sorrows are lifted at last.

> William Henry Draper, 1855–1933

CHRONOLOGY

✠

1516	18 February	Birth of future Mary I
1519	18 June	John Deane ordained priest
1521	25 May	Edict of Worms declares Martin Luther an outlaw
1522	19 October	Cuthbert Tunstall consecrated as Bishop of London
1529	25 October	Thomas More becomes Lord Chancellor
1530	25 March	Cuthbert Tunstall becomes Bishop of Durham
	27 November	John Stokesley consecrated as Bishop of London
	29 November	Death of Cardinal Thomas Wolsey
1531	5 April	Execution of Richard Roose
	4 December	Burning of Richard Bayfield
	20 December	Burning of John Tewkesbury
	27 December	Stephen Gardiner enthroned as Bishop of Winchester
1532	22 March	Richard Rich becomes Clerk of Recognizances
	5 April	Death of Prior William Bolton
	30 April	Burning of James Bainham
	13 May	Richard Rich becomes Attorney General in Wales
	16 May	Thomas More resigns as Lord Chancellor
	28 June	Robert Fuller becomes Prior of St Bartholomew's, Smithfield

	22 August	Death of Archbishop William Warham
1533	25 January	Marriage of Henry VIII and Anne Boleyn
	30 March	Thomas Cranmer consecrated as Archbishop of Canterbury
	23 May	Cranmer pronounces divorce of Henry VIII and Katherine of Aragon
	1 June	Coronation of Anne Boleyn
	8 June	Parliament affirms ending of papal authority in England
	4 July	Burning of John Frith and Andrew Huet
	7 September	Birth of future Elizabeth I
	10 October	Richard Rich becomes Solicitor-General, and is knighted
1534	17 April	Thomas More imprisoned in the Tower
	10 June	Edward Powell imprisoned in the Tower
	December	Thomas Abel and Richard Fetherston imprisoned in the Tower
1535	4 May	Execution of Prior Houghton, Richard Reynolds, John Hale, Augustine Webster and Robert Lawrence
	12 June	Alleged conversation between Thomas More and Richard Rich
	19 June	Execution of Humphrey Middlemore, William Exmewe and Sebastian Newdigate
	22 June	Execution of John Fisher
	6 July	Execution of Thomas More
	27 July	Richard Rich becomes chirographer at Court of Common Pleas
1536	7 January	Death of Katherine of Aragon
	24 April	Richard Rich becomes Chancellor of Court of Augmentations
	19 May	Execution of Anne Boleyn
	30 May	Marriage of Henry VIII and Jane Seymour
	12 June	Richard Rich becomes Speaker of the House of Commons
1537	12 October	Birth of future Edward VI

	24 October	Death of Jane Seymour
1538	22 May	Burning of John Forest
	6 October	Execution of William Tyndale, near Brussels
	16 November	Show trial of John Lambert
	22 November	Burning of John Lambert
1539	8 October	Death of John Stokesley
	25 October	Surrender of St Bartholomew's Priory to the King
1540	6 January	Marriage of Henry VIII and Anne of Cleves
	3 April	Robert Barnes, William Jerome and Thomas Garrett sent to the Tower
	16 April	Edmund Bonner enthroned as Bishop of London
	10 June	Arrest of Thomas Cromwell
	9 July	Marriage of Henry VIII and Anne of Cleves dissolved
	28 July	Execution of Thomas Cromwell. Marriage of Henry VIII and Katherine Howard
	30 July	Burning of Robert Barnes, William Jerome and Thomas Garrett
		Execution of Thomas Abel, Edward Powell and Richard Fetherston
1541	6 May	Henry VIII orders Great Bible to be placed in all churches
	27 May	Execution of Countess of Salisbury
	30 July	Burning of Richard Mekins
1542	13 February	Execution of Katherine Howard
1543	12 July	Marriage of Henry VIII and Katherine Parr
1544	24 April	Richard Rich resigns as Chancellor of Augmentations
	18 June	John Deane becomes Rector of Priory Church of St Bartholomew
1545	10 March	First arrest of Anne Askew

	13 June	Anne Askew re-examined at Guildhall
1546	18 February	Death of Martin Luther
	24 May	Order issued for Anne Askew's rearrest
	19 June	Anne Askew appears before Privy Council
	28 June	Anne Askew arraigned at Guildhall
	11 July	Arrest of George Blagge
	16 July	Burning of Anne Askew, John Lascelles, John Hadlam and John Hemsley
1547	28 January	Death of Henry VIII
	15 February	Richard Rich becomes Baron Rich of Leez
	20 February	Coronation of Edward VI
	12 March	Duke of Somerset becomes Lord Protector
	18 September	Edmund Bonner imprisoned for first time
	23 October	Richard Rich becomes Lord Chancellor
1548	30 June	Stephen Gardiner imprisoned in the Tower
	5 September	Death of Katherine Parr
1549	20 March	Execution of Thomas Seymour
	20 September	Edmund Bonner imprisoned in the Marshalsea
	1 October	Edmund Bonner deprived of bishopric of London
	14 October	Duke of Somerset imprisoned in the Tower
1550	2 May	Burning of Joan Boucher
	13 May	John Rogers becomes Vicar of St Sepulchre-without-Newgate
	15 December	Trial of Stephen Gardiner begins
1551	14 February	Stephen Gardiner deprived of bishopric of Winchester
	25 April	Burning of George van Parris
	24 August	John Bradford becomes Prebendary of St Paul's
	27 August	John Rogers becomes Prebendary of St Paul's
	21 December	Richard Rich resigns as Lord Chancellor

1552	22 January	Execution of Duke of Somerset
	16 May	Richard Rich becomes Lord Lieutenant of Essex
	14 October	Cuthbert Tunstall deprived of bishopric of Durham
1553	6 July	Death of Edward VI
	10 July	Lady Jane Grey proclaimed Queen
	19 July	Mary I proclaimed Queen
	5 August	Edmund Bonner returns as Bishop to St Paul's
	8 August	Funeral of Edward VI
	13 August	Gilbert Bourne preaches at Paul's Cross; riot
	16 August	John Rogers placed under house arrest
	21 August	Execution of Duke of Northumberland
	23 August	Stephen Gardiner becomes Lord Chancellor
	1 October	Coronation of Mary I
	13 November	Thomas Cranmer, Lady Jane Grey, Guildford Dudley, Ambrose Dudley and Henry Dudley arraigned at Guildhall
1554	25 January	Start of Sir Thomas Wyatt's rebellion
	27 January	John Rogers imprisoned in Newgate
	7 February	Collapse of Wyatt's rebellion
	12 February	Execution of Lady Jane Grey
	11 April	Execution of Sir Thomas Wyatt
	17 April	Trial of Nicholas Throckmorton at Guildhall
	25 July	Marriage of Mary I to Philip II of Spain
	30 November	Church in England reunited with Church of Rome
1555	28 January	Beginning of trials in Southwark of 'Protestant preachers'
	4 February	Burning of John Rogers
	16 March	Burning of Thomas Tomkins
	14 April	William Flower attacks priest at St Margaret's, Westminster

	24 April	Burning of William Flower at Westminster
	30 May	Burning of John Cardmaker and John Warne
	1 July	Burning of John Bradford and John Leaf
	23 August	Burning of Elizabeth Warne at Stratford-atte-Bow
	16 October	Burning of Nicholas Ridley and Hugh Latimer in Oxford
	12 November	Death of Stephen Gardiner
	18 December	Burning of John Philpot
1556	*27 January*	Burning of Thomas Whittle, John Tudson, Thomas Browne, Bartlet Green, John Went, Isobel Foster and Joan Warne (alias Lashford)
	21 March	Burning of Thomas Cranmer in Oxford
	24 April	Burning of Robert Drakes, William Tyms, Richard Spurge, Thomas Spurge, John Cavell and George Ambrose
	16 May	Burning of Katherine Hutt, Joan Horns and Elizabeth Thackwell
1557	*12 April*	Burning of Thomas Loseby, Henry Ramsey, Thomas Thyrtell, Margaret Hyde and Agnes Stanley
	15 September	John Deane becomes Rector of Coulsdon
	30 November	Burning of William Sparrow, John Hallingdale and Richard Gibson
	22 December	Burning of John Rough and Margaret Mearing
1558	*28 March*	Burning of Cuthbert Simpson, Hugh Foxe and John Devenish
	27 June	Burning of Roger Holland, Henry Pond, Reginald Eastland, Robert Southam, Matthew Ricarby, John Floyd and John Holiday
	22 August	Friar William Peryn buried in St Bartholomew's

	17 November	Death of Mary I and Cardinal Reginald Pole
	18 December	Funeral of Lady Rich
1559	*15 January*	Coronation of Elizabeth I
	8 May	Act of Uniformity signed by Elizabeth I
	14 July	Black Friars leave St Bartholomew's, Smithfield
	18 November	Death of Cuthbert Tunstall
1560	*20 April*	Edmund Bonner imprisoned in the Marshalsea
1563	*October*	Death of John Deane
1567	*12 June*	Death of Richard Rich
1569	*5 September*	Death of Edmund Bonner

NOTES

✠

I have made extensive use of the excellent online resource of *The Unabridged Acts and Monuments Online* or *TAMO* (HRI Online Publications, Sheffield, 2011). Available from: http://www.johnfoxe.org. Unless otherwise stated, quotations of the words of the martyrs, though often rewritten by me (see 'A Note on Language' at the beginning of this book), are derived from this source (particularly in Chapters 7, 11, 12, 13 and 14).

Introduction – SETTING THE SCENE

3 **a pleasant cracking** . . . J. G. Nichols (ed.), *Narratives of the Days of the Reformation*, Camden Society, 1869, p. 44.

9 **a new paradigm** . . . Vit Šisler, 'The Internet and the construction of Islamic knowledge in Europe', *Masaryk University Journal of Law and Technology*, Vol. 1, No. 2, 2007. http://www.digitalislam.eu/article.do?articleId=1422 [accessed 20 June 2016].

See also:

Peter Ackroyd, *The Life of Thomas More*, Chatto & Windus, 1998.

R. H. Bainton, 'The Left Wing of the Reformation', *The Journal of Religion* 21 (2), 1941, pp. 124–34.

J. Dillon, 'Clerkenwell and Smithfield as a Neglected Home of London Theater', *Huntington Library Quarterly* 71 (1), 2008, pp. 115–35.

Judith Etherton, 'Bolton, William (*d.* 1532)', *Oxford Dictionary of National Biography*, Oxford University Press, 2004. http://www.oxforddnb.com.ezproxy2.londonlibrary.co.uk/view/article/2809 [accessed 19 June 2016].

J. A. Galloway, D. Keene and M. Murphy, 'Fuelling the City: Production and Distribution of Firewood and Fuel in London's Region, 1290–1400', *The Economic History Review* New Series 49 (3), 1996, pp. 447–72.

W. Hooper, 'The Tudor Sumptuary Laws', *The English Historical Review* 30 (119), 1915, pp. 433–49.

John Stow, *Stow's Survey of London*, Dent, 1960.

E. A. Webb, 'The sixteenth century: Prior William Bolton', in *The Records of St. Bartholomew's Priory and St. Bartholomew the Great, West Smithfield: Volume 1*, Oxford University Press, 1921, pp. 223–38. *British History Online*. http://www.british-history.ac.uk/st-barts-records/vol1/pp223–38 [accessed 19 June 2016].

One – BOILING, BURNING AND AMBITION

14 **locked in a chain** . . . J. G. Nichols (ed.), *Chronicle of the Grey Friars of London*, Camden Society, 1852, p. 35.

19 *latine aliquid intelligit* M. Cox, *A history of Sir John Deane's Grammar School, Northwich, 1557–1908*, Manchester University Press, 1975, p. 11.

22 **probably sometime a member** . . . See http://venn.lib.cam.ac.uk/.

22 **does not seem to have been** . . . E. A. Webb, 'Sir Richard Rich', in *The Records of St. Bartholomew's Priory and St. Bartholomew the Great, West Smithfield: Volume 1*, Oxford University Press, 1921, pp. 289–97. *British History Online*. http://www.british-history.ac.uk/st-barts-records/vol1/pp289–97 [accessed 19 June 2016].

22 **through life a very consistent character** . . . J. L. Campbell, *The Lives of the Lord Chancellors and Keepers of the Great Seal of England*, Vol. 2, John Murray, 1846, p. 9.

24 **'aggressive' or 'tough-minded'** J. F. Davis, 'The Trials of Thomas Bylney and the English Reformation', *The Historical Journal* 24 (4), 1981, p. 775.

25 **No one would trouble Luther** . . . G. W. Bernard, *The King's Reformation: Henry VIII and the remaking of the English Church*, Yale University Press, 2005, p. 238.

26 **little rigor and much mercy** Thomas More, *A Dialogue Concerning Heretics* [1529], in *The Complete Works of St Thomas More*, ed. Thomas M. C. Lawler, Germain Marc'hadour and Richard C. Marius, Yale University Press, Vol. 6, Pt. 1, 1981, p. 416.

26 **when they be drunken down** . . . Thomas More, *The Confutation of Tyndale's Answer* [1532], in *Complete Works of St Thomas More*, ed. Louis A. Schuster et al., Yale University Press, Vol. 8, Pt. 1, 1973, p. 38.

26 **every heretic was related** . . . C. W. D'Alton, 'Charity or Fire? The Argument of Thomas More's 1529 Dyalogue', *The Sixteenth Century Journal* 33 (1), 2002, p. 58.

27 **At the heart of both faiths** . . . Susan Brigden, *London and the Reformation*, Clarendon Press, 1989, p. 122.

28 **I find that breed of men** . . . E. F. Rogers (ed.), *St Thomas More: Selected Letters*, Yale University Press, 1961, p. 180.

29 **it is not necessary** . . . 'Henry VIII: June 1530, 17–30', in *Letters and Papers, Foreign and Domestic, Henry VIII, Volume 4, 1524–1530*, ed. J. S. Brewer (London, 1875), pp. 2902–21. *British History Online*. http://www.british-history.ac.uk/letters-papers-hen8/vol4/pp2902-21 [accessed 19 June 2016].

30 **showed signs of not always** . . . Andrew Hope, 'Bayfield, Richard (d. 1531)', *Oxford Dictionary of National Biography*, Oxford University Press, 2004. http://www.oxforddnb.com.ezproxy2.londonlibrary.co.uk/view/article/1745 [accessed 19 June 2016].

33 **There was never a wretch** . . . Preface to Thomas More's *Confutation to Tyndale's Answer*, in *The English Works of Sir Thomas More*, ed. Rastell/Campbell, Eyre & Spottiswoode, 1931, p. 348.

34 **Please continue your goodness** . . . 'Henry VIII: May 1532, 16–31', in *Letters and Papers, Foreign and Domestic, Henry VIII, Volume 5, 1531–1532*, ed. James Gairdner (London, 1880), pp. 470–87. *British History Online*. http://www.british-history.ac.uk/letters-papers-hen8/vol5/pp470-87 [accessed 24 June 2016].

34 **gratifying his Royal Highness** . . . See E. A. Webb, 'The sixteenth century: Prior Robert Fuller', in *The Records of St. Bartholomew's Priory and St. Bartholomew the Great, West Smithfield: Volume 1* (Oxford, 1921), pp. 238–52. *British History Online*. http://www.british-history.ac.uk/st-barts-records/vol1/pp238-52 [accessed 24 June 2016].

35 **so difficult to agree upon** Ibid.

35 **not wishing further** . . . Ibid.

35 **It seems to have been** . . . E. A. Webb, 'The sixteenth century: Prior Robert Fuller', in *The Records of St. Bartholomew's Priory and St. Bartholomew the Great, West Smithfield: Volume 1* (Oxford, 1921), pp. 238–52. *British History Online*. http://www.british-history.ac.uk/st-barts-records/vol1/pp238-52 [accessed 24 June 2016].

36 **making, writing and enrolment** . . . 'Henry VIII: March 1532, 21–31', in *Letters and Papers, Foreign and Domestic, Henry VIII, Volume 5, 1531–1532*, ed. James Gairdner (London, 1880), pp. 415–30. *British History Online*. http://www.british-history.ac.uk/letters-papers-hen8/vol5/pp415-30 [accessed 7 June 2016].

37 **For we long dwelled** . . . William Roper, *The Life of Sir Thomas More*, *c.*1556, ed. Gerard B. Wesemer and Stephen W. Smith, Center for Thomas More Studies, 2003. http://www.thomasmorestudies.org/docs/Roper.pdf [accessed 24 June 2016].

37 **wealthy sinecure** J. L. Campbell, *The Lives of the Lord Chancellors*, p. 11.

38 **woman sole** 'Henry VIII: January 1536, 16–20', in *Letters and Papers, Foreign and Domestic, Henry VIII, Volume 10, January–June 1536*, ed. James Gairdner (London, 1887), pp. 38–47. *British History Online*. http://www.british-history.ac.uk/letters-papers-hen8/vol10/pp38–47 [accessed 24 June 2016].

38 **the King cannot therefore** . . . Ibid.

38 **whether the King** . . . Ibid.

38 **dare not say** Ibid.

38 **Henry might seize** . . . Ibid.

38 **execute the King's orders** . . . Ibid.

38 **The houses** . . . David Loades, *Thomas Cromwell: Servant to Henry VIII*, Amberley, 2013, p. 181.

39 **first care was to augment** . . . J. L. Campbell, *The Lives of the Lord Chancellors*, p. 11.

40 **enjoyed by Thomas Ellys** . . . 'Henry VIII: May 1536, 26–31', in *Letters and Papers, Foreign and Domestic, Henry VIII, Volume 10, January–June 1536*, ed. James Gairdner (London, 1887), pp. 402–20. *British History Online*. http://www.british-history.ac.uk/letters-papers-hen8/vol10/pp402–420 [accessed 24 June 2016].

40 **a continual fire** . . . W. C. Waller, 'An Essex Alchemist', *The Essex Review* 13, 1904, pp. 19–20.

41 **an insult** . . . J. L. Campbell, *The Lives of the Lord Chancellors*, p. 11.

See also:

J. D. Alsop, 'Blagge, Robert (*d.* 1522)', *Oxford Dictionary of National Biography*, Oxford University Press, 2004; online edn, May 2010. http://www.oxforddnb.com.ezproxy2.londonlibrary.co.uk/view/article/2555 [accessed 24 June 2016].

A. P. Baggs, Diane K. Bolton, Eileen P. Scarff and G. C. Tyack, *A History of the County of Middlesex: Volume 5, Hendon, Kingsbury, Great Stanmore, Little Stanmore, Edmonton, Enfield, Monken Hadley, South Mimms, Tottenham*, ed. T. F. T. Baker and R. B. Pugh (London, 1976) *British History Online*. http://www.british-history.ac.uk/vch/middx/vol5 [accessed 24 June 2016].

G. W. Bernard, *The King's Reformation*, Yale University Press, 2005, p. 190.

T. Cooper, *The Last Generation of English Catholic Clergy: Parish Priests in the Diocese of Coventry and Lichfield in the Early Sixteenth Century*, Boydell Press, 1999, p. 7.

C. Harper-Bill, *The Pre-Reformation Church in England 1400–1530*, Longman, 1996, p. 79.

History of Parliament Online, especially: http://www.historyofparliamentonline.org/volume/1509-1558/member/rich-richard-149697-1567.

K. J. Kesselring, 'A Draft of the 1531 "Acte for Poysoning"', *The English Historical Review* 116 (468), 2001, p. 894.

J. F. McCue, 'The Doctrine of Transubstantiation from Berengar through Trent: The Point at Issue', *The Harvard Theological Review* 61 (3), 1968, p. 413.

L. Miles, 'Persecution and the Dialogue of Comfort: A Fresh Look at the Charges against Thomas More', *Journal of British Studies* 5 (1), 1965, p. 21.

C. Rawcliffe and S. Flower, 'English Noblemen and Their Advisers: Consultation and Collaboration in the Later Middle Ages', *Journal of British Studies* 25 (2), 1986, pp. 164–6.

S. Wabuda, 'Bishops and the Provision of Homilies, 1520 to 1547', *The Sixteenth Century Journal* 25 (3), 1994, pp. 553–5.

Two – FUEL FOR THE FIRE

43 **Most lamentably complaineth** . . . Simon Fish, *A Supplication for the Beggars*, 1529. http://www.gutenberg.org/files/32464/32464-h/32464-h.htm [accessed 5 May 2015].

44 **Abbots, Priors, Deacons** . . . Ibid.

44 **ravenous wolves** . . . Ibid.

44 **these greedy sort** . . . Ibid.

44 **Every man and child** . . . Ibid.

44 **translate[d] all rule** . . . Ibid.

45 **a large oak frame** . . . L. A. Parry, *The History of Torture in England*, Sampson Low, Marston & Co., 1933, pp. 76–7.

45 **ordered the rack** . . . Church of England Tract Society, *Some account of the Life and Martyrdom of James Bainham, of the Middle Temple, Esquire, who was burnt at Smithfield, London, April 30th, 1532* (Bristol, 1815), pp. 2–4.

45 **Given the source** . . . See Thomas More, *The Apology*, ed. J. B.

Trapp, *The Complete Works of St. Thomas More* 9, (Yale University Press, 1974) pp. 117–20.

49 **in the stocks** . . . *Some account of the Life and Martyrdom of James Bainham*, pp. 10–11.

49 **chained to a post** . . . Ibid.

49 **cruelly used** Ibid.

49 **where he lay a fortnight** . . . Ibid.

51 **the treasures of his shrine** . . . 'Henry VIII: August 1538, 16–20', in *Letters and Papers, Foreign and Domestic, Henry VIII, Volume 13 Part 2, August–December 1538*, ed. James Gairdner (London, 1893), pp. 37–57. *British History Online.* http://www.british-history.ac.uk/letters-papers-hen8/vol13/no2/pp37–57 [accessed 14 June 2016].

52 **if he committed her** . . . 'Henry VIII: Appendix', in *Letters and Papers, Foreign and Domestic, Henry VIII, Volume 5, 1531–1532*, ed. James Gairdner (London, 1880), pp. 763–77. *British History Online.* http://www.british-history.ac.uk/letters-papers-hen8/vol5/pp763–77 [accessed 2 June 2016].

55 **Of the presence of Christ's body** . . . 'Henry VIII: April 1533, 26–30', in *Letters and Papers, Foreign and Domestic, Henry VIII, Volume 6, 1533*, ed. James Gairdner (London, 1882), pp. 177–93. *British History Online.* http://www.british-history.ac.uk/letters-papers-hen8/vol6/pp177–93 [accessed 2 June 2016].

55 **good young Father Frith** . . . More, *Confutation of Tyndale's Answer*, ed. Schuster et al., p. 35.

56 **Although he lacks irons** . . . 'Henry VIII: October 1532, 21–25', in *Letters and Papers, Foreign and Domestic, Henry VIII, Volume 5, 1531–1532*, ed. James Gairdner (London, 1880), pp. 615–19. *British History Online.* http://www.british-history.ac.uk/letters-papers-hen8/vol5/pp615–19 [accessed 2 June 2016].

56 **The will of God** . . . 'Henry VIII: May 1533, 1–10', in *Letters and Papers, Foreign and Domestic, Henry VIII, Volume 6, 1533*, ed. James Gairdner (London, 1882), pp. 193–211. *British History Online.* http://www.british-history.ac.uk/letters-papers-hen8/vol6/pp193–211 [accessed 2 June 2016].

57 **See, you are not alone** Ibid.

57 **Sir, your wife** . . . Ibid.

58 **obstinate heretics** 'Henry VIII: July 1533, 1–10', in *Letters and Papers, Foreign and Domestic, Henry VIII, Volume 6, 1533*, ed. James Gairdner (London, 1882), pp. 334–52. *British History Online.* http://www.british-history.ac.uk/letters-papers-hen8/vol6/pp334–52 [accessed 2 June 2016].

59 **a very simple** . . . E. Hall, *Chronicle*.

61 **one Doctor Cooke** . . . E. Hall's *Chronicle*.

62 **God, into whose hands** . . . James Anthony Froude, *History of England from the fall of Wolsey to the death of Elizabeth*, Vol. 2, 1856 (reprinted by Nabu Press, 2011), p. 90.

62 **Item moreover** . . . Common Council record of 13 May 1533, quoted in email to author from Howard Doble, Senior Archivist (City Records), London Metropolitan Archives.

63 **And if a man** . . . Leviticus 20:21.

64 **The functional argument** . . . David Loades, *The Oxford Martyrs*, B. T. Batsford, 1970, pp. 24–5.

66 **therefore ensured that** . . . Tracy Borman, *Thomas Cromwell: The untold story of Henry VIII's most faithful servant*, Hodder & Stoughton, 2014, p. 150.

67 **that they be the Church** . . . *The whole workes of W. Tyndall, John Frith, and Doct. Barnes*, ed. J. Foxe (1572–3), p. 126.

67 **extended the definition** . . . David Knowles, *The Religious Orders in England, Volume III: The Tudor Age*, Cambridge University Press, 1959, p. 230.

68 **was she not too familiar** . . . See Knowles, *The Religious Orders in England*, p. 230.

69 **the first whole-hearted defence** . . . Claire Cross, *Church and People, 1450–1660: The Triumph of the Laity in the English Church*, Harvester Press, 1976, p. 62.

69 **The powers that be** . . . William Tyndale, *The Obedience of a Christen man, and how Christen rulers ought to govern, wherein also (if thou mark diligently) thou shalt find eyes to percieve the crafty convience of all iugglers*, 1528. http://www.godrules.net/library/tyndale/19tyndale7.htm [accessed 27 June 2016].

71 **Dost thou not see** . . . Roper, *The Life of Sir Thomas More*.

72 **formulation and debate** . . . Wilfrid R. Prest, 1972, *The Inns of Court under Elizabeth I and the Early Stuarts 1590–1640*, Longman, 1972, p. 116.

72 **Supposing that it were enacted** . . . 'Henry VIII: July 1535, 1–10', in *Letters and Papers, Foreign and Domestic, Henry VIII, Volume 8, January–July 1535*, ed. James Gairdner (London, 1885), pp. 379–402. *British History Online*. http://www.british-history.ac.uk/letters-papers-hen8/vol8/pp379–402 [accessed 2 June 2016].

73 **I, as you know** . . . R. S. Sylvester and D. P. Harding (eds), *Two early Tudor lives*, Yale University Press, 1962, pp. 245–6.

74 **denied the King's supremacy** . . . *Harpsfield's The Life and Death of*

Sir Thomas More, Knight, Sometymes Lord High Chancellor of England,
Oxford University Press, 1963, p. 274.

75 **whosoever being once taught** . . . C. Lloyd (ed.), *Formularies of
faith put forth by authority during the reign of Henry VIII,* Oxford, 1825,
p. 61.

75 **how the bishop of Rome's** . . . J. Block, 'Thomas Cromwell's
Patronage of Preaching', *The Sixteenth Century Journal* 8 (1), 1977,
p. 38.

77 **I am not able** . . . 'Henry VIII: June 1532, 16–30', in *Letters and
Papers, Foreign and Domestic, Henry VIII, Volume 5, 1531–1532,* ed. James
Gairdner (London, 1880), pp. 494–510. *British History Online.* http://
www.british-history.ac.uk/letters-papers-hen8/vol5/pp494–510
[accessed 2 June 2016].

78 **Father Forest, who neither loves** . . . 'Henry VIII: November
1532, 1–15', in *Letters and Papers, Foreign and Domestic, Henry VIII,
Volume 5, 1531–1532,* ed. James Gairdner (London, 1880), pp. 637–50.
British History Online. http://www.british-history.ac.uk/letters-
papers-hen8/vol5/pp637–50 [accessed 2 June 2016].

78 **I think the chancellor** . . . Ibid.

79 **Today or tomorrow** . . . 'Henry VIII: September 1532, 16–30', in
Letters and Papers, Foreign and Domestic, Henry VIII, Volume 5, 1531–1532,
ed. James Gairdner (London, 1880), pp. 571–89. *British History Online.*
http://www.british-history.ac.uk/letters-papers-hen8/vol5/pp571–89
[accessed 6 June 2016].

79 **If he do come** . . . 'Henry VIII: November 1532, 16–30', in *Letters
and Papers, Foreign and Domestic, Henry VIII, Volume 5, 1531–1532,* ed.
James Gairdner (London, 1880), pp. 650–69. *British History Online.*
http://www.british-history.ac.uk/letters-papers-hen8/vol5/pp650–69
[accessed 2 June 2016].

79 **It grieves me sore** . . . 'Henry VIII: February 1533, 1–5', in *Letters
and Papers, Foreign and Domestic, Henry VIII, Volume 6, 1533,* ed. James
Gairdner (London, 1882), pp. 45–56. *British History Online.* http://
www.british-history.ac.uk/letters-papers-hen8/vol6/pp45–56
[accessed 10 June 2016].

80 **In my judgment** . . . Ibid.

80 **I hear you have conceived** . . . 'Henry VIII: Miscellaneous, 1532',
in *Letters and Papers, Foreign and Domestic, Henry VIII, Volume 5,
1531–1532,* ed. James Gairdner (London, 1880), pp. 700–46. *British
History Online.* http://www.british-history.ac.uk/letters-papers-hen8/
vol5/pp700–746 [accessed 2 June 2016].

80 **[Forest] says that he will** . . . 'Henry VIII: February 1533, 11–20',

in *Letters and Papers, Foreign and Domestic, Henry VIII, Volume 6, 1533*, ed. James Gairdner (London, 1882), pp. 68–79. *British History Online.* http://www.british-history.ac.uk/letters-papers-hen8/vol6/pp68–79 [accessed 2 June 2016].

80 **I wish you to burn . . .** Ibid.

81 **Since you first rebuked . . .** Ibid.

81 **I have written my mind . . .** 'Henry VIII: April 1533, 11–20', in *Letters and Papers, Foreign and Domestic, Henry VIII, Volume 6, 1533*, ed. James Gairdner (London, 1882), pp. 151–70. *British History Online.* http://www.british-history.ac.uk/letters-papers-hen8/vol6/pp151–70 [accessed 2 June 2016].

82 **prosperous state, both spiritual and corporal** 'Henry VIII: February 1533, 1–5', in *Letters and Papers, Foreign and Domestic, Henry VIII, Volume 6, 1533*, ed. James Gairdner (London, 1882), pp. 45–56. *British History Online.* http://www.british-history.ac.uk/letters-papers-hen8/vol6/pp45–56 [accessed 10 June 2016].

82 **he took his oath . . .** See G. W. Bernard, *The King's Reformation: Henry VIII and the remaking of the English Church*, Yale University Press, 2005, p. 156.

82 **Broadly defined . . .** Peter Marshall, 'Papist As Heretic: The Burning of John Forest', *The Historical Journal* 41 (2), 1998, p. 363.

83 **prisoner of the mass** See www.turveybeds.com/mordaunts.html and www.historyofparliamentonline.org/volume/1509-1558/member/mordaunt-sir-john [accessed 14 June 2016].

83 **And as for the Bishop of Rome . . .** B. Camm, *Lives of the English Martyrs, declared Blessed by Pope Leo XIII in 1886 and 1895*, Longmans, Green & Co., 1914, pp. 294–5; also A. Cuddon, *Modern British Martyrology*, 1838, i, pp. 103–4.

84 **Your Lordship spoke to me . . .** 'Henry VIII: April 1538, 26–30', in *Letters and Papers, Foreign and Domestic, Henry VIII, Volume 13 Part 1, January–July 1538*, ed. James Gairdner (London, 1892), pp. 311–30. *British History Online.* http://www.british-history.ac.uk/letters-papers-hen8/vol13/no1/pp311–30 [accessed 14 June 2016].

84 **might not lawfully . . .** 'Henry VIII: May 1538, 21–25', in *Letters and Papers, Foreign and Domestic, Henry VIII, Volume 13 Part 1, January–July 1538*, ed. James Gairdner (London, 1892), pp. 384–93. *British History Online.* http://www.british-history.ac.uk/letters-papers-hen8/vol13/no1/pp384–93 [accessed 20 March 2016].

84 **To know the King's pleasure . . .** 'Henry VIII: April 1538, 26–30', in *Letters and Papers, Foreign and Domestic, Henry VIII, Volume 13 Part 1, January–July 1538*, ed. James Gairdner (London, 1892), pp. 311–30.

British History Online. http://www.british-history.ac.uk/letters-papers-hen8/vol13/no1/pp311–30 [accessed 14 June 2016].

84 **by his outward man** . . . 'Henry VIII: May 1538, 21–25', in *Letters and Papers, Foreign and Domestic, Henry VIII, Volume 13 Part 1, January–July 1538*, ed. James Gairdner (London, 1892), pp. 384–93. *British History Online.* http://www.british-history.ac.uk/letters-papers-hen8/vol13/no1/pp384–93 [accessed 20 March 2016].

84 **in a fair chamber** . . . 'Henry VIII: May 1538, 16–20', in *Letters and Papers, Foreign and Domestic, Henry VIII, Volume 13 Part 1, January–July 1538*, ed. James Gairdner (London, 1892), pp. 372–83. *British History Online.* http://www.british-history.ac.uk/letters-papers-hen8/vol13/no1/pp372–83 [accessed 20 March 2016].

84 **Some think he is** . . . Ibid.

85 **This year, the 12th day of May** . . . Charles Wriothesley, *A Chronicle of England during the reigns of the Tudors, from A.D.1485 to 1559*, ed. W. D. Hamilton, Camden Society, Vol. 1, pp. 78–9.

86 **the place of execution** . . . Wriothesley, Vol. 1, pp. 80–1.

86 **wish his pardon** . . . 'Henry VIII: May 1538, 16–20', in *Letters and Papers, Foreign and Domestic, Henry VIII, Volume 13 Part 1, January–July 1538*, ed. James Gairdner (London, 1892), pp. 372–83. *British History Online.* http://www.british-history.ac.uk/letters-papers-hen8/vol13/no1/pp372–83 [accessed 20 March 2016].

86 **And being asked** . . . Wriothesley, Vol. 1, pp. 79–80.

87 **Neither fire, nor faggot** . . . Camm, *Lives of the English Martyrs*, p. 320.

88 **There is a belief** . . . 'Henry VIII: April 1538, 6–10', in *Letters and Papers, Foreign and Domestic, Henry VIII, Volume 13 Part 1, January–July 1538*, ed. James Gairdner (London, 1892), pp. 260–76. *British History Online.* http://www.british-history.ac.uk/letters-papers-hen8/vol13/no1/pp260–76 [accessed 5 May 2016].

88 **like a man of arms** . . . Wriothesley, Vol. 1, p. 80.

88 **great wooden saint** . . . Camm, *Lives of the English Martyrs*, p. 318.

88 **Forest the Friar** . . . Ibid., p. 305.

88 **Then they began to set fire** . . . Ibid., p. 320.

89 **would talk with his wife** . . . Roper, *The Life of Sir Thomas More*.

See also:

Peter Ackroyd, *The Life of Thomas More*, Chatto & Windus, 1998, pp. 384–5.

E. Berry, 'Thomas More and the Legal Imagination', *Studies in Philology* 106 (3), 2009, pp. 316–40.

Susan, Brigden, 'Popular Disturbance and the Fall of Thomas Cromwell and the Reformers, 1539–1540', *The Historical Journal* 24 (2), 1981, pp. 259–60.

Susan Brigden, 'Youth and the English Reformation', *Past and Present* 95, 1982, pp. 43–4.

S. Byman, 'Ritualistic Acts and Compulsive Behavior: The Pattern of Tudor Martyrdom', *The American Historical Review* 83 (3), 1978, p. 627 (fn).

Christian Classics Ethereal Library – www.ccel.org.

David Daniell, 'Frith, John (1503–1533)', *Oxford Dictionary of National Biography*, Oxford University Press, 2004; online edn, Oct 2006. http://www.oxforddnb.com.ezproxy2.londonlibrary.co.uk/view/article/10188 [accessed 27 June 2016].

Galloway et al., 'Fuelling the City', 1996, pp. 451–3.

Brad Gregory, *Salvation at Stake: Christian Martyrdom in Early Modern Europe*, Harvard University Press, 1999, pp. 256–9.

E. Hall, 1809, *Chronicle; containing the History of England . . .* (London).

N. Harpsfield, *Life and Death of Sir Thomas More*, pp. 182–3.

D. Josephson, 'In Search of the Historical Taverner', *Tempo* New Series 101, 1972, pp. 40–52.

J. R. Knott, 'John Foxe and the Joy of Suffering', *The Sixteenth Century Journal* 27 (3), 1996, p. 731 (fn).

Peter Marshall, 'Papist As Heretic: The Burning of John Forest', *The Historical Journal* 41 (2), 1998, pp. 351–74.

L. Miles, 'Persecution and the Dialogue of Comfort: A Fresh Look at the Charges against Thomas More', *Journal of British Studies* 5 (1), 1965, pp. 19–30.

M. Riordan and A. Ryrie, 'Stephen Gardiner and the Making of a Protestant Villain', *The Sixteenth Century Journal* 34 (4), 2003, p. 1045.

J. J. Scarisbrick, 'Warham, William (1450?–1532)', *Oxford Dictionary of National Biography*, Oxford University Press, 2004; online edn, May 2015. http://www.oxforddnb.com.ezproxy2.londonlibrary.co.uk/view/article/28741 [accessed 27 June 2016].

Three – THE MAKING OF MARTYRS

93 **The martyrs died** . . . Gregory, *Salvation at Stake*, p. 137.

94 **Accordingly, in the psalm** . . . Retrieved from http://www.ccel.org/ccel/schaff/npnf104.v.vi.iv.html#fna_v.vi.iv–p13.2 [accessed 15 March 2016].

94 **death for true Christianity** . . . Gregory, *Salvation at Stake*, p. 334.

94 **dying for opinions** . . . Quoted in ibid., pp. 334–5.

95 **gladly go to the fire** . . . Quoted in ibid., pp. 335–6.

95 **noted that if Satan** . . . Ibid., p. 336.

95 **universal public opinion** . . . Henry C. Lea, *A History of the Inquisition of the Middle Ages*, 3 vols, Macmillan, 1922, Vol. 1, p. 234.

96 **before the people** . . . See http://www.ric.edu/faculty/rpotter/heretico.html [accessed 27 May 2015].

96 **Heresy is an opinion** . . . Quoted in Pierre Zagorin, *How the Idea of Religious Toleration Came to the West*, Princeton University Press, 2003, p. 40.

96 **As an exponent** . . . Ibid., p. 20.

97 **This rule** . . . Translated by Peter Holmes. From *Ante-Nicene Fathers*, Vol. 3. Edited by Alexander Roberts, James Donaldson and A. Cleveland Coxe (Buffalo, NY: Christian Literature Publishing Co., 1885). Revised and edited for New Advent by Kevin Knight. http://www.newadvent.org/fathers/0311.htm [accessed 15 March 2016].

97 **a word used in the sense** . . . Ibid.

98 **And these shall go** . . . Matthew 25:46 [Matthew Bible].

99 **like peering through a window** . . . M. Flynn, 'Mimesis of the Last Judgment: The Spanish Auto de fe', *The Sixteenth Century Journal* 22 (2), 1991, p. 293.

99 **If there arise among you** . . . Deuteronomy 13:1–3, 5 [Matthew Bible].

100 **If thy brother** . . . Deuteronomy 13:6–10 [Matthew Bible].

101 **Another similitude** . . . Matthew 13:24–30 [Matthew Bible].

102 **What then does the Master?** . . . Translated by George Prevost and revised by M. B. Riddle. From *Nicene and Post-Nicene Fathers*, First Series, Vol. 10. Edited by Philip Schaff (Buffalo, NY: Christian Literature Publishing Co., 1888). Revised and edited for New Advent by Kevin Knight. http://www.newadvent.org/fathers/200146.htm [accessed 15 March 2016].

102 **in whom there is yet room** . . . Ibid.

102 **stopping the mouths** Ibid.

102 **taking away** . . . Ibid.

102 **breaking up** . . . Ibid.

102 **O you Christians** . . . Translated by R. G. MacMullen. From *Nicene and Post-Nicene Fathers*, First Series, Vol. 6. Edited by Philip Schaff (Buffalo, NY: Christian Literature Publishing Co., 1888). Revised and edited for New Advent by Kevin Knight. http://www.newadvent.org/fathers/160323.htm [accessed 15 March 2016].

103 **We are but men** . . . Ibid.

103 **Let the good tolerate** . . . Ibid.

103 **Again I ask** . . . Retrieved from http://www.ccel.org/ccel/schaff/npnf104.v.vi.iv.html#fna_v.vi.iv–p13.2 [accessed 16 March 2016].

104 **Moreover, she** . . . Ibid.

104 **What then is the function** . . . Retrieved from http://www.ccel.org/ccel/schaff/npnf104.v.vi.v.html [accessed 16 March 2016].

104 **It is indeed better** . . . Retrieved from http://www.ccel.org/ccel/schaff/npnf104.v.vi.viii.html [accessed 16 March 2016].

105 **Where is what the Donatists** . . . Ibid.

106 **The persecutor, said Augustine** . . . Ronald H. Bainton, ed., *Concerning Heretics: Whether they are to be persecuted and how they are to be treated. A collection of the opinions of learned men, Both ancient and modern, An anonymous work attributed to Sebastian Castellio*, Octagon Books Inc., 1965, pp. 24–5.

107 **Convicted heretics, unless** . . . Zagorin, pp. 38–9. See also R. I. Moore, *The War on Heresy: Faith and Power in Medieval Europe*, Profile Books, 2012, p. 2.

108 **Abraham did not wish** . . . G. G. Coulton, *The Death Penalty for Heresy from 1184 to 1917*, Simpkin, Marshall, Hamilton, Kent & Co., 1924, p. 13.

108 **If it be urged** . . . Quoted in Coulton, *The Death Penalty for Heresy*, pp. 13–14.

109 **For it is a much more serious** . . . Aquinas, *Summa Theologica*, Second Part of the Second Part, Question 11, Article 3: Aquin.: SMT SS Q[11] A[3] Body Para. 1/2. http://www.intratext.com/IXT/ENG0023/_P7Y.HTM [accessed 16 March 2016].

109 **the same harsh interpretation** . . . Zagorin, p. 43.

110 **Yet if heretics be altogether** . . . Aquinas, *Summa Theologica*, Second Part of the Second Part, Question 11, Article 3. http://www.newadvent.org/summa/3011.htm#article3 [accessed 16 March 2016].

110 **should be admitted** . . . Zagorin, p. 43.

110 **Again this Gospel** . . . *The Sermons of Martin Luther*, Vol. II, p. 102. http://www.sacred-texts.com/chr/luther/wheat.htm [accessed 16 March 2016].

111 **overcome with holy knowledge** . . . See http://berkleycenter.georgetown.edu/quotes/balthasar-hubmaier-concerning-heretics-and-those-who-burn-them-on-dealing-with-the-godless [accessed 27 May 2015].

112 **If a man bide not** . . . John 15:6 [Matthew Bible].

112 **The ancient Britons** . . . Parry, *The History of Torture in England*, p. 146.

112 **that such punishment** . . . See http://www.ric.edu/faculty/
     rpotter/heretico.html [accessed 27 May 2015].
113 **An anonymous Mishnah rule** . . . I. M. Rosenberg and Y. L.
     Rosenberg, 'Of God's Mercy and the Four Biblical Methods of
     Capital Punishment: Stoning, Burning, Beheading, and Strangulation',
     Tulane Law Review, 78 TUL.L. REV. 1169, 2004, pp. 27–8.
113 **stoning is the most severe** . . . Ibid., pp. 28–9.
113 **The defendant is put in manure** . . . Ibid., p. 51.
114 **speedier** . . . **less painful** . . . Ibid., p. 54.
114 **As the convicted person** . . . Ibid., pp. 34–5.
116 **If the arms were free** . . . Email to author from Elayne Pope PhD,
     20 January 2015.
116 **For extremities** . . . Elayne Pope et al. http://www.burnedbone.
     com/downloads/ExplodingSkulls.pdf [accessed 27 February 2015].
116 **Smaller muscles of the head** . . . Ibid.

See also:

Ronald H. Bainton, 'The Parable of the Tares as the Proof Text for
     Religious Liberty to the End of the Sixteenth Century', *Church
     History* 1 (2), 1932, pp. 67–89.
C. Duncan, 'The Persecutor's Wager', *The Philosophical Review* 116 (1), 2007,
     pp. 1–50.
John Edwards, *Mary I: England's Catholic Queen*, Yale University Press, 2011,
     pp. 255–6.
Linda Geddes, 'Body burners: The forensics of fire', *New Scientist*, 24 May
     2009. http://www.sott.net/article/185067-Body-burners-The-
     forensics-of-fire [accessed 27 February 2015].
Gregory, *Salvation at Stake*, pp. 82–3, 139, 330–1, 332–3, 337–8.
P. Saukko and B. Knight, *Knight's Forensic Pathology*, Third Edition Arnold,
     2004, p. 316.
Latimer, 'Fourth Sermon preached before King Edward VI', in *Sermons*,
     p. 160.
J. J. Megivern, 'Capital Punishment: The Curious History of Its Privileged
     Place in Christendom', *Proceedings of the American Philosophical Society*
     147 (1), 2003, pp. 3–12.
Susan Wabuda, 'Bishops and the Provision of Homilies, 1520 to 1547', *The
     Sixteenth Century Journal* 25 (3), 1994, pp. 551–66.
Zagorin, *How the Idea of Religious Toleration Came to the West*, pp. 23, 29, 37,
     39, 41, 64–5.

Four – RECANTATIONS AND REVERSALS

118 **One of the most perplexing** . . . Knowles, *The Religious Orders in England*, p. 205.

118 **for great heresy** *Chronicle of the Grey Friars*, p. 42.

125 **One Lambert** . . . 'Henry VIII: March 1536, 11–15', in *Letters and Papers, Foreign and Domestic, Henry VIII, Volume 10, January–June 1536*, ed. James Gairdner (London, 1887), pp. 182–95. *British History Online*. http://www.british-history.ac.uk/letters-papers-hen8/vol10/pp182–95 [accessed 1 June 2016].

126 **This day, in the King's Hall** . . . 'Henry VIII: November 1538, 16–20', in *Letters and Papers, Foreign and Domestic, Henry VIII, Volume 13 Part 2, August–December 1538*, ed. James Gairdner (London, 1893), pp. 353–69. *British History Online*. http://www.british-history.ac.uk/letters-papers-hen8/vol13/no2/pp353–69 [accessed 23 June 2016].

130 **It was a wonder** . . . 'Henry VIII: November 1538, 26–30', in *Letters and Papers, Foreign and Domestic, Henry VIII, Volume 13 Part 2, August–December 1538*, ed. James Gairdner (London, 1893), pp. 378–409. *British History Online*. http://www.british-history.ac.uk/letters-papers-hen8/vol13/no2/pp378–409 [accessed 18 June 2016].

131 **rude letter** 'Henry VIII: November 1538, 16–20', in *Letters and Papers, Foreign and Domestic, Henry VIII, Volume 13 Part 2, August–December 1538*, ed. James Gairdner (London, 1893), pp. 353–69. *British History Online*. http://www.british-history.ac.uk/letters-papers-hen8/vol13/no2/pp353–69 [accessed 23 June 2016].

131 **causing the Gospel** . . . *Ibid*.

131 **When breakfast was ended** . . . Foxe's *Acts and Monuments*, reproduced in Anon., *The history of the worthy martyr of God the Reverend John Nicolson, better known by the name of John Lambert, who was burned in Smithfield, in the year 1538*, Church of England Tract Society, 1816, p. 9.

131 **And the 30th day** . . . *Chronicle of the Grey Friars*, p. 44.

133 **a trim minion friar** . . . J. A. Muller, *The Letters of Stephen Gardiner*, Cambridge University Press, 2013, p. 165.

133 **Heresy is a perilous weed** . . . John Fisher, *A sermon had at Paulis by the commandment of the most reverend father in god my lord legate* . . . [Thomas Berthelet, London, 1526?], in *The English Works of John Fisher*, ed. John E. B. Mayer, Early English Text Society, extra series, no. 27, N. Trubner, 1876, p. 434.

134 **My duty is to endeavour me** . . . *Ibid*.

135 **Look well upon** . . . 'Henry VIII: November 1531, 1–30', in *Letters and Papers, Foreign and Domestic, Henry VIII, Volume 5, 1531–1532*, ed. James Gairdner (London, 1880), pp. 238–56. *British History Online*. http://www.british-history.ac.uk/letters-papers-hen8/vol5/pp238–56 [accessed 2 June 2016].

135 **Only faith justifieth** . . . W. D. J. Cargill Thompson, 'The sixteenth-century editions of *A Supplication unto King Henry the Eighth* by Robert Barnes, DD: A footnote to the history of the Royal Supremacy', *Transactions of the Cambridge Bibliographical Society* 3 (2), 1960, pp. 135–6.

137 **nothing and nobody** . . . 'Henry VIII: May 1536, 11–15', in *Letters and Papers, Foreign and Domestic, Henry VIII, Volume 10, January–June 1536*, ed. James Gairdner (London, 1887), pp. 349–71. *British History Online*. http://www.british-history.ac.uk/letters-papers-hen8/vol10/pp349–71 [accessed 17 June 2016].

137 **I beg you to remember me** . . . 'Henry VIII: June 1536, 21–25', in *Letters and Papers, Foreign and Domestic, Henry VIII, Volume 10, January–June 1536*, ed. James Gairdner (London, 1887), pp. 491–504. *British History Online*. http://www.british-history.ac.uk/letters-papers-hen8/vol10/pp491–504 [accessed 7 June 2016].

139 **A private matter** . . . 'Henry VIII: June 1536, 21–25', in *Letters and Papers, Foreign and Domestic, Henry VIII, Volume 10, January–June 1536*, ed. James Gairdner (London, 1887), pp. 491–504. *British History Online*. http://www.british-history.ac.uk/letters-papers-hen8/vol10/pp491–504 [accessed 7 June 2016].

140 **butterflies, fools** . . . 'Henry VIII: March 1540, 21–31', in *Letters and Papers, Foreign and Domestic, Henry VIII, Volume 15, 1540*, ed. James Gairdner and R. H. Brodie (London, 1896), pp. 150–81. *British History Online*. http://www.british-history.ac.uk/letters-papers-hen8/vol15/pp150–81 [accessed 6 June 2016].

141 **perplexed, he was not** . . . Ibid.

143 **detestable heretics** . . . 'Henry VIII: April 1540, 11–20', in *Letters and Papers, Foreign and Domestic, Henry VIII, Volume 15, 1540*, ed. James Gairdner and R. H. Brodie (London, 1896), pp. 209–51. *British History Online*. http://www.british-history.ac.uk/letters-papers-hen8/vol15/pp209–51 [accessed 5 June 2016].

143 **They were brought** . . . 'Henry VIII: February 1541, 26–28', in *Letters and Papers, Foreign and Domestic, Henry VIII, Volume 16, 1540–1541*, ed. James Gairdner and R. H. Brodie (London, 1898), pp. 267–81. *British History Online*. http://www.british-history.ac.uk/letters-papers-hen8/vol16/pp267–81 [accessed 7 June 2016].

144 **all Christians put no trust** . . . Quoted in Bernard, *The King's Reformation*, p. 573.

144 **search out the truth** E. Hall, *A Chronicle of England*.

144 **And as I said before** . . . Ibid.

145 **This year, the thirtieth day** . . . Wriothesley, Vol. 1, pp. 120–1.

146 **Your Grace knows** . . . 'Henry VIII: June 1540, 11–20', in *Letters and Papers, Foreign and Domestic, Henry VIII, Volume 15, 1540*, ed. James Gairdner and R. H. Brodie (London, 1896), pp. 364–76. *British History Online.* http://www.british-history.ac.uk/letters-papers-hen8/vol15/pp364–76 [accessed 29 April 2016].

150 **My Lord, I beseech** . . . 'Henry VIII: March 1537, 1–5', in *Letters and Papers, Foreign and Domestic, Henry VIII, Volume 12 Part 1, January–May 1537*, ed. James Gairdner (London, 1890), pp. 254–67. *British History Online.* http://www.british-history.ac.uk/letters-papers-hen8/vol12/no1/pp254–67 [accessed 24 March 2016].

151 **It was wonderful to see** . . . 'Henry VIII: August 1540, 1–10', in *Letters and Papers, Foreign and Domestic, Henry VIII, Volume 15, 1540*, ed. James Gairdner and R. H. Brodie (London, 1896), pp. 481–8. *British History Online.* http://www.british-history.ac.uk/letters-papers-hen8/vol15/pp481–88 [accessed 28 April 2016].

See also:

Anon., *The history of the worthy martyr of God the Reverend John Nicolson, better known by the name of John Lambert, who was burned in Smithfield, in the year 1538*, 1816, Church of England Tract Society.

Bernard, *The King's Reformation*, pp. 572–3.

Tom Betteridge, 'Lambert, John (*d.* 1538)', *Oxford Dictionary of National Biography*, Oxford University Press, 2004. http://www.oxforddnb.com.ezproxy2.londonlibrary.co.uk/view/article/15938 [accessed 29 June 2016].

Susan Brigden, 'Popular Disturbance and the Fall of Thomas Cromwell and the Reformers, 1539–1540', 1981, pp. 266 and 277.

Susan Brigden, *London and the Reformation*, Clarendon Press, 1989, pp. 317–18.

S. Brigden and N. Wilson, 'New Learning and Broken Friendship', *The English Historical Review* 112 (446), 1997, p. 397.

P. R. N. Carter, 'Rich, Richard, first Baron Rich (1496/7–1567)', *Oxford Dictionary of National Biography*, Oxford University Press, 2004. http://www.oxforddnb.com.ezproxy2.londonlibrary.co.uk/view/article/23491 [accessed 25 June 2016].

J. L. Chester, *John Rogers: The Compiler of the First Authorised English Bible, the Pioneer of the English Reformation, and its First Martyr, embracing a genealogical account of his family, biographical sketches of some of his principal descendants, his own writings etc. etc.*, Longman, Green, Longman & Roberts, 1861, pp. 211–12 and 219–21.

C. W. D'Alton, 'Cuthbert Tunstal and Heresy in Essex and London, 1528', *Albion: A Quarterly Journal Concerned with British Studies* 35 (2), 2003, p. 221.

Howard Leithead, 'Cromwell, Thomas, earl of Essex (*b.* in or before 1485, *d.* 1540)', *Oxford Dictionary of National Biography*, Oxford University Press, 2004; online edn, May 2009. http://www.oxforddnb.com.ezproxy2.londonlibrary.co.uk/view/article/6769, [accessed 29 June 2016].

David Loades, *Thomas Cromwell*, p. 223.

Riordan and Ryrie, 'Stephen Gardiner and the Making of a Protestant Villain', 2003, p. 1049.

Ethan H. Shagan, 'Fetherston, Richard (*d.* 1540)', *Oxford Dictionary of National Biography*, Oxford University Press, 2004. http://www.oxforddnb.com.ezproxy2.londonlibrary.co.uk/view/article/9374 [accessed 29 June 2016].

Ethan H. Shagan, 'Powell, Edward (*c.*1478–1540)', *Oxford Dictionary of National Biography*, Oxford University Press, 2004; online edn, Jan 2008. http://www.oxforddnb.com.ezproxy2.londonlibrary.co.uk/view/article/22644 [accessed 29 June 2016].

Susan Wabuda, 'Latimer, Hugh (*c.*1485–1555)', *Oxford Dictionary of National Biography*, Oxford University Press, 2004; online edn, May 2009. http://www.oxforddnb.com.ezproxy2.londonlibrary.co.uk/view/article/16100 [accessed 29 June 2016].

Five – DISSOLUTION AND DISCIPLINE

152 **From all sedition . . .** Retrieved from justus.anglican.org [accessed 28 March 2015].

152 **To all the faithful . . .** See E. A. Webb, 'The suppression', in *The Records of St. Bartholomew's Priory and St. Bartholomew the Great, West Smithfield: Volume 1* (Oxford, 1921), pp. 253–61. *British History Online.* http://www.british-history.ac.uk/st-barts-records/vol1/pp253–61 [accessed 31 May 2016].

154 **clerk of the church . . .** See E. A. Webb, 'The sixteenth century: Prior Robert Fuller', in *The Records of St. Bartholomew's Priory and St. Bartholomew the Great, West Smithfield: Volume 1* (Oxford, 1921), pp. 238–52. *British History Online.* http://www.british-history.ac.uk/st-barts-records/vol1/pp238–52 [accessed 22 June 2016].

154 **I Richard Bellamy** . . . See E. A. Webb, 'The parish: Inhabitants', in *The Records of St. Bartholomew's Priory and St. Bartholomew the Great, West Smithfield: Volume 2* (Oxford, 1921), pp. 248–91. *British History Online.* http://www.british-history.ac.uk/st-barts-records/vol2/pp248–91 [accessed 15 June 2016].

155 **Thus with the surrender** . . . E. A. Webb, 'The suppression', in *The Records of St. Bartholomew's Priory and St. Bartholomew the Great, West Smithfield: Volume 1* (Oxford, 1921), pp. 253–61. *British History Online.* http://www.british-history.ac.uk/st-barts-records/vol1/pp253–61 [accessed 31 May 2016].

157 **with humility and reverence** . . . 'Henry VIII: May 1541, 11–20', in *Letters and Papers, Foreign and Domestic, Henry VIII, Volume 16, 1540–1541,* ed. James Gairdner and R. H. Brodie (London, 1898), pp. 395–404. *British History Online.* http://www.british-history.ac.uk/letters-papers-hen8/vol16/pp395–404 [accessed 19 March 2016].

158 **very wrong** . . . A Tractarian British Critic, *The Life and Defence of the Conduct and Principles of the Venerable and Calumniated Edmund Bonner, Bishop of London, in the reigns of Henry VIII, Edward VI, Mary, and Elizabeth; in which is considered the best mode of again changing the religion of this nation,* Seeley and Burnside, 1842, p. 55.

158 **Bonner did not** . . . Ibid.

159 **the story of the Queen's misdemeanour** 'Henry VIII: November 1541, 11–20', in *Letters and Papers, Foreign and Domestic, Henry VIII, Volume 16, 1540–1541,* ed. James Gairdner and R. H. Brodie (London, 1898), pp. 613–29. *British History Online.* http://www.british-history.ac.uk/letters-papers-hen8/vol16/pp613–29 [accessed 24 March 2016].

159 **queen of England** . . . 'Henry VIII: December 1541, 1–5', in *Letters and Papers, Foreign and Domestic, Henry VIII, Volume 16, 1540–1541,* ed. James Gairdner and R. H. Brodie (London, 1898), pp. 644–60. *British History Online.* http://www.british-history.ac.uk/letters-papers-hen8/vol16/pp644–60 [accessed 20 March 2016].

160 **rehearse sermons** . . . 'Henry VIII: April 1542, 26–30', in *Letters and Papers, Foreign and Domestic, Henry VIII, Volume 17, 1542,* ed. James Gairdner and R. H. Brodie (London, 1900), pp. 153–68. *British History Online.* http://www.british-history.ac.uk/letters-papers-hen8/vol17/pp153–68 [accessed 5 May 2016].

See also:

P. R. N. Carter, 'Rich, Richard, first Baron Rich (1496/7–1567)', *Oxford Dictionary of National Biography,* Oxford University Press, 2004.

http://www.oxforddnb.com.ezproxy2.londonlibrary.co.uk/view/
article/23491 [accessed 25 October 2016].

Paul Doe and David Allinson, 'Tallis, Thomas', *Grove Music Online. Oxford Music Online*, Oxford University Press. http://www.
oxfordmusiconline.com/subscriber/article/grove/music/27423
[accessed 30 June 2016].

M. F. Sherr, 'Bishop Edmund Bonner: A Quasi Erasmian', *Historical Magazine of the Protestant Episcopal Church* 43 (4), 1974, p. 361.

W. Winters, 'Historical Notes on Some of the Ancient Manuscripts Formerly Belonging to the Monastic Library of Waltham Holy Cross', *Transactions of the Royal Historical Society* 6, 1877, pp. 203–66.

Six – 'Lo, faithless men against me rise'

162 **Lo, faithless men** . . . E. V. Beilin ed., *The Examinations of Anne Askew*, Oxford University Press, 1996, p. 72.

164 **For my friends** . . . Ibid., p. 56.

165 **And the woman** . . . 1 Corinthians 7:13–15 [Matthew Bible].

165 **could not think him worthy** . . . Quoted in B. M. Berry, 'Of the Manner in Which Anne Askew "Noised It"', *The Journal of English and Germanic Philology* 96 (2), 1997, p. 193.

165 **to gad up and down** . . . *Narratives of the Days of the Reformation*, p. 309.

166 **put that man Lascelles** . . . Brigden and Wilson, 'New Learning and Broken Friendship', p. 401.

166 **light both in living** . . . *Proceedings . . . of the Privy Council*, 7.353, quoted in Alec Ryrie, 'Lassells, John (*d.* 1546)', *Oxford Dictionary of National Biography*, Oxford University Press, 2004; online edn, Jan 2008. http://www.oxforddnb.com.ezproxy2.londonlibrary.
co.uk/view/article/68897 [accessed 30 June 2016].

168 **God that made the world** . . . Acts 17:24 [Matthew Bible].

168 **Give not that which is holy** . . . Matthew 7:6 [Matthew Bible].

168 **the one did greatly** . . . Beilin, ed., *The Examinations*, p. 21.

168 **what I said to the Sacrament** . . . Ibid., p. 24.

168 **perceived him** . . . Ibid.

169 **And then I asked him** . . . Ibid., p. 30.

170 **And I told him** . . . Ibid., p. 32.

170 **By communing with the wise** . . . Ibid., p. 33.

170 **I told him, I was** . . . Ibid., p. 34.

172 **And therefore he bade me** . . . Ibid., p. 45.

172 **suddenly shift gears** . . . Murphy, *God's Jury*, pp. 51–2.

173 **I answered, that my conscience** . . . Beilin, ed., *The Examinations*, p. 45.

173 **My lord without faith** . . . Ibid., p. 46.

174 **Then he laid unto me** . . . Ibid., pp. 47–8.

174 **Then asked he me** . . . Ibid., p. 49.

175 **I answered, that it was against** . . . Ibid., p. 54.

175 **Be it known** . . . Ibid., p. 59.

177 **the addition of a few** . . . Meg Hickerson, *Making Women Martyrs in Tudor England*, Palgrave Macmillan, 2005, p. 59.

177 **So with much ado** . . . Beilin, ed., *The Examinations*, p. 63.

179 **for that she was very obstinate** . . . Quoted in T. D. Kemp, 'Translating (Anne) Askew: The Textual Remains of a Sixteenth-Century Heretic and Saint', *Renaissance Quarterly* 52 (4), 1999, pp. 1023–4.

181 **The Bishop of Winchester** . . . Beilin, ed., *The Examinations*, p. 93.

181 **Then the Bishop said** . . . Ibid., p. 97.

182 **Then the Bishop said** . . . Ibid., p. 98.

183 **Ye may not here** . . . Ibid., p. 99.

184 **And though he did say** . . . Ibid.

184 **some wiser man** Ibid., p. 101.

185 **And as for that ye call** . . . Ibid., pp. 110–11.

185 **But who they were** . . . Ibid., p. 124.

185 **Then they said** . . . Ibid., pp. 125–6.

186 **Then they did put me** . . . Ibid., p. 127.

187 **Then the lieutenant** . . . Ibid., p. 130.

187 **to the intent the world** . . . Bishop Bonner's Register, London Metropolitan Archives, DL/A/A/006/MS09531/012/001, 109r.

188 **Oh friend most dearly beloved** . . . Beilin, ed., *The Examinations*, p. 133.

188 **Then was I brought** . . . Ibid., p. 132.

189 **But they both say** . . . Ibid., p. 140.

189 **Yea, and as St Paul** . . . Ibid., p. 142.

189 **But as concerning your Mass** . . . Ibid., p. 144.

189 **a substantial stage** . . . London Metropolitan Archives, Court of Aldermen, Repertory COL/CA/01/01/011, fol.298.

See also:

M. Bassett, 'Newgate Prison in the Middle Ages', *Speculum* 18 (2), 1943, p. 239.

Beilin, Introduction to *The Examinations*, pp. xvii and xxii.

Blench, *Preaching in England*, p. 249.

T. S. Freeman and S. E. Wall, 'Racking the Body, Shaping the Text: The Account of Anne Askew in Foxe's "Book of Martyrs"', *Renaissance Quarterly* 54 (4), 2001, pp. 1165–96.

http://www.historyofparliamentonline.org/volume/1509–1558/member/askew-(ayscough)-sir-william-1486–1540.

Wabuda, 'Bishops and the Provision of Homilies, 1520 to 1547', p. 564.

Diane Watt, 'Askew, Anne (*c.*1521–1546)', *Oxford Dictionary of National Biography*, Oxford University Press, 2004. http://www.oxforddnb.com.ezproxy2.londonlibrary.co.uk/view/article/798 [accessed 30 June 2016].

Seven – DENUNCIATIONS AND NEAR-ESCAPES

194 **first known eminent resident** A. P. Baggs, Diane K. Bolton, M. A. Hicks and R. B. Pugh, 'Hornsey, including Highgate: Highgate', in *A History of the County of Middlesex: Volume 6, Friern Barnet, Finchley, Hornsey With Highgate*, ed. T. F. T. Baker and C. R. Elrington (London, 1980), pp. 122–35. *British History Online.* http://www.british-history.ac.uk/vch/middx/vol6/pp122–35 [accessed 7 June 2016].

Eight – PROTESTANTISM IN THE ASCENDANT

198 **Item the 20th day** . . . *Chronicle of the Grey Friars*, p. 53.

201 **which the popish priests** . . . Wriothesley, Vol. 2, p. 1.

202 **did the office** . . . *Chronicle of the Greyfriars*, p. 62.

203 **he went the same day** . . . Ibid., p. 63.

204 **the censing in Paul's** . . . Wriothesley, Vol. 2, p. 3.

204 **the English procession** Ibid.

204 **Item the 20th day** . . . *Chronicle of the Greyfriars*, p. 59.

206 **it were more commendable** . . . Campbell, *Lives of the Lord Chancellors*, p. 16.

206 **called all the parsons** . . . Wriothesley, Vol. 2, p. 38.

209 **for the defence** . . . London Metropolitan Archives, Court of Common Council, Journal COL/CC/01/01/016, ff.36–7.

209 **the great abuses** . . . Wriothesley, Vol. 2, pp. 25–6.

210 **promised their aid** . . . *Acts of the Privy Council*, Vol. II, pp. 336–7.

210 **presided at the examinations** . . . Campbell, *Lives of the Lord Chancellors*, p. 22.

211 **be had from thence** . . . Wriothesley, Vol. 2, pp. 33–4.

212 **It is a goodly matter** . . . Chester, *John Rogers*, pp. 70–1.

217 **if God were a man** . . . *Chronicle of the Greyfriars*, p. 63.

220 **it is advisable** . . . Della Casa, *Il Galateo*. I'm grateful to Dr Mary Hogan Camp for drawing attention to this text in her thesis, 'Superare la natura: The Portraits of Jacopo Pontormo' (Courtauld Institute of Art, 2015).

220 **It is easy enough** . . . Chester, *John Rogers*, p. 71.

220 **a gentleman . . . set on the pillory** . . . Wriothesley, Vol. 2, pp. 79–80.

221 **This day all copes** . . . Ibid., pp. 78–9.

222 **exhorting and beseeching** . . . Chester, *John Rogers*, pp. 64–5.

222 **Well, perchance** . . . Ibid., p. 65.

See also:

C. D. C. Armstrong, 'Gardiner, Stephen (*c.*1495–1555)', *Oxford Dictionary of National Biography*, Oxford University Press, 2004; online edn, Jan 2008. http://www.oxforddnb.com.ezproxy2.londonlibrary.co.uk/view/article/10364 [accessed 30 June 2016].

Bassett, 'Newgate Prison in the Middle Ages', p. 246.

S. Byman, 'Guilt and Martyrdom: The Case of John Bradford', *The Harvard Theological Review* 68 (3/4), 1975, pp. 305–31.

Campbell, *Lives of the Lord Chancellors*, pp. 13–14, 26.

Kenneth Carleton, 'Bonner, Edmund (*d.* 1569)', *Oxford Dictionary of National Biography*, Oxford University Press, 2004; online edn, May 2006. http://www.oxforddnb.com.ezproxy2.londonlibrary.co.uk/view/article/2850 [accessed 30 June 2016].

P. R. N. Carter, 'Rich, Richard, first Baron Rich (1496/7–1567)', *Oxford Dictionary of National Biography*, Oxford University Press, 2004. http://www.oxforddnb.com.ezproxy2.londonlibrary.co.uk/view/article/23491 [accessed 25 October 2016].

M. Cox, *A history of Sir John Deane's Grammar School, Northwich, 1557–1908*, Manchester University Press, 1975.

Edwards, *Mary I*, pp. 74–5.

Thomas S. Freeman, 'Cardmaker, John (*c.*1496–1555)', *Oxford Dictionary of National Biography*, Oxford University Press, 2004. http://www.oxforddnb.com.ezproxy2.londonlibrary.co.uk/view/article/4613 [accessed 30 June 2016].

Dale Hoak, 'Edward VI (1537–1553)', *Oxford Dictionary of National Biography*, Oxford University Press, 2004; online edn, May 2014. http://www.oxforddnb.com.ezproxy2.londonlibrary.co.uk/view/article/8522 [accessed 30 June 2016].

Andrew Hope, 'Bocher, Joan (*d.* 1550)', *Oxford Dictionary of National Biography*, Oxford University Press, 2004. http://www.oxforddnb.com. ezproxy2.londonlibrary.co.uk/view/article/2744 [accessed 30 June 2016].

E. W. Ives, 'Henry VIII's Will: The Protectorate Provisions of 1546–7', *The Historical Journal* 37 (4), 1994, pp. 901–14.

John N. King, 'Bale, John (1495–1563)', *Oxford Dictionary of National Biography*, Oxford University Press, 2004; online edn, Oct 2009. http://www.oxforddnb.com.ezproxy2.londonlibrary.co.uk/view/article/1175 [accessed 30 June 2016].

Loades, *The Oxford Martyrs*, p. 127.

Diarmaid MacCulloch, *Tudor Church Militant: Edward VI and the Protestant Reformation*, Allen Lane Penguin Press, 1999, pp. 77, 86, 95–6, 101.

Andrew Pettegree, 'Parris, George van (*d.* 1551)', *Oxford Dictionary of National Biography*, Oxford University Press, 2004. http://www. oxforddnb.com.ezproxy2.londonlibrary.co.uk/view/article/21407 [accessed 30 June 2016].

A. J. Slavin, 'The Fall of Lord Chancellor Wriothesley: A Study in the Politics of Conspiracy', *Albion: A Quarterly Journal Concerned with British Studies* 7 (4), 1975, pp. 265–86.

V. F. Snow, 'Proctorial Representation in the House of Lords during the Reign of Edward VI', *Journal of British Studies* 8 (2), 1969, p. 14.

E. A. Webb, 'Sir Richard Rich', in *The Records of St. Bartholomew's Priory and St. Bartholomew the Great, West Smithfield: Volume 1* (Oxford, 1921), pp. 289–97. *British History Online.* http://www.british-history.ac.uk/st-barts-records/vol1/pp289–297 [accessed 30 May 2016].

Nine – 'Turn, and turn, and turn again'

224 Then [the Privy Council] . . . Wriothesley, *Chronicle of England*, Vol. 2, pp. 88–9.

225 The 5 of August . . . Ibid., p. 96.

226 The 5 of August . . . Nichols, *Chronicle of the Grey Friars*, p. 82.

233 Item the 13 day of August . . . Ibid., p. 83.

234 The 13 day of August . . . J. G. Nichols, ed., *The Diary of Henry Machyn, Citizen and Merchant Taylor of London, from AD 1550 to AD 1563*, Camden Society, 1848, p. 41.

234 Sunday the 13 of August . . . Wriothesley, Vol. 2, pp. 97–8.

235 This business was so . . . Ibid., pp. 98–9.

236 **John Rogers, *alias* Matthew** . . . Quoted in Chester, *John Rogers*, p. 113.

236 **When he hears** . . . *Calendar of Letters, Despatches, and State Papers relating to the Negotiations between England and Spain*, London, 1862–1954, Vol. 10, p. 217, quoted in S. Covington, 'Heretic Hunting beyond the Seas: John Brett and His Encounter with the Marian Exiles', *Albion: A Quarterly Journal Concerned with British Studies* 36 (3), 2004, p. 414.

237 **The 21 day of August** . . . *Diary of Henry Machyn*, p. 42.

237 **the sacrament of the body** . . . Wriothesley, Vol. 2, p. 104.

238 **And this was their penance** . . . *Chronicle of the Grey Friars*, p. 92.

240 **the evil savours** . . . *Narratives of the days of the Reformation*, pp. 149–50.

241 **after a short address** . . . Edwards, *Mary I*, p. 225.

241 **The 2 day of December** . . . *Diary of Henry Machyn*, p. 77.

242 **No, my Lord** . . . I have used Rogers's account as recorded in Chester, *John Rogers*, pp. 299–305, as the basis for the following version of this interrogation.

257 **Some of the onlookers** . . . Quoted in Eamon Duffy, *Fires of Faith: Catholic England under Mary Tudor*, Yale University Press, 2009, pp. 112–13.

257 **a great company** . . . *Diary of Henry Machyn*, p. 81.

See also:

Bassett, 'Newgate Prison in the Middle Ages', pp. 244–5.

Sabine Cassola (ed.), '*Te spectant, Reginalde, poli*' by Orlando di Lasso [http://www1.cpdl.org/wiki/index.php/Te_spectant,_Reginalde,_poli_(Orlando_di_Lasso)].

David Daniell, 'Rogers, John (*c.*1500–1555)', *Oxford Dictionary of National Biography*, Oxford University Press, 2004. http://www.oxforddnb.com.ezproxy2.londonlibrary.co.uk/view/article/23980 [accessed 30 June 2016].

Edwards, *Mary I*, pp. 116–22, 235, 258.

David Loades, 'The Marian Episcopate', in E. Duffy and D. M. Loades (eds), *The Church of Mary Tudor*, Ashgate, 2006, pp. 33–4.

Angelo J. Louisa, 'Bourne, Gilbert (*c.*1510–1569)', *Oxford Dictionary of National Biography*, Oxford University Press, 2004; online edn, Jan 2008. http://www.oxforddnb.com.ezproxy2.londonlibrary.co.uk/view/article/3003 [accessed 30 June 2016].

J. W. Martin, 'The Marian Regime's Failure to Understand the Importance of Printing', *Huntington Library Quarterly* 44 (4), 1981, p. 234.

Ten – DOMINICANS IN SMITHFIELD

259 **Grant me, good Lord** . . . Nicolas van Essche, *Spirituall exercyses and goostly meditations and a neare way to come to perfection and lyfe contemplative. Collected and set foorthe by the helpe of God, and diligente laboure of F. Wyllyam Perin Bacheler of divinitie and Prior of the Friers preachers of greate Saynte Bartholomes in Smythfyelde*, Peter le Chandelier, 1598, p. 17v.

262 **Yet such is the untowardness** . . . Quoted in Blench, *Preaching in England*, pp. 141–2.

263 **Thou shalt also** . . . Essche, *Spirituall exercyses and goostly meditations*, f.20r.

264 **delivered a pudding** *Chronicle of the Grey Friars*, p. 95.

264 **ran about the country** . . . Wriothesley, Vol. 2, p. 128.

265 **What dost thou give them?** Nichols, *Diary of Henry Machyn*, pp. 84–5.

266 **a barbarous and heretical race** . . . David Loades, ed., *The chronicles of the Tudor Queens*, Stroud: Sutton Publishing, 2002, p. 46.

266 **white, pink and quarrelsome** H. Kamen, *Philip of Spain*, Yale University Press, 1997, p. 58.

266 **at 8 of the clock** . . . *Diary of Henry Machyn*, p. 74.

267 **because he saw him** . . . Quoted in Edwards, *Mary I*, p. 262.

See also:

Cox, *A history of Sir John Deane's Grammar School*, pp. 15–16.

Duffy, *Fires of Faith*, pp. 118–19, 191–2.

Loades, 'The English Church during the reign of Mary', in *Reforming Catholicism*, pp. 42–3.

Loades, *The Oxford Martyrs*, pp. 157–8.

R. H. Pogson, 'Reginald Pole and the Priorities of Government in Mary Tudor's Church', *The Historical Journal* 18 (1), 1975, pp. 8–9.

L. E. C. Wooding, 'Peryn, William (d. 1558)', *Oxford Dictionary of National Biography*, Oxford University Press, 2004. http://www.oxforddnb.com. ezproxy2.londonlibrary.co.uk/view/article/22007 [accessed 30 June 2016].

Eleven – CEREMONIES OF MARTYRDOM

276 **a grievous and bitter cup** . . . Quoted in Duffy, *Fires of Faith*, p. 84.

277 **of a more soft** . . . Marcus L. Loane, *Pioneers of the Reformation in England*, Church Book Room, 1964, p. 159.

287 **After this I beheld** . . . Revelation 7: 9–17 [Matthew Bible].

290 **What is this life** . . . John Bradford, *Writings,* The Religious Tract Society, 1827, p. 420.

See also:

A. A. Dudley, 'The Attitude to the State in Anglican Literature from 1525 to 1550', *Economica* 25, 1929, p. 44.

Duffy, *Fires of Faith*, pp. 90, 91, 98.

T. Freeman, 'Texts, Lies, and Microfilm: Reading and Misreading Foxe's "Book of Martyrs"', *The Sixteenth Century Journal* 30 (1), 1999, pp. 39–40.

Thomas S. Freeman, 'Cardmaker, John (*c.*1496–1555)', *Oxford Dictionary of National Biography*, Oxford University Press, 2004. http://www. oxforddnb.com.ezproxy2.londonlibrary.co.uk/view/article/4613 [accessed 25 June 2016].

Thomas Fuller, *The History of the Worthies of England*, ed. P. Austin Nuttall, Oxford, 1849, Vol. 2, pp. 158–9.

Loades, *The Oxford Martyrs*, pp. 128, 175–6.

D. Andrew Penny, 'Bradford, John (*c.*1510–1555)', *Oxford Dictionary of National Biography*, Oxford University Press, 2004. http://www. oxforddnb.com.ezproxy2.londonlibrary.co.uk/view/article/3175 [accessed 30 June 2016].

Riordan and Ryrie, 'Stephen Gardiner and the Making of a Protestant Villain', p. 1056.

Twelve – 'I WILL PAY MY VOWS TO THEE, OH SMITHFIELD'

292 **The bishop's task** . . . Quoted in R. H. Bainton, 'The Parable of the Tares as the Proof Text for Religious Liberty to the End of the Sixteenth Century', *Church History* 1 (2), 1932, p. 83.

293 **this Latin service** . . . Bradford, *Writings*, p. 100.

294 **My dearly beloved** . . . Ibid., p. 109.

310 **The 21 day of November** . . . *Diary of Henry Machyn*, p. 97.

See also:

I. R. Bartlett, 'John Foxe as Hagiographer: The Question Revisited', *The Sixteenth Century Journal* 26 (4), 1995, p. 783.

Duffy, *Fires of Faith*, pp. 107, 162.

Ronald H. Fritze, 'Philpott, John (1515/16–1555)', *Oxford Dictionary of National Biography*, Oxford University Press, 2004; online edn, Jan

2008. http://www.oxforddnb.com.ezproxy2.londonlibrary.co.uk/view/article/22182 [accessed 30 June 2016].

D. R. Kelley, 'Martyrs, Myths, and the Massacre: The Background of St Bartholomew', *The American Historical Review* 77 (5), 1972, p. 1328.

Loades, *The Oxford Martyrs*, p. 189.

THIRTEEN – MATTERS OF CONSCIENCE

323 **with a dozen of scutcheons . . .** *Diary of Henry Machyn*, p. 164.

323 **a good and venerable . . .** W. Munk, *The roll of the Royal College of Physicians of London*, 1861, quoted in Sarah Bakewell, 'Bartlot, Richard (d. 1556)', *Oxford Dictionary of National Biography*, Oxford University Press, 2004. http://www.oxforddnb.com.ezproxy2.londonlibrary.co.uk/view/article/1591 [accessed 30 June 2016].

323 **the making of the church wall** Will of Richard Bartlett, Public Record Office, prob/11/40.

332 **Salafism focuses . . .** C. Bunzel, 'From Paper State to Caliphate: The Ideology of the Islamic State', *The Brookings Project on U.S. Relations with the Islamic World*, Analysis Paper No. 19, Brookings, 2015, p. 8.

332 **Oversimplification: . . .** Retrieved from http://lettertobaghdadi.com/14/english-v14.pdf [accessed 28 November 2015].

333 **Confident in this role . . .** Bunzel, 'From Paper State to Caliphate', p. 11.

335 **at the burning . . .** *Acts of the Privy Council*, Vol. V, p. 104.

336 **a goodly sermon** *Diary of Henry Machyn*, p. 147.

337 **a principal, deviser . . .** *Cobbett's Complete collection of state trials*, ed. T. B. Howell and T. J. Howell, Vol. 1, 1809, p. 892.

339 **good literature . . .** E. A. Webb, 'Rectors and their times: Sixteenth century (1544 onwards)', in *The Records of St. Bartholomew's Priory and St. Bartholomew the Great, West Smithfield: Volume 2* (Oxford, 1921), pp. 298–312. *British History Online*. http://www.british-history.ac.uk/st-barts-records/vol2/pp298–312 [accessed 15 June 2016].

339 **old orders and customs** Ibid.

See also:

Cox, *A history of Sir John Deane's Grammar School*, pp. 16–17, 22, 38–9.

Eamon Duffy, *The Stripping of the Altars: Traditional Religion in England c.1400–c.1580*, Yale University Press, 2005, pp. 543–4.

Thomas S. Freeman, 'Green, Bartholomew (1529/30–1556)', *Oxford Dictionary of National Biography*, Oxford University Press, 2004.

http://www.oxforddnb.com.ezproxy2.londonlibrary.co.uk/view/
    article/11376 [accessed 30 June 2016].

Gregory, *Salvation at Stake*, pp. 92–3.

Stanford Lehmberg, 'Throckmorton, Sir Nicholas (1515/16–1571)', *Oxford
    Dictionary of National Biography*, Oxford University Press, 2004; online
    edn, Jan 2008. http://www.oxforddnb.com.ezproxy2.londonlibrary.
    co.uk/view/article/27394 [accessed 30 June 2016].

Loades, 'The English Church during the reign of Mary', in *Reforming
    Catholicism*, pp. 37–8.

P. M. Took, 'The Government and the Printing Trade, 1540–1560',
    unpublished PhD thesis, University of London, 1978, pp. 279–81.

Fourteen – Constancy and Conflagration

341 **The martyr in his . . .** Oscar Wilde, *De Profundis*, Methuen, 1912,
     pp. 139–40.

348 **not so learned . . .** *John Knox's History of the Reformation in
     Scotland*, ed. W. C. Dickinson, 1949, Vol. 1, p. 42.

355 **In all things give thanks** St John Chrysostom: 'Glory to God for
     all things'. See https://oca.org/saints/lives/2009/11/13/103292-st-
     john-chrysostom-the-archbishop-of-constantinople [accessed 1 June
     2015].

See also:

Duffy, *Fires of Faith*, p. 160.

Edwards, *Mary I*, p. 303.

Richard L. Greaves, 'Rough, John (c. 1508–1557)', *Oxford Dictionary of
    National Biography*, Oxford University Press, 2004. http://www.
    oxforddnb.com.ezproxy2.londonlibrary.co.uk/view/article/24167
    [accessed 30 June 2016].

Epilogue – 'By the light of burning martyrs'

364 **Ô vous, les boutefeux . . .** Retrieved from http://www.
     projetbrassens.eclipse.co.uk/pages/transmourir.html [accessed 18
     March 2016].

366 **Never, for any reason . . .** George Orwell, *1984*, Penguin, 1972
     (first published 1949), p. 192.

369 **All forms of oppression . . .** Retrieved from http://binbayyah.

net/english/2014/09/24/fatwa-response-to-isis [accessed 28 November 2015].

370 **The distinction of martyrs** . . . Adapted from 'Jihad Today' by Menahem Milson (published by MEMRI on 21 December 2007). www.discoverthenetworks.org (*A Guide to the Political Left*) [accessed 27 November 2015].

370 **The 'vast reward'** . . . A. J. Caschetta, 'Does Islam Have a Role in Suicide Bombings?', *Middle East Quarterly*, Summer 2015. http://www.meforum.org/5320/islam-suicide-bombings [accessed 27 November 2015].

370 **Let those fight** . . . Qur'an 4:74.

370 **Let us not then fear death** . . . Nicholas Ridley, 'Farewell Letter from Prison', in *The works of Nicholas Ridley, sometime lord bishop of London, martyr, 1555*, ed. H. Christmas, Parker Society, 1843, p. 426.

372 **carried in a chariot** . . . Nichols, *Diary of Henry Machyn*, p. 184.

372 **The 18 day of December** . . . Ibid.

376 **The act of martyrdom** . . . Gregory, *Salvation at Stake*, p. 351.

378 **because men often sin** . . . Zagorin, *How the Idea of Religious Toleration Came to the West*, p. 136.

379 **For *ecclesiastical and secular*** . . . Gregory, *Salvation at Stake*, p. 346.

380 **To suggest that the course** . . . Ibid., p. 347.

381 **have affirmed and declared** . . . See https://www. churchofengland.org/prayer-worship/worship/texts/ordinal/priests. aspx [accessed 18 March 2016].

381 **Holy Scripture containeth** . . . Book of Common Prayer, p. 613.

381 **The Church hath power** . . . Ibid., pp. 619–20.

381 **the Church of Rome** . . . Ibid., p. 619.

381 **when they be gathered** . . . Ibid., p. 620.

381 **The condition of Man** . . . Ibid., p. 615.

382 **We are accounted righteous** . . . Ibid., p. 616.

382 **cannot put away our sins** Ibid.

382 **godly persons** . . . Ibid., pp. 618–19.

383 **The Romish Doctrine** . . . Ibid., p. 620.

383 **It is a thing** . . . Ibid., p. 621.

383 **two Sacraments** . . . Ibid.

383 **The Sacraments were not** . . . Ibid., p. 622.

383 **though he did say** . . . Beilin, ed., *The Examinations*, p. 99.

384 **The Body of Christ** . . . Book of Common Prayer, p. 623.

384 **all other Christian men** Ibid., p. 625.

385 **It is not necessary** . . . Ibid.

386 **open statement** See http://www.peter-ould.net/2008/10/17/

london–gay–wedding–things–hot–up–in–the–deanery/ [accessed 18 March 2016].

386 **To the representatives** . . . See http://www.peter–ould. net/2008/10/19/martin–dudley–mishandles–donatism/ [accessed 18 March 2016].

387 **The point at issue** . . . See http://www.telegraph.co.uk/news/ uknews/2151211/The–Bishops–letter–in–full.html [accessed 18 March 2016].

389 **blackened as if by fire** . . . E. A. Webb, 'The resuscitation and second suppression', in *The Records of St. Bartholomew's Priory and St. Bartholomew the Great, West Smithfield: Volume 1* (Oxford, 1921), pp. 277–88. *British History Online*. http://www.british–history.ac.uk/ st–barts–records/vol1/pp277–288 [accessed 16 July 2016].

390 **For in the world** . . . John 16:33.

390 **Bring us, O Lord God** . . . John Donne, 'Our Last Awakening', from a sermon preached at Whitehall on 29 February 1628, revised and edited by Eric Milner–White (1884–1964).

See also:

Brigden, *London and the Reformation*, pp. 577–8.

Kenneth Carleton, 'Bonner, Edmund (d. 1569)', *Oxford Dictionary of National Biography*, Oxford University Press, 2004; online edn, May 2006. http://www.oxforddnb.com.ezproxy2.londonlibrary.co.uk/ view/article/2850 [accessed 25 June 2016].

P. R. N. Carter, 'Rich, Richard, first Baron Rich (1496/7–1567)', *Oxford Dictionary of National Biography*, Oxford University Press, 2004. http://www.oxforddnb.com.ezproxy2.londonlibrary.co.uk/view/ article/23491 [accessed 25 June 2016].

Cox, *A history of Sir John Deane's Grammar School*, p. 17.

S. Doran and C. Durston, *Princes, Pastors and People: The church and religion in England 1529–1689*, Routledge, 1991, p. 146.

Edwards, *Mary I*, p. 343.

Knowles, *The Religious Orders in England*, p. 441.

Megivern, 'Capital Punishment: The Curious History of Its Privileged Place in Christendom', p. 6.

Zagorin, *How the Idea of Religious Toleration Came to the West*, pp. 189–90.

BIBLIOGRAPHY

✠

Ackroyd, P., 1998, *The Life of Thomas More* (London: Chatto & Windus).

Ahnert, R., 2009, 'Writing in the Tower of London during the Reformation, *ca.* 1530–1558', *Huntington Library Quarterly* 72 (2), pp. 168–92.

Alsop, J., 1979, 'The Revenue Commission of 1552', *The Historical Journal* 22 (3), pp. 511–33.

Anon., 1816, *The history of the worthy martyr of God the Reverend John Nicolson, better known by the name of John Lambert, who was burned in Smithfield, in the year 1538* (Church of England Tract Society).

Baillie, H., 1962, 'Some Biographical Notes on English Church Musicians, Chiefly Working in London (1485–1560)', *Royal Musical Association Research Chronicle* 2, pp. 18–57.

Bainton, R. H., 1932, 'The Parable of the Tares as the Proof Text for Religious Liberty to the End of the Sixteenth Century', *Church History* 1 (2), pp. 67–89.

———, 1941, 'The Left Wing of the Reformation', *The Journal of Religion* 21 (2), pp. 124–34.

———, 1941, 'The Struggle for Religious Liberty', *Church History* 10 (2), pp. 95–124.

——— (ed.), 1965, *Concerning Heretics: Whether they are to be persecuted and how they are to be treated. A collection of the opinions of learned men, Both ancient and modern, An anonymous work attributed to Sebastian Castellio* (New York: Octagon Books Inc.).

Bartlett, I. R., 1995, 'John Foxe as Hagiographer: The Question Revisited', *The Sixteenth Century Journal* 26 (4), pp. 771–89.

Bassett, M., 1943, 'Newgate Prison in the Middle Ages', *Speculum* 18 (2), pp. 233–46.

Beer, B. L., 1972, 'London and the Rebellions of 1548–1549', *Journal of British Studies* 12 (1), pp. 15–38.

————, 1985, 'John Stow and the English Reformation', *The Sixteenth Century Journal* 16 (2), pp. 257–71.

————, 1986, 'London Parish Clergy and the Protestant Reformation, 1547–1559', *Albion: A Quarterly Journal Concerned with British Studies* 18 (3), pp. 375–93.

Beilin, E. V. (ed.), 1996, *The Examinations of Anne Askew* (New York and Oxford: Oxford University Press).

Bernard, G. W., 2005, *The King's Reformation: Henry VIII and the remaking of the English Church* (New Haven and London: Yale University Press).

————, 2012, *The Late Medieval English Church: Vitality and Vulnerability before the Break with Rome* (New Haven and London: Yale University Press).

Berry, B. M., 1997, 'Of the Manner in Which Anne Askew "Noised It"', *The Journal of English and Germanic Philology* 96 (2), pp. 182–203.

Bethencourt, F., 1992, 'The Auto da Fé: Ritual and Imagery', *Journal of the Warburg and Courtauld Institutes* 55, pp. 155–68.

Blench, J. W., 1964, *Preaching in England in the late Fifteenth and Sixteenth Centuries: A Study of English Sermons 1450–c.1600* (Oxford: Basil Blackwell).

Block, J., 1977, 'Thomas Cromwell's Patronage of Preaching', *The Sixteenth Century Journal* 8 (1), pp. 37–50.

Borman, T., 2014, *Thomas Cromwell: The untold story of Henry VIII's most faithful servant* (London: Hodder & Stoughton).

Boyle, A., 2002, 'Hans Eworth's Portrait of the Earl of Arundel and the Politics of 1549–50', *The English Historical Review* 117 (470), pp. 25–47.

Bradford, J., 1827, *Writings* (London: The Religious Tract Society).

Brigden, S., 1981, 'Popular Disturbance and the Fall of Thomas Cromwell and the Reformers, 1539–1540', *The Historical Journal* 24 (2), pp. 257–78.

————, 1982, 'Youth and the English Reformation', *Past and Present* 95, pp. 37–67.

————, 1989, *London and the Reformation* (Oxford: Clarendon Press).

————, and Wilson, N., 1997, 'New Learning and Broken Friendship', *The English Historical Review* 112 (446), pp. 396–411.

Bunzel, C., 2015, 'From Paper State to Caliphate: The Ideology of the Islamic State', *The Brookings Project on U.S. Relations with the Islamic World*, Analysis Paper No. 19 (Washington DC: Brookings).

Burgess, C. and Wathey, A., 2000, 'Mapping the Soundscape: Church Music in English Towns, 1450–1550', *Early Music History* 19, pp. 1–46.

Byman, S., 1975, 'Guilt and Martyrdom: The Case of John Bradford', *The Harvard Theological Review* 68 (3/4), pp. 305–31.

————, 1978, 'Ritualistic Acts and Compulsive Behavior: The Pattern of Tudor Martyrdom', *The American Historical Review* 83 (3), pp. 625–43.

Camm, B. (ed.), 1914, *Lives of the English Martyrs, declared Blessed by Pope Leo XIII in 1886 and 1895* (London: Longmans, Green & Co.).

Campbell, J. L., 1846, *The Lives of the Lord Chancellors and Keepers of the Great Seal of England*, Vol. 2 (London: John Murray).

Carus-Wilson, E. M., 1933, 'The Origins and Early Development of the Merchant Adventurers' Organization in London as Shown in Their Own Medieval Records', *The Economic History Review* 4 (2), pp. 147–76.

Castellio, S., 1981, '*De arte dubitandi et confidendi ignorantia et sciendi*', with introduction and notes by E. F. Hirsch, *Studies in Medieval and Reformation Thought*, Vol. XXIX (Leiden: E. J. Brill).

Chester, A. G., 1951, 'Robert Barnes and the Burning of the Books', *Huntington Library Quarterly* 14 (3), pp. 211–21.

Chester, J. L., 1861, *John Rogers: The Compiler of the First Authorised English Bible, the Pioneer of the English Reformation, and its First Martyr, embracing a genealogical account of his family, biographical sketches of some of his principal descendants, his own writings etc. etc.* (London: Longman, Green, Longman & Roberts).

Christopherson, J. 1554, *An exhortation to all menne to take hede and beware of rebellion* (London: John Cawood; reprinted by Da Capo Press, 1973).

Church of England Tract Society, 1815, *Some account of the Life and Martyrdom of James Bainham, of the Middle Temple, Esquire, who was burnt at Smithfield, London, April 30th, 1532* (Bristol).

Coles, K. A., 2002, 'The Death of the Author (And the Appropriation of Her Text): The Case of Anne Askew's "Examinations"', *Modern Philology* 99 (4), pp. 515–39.

Collinson, P., 2003, *The Reformation* (London: Weidenfeld & Nicolson).

Cooper, T., 1999, *The Last Generation of English Catholic Clergy: Parish Priests in the Diocese of Coventry and Lichfield in the Early Sixteenth Century* (Woodbridge: The Boydell Press).

Coulton, G. G., 1924, *The Death Penalty for Heresy from 1184 to 1917* (London: Simpkin, Marshall, Hamilton, Kent & Co.).

Covington, S., 2004, 'Heretic Hunting beyond the Seas: John Brett and His Encounter with the Marian Exiles', *Albion: A Quarterly Journal Concerned with British Studies* 36 (3), pp. 407–29.

Cox, M., 1975, *A history of Sir John Deane's Grammar School, Northwich, 1557–1908* (Manchester: Manchester University Press).

Craven, W. F., 1930, 'The Earl of Warwick, a Speculator in Piracy', *The Hispanic American Historical Review* 10 (4), pp. 457–79.

Crook, D., 2009, 'A Sixteenth-Century Catalog of Prohibited Music', *Journal of the American Musicological Society* 62 (1), pp. 1–78.

Cross, C., 1976, *Church and People, 1450–1660: The Triumph of the Laity in the English Church* (Hassocks: The Harvester Press).

D'Alton, C. W., 2002, 'Charity or Fire? The Argument of Thomas More's 1529 Dyalogue', *The Sixteenth Century Journal* 33 (1), pp. 51–70.

———, 2003, 'Cuthbert Tunstal and Heresy in Essex and London, 1528', *Albion: A Quarterly Journal Concerned with British Studies* 35 (2), pp. 210–28.

Davis, E. J., 1925, 'The Beginning of the Dissolution: Christchurch, Aldgate, 1532', *Transactions of the Royal Historical Society* Fourth Series 8, pp. 127–50.

Davis, J. F., 1981, 'The Trials of Thomas Bylney and the English Reformation', *The Historical Journal* 24 (4), pp. 775–90.

Derrett, J. D. M., 1964, 'The Trial of Sir Thomas More', *The English Historical Review* 79 (312), pp. 449–77.

Dickson, G., 1999, 'Encounters in Medieval Revivalism: Monks, Friars, and Popular Enthusiasts', *Church History* 68 (2), pp. 265–93.

Dillon, J., 2008, 'Clerkenwell and Smithfield as a Neglected Home of London Theater', *Huntington Library Quarterly* 71 (1), pp. 115–35.

Dolan, F. E., 1994, '"Gentlemen, I Have One More Thing to Say": Women on Scaffolds in England, 1563–1680', *Modern Philology* 92 (2), pp. 157–78.

Donagan, B., 1976, 'The Clerical Patronage of Robert Rich, Second Earl of Warwick, 1619–1642', *Proceedings of the American Philosophical Society* 120 (5), pp. 388–419.

Donnelly, D. H., 1978, 'The "Size" of More (On His 500th Birthday)', *Albion: A Quarterly Journal Concerned with British Studies* 10, Quincentennial Essays on St Thomas More, pp. 11–26.

Doran, S. and Durston, C., 1991, *Princes, Pastors and People: The church and religion in England 1529–1689* (London and New York: Routledge).

Dudley, A. A., 1929, 'The Attitude to the State in Anglican Literature from 1525 to 1550', *Economica* 25, pp. 41–52.

Duffy, E., 2005, *The Stripping of the Altars: Traditional Religion in England c.1400–c.1580* (New Haven and London: Yale University Press).

———, 2009, *Fires of Faith: Catholic England under Mary Tudor* (New Haven and London: Yale University Press).

———, 2012, *Saints, Sacrilege and Sedition: Religion and Conflict in the Tudor Reformations* (London: Bloomsbury).

———, and Loades, D. (eds), 2006, *The Church of Mary Tudor* (Aldershot: Ashgate).

Duncan, C., 2007, 'The Persecutor's Wager', *The Philosophical Review* 116 (1), pp. 1–50.

Edwards, J., 2006, 'Spanish Religious Influence in Marian England' in Duffy, E. and Loades, D. (eds), *The Church of Mary Tudor* (Aldershot: Ashgate), pp. 201–24.

———, 2011, *Mary I: England's Catholic Queen* (New Haven and London: Yale University Press).

———, and Truman, R., 2005, *Reforming Catholicism in the England of Mary Tudor: The Achievement of Friar Bartolomé Carranza* (Aldershot and Burlington VT: Ashgate).

Essche, N. van, 1598, *Spirituall exercyses and goostly meditations and a neare way to come to perfection and lyfe contemplative. Collected and set foorthe by the helpe of God, and diligente laboure of F. Wyllyam Perin Bacheler of divinitie and Prior of the Friers preachers of greate Sayncte Bartholomes in Smythfyelde* (Caen: Peter le Chandelier).

Faul, D., 1994, 'The Battle of the Dons: Recent Historiography of the English Reformation', *Seanchas Ardmhacha: Journal of the Armagh Diocesan Historical Society* 16 (1), pp. 276–88.

Fisher, R. M., 1981, 'The Reformation of Clergy at the Inns of Court 1530–1580', *The Sixteenth Century Journal* 12 (1), pp. 69–91.

Flynn, M., 1991, 'Mimesis of the Last Judgment: The Spanish Auto de fe', *The Sixteenth Century Journal* 22 (2), pp. 281–97.

Franck, T. M., 1997, 'Is Personal Freedom a Western Value?', *The American Journal of International Law* 91 (4), pp. 593–627.

Fraser, A. M., 1967, 'Self-Immolation as a Political Act: A Note', *Vietnam Perspectives* 3 (2), pp. 28–31.

Freeman, T., 1999, 'Texts, Lies, and Microfilm: Reading and Misreading Foxe's "Book of Martyrs"', *The Sixteenth Century Journal* 30 (1), pp. 23–46.

———, 2000, '"The Good Ministrye of Godlye and Vertuouse Women": The Elizabethan Martyrologists and the Female Supporters of the Marian Martyrs', *Journal of British Studies* 39 (1), pp. 8–33.

Freeman, T. S. and Wall, S. E., 2001, 'Racking the Body, Shaping the Text: The Account of Anne Askew in Foxe's "Book of Martyrs"', *Renaissance Quarterly* 54 (4), pp. 1165–96.

Galloway, J. A., Keene, D. and Murphy, M., 1996, 'Fuelling the City: Production and Distribution of Firewood and Fuel in London's Region, 1290–1400', *The Economic History Review* New Series 49 (3), pp. 447–72.

Gasquet, F. A., 1899, *Henry VIII and the English Monasteries* (London: John C. Nimmo).

Green, P. D., 1972, 'Suicide, Martyrdom, and Thomas More', *Studies in the Renaissance* 19, pp. 135–55.

Gregory, B. S., 1999, *Salvation at Stake: Christian Martyrdom in Early Modern Europe* (Cambridge MA and London: Harvard University Press).

Hall, E., 1809, *Hall's Chronicle; containing the History of England during the reign of Henry the Fourth, and the succeeding monarchs, to the end of the reign of Henry the Eighth, in which are particularly described the manners and customs of those periods. Carefully collated with the editions of 1548 and 1550* (London: Printed for J. Johnson).

Hamilton, W. D. (ed.), 1875 and 1877, *A Chronicle of England during the Reigns of the Tudors by Charles Wriothesley, Windsor Herald*, 2 vols (London: The Camden Society).

Harper-Bill, C., 1996, *The Pre-Reformation Church in England 1400–1530* (London and New York: Longman).

Harris, B. J., 1990, 'Women and Politics in Early Tudor England', *The Historical Journal* 33 (2), pp. 259–81.

Hayden, J. M., 2000, 'Religious Reform and Religious Orders in England, 1490–1540: The Case of the Crutched Friars', *The Catholic Historical Review* 86 (3), pp. 420–38.

Heale, M., 2006, 'Monastic-Parochial Churches in Late Medieval England' in Burgess, C. and Duffy, E. (eds), *The Parish in Late Medieval England: Proceedings of the 2002 Harlaxton Symposium* (Donington: Shaun Tyas).

Hickerson, M. L., 2005, *Making Women Martyrs in Tudor England* (London: Palgrave Macmillan).

———, 2007, 'Negotiating Heresy in Tudor England: Anne Askew and the Bishop of London', *Journal of British Studies* 46 (4), pp. 774–95.

Hoak, D., 1987, 'The Secret History of the Tudor Court: The King's Coffers and the King's Purse, 1542–1553', *Journal of British Studies* 26 (2), pp. 208–31.

Hooper, W., 1915, 'The Tudor Sumptuary Laws', *The English Historical Review* 30 (119), pp. 433–49.

Hurstfield, J., 1953, 'Corruption and Reform under Edward VI and Mary: The Example of Wardship', *The English Historical Review* 68 (266), pp. 22–36.

———, 1967, 'Was There a Tudor Despotism after All?', *Transactions of the Royal Historical Society* Fifth Series 17, pp. 83–108.

Ives, E. W., 1968, 'The Common Lawyers in Pre-Reformation England', *Transactions of the Royal Historical Society* Fifth Series 18, pp. 145–73.

———, 1992, 'Henry VIII's Will – A Forensic Conundrum', *The Historical Journal* 35 (4), pp. 779–804.

———, 1994, 'Henry VIII's Will: The Protectorate Provisions of 1546–7', *The Historical Journal* 37 (4), pp. 901–14.

Jones, N., 1997, 'Living the Reformations: Generational Experience and Political Perception in Early Modern England', *Huntington Library Quarterly* 60 (3), pp. 273–88.

Jones, N. L., 1981, 'Matthew Parker, John Bale, and the Magdeburg Centuriators', *The Sixteenth Century Journal* 12 (3), pp. 35–49.

Jordan, W. K. (ed.), 1966, *The chronicle and political papers of King Edward VI* (London).

Kamen, H., 1997, *Philip of Spain* (New Haven CT/London: Yale University Press).

Kelley, D. R., 1972, 'Martyrs, Myths, and the Massacre: The Background of St Bartholomew', *The American Historical Review* 77 (5), pp. 1323–42.

Kemp, T. D., 1999, 'Translating (Anne) Askew: The Textual Remains of a Sixteenth-Century Heretic and Saint', *Renaissance Quarterly* 52 (4), pp. 1021–45.

Kesselring, K. J., 2001, 'A Draft of the 1531 "Acte for Poysoning"', *The English Historical Review* 116 (468), pp. 894–9.

King, J. N., 2000, 'Religious Dissidence in Foxe's "Book of Martyrs": Humanism or Heresy?', *Religion and Literature* 32 (2), pp. 141–56.

King'oo, C. C., 2014, 'Authenticity and Excess in *The Examinations of Anne Askew*', *Reformation* 19 (1), pp. 21–39.

Kisby, F., 1999, 'Officers and Office-Holding at the English Court: A Study of the Chapel Royal, 1485–1547', *Royal Musical Association Research Chronicle* 32, pp. 1–61.

Knott, J. R., 1996, 'John Foxe and the Joy of Suffering', *The Sixteenth Century Journal* 27 (3), pp. 721–34.

Knowles, D., 1959, *The Religious Orders in England, Volume III: The Tudor Age* (Cambridge: Cambridge University Press).

Kolb, R., 1995, 'God's Gift of Martyrdom: The Early Reformation Understanding of Dying for the Faith', *Church History* 64 (3), pp. 399–411.

Kreps, B., 2003, 'Elizabeth Pickering: The First Woman to Print Law Books in England and Relations within the Community of Tudor London's Printers and Lawyers', *Renaissance Quarterly* 56 (4), pp. 1053–88.

Letters of the Martyrs, The, collected and published in 1564, 1837 (London: John F. Shaw).

Loades, D. M., 1964, 'The Press under the Early Tudors: A Study in Censorship and Sedition', *Transactions of the Cambridge Bibliographical Society* 4 (1), pp. 29–50.

———, 1970, *The Oxford Martyrs* (London: B. T. Batsford).

———, 1974, 'The Theory and Practice of Censorship in Sixteenth-Century England', *Transactions of the Royal Historical Society* Fifth Series 24, pp. 141–57.

———, 1993, 'John Foxe and the Traitors: the Politics of the Marian Persecution' in Wood, D., *Martyrs and Martyrologies* (Oxford: Blackwell), pp. 231–44.

———, 2006, 'The Marian Episcopate' in Duffy, E. and Loades, D. M. (eds), *The Church of Mary Tudor* (Aldershot: Ashgate), pp. 33–56.

———, 2013, *Thomas Cromwell: Servant to Henry VIII* (Stroud: Amberley).

——— (ed.), 1999, *John Foxe: An Historical Perspective* (Aldershot: Ashgate).

——— (ed.), 2002, *The chronicles of the Tudor Queens* (Stroud: Sutton Publishing).

Lutton, R., 2010, 'Heresy and Heterodoxy in Late Medieval Kent' in Sweetinburgh, S. (ed.), *Later Medieval Kent, 1220–1540* (Woodbridge: The Boydell Press and Kent County Council), pp. 167–87.

MacCulloch, D., 1996, *Thomas Cranmer: a life* (New Haven and London: Yale University Press).

———, 1999, *Tudor Church Militant: Edward VI and the Protestant Reformation* (London: Allen Lane Penguin Press).

Macek, E., 1988, 'The Emergence of a Feminine Spirituality in the Book of Martyrs', *The Sixteenth Century Journal* 19 (1), pp. 62–80.

Marshall, P., 1998, 'Papist As Heretic: The Burning of John Forest', *The Historical Journal* 41 (2), pp. 351–74.

———, 2003, 'Forgery and Miracles in the Reign of Henry VIII', *Past and Present* 178, pp. 39–73.

Martin, J. W., 1981, 'The Marian Regime's Failure to Understand the Importance of Printing', *Huntington Library Quarterly* 44 (4), pp. 231–47.

McCue, J. F., 1968, 'The Doctrine of Transubstantiation from Berengar through Trent: The Point at Issue', *The Harvard Theological Review* 61 (3), pp. 385–430.

McNeill, J. T., 1974, 'John Foxe: Historiographer, Disciplinarian, Tolerationist', *Church History* 43 (2), pp. 216–29.

Megivern, J. J., 2003, 'Capital Punishment: The Curious History of Its Privileged Place in Christendom', *Proceedings of the American Philosophical Society* 147 (1), pp. 3–12.

Moore, R. I., 2012, *The War on Heresy: Faith and Power in Medieval Europe* (London: Profile Books).

More, T., 1529, *A Dialogue Concerning Heretics* in Lawler, T. M. C., Marc'hadour, G. and Marius, R. C. (eds), 1981, *The Complete Works of St Thomas More*, Vol. 6, Pt. 1. (New Haven: Yale University Press).

———, 1532, *The Confutation of Tyndale's Answer* in Schuster, Louis A. et al. (eds), 1973, *Complete Works of St Thomas More*, Vol. 8, Pt. 1 (New Haven: Yale University Press).

———, 1557/1931, *The English works of Sir Thomas More*, ed. William Rastell (1557) and W. E. Campbell (1931), 2 volumes (London: Eyre and Spottiswoode).

Mozley, J. F., 1953, *Coverdale and his bibles* (Lutterworth).

Murphy, C., 2012, *God's Jury: The Inquisition and the Making of the Modern World* (London: Allen Lane).

Naji, Abu Bakr, 2006, *The Management of Savagery: The Most Critical Stage Through Which the Umma Will Pass*, tr. McCants, W. (funding for translation provided by the John M. Olin Institute for Strategic Studies at Harvard University). Available online at various sites, including http://www.physics.wisc.edu/undergrads/courses/206-f07/files/reference_chapter07/Management_of_Savagery.pdf [accessed 18 March 2016].

Nichols, J. G. (ed.), 1848, *The Diary of Henry Machyn, Citizen and Merchant Taylor of London, from AD 1550 to AD 1563* (London: Camden Society).

——— (ed.), 1852, *Chronicle of the Grey Friars of London* (London: Camden Society).

——— (ed.), 1857, *Literary Remains of King Edward the Sixth* (London: Roxburghe Club).

——— (ed.), 1869, *Narratives of the Days of the Reformation* (London: Camden Society).

Novak, M., 1995, 'Aquinas and the heretics', *First Things* (New York: The Institute on Religion and Public Life, December 1995).

Parry, L. A., 1933, *The History of Torture in England* (London: Sampson Low, Marston & Co.).

Penny, D. A., 1996, 'Family Matters and Foxe's Acts and Monuments', *The Historical Journal* 39 (3), pp. 599–618.

Pineas, R., 'John Frith's Polemical Use of Rhetoric and Logic', *Studies in English Literature, 1500–1900* 4 (1), pp. 85–100.

Pogson, R. H., 1975, 'Reginald Pole and the Priorities of Government in Mary Tudor's Church', *The Historical Journal* 18 (1), pp. 3–20.

Pollard, A. F., 1923, 'Council, Star Chamber, and Privy Council under the Tudors III. The Privy Council', *The English Historical Review* 38 (149), pp. 42–60.

Pollard, A. W. (ed.), 1911, *Records of the English Bible: the documents relating to the translation and publication of the Bible in English, 1525–1611* (reprinted by Forgotten Books, 2016).

Porter, H. C., 1964, 'The Nose of Wax: Scripture and the Spirit from Erasmus to Milton', *Transactions of the Royal Historical Society* Fifth Series 14, pp. 155–74.

Rawcliffe, C. and Flower, S., 1986, 'English Noblemen and Their Advisers: Consultation and Collaboration in the Later Middle Ages', *Journal of British Studies* 25 (2), pp. 157–77.

Raynor, B., 2000, *John Frith, Scholar and Martyr: A biography* (Sevenoaks: Pond View Books).

Rex, R., 2000, 'Jasper Fyloll and the Enormities of the Clergy: Two Tracts Written during the Reformation Parliament', *The Sixteenth Century Journal* 31 (4), pp. 1043–62.

Riordan, M. and Ryrie, A., 2003, 'Stephen Gardiner and the Making of a Protestant Villain', *The Sixteenth Century Journal* 34 (4), pp. 1039–63.

Robertson, M. L., 1990, 'Profit and Purpose in the Development of Thomas Cromwell's Landed Estates', *Journal of British Studies* 29 (4), pp. 317–46.

Rogers, J., 1537, *Thomas Matthew Bible* (Kindle Edition: First Gospel Publications, 2012).

Roper, W., *c.*1556, *The Life of Sir Thomas More*, ed. Wesemer, G. B. and Smith, S. W., 2003 (Center for Thomas More Studies). http://www.thomasmorestudies.org/docs/Roper.pdf [accessed 24 June 2016].

Rosenberg, I. M. and Rosenberg, Y. L., 2004, 'Of God's Mercy and the Four Biblical Methods of Capital Punishment: Stoning, Burning, Beheading, and Strangulation', *Tulane Law Review*, 78 TUL.L. REV. 1169.

Rubin, R., 1993, 'Choosing Death? Experiences of Martyrdom in Late Medieval Europe' in Wood, D. (ed.), *Martyrs and Martyrologies* (Oxford: Blackwell), pp. 152–82.

Russell, C., 1972, 'English Land Sales, 1540–1640: A Comment on the Evidence', *The Economic History Review* 25 (1), pp. 117–21.

Sabine, E. L., 1933, 'Butchering in Mediaeval London', *Speculum* 8 (3), pp. 335–53.

Saukko, P. and Knight, B., 2004, *Knight's Forensic Pathology*, Third Edition (London: Arnold).

Scarisbrick, J. J., 1985, *The Reformation and the English People* (Oxford: Blackwell).

Sherr, M. F., 1974, 'Bishop Edmund Bonner: A Quasi Erasmian', *Historical Magazine of the Protestant Episcopal Church* 43 (4), pp. 359–66.

Shuger, D., 2008, 'The Reformation of Penance', *Huntington Library Quarterly* 71 (4), pp. 557–71.

Slavin, A. J., 1975, 'The Fall of Lord Chancellor Wriothesley: A Study in the Politics of Conspiracy', *Albion: A Quarterly Journal Concerned with British Studies* 7 (4), pp. 265–86.

Snow, V. F., 1969, 'Proctorial Representation in the House of Lords during the Reign of Edward VI', *Journal of British Studies* 8 (2), pp. 1–27.

Stone, L., 1952, 'The Elizabethan Aristocracy – A Restatement', *The Economic History Review* 4 (3), pp. 302–21.

Stow, J., 1960, *Stow's Survey of London* (London: Dent).

Strong, R., 1969, *Tudor and Jacobean Portraits*, 2 vols (London: HMSO).

Thompson, W. D. J. Cargill, 1960, 'The sixteenth-century editions of *A Supplication unto King Henry the Eighth* by Robert Barnes, DD: A footnote to the history of the Royal Supremacy', *Transactions of the Cambridge Bibliographical Society* 3 (2), pp. 133–42.

Thoms, W. J. (ed.), 1842, *A Survey of London, written in the year 1598, by John Stow* (London: Whittaker and Co.).

Tighe, W. J., 1989, 'Courtiers and Politics in Elizabethan Hertfordshire: Sir James Croft, His Friends and His Foes', *The Historical Journal* 32 (2), pp. 257–79.

Tractarian British Critic, A, 1842, *The Life and Defence of the Conduct and Principles of the Venerable and Calumniated Edmund Bonner, Bishop of London, in the reigns of Henry VIII, Edward VI, Mary, and Elizabeth; in which is considered the best mode of again changing the religion of this nation* (London: Seeley and Burnside).

Trevor-Roper, H. R., 1951, 'The Elizabethan Aristocracy: An Anatomy Anatomized', *The Economic History Review* New Series 3 (3), pp. 279–98.

———, 1982, 'Upstairs Downstairs in the Sixteenth Century. The Lisle Letters. 6 volumes by Muriel St Clare Byrne', *The American Scholar* 51 (3), pp. 410–23.

Victoria County History: A History of the County of Essex, Vol. 2, 1907 (British History Online).

Victoria County History: A History of the County of Middlesex, Vol. 5, 1976 (British History Online).

Wabuda, S., 1994, 'Bishops and the Provision of Homilies, 1520 to 1547', *The Sixteenth Century Journal* 25 (3), pp. 551–66.

Wall, A., 1988, 'Patterns of Politics in England, 1558–1625', *The Historical Journal* 31 (4), pp. 947–63.

Whatmore, L. E., 1983, *The Carthusians under King Henry the Eighth* (Salzburg: University of Salzburg).

Whitelock, A. and MacCulloch, D., 2007, 'Princess Mary's Household and the Succession Crisis, July 1553', *The Historical Journal* 50 (2), pp. 265–87.

Williamson, M., 2006, 'Liturgical Music in the Late Medieval English Parish: Organs and Voices, Ways and Means' in Burgess, C. and Duffy, E. (eds), *The Parish in Late Medieval England: Proceedings of the 2002 Harlaxton Symposium* (Donington: Shaun Tyas).

Winters, W., 1877, 'Historical Notes on Some of the Ancient Manuscripts Formerly Belonging to the Monastic Library of Waltham Holy Cross', *Transactions of the Royal Historical Society* 6, pp. 203–66.

———, 1880, 'Notices of the Ministers of the Church of Waltham Holy Cross', *Transcriptions of the Royal Historical Society* 8, pp. 356–84.

Wooding, L. E. C., 2000, *Rethinking Catholicism in Marian England* (Oxford: Clarendon Press).

Wriothesley, C., 1875 and 1877, *A Chronicle of England during the reigns of the Tudors, from A.D. 1485 to 1559*, 2 vols, ed. W. D. Hamilton (London: Camden Society).

Wunderli, R. and Broce, G., 1989, 'The Final Moment before Death in Early Modern England', *The Sixteenth Century Journal* 20 (2), pp. 259–75.

Youings, J. A., 1954, 'The Terms of the Disposal of the Devon Monastic Lands, 1536–58', *The English Historical Review* 69 (270), pp. 18–38.

Zagorin, P., 2003, *How the Idea of Religious Toleration Came to the West* (Princeton and Oxford: Princeton University Press).

INDEX

✠